Canadian

CONTENT

Canadian

CONTENT

Fifth edition

Nell Waldman
Sarah Norton

THOMSON

™

NELSON

tralia   Canada   Mexico   Singapore   Spain   United Kingdom   United States

Canadian Content, Fifth Edition
by Nell Waldman and Sarah Norton

Editorial Director and Publisher:
Evelyn Veitch

Acquisitions Editor:
Anne Williams

Marketing Manager:
Lenore Taylor

Senior Developmental Editor:
Mike Thompson

Senior Production Editor:
Bob Kohlmeier

Copy-Editor:
Sarah Robertson

Proofreader:
Margaret Crammond

Creative Director:
Angela Cluer

Interior-Design Modifications:
Katherine Strain

Cover Design:
Gabriel Sierra

Cover Image:
First Flights over Desolate Ice, by
Lotti Thomas

Compositors:
Alicja Jamorski, Carol Magee

Production Coordinator:
Hedy Sellers

Permissions Coordinator:
Cindy Howard

Printer:
Transcontinental Printing Inc.

**National Library of Canada
Cataloguing in Publication Data**

Canadian content / [edited by]
Nell Waldman and Sarah Norton.
— 5th ed.

Includes index.
ISBN 0-17-622531-5

1. College readers. 2. English
language—Rhetoric—Textbooks.
I. Norton, Sarah, [date]
II. Waldman, Nell Kozak, [date]

PE1417.C25 2003   808'.0427
C2003-900653-0

PREFACE

To the Instructor

Canadian Content, Fifth Edition, is a reader intended for Canadian college or university students who are studying English composition. Fourteen of the twenty new selections are by Canadians, including some of our country's best and most thoughtful writers (Michael Ignatieff, Malcolm Gladwell, Douglas Coupland, Mark Kingwell, Denise Chong, Rex Murphy, and Adam Gopnik) as well as student writers (Shandi Mitchell, Danny Irvine, and Rita Klein-Geltink). The remaining new selections by British and American writers supplement the international essays retained from previous editions.

We've borrowed our title, *Canadian Content*, from the Canadian Radio-television and Telecommunications Commission (CRTC), the federal broadcasting regulatory agency whose guidelines require that broadcasters provide a minimum of 70 percent Canadian content in their programming. Although print materials are not governed by this regulation, we thought that the CRTC's "70 percent" minimum requirement was a worthy goal for a college text.

This edition features some significant changes. "How to Read with Understanding" and "How to Write with Understanding" provide a simplified approach, free of obscure technical terms, to the complex tasks of reading and writing. "How to Write a Documented Essay" has been updated and now concludes with a documented essay from an academic journal. The unit introductions offer short, accessible explanations of the prose structures on which they focus, and each is supported by quotations from essays within the unit.

Unit 1 represents a major change from previous editions. In this unit, we introduce, explain, and exemplify narration, description, and example—three strategies that are basic to all writing. Units 2 through 6 focus on traditional expository patterns: process analysis, classification and division, comparison and contrast, causal analysis, and definition. Unit 7 is devoted to argument and persuasion. The essays within each unit are arranged from simplest to most complex, so instructors can either assign readings appropriate to the level of the class or lead the class through progressively challenging readings based on a single rhetorical pattern. Many instructors prefer to organize their courses around themes rather than structural patterns; to accommodate them, we have included a thematic table of contents.

Each unit introduction is followed by a short model essay that illustrates the organizational pattern under consideration. Together, these model essays demonstrate how a single topic—in this case, communication—can be approached from different points of view and supported in different ways. The model essays also exemplify the various introductory and concluding strategies explained in the List of Useful Terms at the back of the book. Terms that appear in small capital letters throughout the text (AUDIENCE, DICTION, METAPHOR, and THESIS, for example) are defined in the List of Useful Terms.

Within the units, each essay is now preceded by a short biographical note and followed by Words and Meanings—contextual definitions of words and phrases that students are likely to find unfamiliar. As in previous editions, the remaining pedagogical apparatus consists of two sets of questions (Structure and Strategy, Content and Purpose) and Suggestions for Writing. Each unit concludes with Additional Suggestions for Writing.

A separate Instructor's Manual includes suggestions for course planning, sample assignments, an alternate set of model essays, suggested answers to questions in the text, and a testbank of questions on the essays.

ACKNOWLEDGMENTS

We thank the students and teachers across Canada whose feedback has encouraged and helped us to keep refining this text. We are particularly grateful to our reviewers—Jim Andersen, University College of the Fraser Valley; Roger Farr, Capilano College; Peter Miller, Seneca College; Barbara Morris, Humber College; Megan Otton, Langara College; and Valerie Spink, Grant MacEwan College—whose comments, criticisms, and suggestions have made the book more useful and enjoyable than it otherwise might have been. The authors and editors also thank Lazaros and Juanita Simeon, Sarah Robertson, and Margaret Crammond for their invaluable contributions to this book.

CONTENTS

By Unit

UNIT 3: CLASSIFICATION AND DIVISION

UNIT 4: COMPARISON AND CONTRAST

UNIT 5: CAUSAL ANALYSIS

UNIT 6: DEFINITION

UNIT 7: ARGUMENT AND PERSUASION

UNIT 8: FURTHER READING

CONTENTS

By Theme

ON GENDER AND RELATIONSHIPS

ON COMMUNICATION AND WRITING

ON MEDIA AND THE ARTS

ON NATURE, SCIENCE, AND TECHNOLOGY

ON POLITICS

ON SPORTS

INTRODUCTION

1. How to Read with Understanding

Every college student knows how to read—sort of. The trouble is that many of us don't read very efficiently. We don't know how to adapt our reading style to our reading purpose. Most people aren't even aware that there are different ways to read for different purposes.

Basically, there are two kinds of reading: **surface reading,** which is casual reading for pleasure or for easy-to-find facts. This is the kind of reading we do when we enjoy a novel or read a newspaper. The second kind of reading is **deep reading.** This is the type required in college courses and on the job: reading to acquire the facts, ideas, and knowledge we need in order to understand a topic. Deep reading has practical rather than recreational purposes. Both kinds of reading can be satisfying, but the second kind takes more time. It also brings greater rewards. Good readers (and writers) tend to do well not only in college but also in their careers.

Learning to read analytically is a skill that can be mastered. There are three general guidelines to follow:

- figure out as much about the piece as you can *before* reading it;
- identify what you don't understand *while* reading it; and
- review the piece *after* reading it.

There are seven steps to reading and understanding the selections in this text. (These same steps will help you read and understand any piece of academic or professional prose.)

STEP 1: REMOVE DISTRACTIONS

Students new to college often claim that they can read perfectly well while listening to music, watching television, or talking on the phone. They are only partly right: they can read under those circumstances, but they can't read for understanding. Unlike watching TV, which uses less mental energy than eating, reading for understanding is an *active* process. It requires your full concentration and participation.

Here's what you need before you begin to work:

- a quiet place
- a good reading light
- a pencil
- a current, comprehensive dictionary.[1]

STEP 2: PREVIEW BEFORE YOU READ

You cannot learn facts, ideas, or even words in isolation. You need a CONTEXT, a sense of the whole into which each new piece of information fits. The more familiar you are with the context and content of a piece before you begin to read, the better you will understand what you read.

To find out as much as you can before you start reading, look through the essay to get a quick sense of the following:

- *How long is the piece?* You'll want to estimate how much time you'll need to complete it.
- *What is the title?* The title often points to something significant about the content of the essay.
- *Who wrote the essay?* Knowing something about the author may help you predict the kind of essay you're dealing with. Is the author dead or alive? What is his or her nationality? Is the author a humorist or a social critic? A journalist or an academic? A specialist in a particular field?
- *What about the BODY of the piece?* Are there subheadings or other visual cues that indicate the division of the topic into KEY IDEAS?

In addition, read the short unit introductions to discover the *how, what,* and *why* of each essay's organization and development. (You'll also find that many of the essays included in each unit are discussed as examples in the unit introductions.) Remember that terms printed

---

[1] The *Gage Canadian Dictionary* is a convenient portable dictionary, available in an inexpensive paperback edition. For your desk, we recommend either *The Canadian Oxford Dictionary* (1998) or Nelson's *Canadian Dictionary of the English Language* (1997). ESL students will find the *Oxford Advanced Learner's Dictionary of Current English* (2000) a useful reference.

in SMALL CAPITALS in the introductions and in the questions following the selections are explained in the List of Useful Terms at the end of the book. Look them up if you're not sure what they mean.

STEP 3: READ THE SELECTION ALL THE WAY THROUGH

For many people, step 3 is not easy. Most inexperienced readers have a fairly short attention span—about eight to ten minutes—and they need to train themselves to increase it. You need to read a piece all the way through in order to get a sense of the whole; otherwise, you cannot fully understand either the essay or its parts. Here's how to approach your first reading of essays in the book.

- *Note the words marked with a °.* This symbol indicates that the meaning of the word or phrase is given in the Words and Meanings section following the essay. If you're unfamiliar with the term, check the definition we've provided and keep reading. Underline any other words whose meaning you cannot figure out from the CONTEXT. You can look them up later.
- *Withhold judgment.* Don't allow your prejudices—in the root sense of the word, "prejudgments"—to affect your response at this stage. If you decide in advance that the topic is boring ("Who cares about toothpaste?") or the style is too demanding ("I couldn't possibly understand anything entitled 'The Evolution of Evolution'"), you cheat yourself out of a potentially rewarding experience. Give the writer a chance. Part of an author's responsibility is to make the writing interesting and accessible to the reader.
- *Use your pencil.* Make notes, underline, and jot down questions in the margin. Try to identify the THESIS of the essay as you read. When you come across a sentence or passage you don't understand, put a question mark in the margin.

Good writers set up their material for you: they usually identify their topic early and indicate the scope of their essay. Note, however, that your first read-through is not the time to stop and analyze the structure and writing strategies in detail. You need to read the piece a second or even a third time to accomplish such analysis successfully.

STEP 4: LOOK UP THE MEANING OF WORDS YOU DON'T UNDERSTAND

If you can't figure out the meaning of a word from its context, and if you need to know the meaning to understand a sentence or paragraph, it's time to use your dictionary. Don't assume that the first definition listed is the meaning the author intended. Note that some words can be used both as nouns and as verbs. Only one set of meanings will be appropriate in the context you are reading. When you're satisfied you've located the appropriate definition, jot it down in the margin beside the mystery word.

STEP 5: READ THE QUESTIONS FOLLOWING THE SELECTION

After you've answered your own questions about the piece, go through the questions that follow the selection. Our questions are divided into two sections. The Structure and Strategy questions will help you understand the **form** and **style** of the essay—the techniques the writer has used to accomplish his or her PURPOSE. The Content and Purpose questions will help you understand the **meaning** of the essay—what the writer wanted to communicate and why. Together, these questions will guide you to a thorough understanding of the piece.

At this point, you won't be able to answer all the questions we've provided, but don't panic. The purpose of reading our questions now is to prepare yourself for a second, closer reading of the essay. All you need to know at this stage is the kind of questions you'll be considering after your second reading.

STEP 6: READ THE SELECTION A SECOND TIME— SLOWLY, CAREFULLY

Got your pencil ready? The physical act of writing as you read helps keep your attention focused on the essay and serves to deepen your understanding of its content and structure. Here are some guidelines to follow as you read the essay a second time:

1. Identify the INTRODUCTION of the essay. What strategy has the writer used to establish the topic, the limits of the topic, and the TONE?
2. Underline the author's THESIS if you haven't already done so on the first reading.
3. Make notes in the margins. Use the margins to jot down, in point form, an outline of the piece, to add supplementary (or contradictory) evidence, or to call attention to especially significant or eloquently expressed ideas.
4. Circle key TRANSITIONS (linking words and phrases). Transitions signal to the reader that the writer has concluded one idea and is moving on to another.
5. Identify the writer's main PURPOSE. Is it to explain, to persuade, to entertain, or does it reflect a combination of purposes?

6. Identify the AUDIENCE the writer is addressing. Are you included in the group for whom the writer intended the essay? If not, you should remember that your reactions to and interpretations of the piece may differ from those of the intended readers.
7. Notice how the writer develops the KEY IDEAS. Be sure you can distinguish between main ideas and supporting details—the examples, ILLUSTRATIONS, definitions, and ANALOGIES, and so on—that the writer has used to make the ideas clear to the reader.
8. As you read, be conscious of the writer's TONE. Is it humorous or serious, impassioned or objective, formal or informal? Good writers choose their tone very carefully, since it directly affects the reader's response, probably more than any other technical aspect of writing.
9. Consider the CONCLUSION. Does it restate the thesis or expand on it in some way? Are you left with a sense of the essay's completeness, a feeling that all questions raised in the piece have been satisfactorily answered? Or do you feel that you've been left dangling, that some of the loose ends have yet to be tied up?

At this point, you have a decision to make. Are you satisfied that you understand the essay? Are the writer's purpose, thesis, key ideas, and method of development all clear to you? If so, move on to step 7. If not—as often happens when you are learning to read analytically, or when you encounter a particularly challenging piece—go back and read the essay a third time.

STEP 7: ANSWER THE QUESTIONS FOLLOWING THE SELECTION

Consider the questions carefully, one by one, and think about possible answers. Refer to the selection often to keep yourself on the right track. Most of the questions do not have simple or single answers. Some of them ask for your opinion. Write the answers to them in full if that is your assignment. Otherwise, jot down your answers in point form or in short phrases in a notebook or in the margins of the text.

The purpose of the questions is to engage you as deeply as possible in the structure and meaning of each piece. As you analyze *what* the writer has said (the content and purpose) and *how* he or she has said it (the structure and strategies), you will come as close as you can to full understanding. At this point, you are ready to test your understanding in classroom discussion or through writing a paper of your own.

2. How to Write to Be Understood

Learning to read for understanding will help you to write clear, well-organized prose. As you learn the techniques readers use to make sense of a piece of writing, you become increasingly skilled at predicting and satisfying the information needs of *your* readers. For years, you've probably been told to keep your AUDIENCE in mind as you write. By itself, this is not a particularly helpful piece of advice. You need to know not only *who your audience is,* including how much they know and how they feel about your topic, but also *how readers read.* These two pieces of information are the keys to writing understandable prose. (We are assuming here that you have a firm grasp of your topic. You cannot write clearly or convincingly about something you don't understand.)

Once you have decided what you are writing about and whom you are writing for, there are five steps (discussed below) you can take to ensure that your readers will understand what you say. Writing a paper is like going on a journey: it makes sense—and it's certainly more efficient—to choose your destination and plan your route before you begin. Your THESIS is your destination. Your KEY IDEAS establish the route you have selected to get to your destination. Together, your thesis and key ideas determine the kind of paper you are going to write.

In this book, we introduce you to three writing strategies—narration, description, and example—that are useful in every kind of writing. Then we explain and illustrate six ways to approach a topic. Something we want to emphasize is that there is no *one* way to explain a topic. Like a geographical destination, a topic can be approached via several routes.

Take communication, for example. It is a broad, general topic. If you flip through the introductions to Units 1 to 7, you will see that each contains a model essay illustrating the kind(s) of writing explained in that unit. The model essays all discuss communication skills, but they are all different. Read these model essays carefully, and you'll discover how the organizational pattern discussed in each unit can lend COHERENCE and UNITY to the topic you are writing about.

As you have already discovered, people who are reading analytically don't like surprises: they don't want to find sudden shifts in direction or dead ends. They want to find a smooth, well-marked path through the writer's prose. So your task is to identify the destination for them, set them on the path to that destination, and guide them through to the end. If you can keep them interested on their journey, so much the better. As you read through the selections in this book, you will encounter a variety of stylistic devices that you can use to add interest and impact to your own writing.

Rhetoric means the art of using language effectively. RHETORICAL MODES are the four classic kinds of non-fiction writing: NARRATION, DESCRIPTION, EXPOSITION, and ARGUMENT (or PERSUASION). A writer chooses a particular mode depending on the purpose of his or her piece.

RHETORICAL MODE	PURPOSE
Narration	To tell a story
Description	To create a sensory picture for the reader
Exposition	To inform the reader (explain a topic)
Argument/Persuasion	To convince the reader of a particular point of view

Expository pattern refers to one of the organizational patterns frequently used in writing that is intended to inform: process analysis, classification and division, comparison and contrast, causal analysis, and definition. Units 2 through 6 contain essays based on these patterns. (A sixth expository pattern, example, is explained in the introduction to Unit 1.) While the rhetorical modes are useful for classifying and describing different writing techniques, most writing is a blend of modes and purposes.

Here are the five steps to clear, well-organized writing:

1. Clarify your topic.
2. Discover your thesis.
3. Develop your thesis statement (and include, where possible, a preview of your key ideas)
4. Write the first draft.
5. Revise, edit, and proofread your paper.

The first three steps are the *preparation* stage of the writing process. Be warned: these steps will take you as long as—if not longer than—steps 4 and 5, which involve the actual *writing*. There is a general rule that governs academic and professional writing: the longer you spend on preparation, the less time the writing will take, and the better your paper will be.

STEP 1: CLARIFY YOUR TOPIC

The topic of your paper or report may be assigned by a teacher or someone else. If this is the case, don't grumble—be grateful! A large part of the work has already been done for you. You have been given a limited topic and advice on how to approach it. **Direction words** are reliable clues to the kind of paper your instructor or supervisor is looking for:

DIRECTION WORD	APPROACH TO TAKE
Compare/Contrast	Show similarities/differences between things, events, concepts, etc. (Unit 4).
Define	Give the formal meaning of a term, with examples (Unit 6).
Describe	Give a detailed explanation of the topic—often its physical appearance (Unit 1) or how it happened (Unit 2).
Discuss/Explain	Give details and, if relevant, the pros and cons of the topic, supported by EVIDENCE (Units 1, 3, 5, and 7).
Evaluate	Give the positive and negative points of the topic; identify which position is stronger and why (Units 3 and 7).
Illustrate	Explain by giving detailed examples (Unit 1).
Justify	Give reasons, supported by evidence (Unit 7).

What should you do if you are asked to come up with a topic of your own? Choosing a satisfactory topic is a critical part of writing an understandable paper. Inexperienced writers often choose a topic that is far larger than either their knowledge or the assigned word limit can accommodate.

A suitable topic is one that is both *specific* and *supportable*. A detailed discussion of a specific topic is much more satisfying to read than a superficial treatment of a broad one. This is why, in "The End of the Wild," Wade Davis chose to discuss three highly specific examples rather than to generalize about ecological disasters (see page 44). You can narrow a broad topic by applying one or more limiting factors to it. Think of your topic in terms of a specific *kind,* or *time,* or *place,* or *number,* or *person* associated with it. Davis, for example, limited his topic in terms of *kinds* (passenger pigeon, buffalo, and rainforest), *time* (twentieth century), and *place* (the North American continent).

A topic is supportable if you can develop it with examples, facts, quotations, descriptions, ANECDOTES, comparisons, definitions, and other supporting details. These supporting details are called *evidence*. Evidence, combined with good organization, is what makes your explanation of a topic both clear and convincing.

STEP 2: DISCOVER YOUR THESIS

Once you've chosen a suitable topic, you need to decide what you want to say about it. A THESIS is an *idea about* a limited topic; it is a viewpoint that needs to be explained or proved. There are three ways to go about discovering a thesis. The first two are **freewriting** and **brainstorming,** techniques with which most college students are already familiar. A more structured strategy called **questioning** involves asking lead-in questions about your topic. A **lead-in question** is one that guides you and your reader into your topic by pointing to an angle or viewpoint that you can explore in your paper. Traditionally, journalists have relied on the lead-in questions *when, where, who, how, what,* and *why* to help them discover what they can say about a topic.

ANSWERING THE QUESTIONS *WHEN, WHERE,* AND *WHO*
The answers to the questions *when, where,* and *who* are basic to every kind of writing. In Unit 1, you will learn how to answer the question *when* by locating a topic in time (NARRATION); the question *where* by locating a topic in space (DESCRIPTION); and the question *who* (or sometimes *what*) by providing examples to help your reader understand your point.

ANSWERING THE QUESTION *HOW*
To answer the question *how* (how something works, or how to do or make something), you will write a process analysis. Unit 2 explains how to go about it.

ANSWERING THE QUESTION *WHAT*
The question *what* can be answered in different ways, depending on the angle or viewpoint you wish to explore in your paper. Here are the four main approaches:

1. If you want to explain the *kinds* or *parts* or *important features* of your topic, you will write a classification or division paper. (See Unit 3.)
2. If you want to explain the *similarities* or *differences* between your topic and something else, you will write a comparison or contrast paper. (See Unit 4.)

3. If you want to explain what *caused* some event or circumstance, or what the *consequences* were (or will be), you will write a causal analysis. (See Unit 5.)

4. If you want to explain precisely what your topic *means*, you will write an extended definition. (See Unit 6.)

ANSWERING THE QUESTION *WHY*

To answer the question *why*, you need to develop an ARGUMENT. There are two kinds of argument: one is intended to convince the reader that your opinion is valid; the other is intended to change the reader's behaviour in some way. As you will see in Unit 7, building a successful argument is a challenging but highly rewarding task.

STEP 3: DEVELOP YOUR THESIS STATEMENT

A thesis statement is the most efficient way to organize a short paper. It plans your paper for you, and it tells your reader what he or she is going to read about. To continue the analogy between reading an essay and taking a trip, the thesis statement is a kind of map: it identifies your destination and the route you are going to take. Like a map, it keeps your reader (and you) on the right track. To be specific, a thesis statement does two things:

A.   It states the THESIS of your paper.
B.   It previews the KEY IDEAS of your paper.[1]

A. STATING YOUR THESIS

As concisely as possible, identify the topic of your paper and what you intend to explain or prove about that topic. Here are condensed versions of thesis statements taken from two essays in this collection:

Men and women talk differently. ("She Said, He Said," Model Essay, page 136)

Despite what many people think, marriage is good for everyone involved. ("The Case for Marriage," page 242)

Be sure to state your *idea* or *opinion* about your topic; don't just announce it and leave the reader wondering how you intend to approach it. *Do not* write, for example, "I'm going to discuss how men and women talk" or "This paper is about marriage." These are bald expressions of topic, not thesis statements.

---

[1] Sometimes the order of the two parts is reversed. For example, the following thesis statement about the topic "body language" states the key ideas before the thesis: "Your head, hands, and feet signal your feelings by sending strong non-verbal messages."

Once you've stated your thesis, take a close look at it. Is it the right size and scope for your assignment? More specifically, is it appropriate for the length of your paper and the amount of time you've been given to write it? Beware of a thesis that is too broad ("Life is good") or too narrow ("I can hardly wait to go shopping for my wedding dress").

B. PREVIEWING YOUR KEY IDEAS

The second part of a thesis statement identifies the key ideas you intend to discuss and the ORDER in which you will discuss them. To write this part, go back to your lead-in question (*when, where, who, how, what,* or *why*) and make a note of the three or four best answers to that question. The answers to the question are your KEY IDEAS.

After you've arranged your key ideas in an appropriate order, you are ready to expand your initial statement of thesis into a full thesis statement. Compare the following complete thesis statements (thesis + preview of key ideas) with the initial thesis statements we provided above. (To highlight the difference between the two, we've underlined the key idea previews in the statements below.)

When men and women engage in that intrinsically human activity called "talking," there is much that is different in <u>why they talk</u>, <u>the way they talk</u>, and <u>what they talk about</u>." ("She Said, He Said," Model Essay, page 136)

Contrary to what many Americans now believe, getting and staying married is good for men, women, and children. Marriage, it turns out, is by far <u>the best bet for ensuring a healthier</u>, <u>wealthier</u>, and <u>sexier life</u>. ("The Case for Marriage," page 242)

Note that the key ideas in a thesis statement are expressed in the same grammatical form: all nouns, all phrases, or all clauses. (See PARALLELISM.)

Not all essays contain full thesis statements. In many of the selections in this book, for example, you will find a statement of thesis but not a preview of the key ideas. Why? Because professional writers don't need the organizational apparatus that non-professionals do. Through experience, they have learned less visible techniques to keep their readers on track. We recommend, however, that you include a full thesis statement in the papers you write. (The best place to put it is at the end of your introductory paragraph.) There is probably no writing strategy you can use that is more helpful to your readers' understanding of what you have to say.

STEP 4: WRITE THE FIRST DRAFT: PARAGRAPH DEVELOPMENT, TRANSITIONS, AND TONE

Writers draft and revise—sometimes sequentially, sometimes simultaneously. Your objective in writing a first draft is to get something down on paper that you can work with until you have created a well-organized paper with solid PARAGRAPHS, effective TRANSITIONS, and an appropriate TONE.

A. DEVELOPING YOUR PARAGRAPHS

Each of your KEY IDEAS should be developed in a paragraph (sometimes two or three paragraphs may be needed) that contains a TOPIC SENTENCE clearly stating the key idea of that paragraph. Often, the topic sentence comes at the beginning of the paragraph so that the reader knows at the outset what to expect. The sentences that follow the topic sentence should support and develop the central idea. The key to making your paragraph unified (see UNITY) is to be sure that every supporting sentence relates directly to the topic sentence. An adequately developed paragraph includes enough EVIDENCE to make its main idea clear to the reader.

How do you decide what is the best way to develop a particular paragraph? How much evidence should you include? What kind of support should it be? To make these decisions, put yourself in your reader's place. What does the reader need to know in order to fully understand your point? If you ask yourself the questions listed below, you'll be able to decide what and how much evidence you need to develop your topic sentence.

1. Would **narrating a story** be an effective way of getting your idea across? Everyone likes to read a story if it's well told and relevant to what's being discussed. Using a personal ANECDOTE to illustrate an idea can be an effective way of helping your readers to understand and remember your point. The introduction to Unit 1 will give you guidelines to follow when using NARRATION to develop a point.

2. Would **specific details** be useful? Providing your reader with concrete, specific, descriptive details can be effective in developing your key idea and in establishing the mood you are trying to convey. In some paragraphs, facts or statistics can be helpful in supporting your point. See the introduction to Unit 1 for instructions on writing effective DESCRIPTION.

3. Would two or three **examples** help communicate your idea? Providing examples is probably the most common method of developing a key idea (and of avoiding vague or unsupported

generalizations). The introduction to Unit 1 will show you how to use examples effectively.

4. Is a **series of steps or stages** involved? Are you explaining a process to your reader? Sometimes the most logical way to make your point clear is to explain how something is done or how something works—that is, to relate, in order, the steps involved. The introduction to Unit 2 will give you detailed directions for this kind of development.

5. Would a **comparison** or **contrast** help make your explanation clearer? A *comparison* points out similarities between objects, people, or ideas; a *contrast* shows how the objects, people, or ideas are different. The introduction to Unit 4 provides a detailed description of this technique.

6. Is a **definition** needed? If you're using a term that may be unfamiliar to your readers, you should define it—phrasing it in your own words rather than giving a quotation you've found in a dictionary. See the introduction to Unit 6.

7. Would a **quotation** or PARAPHRASE be appropriate? Would your reader be convinced by reading the words of someone else who shares your opinion? As long as they are kept short and not used too frequently, quotations can not only support but also add EMPHASIS to an idea. Whenever you use a quotation or a paraphrase, of course, you must acknowledge your source. See "How to Write a Documented Essay" (page xxix) for instructions on how to find and use source materials.

Note that the methods of paragraph development outlined above are almost the same as the organizational patterns on which whole essays are based. The two sets of strategies are similar because good writing, whether short or long, is based on the same principles.

The methods you choose to develop a key idea should be determined by your readers' needs and expectations. You can, of course, use more than one method to develop a paragraph; sometimes a comparison can be effectively coupled with a quotation, for example. There is no fixed rule that governs the kind or number of development strategies required in any particular paragraph or essay. The decision is up to you. Your responsibility as a writer is to keep in mind what your readers already know and what they need to know in order to understand your THESIS.

Once you have developed your key ideas, you will add two important paragraphs: the INTRODUCTION and CONCLUSION. All too often, these parts of a paper are dull, clumsy, or repetitive. But they shouldn't be and they needn't be. If carefully constructed, these paragraphs can effectively catch your reader's attention and clinch your discussion. The List of Useful Terms contains specific strategies you can choose from when crafting a beginning and ending for your paper.

B. SUPPLYING TRANSITIONS

As you write your paragraphs, keep in mind that you want to make it as easy as possible for your reader to follow you through your paper. *Transitions* are words or phrases that show the relationship between one point and the next, causing a paragraph or a paper to hang together and read smoothly. Like the turn signals on a car, transitions such as *first, next, therefore, however,* and *finally* tell the person following you where you're going. (Don't overuse them, however, or you'll confuse your reader, who won't know after a while which way—or even if—you're going to turn!) The List of Useful Terms will give you suggestions for appropriate transitional phrases, depending on the kind of relationship between ideas that you want to signal.

C. ESTABLISHING AND MAINTAINING AN APPROPRIATE TONE

The writer's attitude toward his or her topic is called *tone*. A writer may feel angry about a topic, or amused, or nostalgic, and this attitude is reflected in the words, examples, quotations, and other supporting details he or she chooses to support the key ideas. Good writing is usually modulated in tone; the writer addresses the reader with respect, in a calm, reasonable way. Highly emotional writing is often not convincing to readers—what gets communicated is the strength of the writer's feelings rather than depth of knowledge or validity of opinion.

Tone is a complex idea to understand, and control of it is a difficult skill to master. To learn what tone means, read the selections in this book carefully and observe how skilled writers convey a range of emotions. For example, in "Edith," Rachel Manley remembers the woman who cared for her as a child. What is Manley's attitude toward Edith, and how does the reader come to feel it in the essay? Judy Brady's "Why I Want a Wife" is humorous, yet readers can sense fury beneath her words. How does she accomplish this combination of wit and rage? In "The Rake," David Mamet writes about the abuse that took place in his home as he was growing up. Yet his tone is not angry; it is carefully modulated, and the effect is more chilling than if he had openly denounced his mother and stepfather.

STEP 5: REVISE, EDIT, AND PROOFREAD YOUR PAPER

At last you've reached the final step in the writing process. Even though you are by now probably sick of the whole project and eager to be done with it, *do not* omit this important final step. Revising (which means "looking back") is essential before your paper is ready to be sent into the world. Ideally, you should revise your paper several days after writing it. After a cooling-off period, you'll be able to see your work more objectively.

A. REVISING

Thorough revision requires at least two reviews of your paper. The first time you go over it, read it aloud, slowly, from beginning to end, keeping your AUDIENCE in mind as you read. Is your THESIS clear? Are the KEY IDEAS arranged in an appropriate ORDER? Are all points adequately explained? Has anything been left out? Are the PARA-GRAPHS unified and coherent? Are there any awkward sentences that should be rephrased?

B. EDITING

Begin editing by running your essay through the grammar- and spell-check functions of your computer. Don't just go through the document replacing your words with the computer's suggestions, however. Computers are programmed to question, not to decide, the appropriateness of a writer's choices. You must decide for yourself if the computer's suggestions are write—oops, right.

The second time you read through your paper, read it with the Editing Checklist (on the inside of the front cover) in front of you for easy reference. Pay special attention to the points that tend to give you trouble: for example, sentence fragments, verb errors, apostrophes, or dangling modifiers. (For help with basic writing skills, log on to www.englishresources.nelson.com.) Most writers know their weaknesses. Unfortunately, it's human nature to try to gloss over our weaknesses and focus on our strengths. That is why editing your work can be a painful process. Nevertheless, it is an absolutely essential task. You owe it both to yourself and to your reader to find and correct any errors in your writing.

C. PROOFREADING

If your spelling, punctuation, or keyboarding skills are not strong, you will need to read your paper a third time. Grammar- and spell-check it again. Then read it through from the end to the beginning to check every sentence. When reading from back to front, you're forced to look at each sentence individually, not in CONTEXT, and thus you are more likely to spot your mistakes. It's also a good idea to ask a friend or someone else to go over your paper and identify any remaining errors.

A final word of advice: whether you are in school or on the job, always make a hard copy of your paper for your files.

If you follow these five steps carefully, you and your reader will arrive at your destination without any accident, mishap, or wrong turns. The journey should be relatively painless for you and informative, perhaps even enjoyable, for your reader. Good luck!

3. How to Write a Documented Essay

For some essays or research assignments, you will be required to locate and integrate other people's ideas, knowledge, or expert opinion into your paper. You will use the written (or, occasionally, spoken) words of external sources to help make your ideas clear and to prove your point to your reader. As any good lawyer knows, proving a point depends on two things: finding enough EVIDENCE and presenting it effectively. The kind and quality of the evidence you assemble and the way you incorporate it into your own writing will determine the success or failure of your documented essay.

Keep in mind that the reason most instructors assign research papers is to give you an opportunity to demonstrate how well you can find, analyze, and evaluate source material; synthesize it; and use it to support your own conclusions about a topic. Very few research assignments require you simply to report other people's findings on a topic. Normally, you are expected to use your source material as evidence to support your THESIS. Writing a documented essay requires the use of high-order thinking skills: interpreting, summarizing, analyzing, and evaluating. That is why a research paper or term paper so often serves as the culminating test of learning in college courses. Such papers are good practice for the world of work, too. The critical thinking skills required of students to produce a documented essay are the same skills required of professionals on the job.

STEP 1: GATHERING THE EVIDENCE

Your first task is to find, evaluate, and make notes on source material that supports your thesis. Usually, you do this work in the library, using computer-based research tools, books, periodicals, or academic journals as your sources. Your librarian will help you search for relevant, up-to-date information.

After you have found a number of promising-looking sources, your next task is to evaluate the material to see if it is appropriate for your paper. Inexperienced writers often get bogged down at this point, spending days or weeks reading each potential source in detail. A more efficient approach is to scan each work quickly and discard whatever is not current, relevant, or reliable.[1] Once you have identified a number of solid supporting sources, read them carefully, using the reading and note-taking suggestions given in "How to Read with Understanding" (page xiii). For every set of notes you make, be careful to record all the source information you need to document your paper accurately. Following are guidelines for print and electronic sources:

- For print sources, you will need the name of the author(s) or editor(s), title, publisher, place and date of publication, and the page(s) on which you found the information you have noted.
- For electronic sources, note the name of the author(s) (if given), document title, title of the database or site, date of publication or last update, name of the institution or organization sponsoring the site (if given), the full URL, and the date you accessed the source.

Keeping detailed and accurate bibliographical records as you read through your sources will save you hours of time and frustration later, when you come to document your paper and can't remember where a crucial piece of information came from. Accurate bibliographical records will also help keep you from falling into the trap of inadvertent plagiarism (more on this later).

STEP 2: PRESENTING THE EVIDENCE

Once your research notes are complete and you have begun your first draft, you need to know how to integrate the information you have found into your own writing. There are three methods you can choose from: summary, paraphrase, or direct quotation. A SUMMARY is a highly condensed version of another person's ideas or observations. A PARAPHRASE is a longer summary. It could include, for example, the KEY IDEA and several supporting details, whereas a summary would present only the key idea. Whether you are summarizing or paraphrasing, however, you must *restate the source information in your own words.* If you use the actual words or phrases of the original, you are *quoting,* and you must signal that fact to the reader by using quotation marks or—for a quotation that runs more than four typed lines in your paper—by indenting the quoted passage 2.5 centimetres from the left margin.

---

[1] Be wary of Internet sources, especially if the source's URL does not end with a recognized domain such as .gov (government) or .edu (educational institution). You can often check the credibility of an author, company, organization, or institution by using an online search engine such as Google.

A word about **plagiarism:** Everyone knows that plagiarism is using someone else's ideas and presenting them as your own. Submitting someone else's term paper or collecting material from various articles and passing it off as your own original thinking are clear examples of academic dishonesty. Not everyone realizes, however, that neglecting to identify your sources, even if the omission is unintentional, is also plagiarism. Whenever you use another writer's ideas in an essay, you need to let your reader know whose ideas they are and where you found them.

Whether you are summarizing, paraphrasing, or quoting, you must acknowledge your sources. This process is called **documentation.** Careful documentation will not only ensure that you avoid plagiarism, it will also ensure that you are given credit for the reading and research you have done.

To document the books, articles, or other information you have used in your paper, you need to follow an approved system of documentation. Two basic styles are used in most colleges and universities: the Modern Language Association (MLA) format, usually required in humanities courses, and the American Psychological Association (APA) format, commonly used in the social sciences. (Both formats have abandoned the old-fashioned and cumbersome footnote system in favour of parenthetical referencing, which means indicating the source in parentheses immediately following the summary, paraphrase, or quotation.)

The natural and physical sciences require a wide variety of documentation formats, and many colleges and universities publish their own style manuals. If your instructor requires a specific format, use the appropriate handbook to guide you through the task of acknowledging source material. Most systems of documentation require, in addition to parenthetical citations, that you list your sources for the paper on a separate page at the end. The format—including spacing, order of information, capitalization, and punctuation—must be followed exactly for both your paper and your list of references. If your instructor leaves the choice of format up to you, choose one of the following style guides:

- Gibaldi, Joseph. *MLA Handbook for Writers of Research Papers.* 6th ed. New York: Modern Language Association, 2003.
- American Psychological Association. *Publication Manual of the American Psychological Association.* 5th ed. Washington: American Psychological Association, 2001.

Detailed information about the MLA and APA documentation styles is available at www.englishresources.nelson.com. For further information and periodic updates, go to the websites of the MLA (www.mla.org) and the APA (www.apa.org).

The following essay by Katherine Murtha[2] is documented in MLA style. It demonstrates (1) how to incorporate summaries, paraphrases, and short and long quotations into your writing; and (2) how to indicate that you have altered a quotation, either by leaving something out (use ellipses) or by adding or changing a word or phrase (use square brackets).

---

[2] A native of Lindsay, Ontario, Katherine Murtha is a workshop facilitator and speaker who holds an M.A. in history and theology from the University of Toronto. She is writing a musical screenplay about women and bicycles entitled *Wheel Women*. "Cycling in the 1890s: An Orgasmic Experience?" was originally published in *Canadian Woman Studies* 21.3 (2001–02): 119–21.

2.5 cm

1.25 cm

2.5 cm

Murtha 1

Katherine Murtha

ENG 101

Professor Norton

7 October 2003

Cycling in the 1890s: An Orgasmic Experience?

Title centred on page

> "Let me tell you what I think of bicy-
> cling," Miss Anthony said, leaning forward and
> laying a slender hand on my arm. "I think it
> has done more to emancipate women than anything
> else in the world. I stand and rejoice every
> time I see a woman ride by on a wheel. It gives
> woman a feeling of freedom and self-reliance.
> The moment she takes her seat she knows she
> can't get into harm unless she gets off her
> bicycle, and away she goes, the picture of free
> untrammeled womanhood." (Anthony 10)

Long quotation indented 2.5 cm from left margin

Full source citation

The "Gay 90s" were made all the more colourful by
the era's bicycle craze. Social historians assert that
the bicycle had a significant levelling effect on
society. Seated on a bicycle, anyone--regardless of
class or social position--could ride through the
streets or in the park, and onlookers found it increasingly difficult to distinguish between the classes.
Nowhere was the role of the bicycle as a vehicle for
social change more apparent than in the lives of women.
By the 1890s, increasing numbers of women had taken to
the road with enthusiasm. The bicycle provided them
with a freedom, mobility, and sense of adventure they
had previously been denied. This phenomenon, however,
did not come to pass without an enormous struggle.

Paper double-spaced throughout

Murtha 2

The newspapers of the time devote an astonishing
amount of space to bicycle news. Writers dedicated hundreds of column inches to women's relationship with the
bicycle, a symbol of modernity. The advent of the
bicycle led to passionate debates about women's
"proper" nature, role, and attire. Clearly, women's
new-found ability to move about unchaperoned threatened
male defenders of the traditional moral order. Taking
direct aim at men's vulnerability, the editor of the
Dominion Medical Monthly warned, "Bicycle riding produces in the female a distinct orgasm." A little further on, he charged that "Toronto's scorching
thoroughfares" made the streets of Sodom and Gomorrah
look "as pure as Salvation Army shelters" (qtd. in
Roberts 16).

Men were not the only ones to express fear and
ridicule of women on wheels. Canada's first woman journalist, Kit Coleman, argued as follows:

> No girl over 39 should be allowed to
> wheel. It is immoral. Unfortunately, it is
> older girls who are ardent wheelers. They love
> to cavort and careen above the spokes,
> twirling and twisting in a manner that must
> remind them of long dead dancing days. They
> have descended from the shelves in myriads and
> in a burst of Indian summer are disporting
> themselves on the highways and byways. (5)

Similar sentiments were expressed worldwide. The terms
loose (meaning without a corset), *town bike*, and *ride*
all come from this period. These derogatory expressions

Short quotation incorporated into text

Abbreviation qtd.in ("quoted in") used for indirect sources

Author of newspaper source

Abbreviated source citation (author's name in text)

Murtha 3

were used to keep women in their "proper" place--immo-
bile and at home (Petty 127). ◄──────────────── *Full source citation (author's name not in text)*

　　That countless anonymous women persisted in riding
in the face of such opposition is remarkable. In keeping
with the egalitarian spirit of the bicycle movement, it
is interesting to note that it was the "sisters, sweet-
hearts, and wives of the young chaps about town, the
clerks, the mechanics and such like" (Denison 281) who
broke through convention and took to the road without
waiting for the example or approval of upper-class
women. The mobility provided by the bicycle also
inspired working-class women to fight for the right to
wear comfortable, pant-like bloomers and the right not
to wear wire-and-whalebone corsets. What was the use of
having a bicycle, they argued, if heavy, constricting
clothing made it virtually impossible to move? The
daring and courageous spirit of these nameless individuals helped to free women from the physical and social
restrictions that had long kept them earthbound.

　　By the summer of 1895, moreover, what had previously been deemed unacceptable became fashionable. The
tide of opinion was turned by the sudden and dramatic
appearance of society's upper echelons on wheels. Once
the bicycle had received the stamp of approval from the
upper classes, the fad became a frenzy. Toronto's
trend-setting society women rode the streets and parks
en masse, parading the latest, most exquisite cycling
costumes before amazed spectators. The papers were full
of information about Toronto's fashion show on wheels.
They took note of the latest "cultured" woman to take

Summary of information from book source

Murtha 4

to the wheel or the most recent fashionable circle to host a bicycle party. These sought-after invitations to bicycle parties often ended with BYOB--bring your own bicycle (Ritchie 161).

Summary of information from three sources, with full citation

The enterprising men of the bicycle industry were eager to tap into the new female market. To counteract the testimony of medical professionals who opposed women's cycling, the bicycle industry sponsored other doctors who publicly attested to the health benefits that were to be derived from bicycle riding. With a little oiling, some doctors were even known to change their opinions. Whereas once the evidence was thought to prove that cycling damaged "the feminine organs of matrimonial necessity" (Larrabee 86) and caused skeletal deformations, hernias, varicose veins, weak hearts, nervous disorders, insomnia, and epilepsy, now it was thought to prove the contrary (Petty 127; Smith 64).

The bicycle fad faded before the turn of the century, but the craze lasted long enough to silence most of the critical voices and create a consensus that cycling was not just acceptable but even beneficial. The ensuing respectability did not come without set backs to women's quest for mobility and freedom. The initial entry of cycling women into the public sphere was marked by a spirit of boldness and independence; once the activity became respectable, however, efforts were renewed to tame women's spirit and restrict their movement. Although by the mid-1890s it was deemed acceptable for women to ride, cycling had to be per

formed in a manner that was considered appropriate for
the female sex. Hence, the controversy surrounding
women and the bicycle continued to rage long after
bicycles had become commonplace.

One controversy was particularly inflammatory: what
could status-conscious female cyclists wear while
riding? "Rational dress" reformers hoped that the social
acceptance of women's cycling would lead to acceptance
of "bloomers," which were far more practical than long
skirts. Many women's hopes were dashed when bloomers
were rejected as being "too masculine." Eventually, a
compromise was reached between the traditionalists and
the reformers: women's skirts were raised two inches,
and elastic undergarments became acceptable alternatives
to punishing whalebone corsets. Understandably, the
corset industry took an interest in the discussions of
the time. Fearing extinction, many companies rallied to
the cause by not only loosening the grip of their
product, but also by offering incentives such as bicycle
insurance with purchases (Smith 66-67).

Paraphrase of information from book source, with full citation

By the latter half of the 1890s, it was generally
agreed that a little exercise was good for the female
sex, if done in moderation. The public nature of bicy-
cling provoked extensive discussions on the subject of
women and athletics. In the end, the traditional view
that women did not benefit from strenuous exercise was
upheld, and any attempt by women to exert themselves ath-
letically was viewed as immoral, if not dangerous. The
following passage, which appeared in *Cycling* in 1893,
expresses the view that came to dominate public opinion:

Murtha 6

A woman can best show what little exertion
is required in propelling her cycle by riding
with modest ease and moderate pace. For feats
of speed and protracted endurance she is . . .
[morally] bound, if she respects her sex, to
avoid anything in the nature of deleterious
excess of exertion. (qtd. in Ritchie 158)

Quoted phrases incorporated into text; full source citations

Women were discouraged from participating in athletics not only by moral strictures, but also by fear
of physical harm. Those who persisted in racing and
competition were threatened with the phenomenon of
"bicycle eyes" or "bicycle face," which, doctors
warned, would result from the strain of cycling. It was
believed that once "wild eyes" were developed, the condition was impossible to cure; the victim would be
marked for life (Smith 69-70; Petty 127).

These restrictions blunted the aspirations of women
who longed to excel in athletics. During the latter
half of the nineteenth century, women had achieved some
success and fame in racing and long-distance riding.
Now, as the consensus around "exercise in moderation"
solidified, the opportunities and recognition that had
been available to women began to disappear. France,
which had witnessed the beginnings of women's bicycle
racing, did not endorse women's events until the 1930s.
The League of American Wheelmen, the organization that
sanctioned bicycle races, blacklisted women. Cycling magazines refused to print the results of women's rallies.
Not until 1958 did the Union Cycliste Internationale

Summary of information from article and full source citation (concluded next page)

Murtha 7

re-establish recognition of women cyclists and resume
recording their achievements. Nevertheless, women refused
to abandon their desire to participate in the sport. A
few who refused to be bound by the dictates of moderation
found an outlet for their skills in the circus, where
women could take their place alongside men, not as assistants, but as equals. Unfortunately, the compromises
forced by public opinion meant that the potential of many
women remained undeveloped. While men's athletic prowess
continued to be celebrated, women had to be content with
awards for "Most Attractive Lady Cyclist" (Browerman 78).

Summary
(conclusion)

Although the bicycle boom died before the new century unfolded, reform movements in which the bicycle had
played a part endured. While the bicycle faded from the
pages of newspapers and magazines, it did not disappear
from women's lives. In the wake of the bicycle craze,
women gained access to cheaper and better vehicles. For
many, the bicycle became a practical means of transportation. It even facilitated political reform: as
Elizabeth Cady Stanton noted, "Many a woman is riding to
the suffrage on a bicycle" (qtd. in Petty 125).

Hanging indents for reference entries

Works Cited

Anthony, Susan B. "Champion of Her Sex." Interview with Nelly Bly. *New York World*. 2 Feb. 1896: 10.

Browerman, Les. "Some Steps in the Long March of the 'Bloomer Brigade.'" *Cycle History: Proceedings of the 8th International Cycle History Conference*. Ed. Rob van der Plas. San Francisco: Bicycle Books, 1998. 78-82.

Coleman, Kit. "Women's Kingdom." *Mail and Empire*. 17 Aug. 1985: 5.

Denison, G. E. "The Evolution of the Lady Cyclist." *Massey's Magazine*. Apr. 1897.

Larrabee, Lisa. "Women and Cycling: The Early Years." *How I Learned to Ride the Bicycle: Reflections of an Influential 19th Century Woman*, by Frances E. Willard. Ed. Carol O'Hare. California: Fair Oaks Publishing Company, 1991. 81-97.

Petty, Ross. "Women and the Wheel." *Cycle History: Proceedings of the 7th International Cycle History Conference*. Ed. Rob van der Plas. San Francisco: Bicycle Books, 1997. 112-33.

Ritchie, Andrew. *King of the Road: An Illustrated History of Cycling*. Berkeley, CA: Ten Speed Press, 1975.

Roberts, Wayne. "Rocking the Cradle for the World: The New Woman and Maternal Feminism, Toronto, 1877-1914." *A Not Unreasonable Claim*. Ed. Linda Kealey. Toronto: The Women's Press, 1979. 15-45.

Smith, Robert A. *A Social History of the Bicycle: Its Early Life and Times in America*. New York: American Heritage Press, 1972.

U N I T

—1—

Three Basic Strategies: Narration, Description, and Example

Narration, description, and example are basic to all writing. Indeed, it would be difficult to write any essay or report without using at least one of these strategies. In this introduction, we use examples from essays in this collection to illustrate what the three strategies are, why we use them, and how to write them.

NARRATION

WHAT IS NARRATION?

Narrative writing tells a story; it relates a sequence of events. Novels and short fiction are narratives, but they are based on imaginary events. In this book, we are concerned with non-fiction— writing that is based on fact. When an essay includes a story (often called an ANECDOTE) to illustrate a KEY IDEA, the reader trusts that the story actually happened. For instance, Douglas Coupland's essay "The Yukon" (page 20) focuses on a trip Coupland took with his father:

When I was young, trips with Dad in the plane often felt like torture, but with hindsight I can see them as an exotic and charmed way to have spent a part of my youth. When I was around thirteen, my father flew my younger brother and me in the Twin Otter up to the Yukon.

WHY DO WE USE NARRATION?

Providing a narrative is often a good way to develop a key idea. For example, the passage below, from David Mamet's "The Rake" (page 55) is an anecdote that illustrates the kind of family the author grew up in.

When we [the family] left the house we left in good spirits. When we went out to dinner, it was an adventure, which was strange to me, looking back, because many of these dinners ended with my sister or myself being banished, sullen or in tears, from the restaurant, and told to wait in the car, as we were in disgrace. . . .

The happy trips were celebrated and capped with a joke. Here is the joke: My stepfather, my mother, my sister, and I would exit the restaurant, my stepfather and mother would walk to the car, telling us that they would pick us up. We children would stand by the restaurant entrance. They would drive up in the car, open the passenger door, and wait until my sister and I had started to get in. They would then drive away.

They would drive ten or fifteen feet, and open the door again, and we would walk up again, and they would drive away again. They sometimes would drive around the block. But they would always come back, and by that time the four of us would be laughing in camaraderie and appreciation of what, I believe, was our only family joke.

This anecdote movingly illustrates the misery and anxiety the children suffered at the hands of their parents.

Focusing on the lead-in question *when*, a writer may use narration as the sole organizing principle of an essay: When did the first event happen? And then what happened? And then . . .? "The Rake" is one example of a narrative essay. Another is Shandi Mitchell's "Baba and Me" (page 10), which tells how the author's grandmother worked to build a life for herself and her children in Canada. A third example is Rachel Manley's "Edith" (page 14), which recounts a story from her Jamaican childhood and her first encounter with the loss of a beloved person.

More often, however, writers use narration to develop a key idea in an essay that is structured as a classification, comparison, causal analysis, or some other pattern. For example, the following anecdote from Brent Staples's causal analysis, "Just Walk On By" (page 169), supports a key idea about the racist assumptions he encountered:

> Another time I was on assignment for a local paper and killing time before an interview. I entered a jewelry store on the city's affluent Near North Side. The proprietor excused herself and returned with an enormous red Doberman pinscher straining at the end of a leash. She stood, the dog extended toward me, silent to my questions, her eyes bulging nearly out of her head. I took a cursory look around, nodded, and bade her good night.

HOW DO WE WRITE NARRATION?

Narration is based on the principles of storytelling. A good story tells a sequence of events in a way that captures the reader's interest and imagination. Good narration re-creates an experience so that readers can see and hear and feel it as if it had happened to them.

Here are five guidelines for writing effective narration:

1. Decide on your THESIS. Every narrative you use should contribute to your thesis by developing one of your key ideas.

2. Select details that are clearly and directly related to your thesis. What you leave out is as important as what you put in. Put yourself in the reader's position and tell enough of the story to make it both clear and vivid, but do not include so many details that the story wanders away from its point. You'll lose your reader's attention if you go on and on. Stay focused on the PURPOSE of your story—the key idea it supports.

3. Arrange the events in the most effective time order. Usually, a story moves in chronological (time) order: first this happened, then this, and finally that. But sometimes a narrative is more effective if the writer begins at the end and then goes back to tell how the story began (this technique is called a **flashback**). It's even possible to begin in the middle of the chronological sequence, introduce a flashback to fill in details that occurred before the point at which the story began, and then proceed to the end. Michael Ignatieff uses this complex sequence in "Deficits" (page 37), an essay about the devastating effects of Alzheimer's disease on his mother. Whatever time order you use, it is important to adhere to the next guideline.

4. Use TRANSITIONS to help your reader follow you as you proceed through the narrative. Provide time-markers (not in every sentence, of course) to indicate the sequence of events: *after, suddenly, next, as soon as,* and *finally* are the kind of useful transitions signals that keep your readers on track.

5. Maintain a consistent POINT OF VIEW. Point of view means the angle of narration: who is telling the story? If you begin your anecdote with yourself as first-person narrator ("I"), continue telling the story yourself. Don't shift to a different narrator, such as a "you" or a "he" or "she." Readers need to experience a story from a single, consistent narrative perspective.

DESCRIPTION

WHAT IS DESCRIPTION?

Descriptive writing creates a picture in words. It tells readers what a person, a place, or a thing looks like. Effective description appeals not only to the reader's visual sense but also to other senses: hearing, taste, smell, and feel. For example, in "Passion Play" (Further Reading, page 314), Lorne Rubenstein describes a golf course in early spring:

> The squishiness of the green, still sodden ground beneath my spiked feet; the earthy scent of the now-fertile soil and the spray of water as my club head contacts the ball; the flight of the ball towards the green; or, often, its helter-skelter path, wind-borne, clasped to the welcome breezes blowing spring warmth onto the course.

Even people who don't golf can get a vivid sense of the experience from this description.

WHY DO WE USE DESCRIPTION?

Description creates a sensory image of a topic. Concrete descriptive details help clarify abstract ideas; they also appeal to the reader on many levels, including the emotional. Description is an excellent way to make a point in a powerful way. Take, for example, Michael Ignatieff's poignant descriptions of his mother when she was young and as she is now:

> She always loved to swim. When she dived into the water, she never made a splash. I remember her lifting herself out of the pool, as sleek as a seal in a black swimsuit, the water pearling off her back. Now she says the water is too cold. . . .

I bathe her when she wakes. Her body is white, soft, and withered. I remember how, in the changing-huts, she would bend over as she slipped out of her bathing suit. Her body was young. Now I see her skeleton through her skin. When I wash her hair, I feel her skull. I help her from the bath, dry her legs, swathe her in towels, sit her on the edge of the bath and cut her nails: they are horny and yellow. Her feet are gnarled. She has walked a long way. ("Deficits")

Things—inanimate objects—can also be described in convincing detail. Consider the following passage and see if you can figure out what common substance David Bodanis is describing:

To keep the glop from drying out, a mixture including glycerine glycol—related to the most common car anti-freeze ingredient—is whipped in with the chalk and water, and to give *that* concoction a bit of substance . . . a large helping is added of gummy molecules from the seaweed *Chrondus crispus*. This seaweed ooze spreads in among the chalk, paint, and anti-freeze, then stretches itself in all directions to hold the whole mass together. A bit of paraffin oil (the fuel that flickers in camping lamps) is pumped in with it to help the moss ooze keep the whole substance smooth. . . .

The only problem is that by itself this ingredient tastes, well, too like detergent. It's horribly bitter and harsh. . . . It's to get around that gustatory discomfort that the manufacturers put in the ingredient they tout perhaps the most of all. This is the flavoring, and it has to be strong. Double rectified peppermint oil is used—a flavorer so powerful that chemists know better than to sniff it in the raw state in the laboratory.

Did you guess that this disgusting-sounding substance is toothpaste? (See Bodanis's essay, "Toothpaste," on page 117.)

Some pieces of writing are entirely descriptive: "Passion Play" (quoted above) is an example. However, description is most often used to support KEY IDEAS within another organizational pattern. "Toothpaste" is a division essay and "Deficits" is primarily a narrative, yet both are enhanced by strong description. Short passages of description—a sentence or two, or just a phrase—can help you ensure that your ideas are clear to the reader. Consider, for example, Jeffrey Moussaieff Masson's description of a penguin's egg in "Dear Dad" (page 83): "Weighing almost a pound [.45 kilograms], and measuring up to 131 millimetres long and 86 millimetres wide, this is one of the largest eggs of any bird." This description helps the reader to visualize the penguin egg in Masson's process analysis.

HOW DO WE WRITE DESCRIPTION?

Description provides details of what your reader needs to visualize in order to understand your point. Good description communicates the writer's attitude to a topic as well as the objective details. Your goal should to be to convey, through the details you choose, a dominant impression that reflects your feelings about the person, place, or thing you are describing. Take another look at the descriptive examples above: Ignatieff's description of his mother, Rubenstein's description of a golf course, and Bodanis's description of toothpaste ingredients. These passages all clearly convey the writers' attitudes toward their topics.

Here are four guidelines for writing good description:

1. Determine your PURPOSE. Are you writing a purely descriptive essay? Or are you using description to develop a key idea in an expository or persuasive essay? Decide whether you want to present a factual, objective picture (Masson's penguin egg, for example) or if you need to create a dominant impression that reflects your feelings.

2. Select the most important physical details. You cannot describe every detail about a topic without losing your focus (and your reader).

3. Arrange your selected details so that your picture emerges coherently. Usually, you will choose a spatial order (from top to bottom, left to right), but sometimes a psychological order (from external features to internal character) is appropriate. Use the arrangement most likely to accomplish your purpose.

4. Use sensory words in your description. What does the topic look, sound, feel, smell, and taste like? Choose words that contribute to the dominant impression you want to convey.

EXAMPLE

WHAT IS EXAMPLE?

An example is something selected from a class of things that is used to show the character of all of them. Examples give concrete form to abstract ideas. In "What I Have Lived For" (page 124), Bertrand Russell writes that he feels "unbearable pity for the suffering of mankind." What does he mean by "the suffering of mankind"? Before we can fully understand Russell's idea, we need examples: "Children in famine, victims tortured by oppressors, helpless old people a hated burden to their sons, and the whole world of loneliness, poverty, and pain make a mockery of what human life should be." In one sentence, Russell gives us three concrete examples that enable us to picture what he means by human suffering.

WHY DO WE USE EXAMPLES?

Good writing is a blend of ABSTRACT and CONCRETE, of general statements and specific examples. It's difficult to imagine *any* kind of writing that doesn't need examples to communicate its KEY IDEAS clearly and effectively.

Examples help to clarify complex ideas so that readers can understand them. In "Altruism" (page 219), Lewis Thomas writes about the instinct that some animals have to surrender their own lives to save the group. He provides several examples to illustrate the mysterious behaviour known as altruism:

> . . . Birds risk their lives, sometimes lose them, in efforts to distract the attention of predators from the nest. Among baboons, zebras, moose, wildebeests, and wild dogs there are always stubbornly fated guardians, prepared to be done in first in order to buy time for the herd to escape.

Writers also use examples to support or back up their generalizations. Notice how Neil Bissoondath uses examples at the beginning of "I'm Not Racist But . . ." (page 211) to support his contention that racism is not limited to a single people, race, or nationality, but is instead a universal human failing:

> Someone recently said that racism is as Canadian as maple syrup. I have no argument with that. History provides us with ample proof. But, for proper perspective, let us remember that it is as American as apple pie, as French as croissants, as Jamaican as ackee, as Indian as aloo, as Chinese as chow mein, as . . . Well, there's an entire menu to be written.

Examples are used to support key ideas in all kinds of essays. Bertrand Russell's essay, for instance, is organized according to the principle of **division;** the organizing principle of Thomas's and Bissoondath's essays is **definition.**

It is also possible to use examples as the organizing principle of an essay. In this case, the examples are usually described at some length and are called **illustrations.** In "The End of the Wild" (page 44), for example, Wade Davis organizes his plea for the environment around three key ideas, each of which is developed as a long example: an animal extinguished by human greed (the passenger pigeon), an animal greatly diminished by human short-sightedness (the buffalo), and a species of tree that is threatened by the logging industry (the rainforest conifers of British Columbia). Davis supports his THESIS with other examples, description, and several narratives, but the main organizing principle of his essay is three carefully arranged illustrations.

HOW DO WE USE EXAMPLE?

Writers use examples taken from research sources, their personal experience, or the experiences of others. Here are three guidelines for choosing good examples:

1. Be sure that any example you use is representative of your topic. Choose typical examples, not unusual or wacky ones.

2. Use examples that are relevant to your topic. There is a good reason why Wade Davis, in "The End of the Wild," did not include species—such as the dinosaurs—that were extinct before humans appeared on Earth. Davis's thesis is that people have recklessly damaged the natural world, and he has chosen examples that directly support this thesis.

3. Limit the number and range of your examples. Include only those examples that support your key ideas. If you include too many examples, you will reduce their effectiveness. Readers need and want the highlights, not the whole catalogue.

Mastering the three basic strategies we have outlined above is well worth your time and effort. Because they answer the fundamental questions readers ask—what happened? what does it look like? who (or what) is involved?—narration, description, and example are three of the most useful tools a writer can use to communicate meaning.

The essay below illustrates how narration, description, and example can be used together to help convey a thesis.

A Cultural Exchange

Introduction (provides descriptive details)

The French bar-café is an institution, a unique national treasure. Its patrons are an eclectic mix of blue-clad workmen in cloth caps or berets; lawyers and stockbrokers in business suits; scruffy individuals who could be students, artists, anarchists, or all three; elderly retired gentlemen in tweeds and moustaches; and farmers in rubber boots. The haze of blue smoke that gives the interior such a warm aura is the most distinctive characteristic of a French bar: the unique smell of French tobacco. The harsh Gauloise produces a tangy, dark aroma that is unforgettable.

Narrative
begins by
describing
situation: a
birthday
celebration

I had entered this tiny bar on the ground floor of a country hotel in a small village in central France on a mission. My wife and I were staying in the hotel overnight, celebrating her fortieth birthday and recovering from lunch. Valerie's celebratory meal had taken place in nearby Roanne at Restaurant Troisgros, one of the gastronomic wonders of the world. "Lunch" had begun at noon and ended nearly four hours later when we staggered out to our car, stuffed with *foie gras,* lobster *breton poché, noisettes* of lamb, a profusion of French cheeses, and a mind-boggling array of rich desserts. Now, some hours later and a few kilometres away, we were ready to cap the big day with a bottle of champagne on the balcony of our room. Unwilling to guzzle the expensive nectar from bathroom tumblers, I had tottered down three flights of stairs to the bar to borrow a pair of proper champagne glasses.

Description
developed by
examples

General
statement
about
communication;
specific
example
concerning
writer's grasp
of French

We take communication for granted—so much so that only when it goes awry do we stop to think about what a complex process it is. My French is adequate, I'm told, so far as accent is concerned, but pathetically weak in grammar and vocabulary. Even the simplest conversation requires extensive rehearsal, so it was with some trepidation that I entered the crowded, smoky bar, muttering to myself the request I was about to make.

Narrative
resumes here

"*Oui, monsieur?*" The bartender was a friendly sort, but possessed of one of those voices that, when pitched just right, can be heard in the next province. Conversation gradually died as everyone turned to watch me struggle through my request.

Narrative
developed by
descriptive
details and
dialogue

I must have done well enough in my broken French accompanied by expressive hand gestures—shaping the glasses in the air and sipping imaginary bubbly—because the bartender grinned, reached under the bar, and produced two large flutes, polishing them elaborately with his apron.

"*Et pour quelle grande célébration désirez-vous deux verres de champagne, monsieur?*" he boomed as he set the glasses in front of me, winking theatrically. By now the entire bar was concentrating on our conversation, eager to hear what great celebration it was that required champagne glasses.

Confident that I was up to the task, I grinned and told the entire company, *"C'est aujourd'hui le quatorzième anniversaire de ma femme!"*

Topic sentence

The bar erupted in cries of congratulation and admiration. Blue-clad, Gauloise-smoking workmen toasted me, hoisting their glasses overhead and shouting their approval. Others, apparently helpless with laughter, sagged against the bar. Several tried to shake my hand, though I was encumbered by the champagne glasses, and more than one slapped my back resoundingly. One older gentleman, nattily dressed in a blue beret and sporting magnificent waxed moustaches, wept with laughter as he tried to pour some of his *pastis* into my precious glasses. The hilarity seemed a bit overdone, I thought, for such a simple announcement . . . until I replayed the conversation in my head and realized that I had given my wife's age not as *quarante*, forty, but as *quatorze*—fourteen.

Examples enhanced by descriptive details

Climactic incident: the "punch line"

Joining the laughter, I bowed deeply, gave my best imitation of a Gallic shrug, and, flourishing my glasses overhead, made my red-faced exit.

Conclusion reinforces thesis: the complexity of communication

Baba and Me

SHANDI MITCHELL

A native of Nova Scotia, author and screenwriter Shandi Mitchell (b. 1964) co-wrote the short film *Gasoline Puddles*, wrote and directed the television drama *Baba's House*, and is developing a feature film. She won the 1991 National Screen Institute Drama Prize and received the Anna Pidruchney Award for New Writers, in 2001, for this essay.

1   In 1922, my father, at the age of two, came to Canada with his parents and five brothers and sisters from the Ukraine. They landed at Pier 21 in Halifax and headed west to homestead in northern Alberta. They lived in a sod-and-log house and suffered the prejudice of the times and the poverty of a barren existence. Forty years later, I was born into a lower-middle-class Canadian existence.

In that short span, the Ukrainian culture had been lost to me.   2
My Baba (grandmother) never learned to speak English and I knew
no Ukrainian. She was as much a stranger to me as were her customs, foods, thoughts, and life. As a child, I was frightened of her.

I knew nothing of her past and none of her secrets. No one   3
spoke of my grandfather. I remember the family visiting a weed-
infested lot set aside from the main cemetery. It wasn't until many
years later that I was told he had killed himself.

It was then 1938: the prairies were choking on dust and Baba   4
was newly widowed, with six children to support. In the next town
over, Old Man Kurik's wife had died in childbirth. And so began
Baba's next marriage. The old man used the kids as field hands and
boxing bags, excepting his own son, whom he schooled to become a
"gentleman." Then World War II exploded. One by one all of Baba's
children left for the cities. They ran from the wheat fields and their
rich, decaying earth.

They ran to the plastic, shiny chrome worlds filled with   5
starched sailors and armed forces personnel. They ran to heroes'
deaths and cowards' retreats. They fell in love and became
"Canadians" or "Americans." They changed their names and
became Marshalls, Smiths, and Longs. They travelled the world
and sent postcards back home to Baba. She saved the exotic images
in a cookie tin under her bed. Eventually, even Baba and Old Man
Kurik moved to town. Baba became a grandmother and was asked
not to speak Ukrainian around her grandchildren.

Baba wrote letters in Ukrainian to the old country, but they   6
remained unanswered. Undaunted by political barriers, she continued to save her pennies, quarters, and nickels for her visit home.
She didn't believe that she wouldn't be let in. Her children shushed
her when she spoke of her Communist brother. It was as if the
world grew up around Baba. Then one day, she found herself a
widow again. That morning, she opened every window and door
in the house and breathed deeply. It was January.

My Baba got old in the seventies. Sometimes, she babysat my   7
brother and me. My parents would drop us off for the weekend. I
hated going there. She didn't speak any English, and I blocked out
her Ukrainian. She dressed funny, she cooked funny, and she
smelled of garlic. She tried to teach me about Ukrainian things. I
didn't want to know. My friends were outside playing, the first
McDonald's in town was opening down the street, and the Bay City
Rollers had a new record. . . . I had better things to do than hang
around with Baba. Back then, I didn't know the word "ashamed."

Baba didn't need English in the town where she lived. There   8
were Ukrainian newspapers, TV and radio stations, stores,

neighbours, churches and all the essentials in this weed of a town poking up out of nowhere in northern Alberta. The town of 1600 was divided neatly into French in the north, Ukrainians in the south, Cree in the east, English in the centre, and everyone else crammed into the west. It was in Baba's town that I first learned about poverty, alcoholism, domestic abuse, and racism.

9   When the old man next door died, his house was boarded up, and it became a popular place to sniff glue and drink aftershave. The neighbours pretended not to see. In the safety of daylight, we kids would venture in and gather up the few bottles amongst the cans and then cash them in at the confectionery for nickel candy. Once, we thought we'd found a dead body, but he had only passed out. Baba tended her garden, seemingly oblivious to the world next door, and kept on planning her trip home to the old country.

10   When the neighbourhood began to gentrify° with condos and supermarkets and it was decided that Baba's best friend, Mrs. Westavich, couldn't keep her chickens anymore, Baba rallied to help her and used her precious savings in the process. When the two old women lost their battle, they took the chickens out to the front yard. Baba swung the axe while Mrs. Westavich held the birds down. They chopped their heads off one by one and let the birds' bodies flail and flop over the manicured lawns.

11   When the family decided it was best for Baba to go into a Home, there was no one left to fight for her. The first place was called Sunnyvale. The kids pulled her out from there when they found that she hadn't been bathed in a month and was covered in bed sores; also, her bank account was unaccountably low. Baba liked the new place better. She had a window box there, and grew tomatoes. I went to visit her, once. I called out, "Hi Baba!" and twenty wizened babas turned expectantly to me.

12   I hear Baba's house rents cheap now. The garden is filled with three cars up on blocks. I don't know what happened to her belongings. Her body is buried in Edmonton. I think the family felt it was a greater tribute to be buried in a city lot.

13   So here I sit in front of my computer with cell phone in hand and a coffeemaker brewing, and wonder about my grandmother. I have only one black and white photograph of her. She is squat and round, with huge breasts. She wears a cotton shift dress. Her nylon stockings are bunched at her ankles. A babushka° covers her head. She stands shyly beside a shiny late-model 1950s car. Next to her is my mother, with dark glasses, over-sized sun hat, and wasp waist, posed very much like Greta Garbo. I stand at the edge of the frame, a skinny kid looking as if I'm about to run.

Words and Meanings

Paragraph

gentrify — to transform an aging neighbourhood into a more prosperous one through remodelling buildings or houses — 10

babushka — a head scarf folded and tied under the chin — 13

Structure and Strategy

1. What kind of INTRODUCTION does Mitchell use in this essay? Is it effective? Why or why not?
2. Identify at least three descriptive details in paragraph 7. How many senses does the DESCRIPTION appeal to? What is the dominant impression that the reader gets from this description?
3. Identify the TRANSITIONS the author uses to link paragraphs 1 to 2, 4 to 5, and 7 to 8. How do they contribute to the effectiveness of the piece?
4. Mitchell develops her THESIS primarily through the use of examples. Choose three that you think are particularly effective and explain how they contribute to the thesis.

Content and Purpose

1. What are the main events of this story? Identify the ORDER in which these events are arranged. Then, in point form, put them in CHRONOLOGICAL ORDER.
2. Baba marries two times. What do you think these marriages were like? Use details from the essay to support your opinions.
3. The northern Alberta town Baba and "Old Man Kurik" move to is described in paragraphs 8 and 9. What kind of place is it? Who lives there? What does Mitchell learn in this town?
4. Why do you think Baba and Mrs. Westavich killed the chickens in the front yard (see paragraph 10)? What is the point of this ANECDOTE?
5. In paragraph 13, the author describes a photograph of her grandmother, her mother, and herself as a child. What do the descriptive details tell you about these people? What does Mitchell imply about the relationships between them?
6. What is Mitchell's PURPOSE in this essay, other than chronicling the life of her grandmother? State in one sentence what you think the "lesson" of the story is. How did the essay affect you?

Suggestions for Writing

1. Write an essay describing an older relative or other person you know (or knew) well. Include physical details, but also describe

the kind of life the person has (or had), as well as your own feelings about him or her.

2. Write an essay explaining the difficulties of being a new immigrant. What does it mean to leave the world one was born into and move to a different country to establish a life for oneself and one's descendants?

Edith

RACHEL MANLEY

Daughter and granddaughter of two of Jamaica's national leaders, Rachel Manley (b. 1947) was raised in Jamaica by her paternal grandparents, Norman and Edna. Her memoir, *Drumblair*, an intimate account of the Manleys' personal and political lives, won the Governor General's Award in 1997. Manley is the author of three books of poetry. Her most recent book, *The Slipstream: A Daughter Remembers*, was published in 2000.

1   There was nothing spectacular about the old wooden two-storey house set far back from the road. It was not even in a fashionable area, but rather poised precariously on the journey between the city and its ghettos, and the lofty slopes of the suburbs. It has often been described as elegant, but it was too visceral° and self-willed a place to be so, for elegance is a product of control. The gate, a plain iron grille hinged to a cracking square cement post, always hung open lazily, despite the thick "Chinese hat" hedge on either side guarding the house from view. The companion post carried the inscription of the name in frank block capitals on a marble inset. The initial slope of the circular driveway was steep enough that even a car needed a burst of new energy to make its way up. And there, at the top of the encircled front lawn, stood the house. It appeared not to take itself very seriously. It was large, but not in the sense of having many rooms—more in the way that you look at a puppy's paws and say, "These are large paws; this will be a big dog." It was just meant to be a large house. It looked out at the world from under a shady sombrero° of shingles. At its waist, a similar frill of roofing adorned it like a fat ballerina's tutu. A veranda enclosed by a criss-cross wooden railing circled the ground floor like the dash of a hasty signature . . . Drumblair.

2   All of my earliest memories lie within that house.

At the back of the house, below the kitchen, was a small basement.   3
Tucked into the damp earth, it was cool and secret. The concrete of
walls and floor was uneven, and the structure slumped into a comfortable shrug under the weight of Drumblair. On a hot day it was a
relief to push open the scraping wooden door and enter the subterranean shadows there. This was the province of Edith—Edith was a
province of Drumblair.

She had arrived as a laundress, and retired slowly over the   4
years into the landscape. The basement, with its great concrete
sinks where she squashed and squeaked clothes to utter softness
before starching them, had become her domain.

Edith also made guava° jelly; she was known in the parish of   5
St. Andrew as the guava-jelly woman. The basement had a Dover
stove at the back, big and black. Here she made her preserves in
huge pots, feeding the oven with wood from time to time, heaving
the latest batch of her vintage across the stove-top and out of the
way. As the wood cracked in the ravenous fire she would observe,
"Yes Lawd, as de sparks fly h'upward. . . ." On replacing the pot,
she would lift the lid to give the lethargic° mixture an encouraging
prod with a wooden spoon.

The smell of clean clothes and hot damp guava.   6

Edith was a huge woman, tall by comparison to my childhood   7
smallness. Over the years, her fat had settled stealthily around her,
giving her the appearance of a complete island setting sail whenever she embarked on a movement. Her skin was soft and creamy, a
gentle brown. It bore no wrinkled tributaries, but stretched thick
and firm across her surface, occasionally falling into a definite fold.
Her face carried no rumour of age, only occasional bunches of
moles like grapes which I enjoyed pointing out to her. She would
smile. Edith always smiled. It seemed that her time on earth was a
state of limbo in which she existed, and which she greatly enjoyed,
without deep commitment. Her life and inner light had a separate
schedule later and beyond.

"When dat great bugle blow, me will be ready!" she'd say.   8

In the meantime she remained patient in her hibernation, sim-   9
mering on a low flame, her bubble of life escaping as slowly as that
of the guava jelly.

When she was not drifting sleepily through her jelly making, or   10
pounding the laundry, she would be in her end room at the back of
the house, singing hymns knowingly to herself.

"No, dear, you can't. Edith's not here today. She's gone to town   11
to see the doctor."

"Is she sick, Aunta°?"   12

13   "Pressure. Terrible pressure," she said, as she lifted her fore-head into lines of acknowledgement that caused her tight bun to bob at the back of her head.

14   Aunta's grey hair looked almost straight when it was scraped back. Straight hair meant good hair on the island. And straight hair, thin lips and a small nose were coveted features of beauty according to the national psyche. There were of course gradations, particularly when it came to the question of colour. The whiter the better. Light was good; dark wasn't. That was how our people saw themselves, through the prism imposed on them by their colonizers. . . .

15   "What's pressure?" I asked, for I was continuously hearing that grown-ups had pressure.

16   "Well," she said, as she frowned at the sock and then shifted her studious gaze to rest on the basket, "it's a thing with the blood. Like it's pushing too hard."

17   "Could it make you burst, Aunta? Will Edith burst?"

18   "No," she laughed, resting the ensocked stone on her lap, "I don't think it's that bad."

19   "Well she mustn't burst before tomorrow. 'Cause what's tomorrow?" I asked.

20   "It's April Fool's Day. And I hope you're not coming with one of your tricks!"

21   "But what else is tomorrow, Aunta?" I repeated, flopping my elbows onto her pint-sized lap with the ailing sock.

22   Struggling to regain the thread now pulled out of the needle, she answered absently, "What else . . . you tell me, child."

23   "It's Edith's birthday!"

24   "Good Lord. . . . You're right, you know. . . . I must see to that at once. . . . You know what you can do for me? Run down to the garden and see if you find Batiste. Ask him to cut a good pineapple for Edith. Tell him to make sure it's sweet. Have you got her a present?"

25   "Mardi° took me to Kong's. I got April Violets."

26   "What's that?"

27   "Powder. Edith likes powder, Aunta." I was becoming exasperated.

28   "Oh, powder! It's *called* April Violets! See what a nice girl you can be." . . .

29   In the evenings, if I was lonely, I would ask Edith to come and stay with me and sing her hymns while I went to sleep. She would promise to try to come, but always later; never then, with me. Sometimes Mardi would ask her to stay with me if she and Pardi were both going out.

30   It was a rare treat when she came.

31   I would hear her lumbering up the stairs, resting after every three or four steps and whispering to the Lord.

I can still hear her: "Lawd, me Jesus, ah comin', ah comin'."   32

Her dresses were often faded from laundering, and so thickly   33
starched that they arrived around the door before she did, like an
annunciating flag. Beneath, her stockings had settled around her
ankles in bunched folds, despairing of travelling farther up those
insurmountable legs.

She would stand at the door for a while, holding her hips and   34
blowing. That is how she arrived that night. She had come to baby-sit.

"Wha' 'appen to Miss Badness dis time?"   35

"Come here, Edith," I shrieked with delight as I bounded out of   36
the small single bed to drag her the last few feet of the way.

"Wait nuh, chile . . . you wan' fe kill me! You doan see dat me   37
can 'ardly ketch me bret . . . me soon a go 'ome to me Lawd, chile."

She slumped heavily into the white chair next to my bed, pro-   38
duced her large plastic fan with a Chinese motif and proceeded to
fan herself in time to the rhythm of her breathing. I jumped back
into bed beside her.

"You jus' wan' company 'cause you Mardi gone an' lef' you   39
again. Weh she gone, chile, she gone a meetin'?"

"I don't know," I singsonged, holding onto the crisp corner of   40
her skirt, feeling the comfort of her presence in the large old house.
Its emptiness at night without Mardi and Pardi seemed to knot its
diffuse° shadows into a silent black fist.

"Are you better, Edith?"   41

"Me nat better! Me did go an' see de Injan doctor today."   42

"Have you got pressure?"   43

"What you know 'bout pressure?" She was laughing. "Yes, 'im   44
say I 'ave pressure. 'Im gimme more pill weh cos' summuch money
an' nu do nuttin'. So coolie man stay!" She sucked her teeth in res-
ignation.

"How old will you be tomorrow?" I asked her.   45

"'Ow ol'? Me na know . . . plenty ol', plenty ol'. . . ."   46

I felt the heaviness of her warm hand on my back as she started   47
to stroke me to sleep. From the very centre of her massive chest her
voice rose sadly, like an old crying practised night after night. Some
bloom of melody succoured the tune within the hoarse cobwebs of
her throat.

"Swing low, sweet chariot . . ."   48

She had once heard Paul Robeson° sing this at Drumblair, "all   49
we ancestor dem weep when it roll out from inside of 'im." It
seemed she was still remembering that evening as she carefully
retrieved each word from its place of memory.

The chariot was coming forth to carry her home, and it was   50
coming forth to carry me to sleep. I did not even feel the corner of
her skirt escape my grasp when she left me.

51   Soon after I opened my eyes the next morning, I remembered Edith's birthday and set off to deliver her present. Before I could cross the hall to start down the stairs, Mardi appeared in the opposite doorway. It seemed such a long time since I'd seen her, though it was really only a day. I ran to her, throwing my arms around the top of her legs. I hugged her and hugged her. But I knew by her gentleness and impotence° that something was wrong.

52   "It's Edith's birthday," I said tentatively. I looked up at her face for an answer.

53   But she told me Edith was gone. She had gone last night. They had taken her away.

54   "But she hasn't got the April Violets!"

55   This seemed to sum up my predicament°. I had never encountered death and had no idea of its implications. But over the following days I began to realize that there would be no more singing at bedtime, no more guava breezes wafting from the basement. Dearest Edith had gone—propelled up into heaven, I presumed, by the pressure of her blood. Or had that chariot come to collect her? Or had whoever ordains these things simply played a cruel trick on me and on Drumblair on April Fool's Day?

Words and Meanings

Paragraph

1	visceral	governed by instincts rather than intellect
	sombrero	wide-brimmed hat
5	guava	tropical fruit
	lethargic	sluggish, slow
12	Aunta	Miss Boyd, housekeeper at Drumblair
25	Mardi	author's grandmother (grandfather is Pardi)
40	diffuse	scattered, spread out
49	Paul Robeson	African-American singer and civil-rights activist
51	impotence	helplessness
55	predicament	difficult situation

Structure and Strategy

1. In what order has Manley arranged the details of her DESCRIPTION of Drumblair (paragraph 1)?

2. What FIGURES OF SPEECH does Manley use in paragraph 1 to describe Drumblair? What overall impression of the house do these details help create?
3. What senses does Manley appeal to in her description of Edith's basement room (paragraphs 3 to 6)?
4. Consider Manley's physical descriptions of Edith (paragraphs 7 to 10 and 31 to 50). What dominant impression do they create? What details tell you that the writer was very young when Edith was part of her life?
5. When does Manley last see Edith? What is the IRONY in the timing of this event?
6. Why do you think Manley relies so heavily on dialogue to convey the story of life at Drumblair? (See paragraphs 15 to 28, for example.) Do you think the dialogue, including the representation of Edith's speech in dialect, is an effective way of telling the story? Why or why not?

Content and Purpose

1. What kinds of work does Edith do at Drumblair? What is the physical problem that threatens her? How does the young narrator learn about it?
2. What characteristics do Drumblair and Edith have in common? How do you think Manley, as an adult, feels about Edith? About life at Drumblair?
3. Describe Edith's character. What kind of woman is she? What motivates her in life?
4. In paragraph 14, Manley comments on the awareness of racial distinctions in Jamaica. Explain the meaning of the last sentence in this paragraph.

Suggestions for Writing

1. Describe your childhood home. Take care to select details that will both create a picture in your reader's mind and communicate the feelings that you have for this home.
2. Describe a person who was important to you when you were a child. Your DESCRIPTION should enable your reader to "see" the person; equally important, it should convey the emotional reasons for this person's importance in your life.
3. Narrate the story of your first encounter with the death of someone who was close to you when you were a child.

The Yukon

DOUGLAS COUPLAND

Douglas Coupland (b. 1961), novelist, short-story writer, journalist, sculptor, and winner of two Canadian National Awards for Excellence in Industrial Design, is perhaps most famous for coining the term "Generation X." His novels include *Generation X* (1991), *Shampoo Planet* (1992), *Microserfs* (1995), and *City of Glass* (2000). "The Yukon" is taken from *Souvenir of Canada* (2002), a collection of photographs and essays about Canadian memorabilia.

1   When my father went civilian in 1966, one of the first things he did, once he could, was to buy a twin-engine de Havilland Otter floatplane. I think he did this to re-create what were the happiest days of his life, paying for his medical school tuition by flying bush planes during the summer in the wilds of northern Quebec and Labrador, into areas then still marked UNMAPPED. He ferried the inhabitants of remote outposts to and from hospitals, as well as Canadian and American military and mining engineers invading Labrador, part of what was then a brand-new Canadian province (Newfoundland) only a few years old.

2   [When I was young], trips with Dad in the plane often felt like torture, but with hindsight I can see them as an exotic and charmed way to have spent a part of my youth. When I was around thirteen, my father flew my younger brother and me in the Twin Otter up to the Yukon. First, we overnighted in Whitehorse, a city of diesel fumes, hamburgers, beige dusty roads and people getting really *really* drunk at the local bars. The Klondike fulfills many expectations. The next day we headed off into Kluane *(kloo-awn-ay)* National Park—a place I never even knew existed, but to fly over it was to apprehend God or the next world or something altogether richer than the suburbs of home. Glaciers drape like mink over feldspar ridges like broken backs, and the twenty-four-hour midnight sun somehow burns paler and whiter than the sun in the south—and the horizon seems to come from a bigger planet. To see a wild landscape like this is to crack open your soul and see larger landscapes inside yourself. Or so I believe. Raw nature must be preserved, so that we never forget the grandeur it can inspire.

Anyway, as we landed at a fishing camp on Tincup Lake, my 3
younger brother and I, a bit young for soul-cracking, were intent on
panning for gold, having boned up on the subject the week before,
becoming experts along the way and doubtlessly destined to tap
the mother lode the locals had missed in all of their adult ignorance. We'd barely docked before we hit the nearest stream, our
pans verily frisbeeing ahead of us.

Several hours later, we were goldless, but as consolation, we 4
played the ancient game of trying to convince each other that the
thin, triangular rocks just found were indeed, *no I swear it, man,*
arrowheads.

The next day boredom set in, and Floyd, the boat boy working 5
for the summer as part of a juvenile rehabilitation program, suggested we ride down to the end of the lake to check out a trapper's
cabin that had only ever been sighted from the air. The thing about
Floyd was that, well, I wasn't sure if he was a living person or the
ghost of a dead boat boy like in a Stephen King novel. Everything
about him was white, and he smoked too much and his breath
didn't steam the morning air like everybody else's. However,
boredom being boredom, we went, with a canoe lying criss-crossed
over the twelve-foot aluminum heap powered by an Evinrude 50.
We set out around four in the afternoon for the 16-kilometre trip to
the end of the lake. Once there, we beached the boat on a gravel bar
and paddled downstream. Maybe 3 kilometres down, we came to
the cabin, not much to speak of, like the Unabomber's shack after a
hundred years of rot.

We parked the canoe and went "inside," quotation marks used 6
because half the roof was gone. At the very least, I expected to find
a skeleton wrapped in mummified beaver pelts, because after all,
I'd canoed to this place with Floyd the Undead. Instead, we found
an old coffee can, the top of a tobacco tin and lots of animal bones
in a pile out behind. None of this was very exciting, but at least
we'd been the first to visit the cabin in probably fifty years, and I
felt what visitors to Shackleton's° Antarctic home must feel.

Fine. 7

Then we portaged up the river's edge maybe ten paces before 8
Floyd the Undead said, "I guess I was wrong. Doug—we can't
portage because there's no path."

Moron. 9

So we ended up wading 3 kilometres upstream in water only a 10
degree above freezing, three steps ahead, two steps back, and it was
past midnight when we finally reached the aluminum boat, which
ran out of gas after three putt-putts. But it was bright outside and

we were young (at least I was—Floyd, being undead, had no age) so we canoed back down the lake, arriving at 4:00 a.m. and expecting a search party in high anxiety. Instead, we found a poker game at the peak of its action.

11   "Hi guys. Have a good trip down the lake?"

12   Mutter mutter.

13   And that is the Yukon. Or a slice of it. Everyone I've ever met from the Yukon is successful: couture designers, actors, builders and private investigators. Something about the place makes people think and act big—the slightly larger horizon makes them look ahead slightly farther. It's a place that delivers the dream.

Words and Meanings

Paragraph
6   Shackleton   Sir Ernest Henry (1874–1922), Irish explorer best known for the perilous journey he undertook to seek help for his stranded crew after his ship, the *Endurance*, was crushed in ice during his third Antarctic expedition, in 1914–16

Structure and Strategy

1. How does the first paragraph set up both the narrative and the TONE of this piece? How would you describe the tone?
2. Paragraph 2 is full of descriptive details. Identify three or four that you think are particularly effective and explain why.
3. In the narrative section of this essay (paragraphs 3 to 12), Coupland tells an ANECDOTE. Several of the paragraphs are one or two words. Why? Are these words intended to represent dialogue or something else? Where does Coupland make clear the point of the anecdote?

Content and Purpose

1. How did Coupland feel about the Yukon wilderness when he was thirteen years old? How does he feel about it as an adult? Where are the two contrasting perspectives highlighted in the essay?
2. Summarize the events of the trip to and from the trapper's cabin (paragraphs 5 to 12). What is the connection between the trip and Coupland's concluding remarks (paragraph 13)?
3. Who is Floyd, and why does Coupland call him "the Undead"? Floyd is the only person in this essay who is described in any detail. What is the similarity between Floyd and the setting in which he lives?

4. What does Coupland think of the Yukon and its people? What connection is there between the landscape and the people?
5. What does Coupland mean by his concluding statement, "It's a place that delivers the dream"?
6. Would Coupland be likely to favour intensive exploration of the Arctic for oil, diamonds, and other natural resources? Why or why not?

Suggestions for Writing

1. Write an essay about a personal experience from your past that seemed difficult, boring, or agonizing at the time but is now a fond memory. Why do you think your feelings about the experience changed?
2. Describe a natural setting you enjoy visiting. What is it about the place that appeals to you?

Dispatches from the Poverty Line

PAT CAPPONI

Author of *Upstairs in the Crazy House, Dispatches from the Poverty Line,* and *The War at Home: An Intimate Portrait of Canada's Poor,* Pat Capponi (b. 1949) is a board member of the Centre for Addiction and Mental Health and a monthly contributor to *NOW* magazine. A survivor of psychiatric illness and long periods of unemployment, Capponi is familiar with the world of the sick and the poor. She was recently awarded the Order of Ontario and the C. M. Hincks Award from the Canadian Mental Health Association.

We live in a time when manipulation of public opinion has been elevated to a science, when stereotypes are accepted as true representatives of their segment of the population. And, as always, stereotypes cause a great deal of pain to those tarred with the same brush. . . .   1

I am not innocent as far as taking refuge in stereotypes goes. As much as I try to catch myself at it, on occasion I'm forced to admit to myself, and sometimes to others, that I've fallen prey to its comforting lure.   2

I've served on many committees, task forces, working groups and boards in my seventeen years of mental health advocacy°. Before consumer involvement became more widely accepted, I was   3 often the only ex-patient at the table, trying to deal with hospital administrators, bureaucrats, psychiatrists, nurses and family groups. I didn't think any board could scare me again, or silence me through intimidation.

4   I was, however, being forced to admit that one hospital board in particular was giving me a great deal of angst°. It left me feeling as though I'd been flung back through time. . . . I used to tell audiences of consumers and mental health staff that one of our biggest problems was that there was no consensus in the system concerning the value of involving clients in the management and delivery of services. One day I'd be working with an agency that possessed the equivalent of New York sophistication around the issues, and the next I'd feel as though I were in Alabama before the civil rights movement got under way. It wasn't unusual for these opposites to be within a few city blocks of each other.

5   That was part of my problem with this board, that it was Alabama-like while believing itself to be cutting edge. But there was more. There were deep and obvious class distinctions, and even though I was, at the time, gainfully employed, a published author, someone who possessed the respect of my community, I felt intimidated, looked down on, stereotyped and all the rest. It got so that I had to force myself to attend.

6   The board was a status board, composed of high-powered bankers, lawyers, publishers and consultants, as well as hospital executives. I was the only one in jeans, in a hat. I was the only one from my particular class and background. I was the only voice expressing criticism of the liberal establishment we were running. . . . Meetings were corporate°; when I would leave for a cigarette I felt I should be bowing and backing up to the door. Nobody laughed, it seemed, ever. Nobody talked out of turn.

7   Then, one afternoon when I had screwed up my courage to attend, I bumped into the "fat cat" lawyer in the hallway. He made a joke, and I made one back before I had time to think about it. We both laughed, and . . . we both stared at each other, surprised at the unlikely evidence of a sense of humour beneath the stereotype. Ice got broken. Then the banker who had offered me lifts home before, which I'd declined—what would I have to talk to him about in the car?—offered again, and I accepted. I even teased him about his brand new BMW and the pervasive smell of leather from the seats. He demonstrated how his car phone responded to voice orders to dial numbers, and I confess I got a kick out of the gimmickry. . . .

8   I remember another kind of breakthrough event at that board. I was trying once again to explain why I needed more people like me (from my class and experience) around the table. How easy it was

to get intimidated in the setting we were in if you didn't find the corporate air invigorating. How easy it was to dismiss the views I was putting forward because it was only me they were hearing them from. How our class differences, our life experiences, created gulfs between us.

My banker friend took umbrage°. He was sure, he said, that he was quite capable of relating to me as a person, as another human being. He felt we were operating on a level playing field°, and that I wasn't giving them enough credit. **9**

My lawyer friend then made a remarkable statement. **10**

"That's not true," he said. "Pat didn't start out on a level **11** playing field with me. I took one look at her and summed her up. It wasn't until later that I started to see her differently."

"And I," I said, "did the same thing, summed up you guys at **12** a glance, and what I felt was your attitude towards me. It got easier to walk around with a chip on my shoulder than to try and relate to you."

Even the publisher chimed in: **13**

"I understand what you mean about intimidation. I never saw myself as intimidating, I like to think I'm an easygoing, friendly guy. But some of my staff have been pointing out to me that people who work for me don't have that same picture, because I have power over them. It's not easy or comfortable to realize that you may scare people, but a lot of times it's true."

Only the banker held out for the level playing field precept, but **14** of course the conversation was ruled out of order and we were on to the next item on the agenda°.

A month or two later, I decided to transfer my bank account to a **15** branch nearer my residence. To get an account in the first place had been a challenge. I don't have credit cards, or a driver's licence: therefore, I don't have a system-recognized identity. This is a very common dilemma for those who make up the underclass, and it accounts for the prevalence° and huge success of Money Mart cheque-cashing services in poor areas. As long as I've been an advocate, various groups of workers have tried to break through the banking system, to work out generally acceptable ways of identifying clients to tellers through letters of introduction, or special cards, with no real success. . . .

In order for me to get an account in the first place, my pub- **16** lisher, Cynthia Good, had to take me into her branch, where we met with her "personal banking representative," and on the basis of Cynthia's knowledge of me, I got an account in time to deposit the cheque I'd received for the movie rights to my book.

I confess I felt quite mainstream for a while, with my PIN **17** number and cheques and accounts book, as though I'd arrived. It was enough to make me overconfident. I decided it was silly to travel forty minutes to that branch when there was one a few blocks from me. I still had a balance of a little over $5,000, so I didn't anticipate any problems. I walked into my local branch and was soon seated across from yet another "personal banking representative."

18   "What I can do for you today?" she asked, pleasantly.

19   "I'd like to transfer my account to here, please," I responded, handing over my account book and bank card.

20   "I see, um, would you have some identification?"

21   I was puzzled.

22   "Nothing you guys seem to accept. But I only want to transfer, not open, an account."

23   She persists:
"A major credit card? A driver's licence?"

24   I have a birth certificate. I remember trying to rent a video using it, and the owner of the store turning the card over and saying, "Your signature's not on it."

25   I shake my head. I give her the card of the other personal banking representative, the one in whose presence I had been validated. She phones. She shakes her head. That person is on vacation. She purses her lips, not liking to create difficulties for me, but there are rules.

26   "I'm sorry, we really do need identification."

27   I'm getting angry, and I suspect she feels it, which accounts for her visible nervousness. It won't help to get snippy with her. I could just pack it in and leave—it wouldn't be the end of the world, after all. But the battle for reason is under way. It would feel too much like defeat to withdraw now.

28   I try for a reasoned, measured tone.

29   "I don't want to withdraw anything. I have $5,000 in my account. You have my card, my cheques, my account book."

30   I hear steps behind me, I'm sure the security guard is getting ready to pounce.

31   "It's a different branch of the same bank. C'mon, be reasonable."

32   "Don't you even have your Indian Status Card?"

33   "I'm not Indian!"

34   Ordinarily, I would take it as a compliment, being mistaken for one of the First People, but in this context, I know there's some heavy stereotyping, and quite possibly some heavy attitude, going on.

35   I get a flash. I'm terrible about names, remembering names. I can recall the most minute° details of conversations, mannerisms, backgrounds and clothing but not names. But I do remember the division my BMW banker is president of. And I do remember it's this same corporation.

I ask her to look up the name of the guy in charge of ———.   36

"Why?" she asks, immediately suspicious.   37

"I know him, he can tell you I exist."   38

Perhaps to humour me, she flips open a book and recites some   39
names.

"That's him," I cry, vindicated°. "Give him a call, will you?"   40

I suppose it's like telling a private to ring up a general at the   41
request of a possible lunatic, an aboriginal impersonator: it's not
done.

She excuses herself to consult with a superior. Long minutes   42
pass. I feel myself being examined from the glassed-in cubicles
where the decision-makers sit. I feel the breath of the security
officer. I feel renewed determination.

She's back.   43

"I'm sorry for the delay. His secretary had some difficulty   44
reaching him, he's in a meeting. But he is available now."

My understanding smile is as false and strained as her apology.   45

She picks up the phone and annoyingly turns her chair away   46
from me while she speaks in low tones into the receiver. A few
heartbeats, then she passes the phone to me.

Not waiting for his voice, I say: 47

"I told you there's no level playing field."

He laughs, loudly and honestly.   48

In under ten minutes, I have my new account, my new card,   49
cheques and a small degree of satisfaction.

Chalk up one for the good guys.   50

I take refuge in a nearby park, liking and needing the sun and a   51
place to enjoy it. I've checked out the four or five in my neighbourhood, and on days when I need to walk, I go up to the one opposite
the Dufferin Mall. I love the solitude, the birds, the green—a perfect
setting for reading and tanning. Picking an empty bench, away
from small clumps of people dotting the large park, I open my
paperback and disappear into it.

It doesn't seem very long (my watch died a few months ago)   52
before an old fellow, tottering on his cane, shuffles towards me. I look
up at his approach, smile briefly and dive back into P. D. James. I am
dismayed when he chooses to perch on the other end of my bench,
and I try to ignore his presence while my conscience starts bothering
me. Now, I only smiled at him because I am aware that some folks
think I look a bit tough, and I didn't want him worrying, but he
might have mistaken the gesture for a come-chat-with-me invitation.
He's probably lonely, isolated, this is probably his big daily outing.
Would it kill me to spend a couple of minutes talking to him? Damn.

53   I close my book, look over at him looking over at me expectantly.

54   "Beautiful day, isn't it?"

55   I can barely make out his reply, cloaked in a thick accent, but his head bobbing up and down is pretty clear. I'm stuck for the next sentence, but he keeps going enthusiastically. I make out his name, repeating it triumphantly: "Victor! Hi, I'm Pat."

56   One arthritic hand grasps mine briefly, then goes back to rest on his cane with the other one.

57   "I'm retired." He's getting better at speaking clearly, maybe it was just a lack of opportunity that made him rusty. "I was an engineer."

58   "You live around here?"

59   He turns painfully, pointing vaguely over his shoulder.

60   "Right over there, a beautiful place. Very beautiful place."

61   "Good for you."

62   I offer him a cigarette, which he accepts, and we sit in companionable silence in the sun. I'm thinking after the smoke I will move on, find another park, maybe nearer my home.

63   He's talking again, and when I realize what he's saying my jaw drops open.

64   "If you come see my place, I will give you twenty dollars."

65   "Jesus Christ! Are you crazy?" I'm so annoyed, and shocked, and thrown off balance by his offer, that I'm blustering. I want to whack him, except he'd probably fall over, like the dirty-old-man character on *Laugh-In*.

66   "Listen to me," I lecture, as I shake my finger in his face. "First off, you're committing a crime. Secondly, it's stupid and dangerous for you. You can't go around offering money to people you don't know for things I don't want to think about. You've insulted me. I could have you arrested! Do you understand?"

67   Now I'm pretty sure what his daily tour of the park is about, and I worry about the school-age girls that hang out at lunch time.

68   "If I see you doing this to anyone else, I will report you, do you get that? I'll be watching you!"

69   He's stuttering out an apology, which I don't believe, and I refrain from kicking his cane, though I really want to.

70   On my way home, in between feeling outraged and feeling dirtied, I start to laugh at my own stereotyping of a lonely old man in need of conversation in juxtaposition° with his own stereotyping of me.

71   People ought to wear summing-up signs sometimes, just so you'd know what to expect.

Words and Meanings

		Paragraph
mental health advocacy	working for improvement in the lives of people with mental illnesses	3
angst	anxiety	4
corporate	formal, businesslike	6
took umbrage	objected	9
operating on a level playing field	business jargon for "equal"	
agenda	list of topics to be discussed at a meeting	14
prevalence	widespread existence	15
minute	tiny, insignificant	35
vindicated	justified, cleared of suspicion	40
in juxtaposition	occurring close together	70

Structure and Strategy

1. This piece consists of two distinct narrative ILLUSTRATIONS. The first takes place in paragraphs 1 to 50, the second in paragraphs 51 to 71. What links the two examples?
2. Identify the author's thesis statement.
3. Why does Capponi introduce her discussion of stereotyping with a CLICHÉ ("tarred with the same brush," paragraph 1)? What does this cliché mean?
4. Why do you think the author describes her experience as a mental health advocate in Canada in terms of a contrast between "New York sophistication" and "Alabama before the civil rights movement" (paragraph 4)? Are these comparisons meaningful to the Canadian audience she is writing for? Are they original or are they STEREOTYPES?
5. Capponi relies primarily on dialogue to tell her story. Why do you think she chooses to re-create her experiences for the reader through dialogue rather than to summarize them through DESCRIPTION and NARRATION?

Content and Purpose

1. Based on the hints given in the essay, what do you think Capponi looks like? How does she dress? Given her appearance and behaviour, how might people STEREOTYPE her?

2. Paragraph 7 contains two examples of stereotyping. What are they, and who is responsible for them? What succeeds in breaking through these stereotypes? What other "breakthrough events" does Capponi relate in this essay?
3. How does Capponi succeed in opening her first bank account? Why is banking a problem for her? Does she think it is a problem for others? If so, why and for whom?
4. Why does the "personal banking representative" not want to transfer Capponi's account to her branch? In what ways does this woman stereotype Capponi?
5. How is the standoff with the banking representative resolved? How does Capponi feel about the resolution? What solutions do you think might be available to other victims of stereotyping?
6. In the second ILLUSTRATION (paragraphs 51 to 71), what does Capponi think the old man in the park is looking for? What is he really looking for? How does Capponi react to the misunderstanding? Does she learn anything from this experience?

Suggestions for Writing

1. Have you ever experienced stereotyping because of the way you look? Write an essay that recounts your experience and your response to it.
2. Have you ever wrongly stereotyped someone based on his or her appearance or behaviour? Write an essay that tells the story of your experience and indicates what you learned from it.

Bush League Business

BASIL JOHNSTON

Scholar and storyteller Basil Johnston was born on Parry Island Sound Indian Reserve in 1929. One of the few living speakers of the ancient Ojibway (Chippewa) language, he is the author of many stories, essays, and books on First Nations culture and history, including *Ojibway Heritage* (1976) and *Indian School Days* (1988), an autobiographical account of his childhood experiences at a residential school run by Jesuit priests in Spanish, Ontario. His most recent book, *Crazy Dave* (1999), is a family memoir.

A t the end of March 1945, three months short of completing
Grade 9, I dropped out of [school] to return to the sanc-
tuary° and comfort of Cape Croker°.

In the fall of the same year, when my father left the reserve to
seek his fortune in the lumber camps, I was left in sole possession
and proprietorship of the family estate, which consisted of a log
house, a log barn and a log privy situated on a parcel of land of
twenty-five acres, more or less. Formerly my grandmother, Rosa,
had owned it.

Upon my father's departure, survival—mine—became my first
and only object in the sixteenth year of my life. With trout near
extinction in Georgian Bay and pulp depleted, opportunities for
survival were scarce for everyone but farmers. To go on "relief," as
welfare was known in those days, was unthinkable. No man
worthy of the name would ever think of asking for relief, and
people at the Cape proudly boasted that only two people got relief
during the Depression.

I would make the people of the Cape proud of me. In the waning
days of August I began to assess the community's business needs, its
resources and my expertise. In training I had Grade 8 and half of
Grade 9, which was of no value to anyone. According to my analysis
there was one constant need in winter: fuel. And as far as my keen
eye could see, the resources were limitless. All that was required in
the way of capital expenditures was an axe. I already had an axe.

Before launching my timbering operation, I conducted a mental
market-research survey, in accordance with the finest business and
economic principles. There were Pulch (Mrs. Isadore Pitawaniquot),
Meeks (Stanley McLeod, my uncle), Shabow (Mr. Francis
Nadjiwon), Bee Dee (Peter Nadjiwon), Kitchi-Flossie (Mrs. William
Akiwenzie), Chick (Walter Johnston, my uncle), Kitchi-Susan (Mrs.
Susan Taylor), Shawnee (Charles Jones), Kitchi-Low See (Mrs. Lucy
Nawash), Christine Keeshig (my grandmother's sister), Maggie
(Mrs. Desjardins), Eezup (Andrew Akiwenzie), Pollock (Mrs. E.
Akiwenzie), and many, many more.

Revenue! More than I had realized. I calculated that I could cut
a load of poles every day. At three dollars a load, less a dollar to the
teamster for delivery, that was sixty dollars a month—a handsome
profit. I'd survive. More than survive! Except that there were
Sundays and Saturdays, and that my potential customers would
not burn a load of fuel each day. I reduced my estimates accordingly. Then I realized that many of my potential customers cut their

own wood, and that I would be in direct competition with my Uncle Stanley. There wasn't as much revenue in cutting wood as I had originally thought.

7   I needed advice. I went to my Uncle Stanley, who was an expert in survival. He suggested that I go into the fur industry, at the primary level, trapping or harvesting raccoons. And he showed me a price list issued by one of the fur buyers on Spadina Avenue in Toronto to illustrate how profitable the raccoon industry was: up to twenty-four dollars for a prime pelt. I panted and drooled. Uncle was willing to share both his expertise and his resources. There were more raccoons than my uncle and I together could harvest. All I needed was to kill one fat raccoon every day and I'd be in business.

8   Uncle was generous. He conceded° to me as my own hunting territory the ridge, a part of the Niagara Escarpment formation that extended from the Lighthouse to Cove of Cork, bending inward as it followed the contour of Little North Bay, outward to Benjamin's Point and then south-west until it sloped into the flat sedimentary rocks at Pine Tree Point. In addition, all the territory between was mine to hunt.

9   One of the advantages of this kind of enterprise is that little capital investment is required. My total capital equipment consisted of two enthusiastic but inexperienced dogs and an axe. But that was all that was needed for this kind of business.

10   After the trawling season was over it was my daily routine to set out with a lunch in an old army haversack, axe in hand and preceded by two exuberant dogs who raced ahead and ranged the bushes in search of any beast worth barking at: squirrels, rabbits, chipmunks, groundhogs, skunks, porcupines, foxes, partridge— anything, so long as it was alive. I had to investigate every round of barking, otherwise the dogs would not leave the quarry; or worse, they would mutiny and go home. Instead of walking ten to twelve miles, which would have constituted the whole round-trip distance of my beat, I frequently walked anywhere between twenty and twenty-five miles, often for nothing.

11   On returning home in the evening I had to cut wood, make a fire, cook a meal, and, if I had got a raccoon, skin and clean the beast and stretch the pelt on the roof or side of the barn. By the time I had completed these operations, I was ready for sleep.

12   My hunting technique was primitive and simple, but effective. If the dogs treed a raccoon, I'd chop the tree down and, if need be, two or three other trees. As soon as tree and quarry fell to earth my assistants would be instantly upon the raccoon, holding the victim for the coup de grâce°, which I delivered with the flat of my axe. If the dogs ran the raccoon into a cave or burrow, a torch made from a

mixture of leaves and pine gum stuck at the end of a pole would flush it out. Once the raccoon emerged, my assistants would seize it and hold it fast in their jaws for execution. Once, as I delivered the fatal blow, my dog Chalk sprang at my victim for one extra bite. I hit Chalk instead of the raccoon. From the way my dog quivered and convulsed, I thought I had killed him.

Despite their numbers, I didn't kill as many raccoons as I expected. Nevertheless, I killed enough to cover the roof and sides of the barn with raccoon hides. 13

Only once did I kill more than two in a day; on that occasion I killed six in one cave. Killing an enormous moose or catching a net full of fish may be the dream of most hunters or fishermen, but the dream may turn into a bad dream. I killed the six raccoons at Benjamin's Point on my return patrol. I looked at my victims with the practised eye of a fur appraiser; at least fifty dollars. My energies were instantly restored. And even though my energies and strength could have borne the total weight of the six raccoons, I could no more carry six flopping raccoon corpses than I could carry two greased monkeys, no matter how I tried. I resorted to the simple expedient° of carrying forward three at a time for some distance, leaving them on the ground, and then returning for the other three. By this means I eventually arrived at the old Bert Ashkewe homestead and corner. It was already dark and I still had a mile to walk. Only the vision of fifty dollars sustained me. While I mentally caressed the bills I heard the snort of horses and the rumble of wagon wheels. It was Charles Jones, Jr., known as Shawnee in the village. I hitched a ride. 14

After I was done skinning the raccoons, I reviewed my production and estimates of revenue for the coming winter—a market forecast of sorts. Up to this point the raccoon division of my fur operations was not yielding as much profit as I had originally anticipated, and it would yield even less during the winter, that was clear. I would have to diversify°. 15

Once more I studied the price list. The only fur bearer on the list that inhabited our reserve in sufficient numbers to justify hunting was the squirrel: black, red, grey and flying. In fact, there was an overpopulation of black squirrels, especially in Peter Nadjiwon's sugar bush. At $1.25 for a prime black-squirrel pelt, there was a tidy profit to be realized. 16

I diversified the very next morning. With only a slingshot I blasted fifteen fat squirrels from the trees before half the afternoon was over. Besides a handsome profit, there was meat. 17

At home I studied the deskinning manuals that my Uncle Stanley had given to me. According to the instructions, squirrels were to be unskinned from the ankles, then over the head, inside 18 out, in much the same way women remove their nightgowns. After the squirrel is unskinned, the pelt should be sheathed inside-out tightly over a pointed arched wooden frame, much as a dress is slipped over a mannequin. Not only would I have to deskin the squirrels, I would have to make the frames. Fortunately, across the road, there was a cedar-rail fence; ample raw material for frames.

19   I couldn't wait to perform surgery; the manual, with its diagrams, made the operation look simple. All one had to do was to follow instructions. Because I did not have the proper instruments, I could not begin immediately. . . .

20   . . . I went across the road to my neighbour, Francis Nadjiwon, to borrow the proper surgical instrument.

21   With proper instruments and as directed by the diagrams, I cut an incision from ankle to ankle, following, as it were, an invisible inseam. Just as the manual had promised, it was easy. Step two was to peel off said squirrel's hide down and over its arms and head. I peeled, but the hide did not peel off as easily as promised in the diagram. As I undressed my patient, tissue, sinew and fat clung to the hide and would not let go. I consulted my manual, but it offered no guidance on a method of removing skin from tough tissue, or of pinning down a limp squirrel long enough to divest it of its skin. I resolved this difficulty by tying the squirrel's hindpaws to a nail. At least I had some control over the beast, and I peeled its pelt off as far as the head where, in my haste, I peeled too indelicately; I tore the skin. Discouraging as was the wasted work and the loss of profit, I consoled myself with the thought that at least I had the meat. I could not indulge in self-pity too long. I had to go on.

22   I operated on the second squirrel without accident. By sawing, chopping, splitting, carving, whittling and shaving I eventually constructed a stretching frame. As gently as I could, I slipped the pelt over the frame, pulled and stretched downward. Either I pulled too hard, or the pelt was too thin; my squirrel pelt split.

23   Two gone and wasted; thirteen to go. It was now 9:30 p.m. As yet I had not eaten. At this rate of deskinning, I would not be done until noon the next day.

24   On I worked, resolved to deskin every little beast, even if I had to work through the night. I had to recover some of my invested time and effort. As a surgeon must take care not to skewer a patient during surgery, so did I operate on squirrel number three.

25   Afterward I mounted my patient on a frame. I felt proud as I earned $1.25, which had taken an hour and a half. By 3:00 a.m. I had deskinned two more.

Hungry, sleepy, cold and stiff-fingered, I decided there and then to close down my squirrel diversification program. To hell with squirrels; raccoons were easier. 26

Maybe it would be better to go back to school. I had heard vague rumours that Spanish° was offering a high-school program. If it were true, I would return. It was my only chance to escape a life of cutting wood. 27

Though raccoons were easier to harvest, they did not generate enough income to support even a marginal existence. To keep from starving and to uphold the image of being a man, capable of self-support, I undertook whatever work was available: trawling the waters of the Cape the entire summer, fishing with nets in the fall with Casimir Taylor, drawing water for Resime Akiwenzie and Herman Taylor during their hog-slaughtering sessions and, finally, working for Frank Nadjiwon as farm-hand. For Frank I made a crooked ladder and dismantled a bicycle I was unable to reassemble. I felled trees with style, dug post-holes with grace and spread manure with finesse. I also told Frank about the high-school program being offered at Spanish, and spoke of my intention to return to an institution to which I had not given a single thought since I left it. 28

Frank said, "Yes! You ought to go back, it's your only chance." I guess he knew better than I suspected that I was never going to be a carpenter, plumber, farmer, blacksmith, mechanic or any kind of tradesman. He knew from his experience in the army that no one ever got very far with only Grade 8, not even soldiers. Spanish, no matter how tough, could never be as bad as the army. 29

Words and Meanings

		Paragraph
sanctuary	safe place	1
Cape Croker	Ojibway reserve on the Bruce Peninsula	
conceded	allotted, gave	8
coup de grâce	final blow	12
expedient	means, solution	14
diversify	branch out into other activities	15
Spanish	town north of Manitoulin Island, location of the residential school Johnston attended	27

Structure and Strategy

1. Assess the DICTION of this piece. How does Johnston's use of business JARGON contribute to the TONE? For example, he uses phrases such as "capital expenditures" (paragraph 4), "market-research survey" (paragraph 5), and "diversify" (paragraph 15) to describe hunting in the Northern Ontario bush. Identify other examples of this technique. What do they say about the author's attitude toward his topic?
2. Reread paragraph 6. Is it funny? Why or why not?
3. To what does Johnston compare skinning and stretching a squirrel pelt in paragraph 18? What's the effect of this incongruous comparison?
4. What function do paragraph 12 and paragraphs 18 to 25 have in common? Why has Johnston included them?

Content and Purpose

1. Paragraphs 2 and 3 summarize the author's predicament. What was it? What choices did he have to solve it? Why didn't he go on welfare? Why didn't he turn to fishing and logging, his community's traditional ways of earning a living?
2. Paragraphs 9 to 13 narrate the events of a typical working day in the life of the young raccoon hunter. What strikes you about the work involved? Identify four or five specific details that make the DESCRIPTION effective and memorable.
3. What made Johnston decide to "diversify" into squirrel hunting? What does he learn from his decision?
4. This piece, taken from Johnston's autobiographical work, *Indian School Days,* is a mature adult's recollection of an experience he had when he was sixteen. Identify four or five passages that clearly relate adolescent experience from an adult's perspective. How would these events be described if they were told from the POINT OF VIEW of a teenager?
5. What decision does the narrator arrive at by the end of the piece? Does anyone support his decision? Why?

Suggestions for Writing

1. Write an essay narrating the story of your first job. What did you learn about the value, fun, or misery of "hard work"? Include a variety of descriptive details that not only communicate your experience but also convey to your readers your PURPOSE in writing the essay.

2. Write an essay exploring some of the problems faced by First Nations peoples who attempt to maintain their traditional livelihood—hunting and trapping. Many Native communities have been decimated by the decline of wildlife populations that sustained them for centuries. Another kind of pressure comes from animal-rights activists who object on principle to harvesting animals. Are trapping and hunting morally indefensible? What are the implications of banning these activities based on principles foreign to First Nations peoples?

Deficits

MICHAEL IGNATIEFF

An award-winning author, historian, and broadcaster, Michael Ignatieff (b. 1947) was educated at the University of Toronto and abroad at Harvard and Cambridge. His books include *The Russian Album* (1987), which received the Governor General's Award; *Scar Tissue* (1993), an expanded and fictionalized treatment of the experience related in "Deficits"; *Isaiah Berlin: A Life* (1998); and *Virtual War: Kosovo and Beyond* (2000). Ignatieff is Carr Professor of Human Rights Practice and director of the Carr Center for Human Rights Policy at Harvard's Kennedy School of Government.

It begins the minute Dad leaves the house.   1
"Where is George?"   2
"He is out now, but he'll be back soon."   3
"That's wonderful," she says.   4
About three minutes later she'll look puzzled: "But George . . ."   5
"He's away at work, but he'll be back later."   6
"I see."   7
"And what are you doing here? I mean it's nice, but . . ."   8
"We'll do things together."   9
"I see."   10
Sometimes I try to count the number of times she asks me these questions but I lose track.   11
I remember how it began, five or six years ago. She was 66 then. She would leave a pot to boil on the stove. I would discover it and find her tearing through the house, muttering, "My glasses, my glasses, where the hell are my glasses?"   12

13   I took her to buy a chain so that she could wear her glasses around her neck. She hated it because her mother used to wear *her* glasses on a chain. As we drove home, she shook her fist at the windscreen.

14   "I swore I'd never wear one of these damned things."

15   I date the beginning to the purchase of the chain, to the silence that descended over her as I drove her home from the store.

16   The deficits, as the neurologists call them, are localized. She can tell you what it felt like when the Model T Ford ran over her at the school gates when she was a girl of seven. She can tell you what her grandmother used to say, "A genteel° sufficiency will suffice°," when turning down another helping at dinner. She remembers the Canadian summer nights when her father used to wrap her in a blanket and take her out to the lake's edge to see the stars.

17   But she can't dice an onion. She can't set the table. She can't play cards. Her grandson is five, and when they play pairs with his animal cards, he knows where the second penguin will be. She just turns up cards at random.

18   He hits her because she can't remember anything, because she keeps telling him not to run around quite so much.

19   Then I punish him. I tell him he has to understand.

20   He goes down on the floor, kisses her feet, and promises not to hit her again.

21   She smiles at him, as if for the first time, and says, "Oh, your kiss is so full of sugar."

22   After a week with him, she looks puzzled and says, "He's a nice little boy. Where does he sleep? I mean, who does he belong to?"

23   "He's your grandson."

24   "I see." She looks away and puts her hand to her face.

25   My brother usually stays with her when Dad is out of town. Once or twice a year, it's my turn. I put her to bed at night. I hand her the pills—small green ones that are supposed to control her moods—and she swallows them. I help her out of her bra and slip, roll down her tights, and lift the nightie over her head. I get into the bed next to hers. Before she sleeps she picks up a Len Deighton and reads a few paragraphs, always the same paragraphs, at the place where she has folded down the page. When she falls asleep, I pick the book off her chest and I pull her down in the bed so that her head isn't leaning against the wall. Otherwise she wakes up with a crick in her neck.

26   Often when I wake in the night, I see her lying next to me, staring into the dark. She stares and then she wanders. I used to try to stop her, but now I let her go. She is trying to hold on to what is left. There is a method in this. She goes to the bathroom every time

she wakes, no matter if it is five times a night. Up and down the stairs silently, in her bare feet, trying not to wake me. She turns the lights on and off. Smooths a child's sock and puts it on the bed. Sometimes she gets dressed, after a fashion, and sits on the downstairs couch in the dark, clutching her handbag.

When we have guests to dinner, she sits beside me at the table, holding my hand, bent forward slightly to catch everything that is said. Her face lights up when people smile, when there is laughter. She doesn't say much any more; she is worried she will forget a name and we won't be able to help her in time. She doesn't want anything to show. The guests always say how well she does. Sometimes they say, "You'd never know, really." When I put her to bed afterward I can see the effort has left her so tired she barely knows her own name. 　27

She could make it easier on herself. She could give up asking questions. 　28

"Where we are now, is this our house?" 　29

"Yes." 　30

"Where is our house?" 　31

"In France." 　32

I tell her: "Hold my hand, I'm here. I'm your son." 　33

"I know." 　34

But she keeps asking where she is. The questions are her way of trying to orient° herself, of refusing and resisting the future that is being prepared for her. 　35

She always loved to swim. When she dived into the water, she never made a splash. I remember her lifting herself out of the pool, as sleek as a seal in a black swimsuit, the water pearling off her back. Now she says the water is too cold and taking off her clothes too much of a bother. She paces up and down the poolside, watching her grandson swim, stroking his towel with her hand, endlessly smoothing out the wrinkles. 　36

I bathe her when she wakes. Her body is white, soft, and withered. I remember how, in the changing-huts, she would bend over as she slipped out of her bathing suit. Her body was young. Now I see her skeleton through her skin. When I wash her hair, I feel her skull. I help her from the bath, dry her legs, swathe her in towels, sit her on the edge of the bath and cut her nails: they are horny and yellow. Her feet are gnarled°. She has walked a long way. 　37

When I was as old as my son is now I used to sit beside her at the bedroom mirror watching her apply hot depilatory° wax to her legs and upper lip. She would pull her skirt up to her knees, stretch her legs out on the dresser, and sip beer from the bottle, while 　38 waiting for the wax to dry. "Have a sip," she would say. It tasted bitter. She used to laugh at the faces I made. When the wax had set, she would begin to peel it off, and curse and wince, and let me collect the strips, with fine black hairs embedded in them. When it was over, her legs were smooth, silky to touch.

39   Now I shave her. I soap her face and legs with my shaving brush. She sits perfectly still; as my razor comes around her chin we are as close as when I was a boy.

40   She never complains. When we walk up the hill behind the house, I feel her going slower and slower, but she does not stop until I do. If you ask her whether she is sad, she shakes her head. But she did say once, "It's strange. It was supposed to be more fun than this."

41   I try to imagine what the world is like for her. Memory is what reconciles° us to the future. Because she has no past, her future rushes toward her, a bat's wing brushing against her face in the dark.

42   "I told you. George returns on Monday."

43   "Could you write that down?"

44   So I do. I write it down in large letters, and she folds it in her white cardigan pocket and pats it and says she feels much less worried.

45   In half an hour, she has the paper in her hand and is showing it to me.

46   "What do I do about this?"

47   "Nothing. It just tells you what is going to happen."

48   "But I didn't know anything of this."

49   "Now you do," I say and I take the paper away and tear it up.

50   It makes no sense to get angry at her, but I do.

51   She is afraid Dad will not come back. She is afraid she has been abandoned. She is afraid she will get lost and never be able to find her way home. Beneath the fears that have come with the forgetting, there lie anxieties for which she no longer has any names.

52   She paces the floor, waiting for lunch. When it is set before her, she downs it before anyone else, and then gets up to clear the plates.

53   "What's the hurry?" I ask her.

54   She is puzzled. "I don't know," she says. She is in a hurry, and she does not know why. She drinks whatever I put before her. The wine goes quickly.

55   "You'll enjoy it more if you sip it gently."

56   "What a good idea," she says and then empties the glass with a gulp.

57   I wish I knew the history of this anxiety. But I don't. All she will tell me is about being sprawled in the middle of Regent Street°

amid the blood and shop glass during an air raid, watching a mother sheltering a child, and thinking: I am alone.

In the middle of all of us, she remained alone. We didn't see it. **58** She was the youngest girl in her family, the straggler in the pack, born cross-eyed till they straightened her eyes out with an operation. Her father was a teacher and she was dyslexic°, the one left behind.

In her wedding photo, she is wearing her white dress and **59** holding her bouquet. They are side by side. Dad looks excited. Her eyes are wide open with alarm. Fear gleams from its hiding place. It was her secret and she kept it well hidden. When I was a child, I thought she was faultless, amusing, regal. My mother.

She thinks of it as a happy family, and it was. I remember them **60** sitting on the couch together, singing along to Fats Waller records. She still remembers the crazy lyrics they used to sing:

> There's no disputin'
> That's Rasputin
> The high-falutin loving man.

I don't know how she became so dependent on him, how she lost so many of the wishes she once had for herself, and how all her wishes came to be wishes for him.

She is afraid of his moods, his silences, his departures, and his **61** returns. He has become the weather of her life. But he never lets her down. He is the one who sits with her in the upstairs room, watching television, night after night, holding her hand.

People say: it's worse for you, she doesn't know what is hap- **62** pening. She used to say the same thing herself. Five years ago, when she began to forget little things, she knew what was in store, and she said to me once, "Don't worry. I'll make a cheerful old nut. It's you who'll have the hard time." But that is not true. She feels everything. She has had time to count up every loss. Every night, when she lies awake, she stares at desolation.

What is a person? That is what she makes you wonder. What **63** kind of a person are you if you only have your habits left? She can't remember her grandson's name, but she does remember to shake out her tights at night and she never lets a dish pass her by without trying to clean it, wipe it, clear it up, or put it away. The house is littered with dishes she is putting away in every conceivable cupboard. What kind of a person is this?

It runs in the family. Her mother had it. I remember going to see **64** her in the house with old carpets and dark furniture on Prince Arthur Avenue. The windows were covered with the tendrils of plants growing in enormous Atlas battery jars, and the parquet° floors shone with wax. She took down the giraffe, the water buffalo, and the leopard—carved in wood—that her father had brought back from Africa in the 1880s. She sat in a chair by the fire and silently watched me play with them. Then—and it seems only a week later—I came to have Sunday lunch with her and she was old and diminished and vacant, and when she looked at me she had no idea who I was.

65   I am afraid of getting it myself. I do ridiculous things: I stand on my head every morning so that the blood will irrigate my brain; I compose suicide notes, always some variant of Captain Oates's: "I may be gone for some time." I never stop thinking about what it would be like for this thing to steal over me.

66   She has taught me something. There are moments when her pacing ceases, when her hunted look is conjured° away by the stillness of dusk, when she sits in the garden, watching the sunlight stream through all the trees they planted together over 25 years in this place, and I see something pass over her face which might be serenity°.

67   And then she gets up and comes toward me looking for a glass to wash, a napkin to pick up, a child's toy to rearrange.

68   I know how the story has to end. One day I return home to see her and she puts out her hand and says: "How nice to meet you." She's always charming to strangers.

69   People say I'm already beginning to say my farewells. No, she is still here. I am not ready yet. Nor is she. She paces the floor, she still searches for what has been lost and can never be found again.

70   She wakes in the night and lies in the dark by my side. Her face, in profile, against the pillow has become like her mother's, the eye sockets deep in shadow, the cheeks furrowed° and drawn, the gaze ancient and disabused°. Everything she once knew is still inside her, trapped in the ruined circuits—how I was when I was little, how she was when I was a baby. But it is too late to ask her now. She turns and notices I am awake too. We lie side by side. The darkness is still. I want to say her name. She turns away from me and stares into the night. Her nightie is buttoned at the neck like a little girl's.

Words and Meanings

Paragraph

16	genteel	polite, well-bred
	suffice	be enough, satisfy
35	orient	find her bearings; figure out where she is in time and space
37	gnarled	knobby, crooked
38	depilatory	hair remover

Structure and Strategy

1. Look up the word "deficits" in a good general dictionary. What meanings of the word apply to Ignatieff's title?
2. Using both NARRATION and DESCRIPTION, Ignatieff describes the effects of Alzheimer's disease on its victims, and on those who care for them. What function does the opening dialogue (paragraphs 1 to 11) serve?
3. This essay contains several passages of dialogue. Each is included because it supports Ignatieff's THESIS in some way. Consider how each of the following passages contributes to the PURPOSE or intended effect of the essay: paragraphs 28 to 35; paragraphs 42 to 49; paragraphs 52 to 56.
4. Paragraphs 37 to 39 present the ironic contrast between Ignatieff's boyhood relationship with his mother and their current relationship. Identify the specific details that you think are most effective in conveying this contrast.
5. How does the author's own fear of contracting Alzheimer's disease affect the TONE of the essay?

Content and Purpose

1. The THESIS of Ignatieff's essay is implied rather than explicitly stated. Sum up the thesis in a one-sentence thesis statement.
2. What was the initial reaction of the mother when the first signs of the disease appeared? Does she maintain this feeling as her confusion and loss of memory increase?
3. Ignatieff includes a number of poignant descriptive details: the toenails, the gnarled feet, the depilatory wax, the bath. Why does he include these intimate aspects of his mother's life and condition? What emotional effect do they have on the reader?
4. What is the fundamental IRONY underlying the relationship between mother and son? Reread paragraphs 25, 27, and 70 for clues.

5. What experiences in the mother's life may be responsible for the "fear [that] gleams from its hiding place" in her eyes?
6. Is Ignatieff comfortable with the task of caring for his mother? Identify specific passages in the essay that point to the writer's personal conflict.

Suggestions for Writing

1. Modelling your essay on the combination of descriptive and narrative techniques that Ignatieff uses in "Deficits," write a paper on the physical and psychological impact of a serious illness on someone you know and on his or her immediate family.
2. Using "Deficits" and "The Way of All Flesh" by Judy Stoffman (Further Reading, page 339) as background material, write an essay explaining how society can and must enable older people to live in dignity, despite physical or mental handicaps.
3. Traditional societies such as the Chinese respect and venerate the old, but progressive Western societies increasingly see the aged as an unwelcome burden. Write an essay in which you identify and explain two or three significant reasons why our society excludes or rejects the elderly.

The End of the Wild

WADE DAVIS

A native of British Columbia, Wade Davis has worked as a logger, park ranger, forestry engineer, researcher, writer, and environmental activist. He is an anthropologist, biologist, botanical explorer, and photographer whose books include *The Serpent and the Rainbow* (1985), *Passage of Darkness* (1988), *Shadows in the Sun* (1993), *Nomads of the Dawn* (1995), *One River* (1996)—short-listed for the Governor General's Award—*The Clouded Leopard* (1998), *Rainforest* (1998), and *Light at the End of the World* (2002). Davis is explorer-in-residence at the National Geographic Society and host and cowriter of *Earthguide*, a television series on the environment.

1   Some time ago at a symposium° in Barbados, I was fortunate to share the podium with two extraordinary scientists. The first to speak was Richard Leakey, the renowned anthropologist who with his mother and father drew from the dust and ashes of

Africa the story of the birth of our species. The meeting concluded with astronaut Story Musgrave, the first physician to walk in space. It was an odd and moving juxtaposition of the endpoints of the human experience. Dr. Musgrave recognized the irony and it saddened him. He told of what it had been like to know the beauty of the earth as seen from the heavens. There he was, suspended 200 miles above the earth, travelling 18,000 miles per hour with the golden visor of his helmet illuminated by a single sight, a small and fragile blue planet enveloped in a veil of clouds, floating, as he recalled, "in the velvet void of space." To have experienced that vision, he said, a sight made possible only by the brilliance of human technology, and to remember the blindness with which we as a species abuse our only home, was to know the purest sensation of horror.

Many believe that this image of the earth, first brought home to   2
us but a generation ago, will have a more profound impact on human thought than did the Copernican revolution of the 16th century, which transformed the philosophical foundations of the western world by revealing that the planet was not the center of the universe. From space, we see not a limitless frontier nor the stunning products of man, but a single interactive sphere of life, a living organism composed of air, water, and earth. It is this transcendent vision which, more than any amount of scientific data, teaches us the earth is a finite place that can endure our foolish ways for only so long.

In light of this new perspective, this new hope, the past and   3
present deeds of human beings often appear inconceivably cruel and sordid. Shortly after leaving Barbados, while lecturing in the midwest of the United States, I visited two places that in a different, more sensitive world would surely be enshrined as memorials to the victims of the ecological catastrophes that occurred there. The first locality was the site of the last great nesting flock of passenger pigeons, a small stretch of woodland on the banks of the Green River near Mammoth Cave, Ohio. This story of extinction is well known. Yet until I stood in that cold, dark forest, I had never sensed the full weight of the disaster, the scale and horror of it.

At one time passenger pigeons accounted for 40% of the entire   4
bird population of North America. In 1870, at a time when their numbers were already greatly diminished, a single flock a mile wide and 320 miles long containing an estimated 2 billion birds passed over Cincinnati on the Ohio River. Imagine such a sight. Assuming that each bird ate half a pint of seeds a day, a flock that size must have consumed each day over 17 million bushels of

grain. Such sightings were not unusual. In 1813, James Audubon°
was travelling in a wagon from his home on the Ohio River to
Louisville, some sixty miles away, when a flock of passenger
pigeons filled the sky so that the "light of noonday sun was
obscured as by an eclipse." He reached Louisville at sunset and the
birds still came. He estimated that the flock contained over 1 billion
birds, and it was but one of several columns of pigeons that black-
ened the sky that day.

5   Audubon visited roosting and nesting sites to find trees two
feet in diameter broken off at the ground by the weight of birds. He
found dung so deep on the forest floor that he mistook it for snow.
He once stood in the midst of a flock when the birds took flight and
then landed. He compared the noise and confusion to that of a gale,
the sound of their landing to thunder.

6   It is difficult now to imagine the ravages of man that over the
course of half a century destroyed this creature. Throughout the
19th century, pigeon meat was a mainstay of the American diet and
merchants in the eastern cities sold as many as 18,000 birds a day.
Pigeon hunting was a full time job for thousands of men. The term
"stool pigeon" derives from a standard killing technique of the era.
A hunter would sew shut the eyes of a living bird, bind its feet to a
pole driven into the ground, and wait in the surrounding grass for
the flocks to respond to its cry. When the birds came, they arrived
in such numbers that the hunter could simply bat them out of the
air with a club. The more affluent classes slaughtered birds for
recreation. It was not unusual for shooting clubs to go through
50,000 birds in a weekend competition; hundreds of thousands of
live birds were catapulted to their death before the diminishing
supply forced skeet shooters to turn to clay pigeons.

7   By 1896, a mere 50 years after the first serious impact of man,
there were only some 250,000 birds left. In April of that year, the
birds came together for one last nesting flock in the forest outside of
Bowling Green, Ohio. The telegraph wires hummed with the news
and the hunters converged. In a final orgy of slaughter over 200,000
pigeons were killed, 40,000 mutilated, 100,000 chicks destroyed. A
mere 5,000 birds survived. The entire kill was to be shipped east but
there was a derailment on the line and the dead birds rotted in their
crates. On March 24, 1900 the last passenger pigeon in the wild was
shot by a young boy. On September 1, 1914, as the Battle of the
Marne consumed the flower of European youth, the last passenger
pigeon died in captivity.

8   When I left the scene of this final and impossible slaughter, I
travelled west to Sioux City, Iowa to speak at Buena Vista College.
There I was fortunate to visit a remnant patch of tall grass prairie, a

180-acre preserve that represents one of the largest remaining ves-
tiges of an ecosystem that once carpeted North America from
southern Canada to Texas. Again it was winter, and the cold wind
blew through the coneflowers and the dozens of species of grass.
The young biology student who was with me was familiar with
every species in that extraordinary mosaic—they were like old
friends to him. Yet as we walked through that tired field my
thoughts drifted from the plants to the horizon. I tried to imagine
buffalo moving through the grass, the physics of waves as millions
of animals crossed that prairie.

As late as 1871 buffalo outnumbered people in North America. 9
In that year one could stand on a bluff in the Dakotas and see
nothing but buffalo in every direction for thirty miles. Herds were
so large that it took days for them to pass a single point. Wyatt Earp
described one herd of a million animals stretched across a grazing
area the size of Rhode Island. Within nine years of that sighting,
buffalo had vanished from the Plains.

The destruction of the buffalo resulted from a campaign of bio- 10
logical terrorism unparalleled in the history of the Americas. U.S.
government policy was explicit. As General Philip Sheridan wrote
at the time, "The buffalo hunters have done in the past two years
more to settle the vexed Indian Question than the regular army has
accomplished in the last 30 years. They are destroying the Indians'
commissary°. Send them powder and lead, and let them kill until
they have exterminated the buffalo." Between 1850 and 1880 more
than 75 million hides were sold to American dealers. No one knows
how many more animals were slaughtered and left on the prairie. A
decade after native resistance had collapsed, Sheridan advised Congress to mint a commemorative medal, with a dead buffalo on one
side, a dead Indian on the other.

I thought of this history as I stood in that tall grass prairie near 11
Sioux City. What disturbed me the most was to realize how effortlessly we have removed ourselves from this ecological tragedy.
Today the people of Iowa, good and decent folk, live contentedly in
a landscape of cornfields that is claustrophobic in its monotony. For
them the time of the tall grass prairie, like the time of the buffalo, is
as distant from their immediate lives as the fall of Rome or the
battle of Troy. Yet the destruction occurred but a century ago, well
within the lifetime of their grandfathers.

This capacity to forget, this fluidity of memory, is a frightening 12
human trait. Several years ago I spent many months in Haiti, a
country that as recently as the 1920s was 80% forested. Today less
than 5% of the forest cover remains. I remember standing with a
Vodoun priest on a barren ridge, peering across a wasteland, a

desolate valley of scrub and half-hearted trees. He waxed eloquent as if words alone might have squeezed beauty from that wretched sight. He could only think of angels, I of locusts. It was amazing. Though witness to an ecological holocaust that within this century had devastated his entire country, this man had managed to endure without losing his human dignity. Faced with nothing, he adorned his life with his imagination. This was inspiring but also terrifying. People appear to be able to tolerate and adapt to almost any degree of environmental degradation. As the farmers of Iowa today live without wild things, the people of Haiti scratch a living from soil that will never again know the comfort of shade.

13   From a distance, both in time and space, we can perceive these terrible and poignant events as what they were—unmitigated ecological disasters that robbed the future of something unimaginably precious in order to satisfy the immediate and often mundane needs of the present. The luxury of hindsight, however, does nothing to cure the blindness with which today we overlook deeds of equal magnitude and folly.

14   As a younger man in Canada I spent a long winter in a logging camp on the west coast of Haida Gwaii, or the Queen Charlotte Islands as they were then commonly known. It was a good life and it put me through school. I was a surveyor, which meant that I spent all of my time far ahead of the loggers in the dense uncut forest, laying out the roads and the falling boundaries, determining the pattern in which the trees would come down. At the time I had already spent more than a year in the Amazon and I can tell you that those distant forests, however immense and mysterious, are dwarfed by the scale and wonder of the ancient temperate rainforests of British Columbia. In the valleys and around the lakes, and along the shore of the inlet where the soil was rich and deep, we walked through red cedar and sitka spruce, some as tall as a 25-storey building, many with over 70 million needles capturing the light of the sun. Miracles of biological engineering, their trunks stored thousands of gallons of water and could be twenty feet or more across at the base. Many of them had been standing in the forest for more than a thousand years, the anchors of an extraordinarily complex ecosystem° of mountains and rain, salmon and eagles, of squirrels that fly, fungi that crawl, and creatures that live on dew and never touch the forest floor. It is a world that is far older, far richer in its capacity to produce the raw material of life, and far more endangered than almost any region of the Amazon.

15   To walk through these forests in the depths of winter, when the rain turns to mist and settles softly on the moss, is to step back in time. Two hundred million years ago vast coniferous° forests

formed a mantle across the entire world. Then evolution took a great leap and the flowers were born. The difference between the two groups of plants involves a mechanism of pollination and fertilization that changed the course of life on earth. In the case of the more primitive conifers, the plant must produce the basic food for the seed with no certainty that it will be fertilized. In the flowering plants, by contrast, fertilization itself sparks the creation of the seed's food reserves. In other words, unlike the conifers, the flowering plants make no investment without the assurance that a viable seed will be produced. As a result of this and other evolutionary advances, the flowering plants came to dominate the earth in an astonishingly short period of time. Most conifers went extinct and those that survived retreated to the margins of the world, where a small number of species managed to maintain a foothold by adapting to particularly harsh conditions. Today, at a conservative estimate, there are over 250,000 species of flowering plants. The conifers have been reduced to a mere 700 species and in the tropics, the hotbed of evolution, they have been almost completely displaced.

On all the earth, there is only one region of any size and significance where, because of unique climatic conditions, the conifers retain their former glory. Along the northwest coast of North America the summers are hot and dry, the winters cold and wet. Plants need water and light to create food. Here in the summer there is ample light for photosynthesis, but not enough water. In the winter, when both water and light are sufficient, the low temperatures cause the flowering plants to lose their leaves and become dormant. The evergreen conifers, by contrast, are able to grow throughout the long winters and since they use water more efficiently than broad-leafed plants, they also thrive during the dry summer months. The result is an ecosystem so rich, so productive, that the biomass° in the best sites is easily four times as great as that of any comparable area of the tropics.

Inevitably there was, at least for me, an almost surrealistic quality to life in our remote camp where men lived away from their families and made a living cutting down in minutes trees that had taken a thousand years to grow. The constant grinding of machinery, the disintegration of the forest into burnt slash and mud, the wind and sleet that froze on the rigging and whipped across the frozen bay, etched patterns into the lives of the men. Still, no one in our camp had any illusions about what we were doing. All the talk of sustained yield and overmature timber, decadent and normal forests we left to the government bureaucrats and the company PR hacks. We used to laugh at the little yellow signs stuck on the sides of roads that only we would ever travel, that announced

16

17

that twenty acres had been replanted, as if it mattered in a clearcut that stretched to the horizon. . . .

18   Everyone knew, of course, that the ancient forests would never come back. One of my mates used to say that the tangle of half-hearted trees that grew up in the slash° no more resembled the forest he'd cut down, than an Alberta wheatfield resembled a wild prairie meadow. But nobody was worried about what they were doing. It was work, and living on the edge of that immense forest, they simply believed that it would go on forever.

19   If anyone in the government had a broader perspective, we never heard about it. Our camp was nineteen miles by water across an inlet from a backroad that ran forty miles to the nearest forestry office. The government had cut back on overtime pay, and, what with the statutory coffee and lunch breaks, the forestry fellows couldn't figure out how to get to our camp and back in less than seven and a half hours. So they didn't try. The bureaucracy within the company wasn't much better. The mills down south kept complaining that our camp was sending them inferior grades of Douglas fir, which was surprising since the species doesn't grow on the Charlottes.

20   There were, of course, vague murmurs of ecological concern that filtered through to our camp. One morning in the cookhouse I ran into a friend of mine, a rock blaster named Archie whose voice had been dusted by ten thousand cigarettes and the dirt from a dozen mine failures. Archie was in a particularly cantankerous mood. Clutching a donut he'd been marinating in caffeine, he flung a three day old newspaper onto the table. The headline said something about Greenpeace.

21   "Fucking assholes," he critiqued.

22   "What's wrong, Arch?" I asked.

23   "Sons of bitches don't know a damn thing about pollution," he said. Archie then proceeded to tell me about working conditions in the hard rock uranium mines of the Northwest Territories shortly after the Second World War. The companies, concerned about the impact of radioactivity, used to put the workers, including Archie, into large sealed chambers and release a gas with suspended particles of aluminum in it. The idea being that the aluminum would coat the lungs and, at the end of the shift, the men would gag it up, together with any radioactive dust.

24   "Now that," growled Archie, "was environmental pollution."

25   In truth, it is difficult to know how much the forest destruction actually affected the men. Some clearly believed blindly in the process and were hardened by that faith. Others were so transient, moving from camp to camp, sometimes on a monthly basis, that

they never registered the full measure of the impact of any one log-ging show. Some just didn't care. The entire industry was so itin-erant° that no one ever developed a sense of belonging to a place. There was no attachment to the land, nor could there be given what we were doing. In the slash of the clearcuts, there was little room for sentiment.

I knew of a veteran faller who, having cut down thousands of   26
trees, finally came upon one giant cedar that was simply too mag-nificent to be felled. When he refused to bring it down, the bull-bucker° threatened to fire him. The faller felt he had no choice. He brought it down and then, realizing what he had done, he sat on the stump and began to weep. He quit that afternoon and never cut another tree.

Like everyone else in our camp, I was there to make money. On   27
weekends, when our survey crew was down, I picked up overtime pay by working in the slash as a chokerman°, wrapping the cables around the fallen logs so the yarders° could drag them to the land-ings° where they were loaded onto the trucks. Setting beads° is the most miserable job in a logging show, the bottom rung of the camp hierarchy.

One Saturday I was working in a setting high up on the moun-   28
tain that rose above the camp. It had been raining all day and the winds were blowing from the southeast, dragging clouds across the bay and up the slope, where they hung up in the tops of giant hem-locks and cedars that rose above the clearcut. We were working the edge of the opening, but the landing was unusually close by. It took no time at all for the mainline to drag the logs in, and for the haulback° to fling the chokers° back to us. We'd been highballing° all day and both my partner and I were a mess of mud, grease and tree sap. He was a native boy, a Nisga'a from New Aiyansh on the Nass River, but that's all I knew about him.

Late in the afternoon, something got fouled up on the landing,   29
and the yarder shut down. Suddenly it was quiet and you could hear the wind that had been driving the sleet into our faces all day. My partner and I abandoned the slash for the shelter of the forest. We found a dry spot out of the wind in a hollow at the base of an enormous cedar and waited for the yarder to start up. We didn't speak. He kept staring off into the forest. All hunched up with the cold, we looked the same—orange hardhats, green-black rain gear, rubber corkboots. We shared a cigarette. I was watching his face as he smoked. It struck me as strange that here we were, huddled in the forest in silence, two young men from totally different worlds. I tried to imagine what it might have been like had we met but a cen-tury before, I perhaps a trader, he a shadow in the wet woods. His

people had made a home in the forest for thousands of years. I thought of what this country must have been like when my own grandfather arrived. I saw in the forest around us a world that my own children might never know, that Nisga'a children would never know. I turned to my partner. The whistle blew on the landing.

30   "What the hell are we doing?" I asked.

31   "Working," he said. I watched him as he stepped back into the clearcut, and then I followed. We finished the shift and, in the falling darkness, rode back to camp together in the back of the company crummy. That was the last I saw of him.

32   Fifteen years have passed since I left that camp and I've often wondered what became of the Nisga'a boy. It's a good bet he's no longer working as a logger. Natives rarely get promoted beyond the landing and, what's more, over the last decade a third of all logging jobs have been lost. The industry keeps saying that environmentalists are to blame, but in reality all the conservation initiatives of the last ten years in B.C. have not cost the union more than a few hundred jobs, if that. Automation and dwindling timber supplies have put almost 20,000 people out of work in this province alone. And still we keep cutting. In Oregon, Washington and California only 10% of the original coastal rainforest remains. In British Columbia roughly 60% has been logged, largely since 1950. In the mere 15 years since I stood in the forest with that Nisga'a boy, over half of all timber ever extracted from the public forests of British Columbia has been taken. At current rates of harvest, the next 20 years will see the destruction of every valley of ancient rainforest in the province.

33   We are living in the midst of an ecological catastrophe every bit as tragic as that of the slaughter of the buffalo and the passenger pigeon. Our government policies are equally blind, our economic rationales equally compelling. Until just recently, forestry policy in British Columbia explicitly called for the complete eradication of the old growth forests. The rotation cycle, the rate at which the forests were to be cut across the province, and thus the foundation of sustained yield forestry, was based on the assumption that all of these forests would be eliminated and replaced with tree farms. In other words, consideration of the intrinsic value of these ancient rainforests had no place in the calculus of forestry planning. Like the buffalo and the passenger pigeon, these magnificent forests were considered expendable°.

34   But while the passenger pigeons are extinct, and the buffalo reduced to a curiosity, these forests still stand. They are as rare and spectacular as any natural feature on the face of the earth, as biologically significant as any terrestrial ecosystem that has ever existed.

If, knowing this, we still allow them to fall, what will it say about us as a people? What will be the legacy of our times?

The truth is, in an increasingly complex and fragmented world we need these ancient forests, alive and intact. For the children of the Nisga'a they are an image of the dawn of time, a memory of an era when raven emerged from the shadow of the cedar and young boys went in search of spirits at the north end of the world. For my own two young girls these forests echo with a shallow history, but one that is nevertheless rich in the struggles of their great grandparents, men and women who travelled halfway around the world to live in this place. Today all peoples in this land are drawn together by a single thread of destiny. We live at the edge of the clearcut, our hands will determine the fate of these forests. If we do nothing, they will be lost within our lifetimes and we will be left to explain our inaction. If we preserve these ancient forests they will stand apart for all generations and for all time as symbols of the geography of hope.

Words and Meanings

Paragraph

symposium	academic conference	1
Audubon	Haitian-born U.S. scientist and artist who painted all the species of birds known in North America in the early nineteenth century	4
commissary	food supply	10
ecosystem	interdependent network of all living things	14
coniferous	pertaining to cone-bearing evergreen trees	15
biomass	weight (density) of all living things in a given area	16
slash	an open space in a forest resulting from logging	18
itinerant	travelling from place to place	25
	The terms in these paragraphs are loggers' jargon to describe the act of getting trees out of the slash. The foreman (bullbucker) supervises the workers who hook the logs onto a cable (choker) that is operated by a machine (yarder). Once the logs reach the "landing," the site from which they are loaded onto trucks, another line (the haulback) returns the empty chokers (or beads) to the site to be reset. Performing these activities at top speed to ensure maximum production is "highballing."	26 to 28
expendable	something we can use up for short-term gain without serious consequences	33

Structure and Strategy

1. Davis introduces his essay with examples of two scientists who spoke, along with the author, at an international conference. Why did he choose to begin with Leakey and Musgrave? What is the "odd and moving juxtaposition" these two men represent?
2. What is the THESIS of this essay? Which sentence in paragraph 3 most clearly expresses it?
3. Which paragraphs detail the extinction of the passenger pigeon? Which deal with the decimation of the plains buffalo herds? What is the third ILLUSTRATION of Davis's point? In what ORDER has he arranged these three main sections of his essay?
4. Identify vivid descriptive details in paragraphs 5, 14, and 17. What is the purpose of the ANECDOTE in paragraph 26?
5. Identify the TOPIC SENTENCES in paragraphs 6, 10, 12, and 16; then determine what kind of support the author uses to develop his topic in each of these paragraphs.
6. How is the topic of paragraph 7 developed? Find another paragraph in the essay that uses the same kind of support to develop the topic. What effect do these paragraphs have on the reader?
7. What is the TONE of paragraph 19? How does the tone contribute to your understanding of the author's opinion of the government?
8. Why does Davis elaborate his third point in such detail, including dialogue and characterization?
9. Besides EXPOSITION, what other RHETORICAL MODE does Davis employ in "The End of the Wild"?
10. Who is the AUDIENCE for this piece? What is its overall tone?

Content and Purpose

1. According to the essay, what does the earth look like from space? (See paragraph 2.) What IRONY is explored in paragraphs 2 and 3? According to Davis, what should we have learned from the image of earth as seen by space travellers?
2. What was the passenger pigeon population in North America in 1870? What happened to them? How? Why?
3. What is a "stool pigeon" (paragraph 6)? What is the meaning of the idiom today?
4. What has North America lost along with the buffalo? (See paragraphs 8, 10, and 11.) How do these paragraphs reinforce Davis's THESIS?
5. Explain in your own words the political purpose of the U.S. government in promoting the slaughter of the buffalo that makes this "biological terrorism" (paragraph 10) so horrific.

6. According to Davis, why are the rainforests of British Columbia even more remarkable and more endangered than those of the Amazon? (See paragraphs 14 to 16.)
7. According to the essay, what are the attitudes of the loggers, the logging companies, the government, and the Native peoples to clearcutting the rainforest?
8. Why do you think Davis includes the narrative involving "a rock blaster named Archie" (paragraphs 20 to 24) and "a native boy, a Nisga'a from New Aiyansh" (paragraphs 28 to 33)? What effect do these narratives have on the reader?
9. Summarize what has happened in the fifteen years since the author worked in the logging industry (see paragraph 32).
10. How does Davis unify his essay in the CONCLUSION (paragraphs 33 to 35)? How does he connect his three examples? Why does he want to preserve the rainforests?

Suggestion for Writing

Using an example from the natural environment (avoid pigeons, buffaloes, and rainforests), write an essay illustrating the interdependence of humanity and the rest of the ecosystem. What, for example, has happened to the groundfish stocks in the North Atlantic? To the salmon fishery in British Columbia? What has caused the depletion, and how has it affected those who have traditionally relied on these resources?

The Rake

DAVID MAMET

U.S. dramatist David Mamet (b. 1947) has taught theatre, founded theatre groups, and written numerous outstanding plays, including the award-winning *American Buffalo, Glengarry Glen Ross,* and *Oleanna.* He is the only major American playwright to succeed as a screenwriter and director. His movies include adaptations of his plays, adventure films (*The Edge,* 1997), and comedies (*Wag the Dog,* 1997).

There was the incident of the rake and there was the incident   1
of the school play, and it seems to me that they both took place at the round kitchen table.

The table was not in the kitchen proper but in an area called   2
"the nook," which held its claim to that small measure of charm by

dint of a waist-high wall separating it from an adjacent area known as the living room.

3   All family meals were eaten in the nook. There was a dining room to the right, but, as in most rooms of that name at that time and in those surroundings, it was never used.

4   The round table was of wrought iron and topped with glass; it was noteworthy for that glass, for it was more than once and rather more than several times, I am inclined to think, that my stepfather would grow so angry as to bring some object down on the glass top, shattering it, thus giving us to know how we had forced him out of control.

5   And it seems that most times when he would shatter the table, as often as that might have been, he would cut some portion of himself on the glass, or that he or his wife, our mother, would cut their hands on picking up the glass afterward, and that we children were to understand, and did understand, that these wounds were our fault.

6   So the table was associated in our minds with the notion of blood.

7   The house was in a brand-new housing development in the southern suburbs. The new community was built upon, and now bordered, the remains of what had once been a cornfield. When our new family moved in, there were but a few homes in the development completed, and a few more under construction. Most streets were mud, and boasted a house here or there, and many empty lots marked out by white stakes.

8   The house we lived in was the development's Model Home. The first time we had seen it, it had signs plastered on the front and throughout the interior telling of the various conveniences it contained. And it had a lawn, and was one of the only homes in the new community that did.

9   My stepfather was fond of the lawn, and he detailed me and my sister to care for it, and one fall afternoon we found ourselves assigned to rake the leaves.

10   Why this chore should have been so hated I cannot say, except that we children, and I especially, felt ourselves less than full members of this new, cobbled-together° family, and disliked being assigned to the beautification of a home that we found unbeautiful in all respects, and for which we had neither natural affection nor a sense of proprietary° interest.

11   We went to the new high school. We walked the mile down the open two-lane road on one side of which was the just-begun suburban community and on the other side of which was the cornfield.

The school was as new as the community, and still under con- 12
struction for the first three years of its occupancy. One of its inno-
vations was the notion that honesty would be engendered° by the
absence of security, and so the lockers were designed and built
both without locks and without the possibility of attaching locks.
And there was the corresponding rash of thievery and many lectures about the same from the school administration, but it was
difficult to point with pride to any scholastic or community tradition supporting the suggestion that we, the students, pull together
in this new, utopian° way. We were, in school, in an uncompleted
building in the midst of a mud field in the midst of a cornfield.
Our various sports teams were called The Spartans; and I played
on those teams, which were of a wretchedness consistent with
their novelty.

Meanwhile my sister interested herself in the drama society. 13
The year after I had left the school she obtained the lead in the
school play. It called for acting and singing, both of which she had
talent for, and it looked to be a signal triumph for her in her otherwise unremarkable and unenjoyed school career.

On the night of the play's opening she sat down to dinner 14
with our mother and our stepfather. It may be that they ate a trifle
early to allow her to get to the school to enjoy the excitement of
the opening night. But however it was, my sister had no appetite,
and she nibbled a bit at her food, and then she got up from the
table to carry her plate back to scrape it in the sink, when my
mother suggested that she sit down, as she had not finished her
food. My sister said she really had no appetite, but my mother
insisted that, as the meal had been prepared, it would be good
form to sit and eat it.

My sister sat down with the plate and pecked at her food and 15
she tried to eat a bit, and told my mother that, no, really, she possessed no appetite whatever, and that was due, no doubt, not to the
food, but to her nervousness and excitement at the prospect of
opening night.

My mother, again, said that, as the food had been cooked, it had 16
to be eaten, and my sister tried and said that she could not; at which
my mother nodded. She then got up from the table and went to the
telephone and looked the number up and called the school and got
the drama teacher and identified herself and told him that her
daughter wouldn't be coming to school that night, that, no, she was
not ill, but that she would not be coming in. Yes, yes, she said, she
knew that her daughter had the lead in the play, and, yes, she was
aware that many children and teachers had worked hard for it, et

cetera, and so my sister did not play the lead in her school play. But I was long gone, out of the house by that time, and well out of it. I heard that story, and others like it, at the distance of twenty-five years.

17   In the model house our rooms were separated from their room, the master bedroom, by a bathroom and a study. On some weekends I would go alone to visit my father in the city and my sister would stay and sometimes grow frightened or lonely in her part of the house. And once, in the period when my grandfather, then in his sixties, was living with us, she became alarmed at a noise she had heard in the night; or perhaps she just became lonely, and she went out of her room and down the hall, calling for my mother, or my stepfather, or my grandfather, but the house was dark, and no one answered.

18   And, as she went farther down the hall, toward the living room, she heard voices, and she turned the corner, and saw a light coming from under the closed door in the master bedroom, and heard my stepfather crying, and the sound of my mother weeping. So my sister went up to the door, and she heard my stepfather talking to my grandfather and saying, "Jack. Say the words. Just say the words . . ." And my grandfather, in his Eastern European accent, saying, with obvious pain and difficulty, "No. No. I can't. Why are you making me do this? Why?" And the sound of my mother crying convulsively.

19   My sister opened the door, and she saw my grandfather sitting on the bed, and my stepfather standing by the closet and gesturing. On the floor of the closet she saw my mother, curled in a fetal position, moaning and crying and hugging herself. My stepfather was saying, "Say the words. Just say the words." And my grandfather was breathing fast and repeating, "I can't. She knows how I feel about her. I can't." And my stepfather said, "Say the words, Jack. Please. Just say you love her." At which my mother would moan louder. And my grandfather said, "I can't."

20   My sister pushed the door open farther and said—I don't know what she said, but she asked, I'm sure, for some reassurance, or some explanation, and my stepfather turned around and saw her and picked up a hairbrush from a dresser that he passed as he walked toward her, and he hit her in the face and slammed the door on her. And she continued to hear "Jack, say the words."

21   She told me that on weekends when I was gone my stepfather ended every Sunday evening by hitting or beating her for some reason or other. He would come home from depositing his own kids back at their mother's house after their weekend visitation, and would settle down tired and angry, and, as a regular matter on those evenings, would find out some intolerable behavior on my sister's part and slap or hit or beat her.

Years later, at my mother's funeral, my sister spoke to our aunt, 22 my mother's sister, who gave a footnote to this behavior. She said when they were young, my mother and my aunt, they and their parents lived in a small flat on the West Side. My grandfather was a salesman on the road from dawn on Monday until Friday night. Their family had a fiction, and that fiction, that article of faith, was that my mother was a naughty child. And each Friday, when he came home, his first question as he climbed the stairs was, "What has she done this week . . .?" At which my grandmother would tell him the terrible things that my mother had done, after which she, my mother, was beaten.

This was general knowledge in my family. The footnote con- 23 cerned my grandfather's behavior later in the night. My aunt had a room of her own, and it adjoined her parents' room. And she related that each Friday, when the house had gone to bed, she, through the thin wall, heard my grandfather pleading for sex. "Cookie, please." And my grandmother responding, "No, Jack." "Cookie, please." "No, Jack." "Cookie, please."

And once, my grandfather came home and asked, "What has 24 she done this week?" and I do not know, but I imagine that the response was not completed, and perhaps hardly begun; in any case, he reached and grabbed my mother by the back of the neck and hurled her down the stairs.

And once, in our house in the suburbs there had been an out- 25 burst by my stepfather directed at my sister. And she had, somehow, prevailed. It was, I think, that he had the facts of the case wrong, and had accused her of the commission of something for which she had demonstrably had no opportunity, and she pointed this out to him with what I can imagine, given the circumstances, was an under-standable, and, given my prejudice, a commendable degree of freedom. Thinking the incident closed she went back to her room to study, and, a few moments later, saw him throw open her door, bat the book out of her hands, and pick her up and throw her against the far wall, where she struck the back of her neck on a shelf.

She was told, the next morning, that her pain, real or pre- 26 tended, held no weight, and that she would have to go to school. She protested that she could not walk, or, if at all, only with the greatest difficulty and in great pain; but she was dressed and did walk to school, where she fainted, and was brought home. For years she suffered various headaches; an X ray taken twenty years later for an unrelated problem revealed that when he threw her against the shelf he had cracked her vertebrae.

*   *   *

27   When we left the house we left in good spirits. When we went out to dinner, it was an adventure, which was strange to me, looking back, because many of these dinners ended with my sister or myself being banished, sullen or in tears, from the restaurant, and told to wait in the car, as we were in disgrace.

28   These were the excursions that had ended, due to her or my intolerable arrogance, as it was then explained to us.

29   The happy trips were celebrated and capped with a joke. Here is the joke: My stepfather, my mother, my sister, and I would exit the restaurant, my stepfather and mother would walk to the car, telling us that they would pick us up. We children would stand by the restaurant entrance. They would drive up in the car, open the passenger door, and wait until my sister and I had started to get in. They would then drive away.

30   They would drive ten or fifteen feet, and open the door again, and we would walk up again, and they would drive away again. They sometimes would drive around the block. But they would always come back, and by that time the four of us would be laughing in camaraderie° and appreciation of what, I believe, was our only family joke.

31   We were raking the lawn, my sister and I. I was raking, and she was stuffing the leaves into a bag. I loathed the job, and my muscles and my mind rebelled, and I was viciously angry, and my sister said something, and I turned and threw the rake at her and it hit her in the face.

32   The rake was split bamboo and metal, and a piece of metal caught her lip and cut her badly.

33   We were both terrified, and I was sick with guilt, and we ran into the house, my sister holding her hand to her mouth, and her mouth and her hand and the front of her dress covered in blood.

34   We ran into the kitchen where my mother was cooking dinner, and my mother asked what happened.

35   Neither of us, myself out of guilt, of course, and my sister out of a desire to avert the terrible punishment she knew I would receive, neither of us would say what occurred.

36   My mother pressed us, and neither of us would answer. She said that until one or the other answered, we would not go to the hospital; and so the family sat down to dinner where my sister clutched a napkin to her face and the blood soaked the napkin and ran down onto her food, which she had to eat; and I also ate my food and we cleared the table and went to the hospital.

37   I remember the walks home from school in the frigid winter, along the cornfield that was, for all its proximity° to the city, part

of the prairie. The winters were viciously cold. From the remove of years, I can see how the area might and may have been beautiful. One could have walked in the stubble of the cornfields, or hunted birds, or enjoyed any of a number of pleasures naturally occurring.

Words and Meanings

		Paragraph
cobbled-together	makeshift, clumsily put together	10
proprietary	sense of ownership	
engendered	produced, encouraged	12
utopian	ideal, visionary	
camaraderie	sense of sharing, of friendship, in a group of people	30
proximity	closeness, nearness	37

Structure and Strategy

1. How does paragraph 1 set up the key events on which this narrative is based?
2. Why does the author spend so much time on the specific place these events occur (paragraphs 1 to 5)? What is the horrible IRONY in paragraph 6?
3. Identify the paragraphs that tell the stories of the two incidents referred to in the first paragraph.
4. Analyze the descriptive details that make up paragraphs 2, 3, 7, 11, and 12. How do these details contribute to the sense of unhappiness, even desperation, of the author's life and that of his sister?
5. What irony is there in the fact that the family lives in "the development's Model Home" (paragraph 8)? Where in the essay are you told how the children feel about the house?
6. The essay contains at least two short narratives besides those the author refers to in paragraph 1. Identify the stories and explain how they contribute to the author's THESIS. Could they have been omitted without affecting the dominant impression of this essay?
7. The concluding paragraph describes the place where the key events of this story occurred. What is implied by the details Mamet includes in this paragraph? Is the CONCLUSION an effective ending to this disturbing essay? Why or why not?
8. David Mamet is a renowned playwright. What characteristics or qualities in "The Rake" reveal his dramatic skills?

Content and Purpose

1. Why do you think Mamet titled his essay "The Rake"?
2. Most analysis of abusive families suggests that violence runs in families, that violent parents breed violent children. How does "The Rake" support this thesis? How many generations are involved?
3. Why is the name of the sports teams in the author's high school particularly appropriate (paragraph 12)? What is the high school like? Is it the "new, utopian" school that it was designed to be?
4. Which specific episodes reveal most clearly the mother's rigidity, her failure to empathize with her children, especially her daughter? Why is it ironic that these episodes occur at the kitchen table?
5. The stepfather commits the most directly brutal acts against the children. Who is the primary victim of his rages? When do his rages occur? What triggers them?
6. In paragraphs 4 and 5, Mamet comments on the responsibility for violence—and the displacement of responsibility—that occurs in abusive families. Who appears to suffer as a result of the stepfather's rage? Who really suffers?
7. In paragraphs 29 and 30, the author describes their one family joke. Why do the children share in the laughter? What effect does the recounting of this "joke" have on the reader?
8. This essay is an adult's reflections on a very unhappy childhood. Find two incidents in which a child encounters something that she or he is unable to comprehend at the time. What details are added twenty-or-so years later? How do these details change the adult's understanding of the incidents?

Suggestions for Writing

1. Write an essay that tells a story from your own childhood (it need not be violent or sad—it could be a happy or humorous recollection). Your narrative should focus on a childhood experience that now, as an adult, you see differently.
2. Write an essay that narrates the effects of a family trauma or disruption on the children.

Additional Suggestions for Writing: Three Basic Strategies

Choose one of the topics below and write a thesis statement based on it. Expand your thesis statement into an essay by selecting specific narrative details, descriptions, and/or examples from your own experience to develop the key ideas.

1. A dangerous spot that you have explored
2. A humorous family story
3. A vacation or holiday you would like to forget
4. An experience that led to success
5. An experience that led to failure
6. A journey that taught you something
7. A place that was special to you when you were a child
8. The birth of a child
9. A sacred place
10. Chat rooms
11. The stupidest thing you ever did
12. A chance encounter
13. People are not always what they appear to be.
14. Travel teaches us about ourselves as well as others.
15. Services offered by your college that help (or don't help) students.
16. Movies reveal some important things about our culture.
17. You are (or are not) what you wear.
18. Young people are exposed to violence every day.
19. You are optimistic (pessimistic) about the world as we move through the first decade of the twenty-first century.
20. "Good fences make good neighbours." (Robert Frost)
21. "All happy families resemble one another, but each unhappy family is unhappy in its own way." (Leo Tolstoy)
22. "Beauty in things exists in the mind which contemplates them." (David Hume)
23. "We are all immigrants to this place, even if we were born here." (Margaret Atwood)
24. "The truths of the past are the clichés of the present." (Ned Rorem)
25. "It is always easier to draw on the storehouse of memory than to find something original to say." (Michel de Montaigne)

Process Analysis

WHAT IS PROCESS ANALYSIS?

Process analysis is writing that explains *how* something happens. It explains the steps or phases of a particular process. For example, the model essay in this unit, "Metamorphosis," explains how a baby learns to talk. It charts the course of a baby named Jeanie from birth to eighteen months of age, explaining the stages that she goes through as she develops from a crying infant to a talking toddler.

WHY DO WE USE PROCESS ANALYSIS?

Process analysis answers the lead-in question *how*. It is a familiar pattern of writing. Just think of the magazines you read and the how-to books that people rush to buy. They are full of instructions for improving your looks, your game, your house, your relationship with your spouse, children, parents, boss, pet—or anything else you can think of.

Process analysis is used for two purposes that lead to two different kinds of essays or reports. A **directional process analysis** —the "how-to-do-it" essay—gives readers the directions they need to perform the process themselves, whether it's building a website or training a dog. One example of a directional process analysis in this unit is Paul Quarrington's "Home Ice," which tells you how to make a backyard skating rink.

The second kind of process analysis provides information about how something happens (or happened). Readers of an **informational process analysis** do not want to perform the process they are reading about; they just want to learn how it is (or was) performed. For example, R. G. Des Dixon's "Martha: One Pillowcase Short of a Pair" describes how the author's mother did the family's laundry in the days before automatic washers and dryers made this chore relatively easy. No one would want to do laundry the old-fashioned way, but Dixon's essay is an interesting account of the backbreaking task of keeping a family clean with nothing more than a wood stove and a clothesline. Jeffrey Moussaieff Masson's "Dear Dad" describes the fascinating role played by male penguins in the reproductive cycle. Again, information (not directions) is the goal of this kind of process analysis.

Some writers use process analysis as a vehicle for humour or social commentary. The conventional how-to-do-it essay can be funny if a writer provides instructions for something no one wants to do, such as become obese or fail in school. A more serious social purpose underlies Danny Irvine's "A Tree-Planting Primer" (a directional process analysis) and Jessica Mitford's "Behind the Formaldehyde Curtain" (an informational process analysis).

HOW DO WE WRITE PROCESS ANALYSIS?

Here are five guidelines for writing an effective process analysis:

1. Think through the whole process carefully and write an outline detailing all the steps involved. If you are writing a directional process analysis, be sure to include any preparatory steps or special equipment the reader should know about.

2. Put the steps of the process into CHRONOLOGICAL ORDER.

3. Write a clear thesis statement. (You need not include a preview of the main steps unless your topic is complex or your instructor specifically requires it.)

4. Write your first draft. Define any specialized or technical terms that may be unfamiliar to your reader. Use TRANSITIONS, or time-markers, to indicate the progression through the steps or stages (*first, next, after,* and so on).

5. Revise your draft carefully. Clarify any steps that cause confusion and revise until the whole paper is both clear and interesting.

The model essay that follows is an informational process analysis.

Metamorphosis

Introduction
(creates a sce-
nario and
introduces the
central
analogy)

Meet newborn Jeanie. Weak and helpless as a caterpillar, Jeanie's only defence against hunger and pain is
the one sound she can make at will: crying. Eighteen
months later, Jeanie will be a busy toddler who asks
questions, expresses opinions, and even makes jokes.
From helplessness to assertiveness: how does this
wondrous transformation take place? To discover how

*Thesis state-
ment*

we learn to speak, let's follow Jeanie as she develops
from infant to toddler, from caterpillar to butterfly.

*First stage
(developed by
definition and
factual details
of speech
development)*

Infancy, the first stage of language development,
literally means "not able to speak." For the first six
months of her life, Jeanie isn't able to talk, but she can
respond to speech. Shortly after birth, she'll turn her
head toward the sound of a voice. By two weeks of
age, she will prefer the sound of a human voice to
non-human sounds. Between two and four months,
she will learn to distinguish the voices of her care-
givers from those of strangers, and she knows
whether those voices are speaking soothingly or
angrily. By the time she is two months old, Jeanie will
have learned to coo as well as cry, and she coos happily when people smile and talk to her. Now she can
express contentment as well as discomfort. At around
four months of age, Jeanie's happy sounds become
more varied and sophisticated: she registers delight on
a scale ranging from throaty chuckles to belly laughs.
All this vocal activity is actually a rehearsal for speech.
As Jeanie cries and coos and laughs, her vocal cords,
tongue, lips, and brain are developing the coordination
required for her to speak her first words.

*Transition
(continues the
analogy)*

Second stage

At six or seven months of age, Jeanie is no longer
an infant; she's moved on to the *baby* stage of language development. Like a pupa in its cocoon, Jeanie
is undergoing a dramatic but (to all but her closest
observers) invisible change. She looks at her mother
when someone says "Mama." She responds to simple
directions: she'll clap her hands or wave "bye-bye" on
request. By the time she is a year old, Jeanie will rec-

*Note defini-
tions and
examples*

ognize at least twenty words. The sounds Jeanie produces at this stage are called *babbling*, a word that
technically describes a series of reduplicated single
consonant and vowel sounds and probably derives its

name from a common example: "ba-ba-ba-ba." About halfway through this stage of her development, Jeanie progresses to *variegated babbling*, in which sounds change between syllables. "Da-dee, da-dee, da-dee," she burbles, to the delight of her father (who doesn't know that Jeanie cannot yet connect the sounds she makes to the meaning they represent to others). But by the time Jeanie celebrates her first birthday, the variety, rhythm, and tone of her babbling have become more varied, and her family begins to sense consistent meaning in the sounds she makes. "Go bye-bye!" is as clearly meant as it is spoken—Jeanie wants to get going!

Third stage (developed with description, examples, dialogue)

Jeanie's recognition of the link between sounds and meanings signals her entry into the *toddler stage*—twelve to eighteen months. At eighteen months, Jeanie will understand approximately 250 words—more than ten times the number she understood at twelve months. Most of what she says are single-word utterances: "kitty" for a cat in her picture book, "nana" for the bananas she loves to squish and eat. But even single words now function as complex communications depending on the intonation Jeanie gives them. "Kitty?" she inquires, looking at a picture of a tiger. She demands a "nana!" for lunch. About halfway through the toddler stage, Jeanie begins to link words together to make sentences. "Mama gone," she cries when her mother leaves for work. "Me no go bed," she tells her father. Though it marks the beginning of trouble for her parents, this development marks a triumph for Jeanie. She has broken out of the cocoon of passive comprehension into the world of active participation.

Reference to metamorphosis analogy contributes to unity

Conclusion (refers back to introduction and completes analogy)

In less than two years, Jeanie has metamorphosed from wailing newborn to babbling baby to talking toddler. Through language, she is becoming her own woman in the world. Now she can fly.

The Magic of Moviegoing

RICK GROEN

Rick Groen (b. 1947) holds an M.A. in English literature from the University of Toronto. He has been an arts critic, reviewing both television and film, at *The Globe and Mail* since the early 1980s. Groen won the National Newspaper Award for critical writing in 1991 and the Stanley McDowell award for writing in 2001.

What movies to watch; whom to watch; where, when and why to watch. Oh, we got it covered, and so does everyone else. Turn to your favourite newspaper or magazine and, on any given week, these cinematic five W's will all be lined up and duly addressed. In the arts no less than the news, they're the standard quintet of queries, forming the foundation for most critical commentary. But there's another question, equally interesting, that seldom gets examined or even asked. It's not the What but the How of the matter: How do we behave during this pop rite of going to the picture show?   1

Let's confine our little inquiry to theatres proper, and exclude living rooms. Obviously, it's a very different experience viewing a film in the bright confines of your home and through the tiny frame of a TV set. There, we tend to watch more forgivingly, more tolerantly. For every majestic opus, every *Lawrence of Arabia*, that suffers when removed from the big screen, there are a myriad humdrum flicks—tepid thrillers, formula comedies—that actually seem more palatable° on the tube. They get better because our expectations get lowered—our investment (of time and money) is just smaller.   2

Clearly, the stakes are raised when the setting shifts to a real movie house. So how do we watch there? Well, indulge me for a second while I pick up a popular line of thought about film theatres, the one that insists on a connection between Where and What. This theory suggests that the architecture of the movie theatre is somehow intrinsically linked to the makeup of the movies. Back in the era of the single-screen theatre, the films neatly fit their abodes—a charming Fred Astaire musical felt right at home in an art-deco palace°. And now, with the switch from unique local cinemas to multiplex malls, these vast generic structures are attracting the product they deserve—loud, look-alike films for loud, look-alike boxes. There, the argument continues, the patrons pick out a movie as they would a channel, and with about as much optimism—18 screens yet nothing to watch.   3

4   I don't think so. Although no fan of the multiplex, I'm leery of such rear-view mirror reasoning, the nostalgic yearning for an illusory past where every screen was silver and every movie golden. Anyway, nostalgia just keeps getting updated. No doubt, a few decades from now, some savage modernist will be tearing down some vintage multiplex, and today's 20-year-olds will be penning tearful odes to the passing of an aesthetic landmark. And they'll be doing so for a good reason. Although where we watch and what we watch have changed radically over time, how we watch has stayed relatively constant. Indeed, for many, the ritual of moviegoing is a large part of the allure, every bit as appealing as the movies themselves.

5   That ritual begins at the box office. Movies were invented as a form of mass entertainment, and there's a nicely democratic quality to the very act of entering a theatre. What you buy is a general admission ticket, not an assigned seat, which invariably leads to that through-the-foyer-into-the-aisle scramble for your preferred location—way up front where actors look like giant celluloid idols, mid-range for a less infantilizing perspective, deep in the far reaches for those with extracinematic pursuits° in mind.

6   Yes, *that* part of the ritual. Moviegoing is a social experience. People tend to go in couples or groups. Always, they want to sit together. Too often, they want to talk together. And usually, they want to eat and drink together. In fact, given the wider variety of fare—the hot dogs, the nachos, the pastries—available at the multiplex, "dinner and a movie" has been replaced by "dinner at the movie." (Thanks to the concessions' inflated prices, the hit to the wallet is about the same.) Last, but hardly least, don't forget to add sex to the social equation. A movie is frequently a date; it's foreplay.

7   But now the picture starts, and a tension immediately develops between two competing interests—between moviegoing, which is primarily a social experience, and movie-watching, which is essentially an individual experience. A film projected onto a screen in a darkened theatre approximates the state of dreaming, and is intensely personal. So when the lights go down, these duelling impulses—to socialize or to watch, to talk with others or to dream alone—begin to meld. As they do, the theatre becomes simultaneously a public and a private space, with people striving to get the balance right and to keep the boundaries straight.

8   We strive for a similar balance inside our automobiles—another hybrid of public and private space. Of course, the car and the motion picture enjoy a shared history. Both came of age through the early part of the last century; both are transporting devices in their separate fashions; and both serve as havens for our sexual desires,

either symbolically or otherwise. Inevitably, their twin paths inter-sected in the steamy atmosphere of the drive-in theatre, a place that typically specialized in showing B-pictures—the kind that weren't too distracting, that prevented the private experience of movie-watching from infringing on the social experience of moviegoing.

Which brings us to a conclusion less obvious than it might seem at first glance: How we behave at a movie is directly influ-enced by what we're viewing. The more engrossing the film, the more that moviegoing gives way to movie-watching. We've all observed, even felt this transition—it's almost palpable. Suddenly, popcorn stops being munched, words stop being exchanged, passes stop being made. As we get lost in the movie, we get lost to our companions. But there's a paradox at work here too. This conver-gence of disparate people turns into an audience, becomes one, only when the various social groupings have disintegrated and its members have splintered off into their private selves. The irony is bald but delicious: When we are most truly alone, we are most truly an audience. 9

That's how we watch movies at our best. And, for me, that's the recurring magic of movies, the alchemical° wizardry that can break down a buzzing crowd into islands of attentive individuals, then re-assemble those islands into the archipelago° of a rapt audience. Funny thing about this wizardry. Disdainful of borders and blind to class, the stuff can pop up anywhere folks gather to find it—at a sprawling multiplex in Dolby surround-sound, or on a white sheet strung between tent poles in the thin open air. The magic may come, or not, but one thing is sure—it's always worth the wait. 10

Words and Meanings

Paragraph

palatable	pleasant, acceptable, or satisfactory	2
art-deco palace	a movie theatre constructed in a decorative art and architectural style—characterized by bold lines, geometric shapes, and strong colours—that was popular in the 1920s and 1930s	3
extracinematic pursuits	interests lying outside of cinema	5
alchemical	miraculously transforming; adjective form of *alchemy*, the medieval pseudo-science that sought to turn base metals into gold and silver	10
archipelago	a large group of islands in the sea; metaphor-ically, a large group of individuals	

Structure and Strategy

1. In his INTRODUCTION, the author refers to the "five W's"—the questions that make up "the foundation for most critical commentary." What are the five W's? What is the other question around which Groen has chosen to structure his KEY POINTS?
2. What stages in the ritual of moviegoing does Groen identify? Which paragraphs describe each stage? Have any stages been left out?
3. Paragraphs 7 and 8 are developed by means of comparison. What two things are compared in paragraph 7? In paragraph 8? Do you agree with the comparisons? Why or why not?
4. Identify the METAPHOR in the last paragraph. Do you think it is effective? Why or why not?

Content and Purpose

1. According to Groen, what is the difference between watching a movie at home and watching a movie in a theatre?
2. Paragraph 3 presents an ARGUMENT about the architecture of theatres and the kinds of movies that are shown in them. Summarize this argument. Does Groen agree with it? Do you? Why or why not?
3. According to the author, how do people choose a seat in a movie theatre?
4. Identify the elements of the "social experience" (paragraph 6) of going to a movie.
5. According to paragraph 9, what is the connection between people's behaviour at a movie and the movie itself?
6. What is the central IRONY expressed in paragraph 9? How is it essential to the "recurring magic of movies" (paragraph 10)? Do you agree with this idea? Why or why not?

Suggestions for Writing

1. Write an essay describing the kinds of movies you like to watch. Why do you find them entertaining?
2. Write an essay on the ritual involved in another form of entertainment (for example, a sports or cultural event, a nightclub, or live theatre).

Martha: One Pillowcase Short of a Pair

R. G. DES DIXON

A fifth-generation Canadian, R. G. Des Dixon was born on a kitchen table in rural Ontario. His novel *Tell Me Who You Are* (1995) echoes the journey from there to end-of-century turmoil in a big-city high school. Another book, *Future Schools* (1992), proposes radical new models of childhood and schooling.

There's a new full-page ad in which we see Martha Stewart° holding a feather-light basket full of dry sheets, fully pressed and folded, that she is either hanging or retrieving from outdoor clotheslines. So we figure Martha is one pillowcase short of a pair or else has been divinely dispatched° to save the masses from unclassiness.

Mother Martha is showing us what fun it is to play old-fashioned house: just casually crisscross your back lawn with snow-white clotheslines and hang out the already-clean contents of your linen cupboard. Be sure to reserve some nicely ironed sheets in a traditional wicker basket that you parade around the yard to show neighbours you've mastered the finer points of laundry chic. While you prance about with your mix-and-match colours and patterns, you smile as Martha does, "I'm so pleased to bring you my collection of beautiful basics."

But the era plundered° so sweetly by Martha's marketing actually mixed and matched bleaker basics with the beautiful. Sixty years ago in rural Ontario, my mother, with a household of four children and three adults, hung out enough sheets every Monday to sail the *Bluenose°*. All white, all wet, all heavy, all work.

Every Sunday afternoon, between basting a 10-pound roast and baking two pies for dinner and a scratch cake° for bedtime snacks, she hand-pumped water in the back yard and filled every bucket, bowl and tub in the house. By 7 a.m. Monday, the great copper boiler was hissing and bubbling on the wood stove and soap-scented steam permeated the kitchen. I ate my oatmeal porridge and watched my perspiring mother, a homemade cigarette stuck to her bottom lip, bash the boiling sheets into spotless submission with lumps of blueing° wrapped in rags and lashed to a sawed-off broom stick.

5   While I was at school, she scrubbed sheets one at a time on a washboard in a galvanized metal tub, rinsed them in three more tubs spread around the kitchen and hand-cranked each through a wringer clamped to a huge bucket. Summer or winter, she repeatedly mounted a wind-swept platform, hair and skirt flying, mouth and apron full of old wooden clothespins, and launched sheet after sheet on a pulley clothesline of heavy braided steel till the first-launched billowed up there where only sea gulls glided the other six days of the week.

6   When I got home from school on winter days, my numb-fingered mother would be placing frozen sheets one at a time like drywall panels into the back kitchen where she stood them against walls beside ice-stiffened long johns standing at attention. From then till supper time, I kept watch and shouted "Ma!" whenever a sheet suddenly collapsed or a suit of long underwear crumpled like a vanquished° enemy soldier. My victorious mother, her toddler tucked under one arm to keep him from the runoff°, scooped up her wrinkled spoils between stirs of simmering supper pots.

7   Monday nights, she washed the supper dishes as usual on the kitchen table in a battered pan, threw the murky water out the back door, hung the pan on a nail behind the wood stove, spat on the stove-heated flat irons to test hotness and attacked the ironing that would not be finished till late Tuesday. There being no other heated room in the house, the rest of us navigated between white mountains and gathered in a safe corner behind the wood box. We sat there on assorted wooden chairs, among the overshoes and rubber boots and car-size radio batteries, glued to wheezy broadcasts till my mother brewed coffee and cocoa and warmed scratch cake in the oven at 9:00.

8   She ironed by lamplight, the starched shirts first, not even pausing while she rolled her next smoke. She rolled each cigarette with one hand (either hand—she was ambidextrous°), glued her handcrafted creation with a swipe of her tongue, and lit it over the chimney of the oil lamp. All without missing a stroke or a wrinkle, without singeing a shirt or an eyebrow.

9   Now that's class.

Words and Meanings

Paragraph

1   Martha Stewart   media personality who tells people how to decorate, cook, and achieve an expensive "back to basics" lifestyle

     divinely dispatched   sent by God

plundered	raided, looted	3
Bluenose	famous Nova Scotia racing schooner	
scratch cake	homemade cake (that is, not from a mix)	4
blueing	colouring agent used, before bleach was available, to keep laundry from yellowing	
vanquished	conquered, defeated	6
runoff	puddles of water that collected on the floor as the laundry thawed	
ambidextrous	able to use both hands with ease	8

Structure and Strategy

1. Is Dixon's essay an example of informational or directional process?
2. What strategy does Dixon use in his INTRODUCTION (paragraphs 1 to 3)?
3. How would you describe the TONE of paragraphs 1 and 2? How and why does the tone change in paragraphs 4 to 9?
4. Paragraph 2 describes how Martha does laundry; paragraph 5 describes how Dixon's mother did it. Underline the verbs in these two paragraphs. How does the difference in DICTION reinforce the contrast Dixon develops?
5. In paragraph 4, Dixon describes his mother "bash[ing] the boiling sheets into spotless submission." Find four more examples of word choice that reinforce the notion that doing laundry in the 1930s was a battle, if not a war.

Content and Purpose

1. Why do you think Dixon gave his essay this title? What does "one pillowcase short of a pair" mean?
2. Identify, in order, the steps in the process of doing laundry in Dixon's home in the 1930s. What are some of the factors that made laundry then so much more work than it is today?
3. What other household tasks did Dixon's mother do? What was the role of her young son who would, many years later, describe these tasks?
4. How do you think Dixon feels about his mother? Was his a happy home? How do you know?
5. What does Dixon mean by his CONCLUSION (paragraph 9)? In a sentence or two, explain how you think he might define "class."
6. Why do you think Dixon wrote this essay? Does he intend only to tell us how his mother did laundry 60 years ago, or does he have another PURPOSE?

Suggestions for Writing

1. Write an informational process analysis detailing the steps involved in doing a chore in an old-fashioned way. In other words, tell the reader how to accomplish a task that is much easier to do today.
2. Write an informational process analysis outlining how you approach a necessary task that you do not want to do, such as cleaning the house, disciplining a child, losing weight, delivering bad news, or studying for a final examination.

Home Ice

PAUL QUARRINGTON

Novelist, playwright, screenwriter, journalist, and critic, Paul Quarrington (b. 1953) is one of Canada's most versatile writers. A former rock musician, he writes song lyrics as well as fiction, non-fiction, plays, and films. His recent works include *Civilization and Its Part in My Downfall* (1994), *Dying Is Easy* (1997), and *The Spirit Cabinet* (1999).

1   Think of it as wintry gardening. Better yet, think of it as nocturnal thaumaturgy°. Focus on the magical aspects, for on a more worldly level, we are about to discuss standing outside on the most bitter of nights with a spurting garden hose in your hand, likely frozen there forever. We are about to discuss making a backyard skating rink.

2   It seems to me that the backyard rink ranks right up there with frozen duck ponds and ice-locked rivers. Which is to say, they have a home not only on the earth but also in our frostbitten imaginations. Dreams of Stanley Cups and figure-skating championships are born there. Local arenas are nice enough places, I suppose, but the important thing is the sense of community. When I think of local arenas, I think of the benches, the snack bars, the people huddled together eating cold hot dogs and blowing on cups of hot chocolate. The ice itself is nothing special—it is quiet and subdued, not like the unruly ice you find in the backyard rink. Curlers and assorted Celts call the outdoor variety "roaring ice." The blades of skates produce sharp-edged howls. The ice of a backyard rink is welted and scarred and unable to smooth the wrinkled face of the planet. It is elemental, having as much claim to the land as rocks or wind.

That is why the process is not really so much "making" or 3
"constructing" a backyard rink; it is more along the lines of
allowing one to come into being, a sort of shivering midwifery.
Some people conceive of the process as imposing the rink on the
ground, which results in that most mundane and dreary objection
to the backyard skating rink: it will ruin the grass. That is not true.
You don't have to take my word for it. I went and asked Peter
Hayward, a landscaper/gardener here in Orillia, Ontario, where
the backyards are huge and backyard rinks commonplace. "No, it
won't ruin the grass," he assured me, although after a moment of
judicious and professional musing, he added, "Might make it grow
a bit *funny*." What he meant was that the grass may grow in
opposing directions in the spring—but only for a time.

Funny grass is a small price to pay. This is something you can 4
do for your children, something meaningful. The magic will not be
lost upon them. They will be delighted that a field of ice has
bloomed during the night. They will stare at it and think, "Geez,
Dad [or Mom] must have frozen his [or her] butt off!" They will be
right. There is little point sugarcoating this truth. If you can't stand
the cold, stay in the kitchen.

I propose to pass on the recipe for the definitive, the quintes- 5
sential, the perfect backyard skating rink. I did not arrive at such a
recipe without a lot of help. I turned to my friend Peter Hayman
(not to be confused with Peter Hayward, although this, perhaps,
cannot be helped), a Toronto filmmaker and father of three young
boys. He was led to make a rink mostly because he remembered
one from his childhood: "Also, there's a rink at the end of our street
that the city is supposed to keep up, and, of course, they never do.
A little thaw, and it's wiped out." I have skated on Hayman's rink
and know it to be first-class. (I have a simple test: any ice that does
not immediately flip me onto my dustcover is first-class.) I also
received a lot of information from Ronn Hartviksen, an art teacher
who lives in Thunder Bay. Hartviksen is the creator of perhaps the
most ambitious and beautiful backyard rink in the world, a huge
thing (about 65 by 110 feet) that has achieved almost legendary
status in the hockey-playing community. The rink is called the
"Bean Pot," a nod to Boston and the Boston Bruins, Hartviksen's
favourite hockey team. An ice artist, he has put the team's distinctive "B" at centre ice.

When Dave King was preparing the Canadian team for the 6
1988 Olympics, he made sure the players found time to visit Hartviksen's place and skate on the Bean Pot. Similarly, he had the team
skate on the Ottawa Canal. Coach King, a man who takes pains to
seem reasonable and sedate°, sometimes talks about "the romance

of the backyard rink" and hints there is something very important to be discovered out on that ice.

7   "The indoor rink," opines King, "is a good place to develop technical skills. But the outdoor rink is the place to acquire a real love for the game. In the new generation of hockey players, this is missing." Despite unpredictable chinooks° in Calgary, where King lives, he continues to make his own backyard rink. Lastly, I went to the guru of the backyard rink, the man who made what is surely the most famous backyard rink in the world, Walter Gretzky°.

8   If you are going to make a backyard rink, decide early in the season, well before winter is actually in sight. This is the easy part, walking outside and choosing the likeliest site. It may be that you have a smallish backyard and are therefore simply going to flood the whole thing. Others may be faced with a larger expanse and should select some portion of it. The guiding principle should arise from the fact that you are going to have to shovel, resurface and otherwise groom your backyard rink, so you should keep it to a manageable size. Twenty by forty feet seems reasonable: large enough for skaters to manoeuvre, even to play a spirited, if congested, game of shinny, but small enough to care for.

9   A prime consideration is flatness. It is not necessary that the ground be perfectly smooth (you will be surprised at how hilly and full of cavities your lawn really is), but there is no getting around the fact that it must be level. Some depressions can, of course, be built up with snow, and small rises will just become part of the rink (I can recall a section of a rink long ago that would supply me with a quick burst of speed, alarming, not to mention astounding, everyone else on the ice), but a slope, even a gentle one, will undermine all your best efforts.

10   The last consideration is proximity° to a water source. Tapping into an inside source is best. If you can run a hose into the basement, for example, and hook up with the washing-machine taps, you will reap a number of benefits. Remember that no nozzle/hose connection is perfect, and imagine some of the nasty things that could happen at an outside connection—such as finding the thing encased in a block of ice. Even if you avoid nightly chipping and hacking, any outside terminal is going to require a bucket or two of hot water just to get the tap cranked. So if you can get to the water inside, so much the better, especially because, in the maintenance stages, you can employ the hot water for resurfacing, a technique I call "the poor man's Zamboni" (a machine used to resurface the ice in arenas). My own experience has taught me the value of hot water to promote a smooth ice surface. Curiously, none of the authorities I talked to used the method.

But let's not worry about maintenance right now; let's get the thing started. Just a couple of quick points here: you probably lack enough hose, because you are used to pulling it up the centre of the lawn. It is now necessary to pull the hose around the outside of a 20-by-40-foot rectangle (you must be able to stand at any point around the perimeter°, hose in hand), so go out and buy another section. It must be a good-quality, thick, heavy rubber hose, because plastic ones are likely to crack open when the world is hung about with ice spikes. 11

Having selected the site, make sure the ground is properly tended, which means mowing and raking. If you don't, you might face what proved to be the bane of my childhood backyard rinks: errant° blades of grass popping through the ice surface. I know this does not seem likely or even possible, but believe me, little green Ninjas will sprout up and flip you onto your backside. So give your lawn a marine cut late in the fall. 12

Here is an optional step, depending on where you live. Ronn Hartviksen—who, you will recall, resides in Thunder Bay—says that sometimes in late fall, he will hose down the naked earth. It's cold enough to freeze, and he has a layer of black ice for his rink's foundation. In other, more southerly places, watering your lawn late fall serves no purpose except to demonstrate to your neighbours that you are fairly strange, so they will not think twice the first time you are out there at midnight and 40 below. 13

Now you wait. 14

You wait for cold temperatures. "It would be lovely to do all this, say, over the Christmas holidays," says Hayman, "but that's usually just not possible here in Toronto. You're more likely going to have to wait until the middle of January." So you wait for the requisite cold temperatures, and you wait for snow. Wait until there is a whole lot of snow, maybe two or three good dumpings. Then clear some of it away from your rectangle, leaving behind anywhere from four to six inches. This clearing supplies you with a little border, something to aid in water retention while flooding. It also gives a comfortable sense of containment and might even keep a puck on the ice, although you and I both know that the puck will hit your little ridge of snow, pick up torque° and be gone into the neighbour's yard. 15

It is best to flatten the snow. Hartviksen sends out a troop of kids to play what he calls "boot hockey." He also possesses a heavy piece of wood that he can drag behind him, smoothing the surface. This is not as crucial a step as some people believe. I recall from childhood when someone—I think maybe Mr. Michaels (the kind of man who locked his garage doors)—rented one of those huge 16 industrial drum rollers. The problem is that snow sticks to things like that; also, those rollers are fairly useless unless you fill them with water, which can cause problems. For instance, it can deprive you of your coffee breaks, lest the water inside the drum freeze. The process of backyard rink building raises the market value of coffee breaks considerably; they soon seem as important as reaching Base Camp while scaling K2°.

17   The foundation of the base is snow. Snow plus water and the chilly, chilly air. I am going to advocate the "slush" approach to base building, which differs slightly from, say, Hartviksen's "sugar-cube" approach. (Hartviksen's approach is really more of an aid to visualization. He gives the snow a heavy watering and imagines each section of snow as a large sugar cube. The darkening on the surface gives a good indication of the degree of saturation.)

18   I am a proponent of the most active sort of base building, getting out there with a hose and creating slush, which is then smoothed flat. You want the slush to be more solid than a Slurpee, just watery enough that snowball construction is out of the question. Do small sections at a time. Hayman's technique is effective here: water the ground, work it into slush with a snow shovel, use the back of the snow shovel to smooth it out, move along, do it again. Work lanes, walking backward across the rink-to-be. Once you get that done, have someone carry you inside to thaw you out in a dry, warm corner.

19   In the morning, it will be slightly hilly—well, let's face it, your rink at this point would baffle most topographical° mapmakers. But that's all right. You have done most of the heavy human work now; it is time to turn things over to Mother Nature and let her smooth everything out. The next night . . . oh, let's clear that up. It is not absolutely necessary to do this at night, although a fierce sun can slow things down even on the coldest day. In my experience, however, backyard rink building is always done at night for various practical reasons (a job being the chief one) and for one very impractical one: Did the elves ever show up at the shoemaker's before midnight?

20   The next night, go out there armed with your hose. Just the hose, no fancy nozzles or sprayers: you have to have the open-ended hose because you want to get as much water on the ground in as short a time as possible. "People are always offering me gadgets to put on the end of my hose," says Hartviksen, "but I find they clog and drip and freeze my pant legs. I always end up with just the hose and my thumb. I alternate thumbs. I'm thinking of getting them insured." You should be able to hit most places without stepping on the ice surface, but if you can't, go ahead and step on it.

Your foot will go through, but the footprints will be filled in as you build layer by layer, and that is a better option than depriving your rink-to-be of an even flooding. Depending on how cold it is, you might be able to do two, even three, floodings that first night. When you have finished do yourself an enormous favour: coil the hose up, and take it inside the house with you.

The next morning, you will find a vaguely flat sheet of ice, **21** although it might be alarmingly pitted, cracked and ravined. Now, in Peter Hayman's words, you "make like a referee." No, he doesn't mean that you get small-minded and petty and order your children to bed early for no good reason (just joking); he means that you get out there on hands and knees—as referees often do during games—grab handfuls of snow and start stuffing the cracks and holes. Stuffing and tamping, tamping and stuffing. It's amazing how much snow even the smallest crack can hold, so don't imagine this is the work of a few moments. However, the more patching you do, the better your rink is going to be.

Now, the ice might look uniformly strong, but it is very **22** doubtful that it is. The roll of the lawn has a lot of influence here, and usually, there are air pockets undermining the structure. I hold to the view that it is best to know about them at this stage of the game—when they can be corrected. So as you do your flood that evening, get out there. Flood the rink, drink cognac and wait until it freezes, flood the rink, drink cognac, drink cognac. . . .

In the morning, you have something that looks like a skating **23** rink. This cheers you up, because you drank too much cognac the night before and are feeling a little poorly. There is still some patching to do, but it seems less fundamental—more like polishing than anything else—and after another couple of floodings that evening, you will have, if not a proper skating rink, what Hayman refers to with caution as "a skateable situation."

Put the lightest family member out there. Hold your breath. **24** Watch as he or she makes a couple of circuits around the outer edges. There will be some creaking, maybe a little cracking—make like a referee, and flood again that evening. And the next. And the next. You need an ice thickness of perhaps six inches to survive sudden thaws. If it should snow, it must be cleared away almost immediately, because a thick blanket can result in an ice-snow commingling° that will ruin the surface.

In time, you will not have to flood every night, or even every **25** other night, but many nights will find you out there, hose in hand, practising a little wintry gardening, a little nocturnal thaumaturgy.

Words and Meanings

1	nocturnal thaumaturgy	nighttime magic
6	sedate	calm, composed, thoughtful, steady
7	chinooks	warm winter winds that blow eastward across the Rocky Mountains into Alberta and Saskatchewan
	Walter Gretzky	father of hockey great Wayne Gretzky
10	proximity	closeness
11	perimeter	outer boundary, the edge around the rink
12	errant	uncontrolled, growing in all directions
15	torque	speed and spin
16	scaling K2	climbing the world's second-highest mountain
19	topographical	showing the surface features of a place or region; for example, mountains or rivers
24	commingling	mixture, blending together

Structure and Strategy

1. What METAPHORS does the author use in the opening paragraph? Do they recur later in the essay? (Hint: are there any other references to magic?) Why does the author choose such sophisticated DICTION ("nocturnal thaumaturgy") to identify his subject?

2. Paragraph 2 is based on a contrast. What is it and why does the author introduce it here? (See paragraph 3.)

3. After the INTRODUCTION (paragraphs 1 to 4), Quarrington moves to the preparation stage (paragraphs 5 to 7). What three "experts" did he consult? What are their qualifications to act as authorities on this topic?

4. In which paragraph does the author's process analysis actually begin? Trace the ten steps involved in creating a backyard rink. Are Quarrington's instructions clear and easy to follow? Do they adhere to the principles described in the introduction to this unit?

5. Quarrington employs several FIGURES OF SPEECH to develop his ideas; for example, "more solid than a Slurpee" (paragraph 18), and "make like a referee" (paragraph 21). Find other examples of figurative language. (Hint: look first at the title.)

6. Quarrington tries to encourage his readers by using humour to modify the impression that making a backyard rink is a long, tedious, and even painful process. Identify three or four examples of humour in this essay.

Content and Purpose

1. What objection to backyard rink building does paragraph 3 refute? What objection cannot be refuted and how does the author suggest the reader deal with it (paragraph 4)?
2. Identify three significant reasons why anyone would go through the trouble and discomfort of making a backyard rink.
3. The first step in the process, deciding where to put the rink, depends on what three factors? (See paragraphs 8 to 10.)
4. How does the author suggest you check to see whether your rink is ready for skating?

Suggestion for Writing

Write a directional process analysis for a multi-step project: for instance, DJ-ing, detailing a car, getting into college, building a deck, designing a webpage, making sushi, doing a body piercing. Make sure that your essay not only explains how to complete the process but also suggests why the process is worthwhile.

Dear Dad

JEFFREY MOUSSAIEFF MASSON

Jeffrey Moussaieff Masson (b. 1941) taught Sanskrit and Indian Studies at the University of Toronto from 1969 to 1980. After graduating from the Toronto Institute of Psychoanalysis in 1978, he served as projects director of the Sigmund Freud Archives. He has demonstrated his fascination with animal psychology in such books as *When Elephants Weep* (1994), *Dogs Never Lie About Love* (1997), and *The Nine Emotional Lives of Cats* (2002).

One reason that so many of us are fascinated by penguins is that they resemble us. They walk upright, the way we do, and, like us, they are notoriously curious creatures. No doubt this accounts for our fondness for cartoon images of penguins dressed up at crowded parties, but as fathers, penguins are our superiors.

Unlike mammals, male birds can experience pregnancy as an intimate matter, with the father in many species helping to sit (brood) the egg. After all, a male can brood an egg as well as a female can. But in no other species does it reach this extreme.

3   The emperors usually wait for good weather to copulate, any time between April 10 and June 6. They separate themselves somewhat from the rest of the colony and face each other, remaining still for a time. Then the male bends his head, contracts his abdomen, and shows the female the spot on his belly where he has a flap of skin that serves as a kind of pouch for the egg and baby chick. This stimulates the female to do the same. Their heads touch, and the male bends his head down to touch the female's pouch. Both begin to tremble visibly. Then the female lies face down on the ice, partially spreads her wings and opens her legs. The male climbs onto her back and they mate for 10 to 30 seconds.

4   They stay together afterward constantly, leaning against one another when they are standing up, or if they lie down, the female will glide her head under that of her mate. About a month later, between May 1 and June 12, the female lays a single greenish-white egg. French researchers noted that the annual dates on which the colony's first egg was laid varied by only eight days in 16 years of observation. Weighing almost a pound [.45 kilograms], and measuring up to 131 millimetres long and 86 millimetres wide, this is one of the largest eggs of any bird. The male stays by the female's side, his eyes fixed on her pouch. As soon as he sees the egg, he sings a variation of what has been called the "ecstatic" display by early observers, and she too takes up the melody.

5   She catches the egg with her wings before it touches the ice and places it on her feet. Both penguins then sing in unison, staring at the egg for up to an hour. The female then slowly walks around the male, who gently touches the egg on her feet with his beak, making soft groans, his whole body trembling. He shows the female his pouch. Gently she puts the egg down on the ice and just as gently he rolls it with his beak between his large, black, powerfully clawed feathered feet, and then, with great difficulty, hoists the egg onto the surface of his feet. He rests back on his heels so that his feet make the least contact with the ice. The transfer of the egg is a delicate operation. If it falls on the ice and rolls away, it can freeze in minutes or it might even be stolen. If it is snatched away by a female penguin who failed to find a mate, its chances of survival are slight because the intruder will eventually abandon the egg, since she has no mate to relieve her.

6   With the egg transfer successfully completed, the happy couple both sing. The male parades about in front of the female, showing her his pouch with the egg inside. This thick fold, densely feathered on the outside and bare inside, now completely covers the egg and keeps it at about 95 degrees Fahrenheit, even when the temperature falls to 95 degrees below zero.

The female begins to back away, each time a little farther. He   7
tries to follow her, but it is hard, since he is balancing the egg.
Suddenly she is gone, moving purposefully toward the open sea.
She is joined by the other females in the colony, who, by the end of
May or June, have all left for the ocean almost 100 kilometres away.
The females have fasted for nearly a month and a half, and have
lost anywhere between 17 to 30 per cent of their total weight. They
are in urgent need of food.

The female must renew her strength and vitality so that she can   8
return with food for her chick. Going to the sea, she takes the
shortest route to reach a polynya (open water surrounded by ice).
Penguins appear to be able to navigate by the reflection of the
clouds on the water, using what has been called a "water sky."

The male penguin, who has also been fasting, is now left with   9
the egg balanced on his feet. The first egg was laid on the first of
May; a chick will emerge in August. Since the seasons are reversed
south of the equator, full winter has arrived, with many violent
blizzards and the lowest temperatures of the year. Emperor penguins are well adapted to the almost unimaginable cold of these 24-
hour Antarctic nights: Their plumage is waterproof, windproof,
flexible and renewed annually. They may not need tents, but as
soon as the bad weather starts, generally in June, the males need
some protection from the bitter cold, and nearly all of them find it
by forming a *tortue*, which is a throng of very densely packed penguins. When the storms come they move in close to one another,
shoulder to shoulder, and form a circle. The middle of the tortue is
unusually warm and one would think that every penguin fights to
be at the epicentre of warmth. But in fact what looks like an immobile mass is really a very slowly revolving spiral. The constantly
shifting formation is such that every penguin, all the while balancing that single precious egg on his feet, eventually winds up in
the middle of the tortue, only to find himself later at the periphery.

What early French explorers noticed during the two- to three-   10
month incubation period is an almost preternatural calm among the
males. This is no doubt necessitated by the long fast that is ahead of
them. Many of them have already fasted, like the females, for two
months or more, and must now face another two months of fasting.
And moving about with an egg balanced on one's feet is difficult at
the best of times.

The only time a father will abandon an egg is if he has reached   11
the maximum limit of his physiological° ability to fast, and would
die if he did not seek food. Not a small number of eggs are left for
this reason, and it would seem that in each case the female is late in
returning.

12   In July or August, after being gone for almost three months, the female emperor returns from the sea, singing as she penetrates various groups of birds, searching for her mate and her chick or egg. The males do not move, but make small peeping noises. When she finds her partner, she sings, she makes little dance steps, then she goes quiet and both birds can remain immobile for up to 10 minutes. Then they begin to move around one another. The female fixes her eyes on the incubatory pouch of her partner, while her excitement grows visibly. Finally, if it is the right bird, the male allows the egg to fall gently to the ice, whereupon the female takes it and then turns her back to the male, to whom, after a final duet, she becomes completely indifferent. The male becomes increasingly irritated, stares at his empty pouch, pecks at it with his beak, lifts up his head, groans, and then pecks the female. She shows no further interest in him and eventually he leaves for the open sea, to break his long fast. The whole affair has lasted about 80 minutes. . . .

13   The miracle is that the mothers usually return on the day their chicks hatch. How is it, one wonders, that the female emperor penguin is able to return just in time for the birth of her chick? As Alexander Skutch notes in his wonderful book, *The Minds of Birds*, it is improbable that she has consciously counted the 63 days or whatever the exact number is between the laying of her egg and the hatching of her chick. "Some subconscious process, physiological or mental, was evidently summing the days to prompt the birds to start homeward when the proper number had elapsed."

14   If the egg has hatched before her arrival and the male already has a chick between his legs, the female is even more excited to hear it peep, and quickly removes it from the male. She immediately regurgitates food to the chick. If she is late in coming, the male, in spite of his near starvation, has a final resource: He regurgitates into the beak of his peeping newborn a substance known as penguin milk, similar to pigeon's milk, or crop milk, which is secreted from the lining of his esophagus. The secretion is remarkably rich, containing essential amino acids, much like the milk of marine mammals such as seals and whales. These feedings allow the young birds to survive for up to two weeks after hatching. Many of these males have now fasted for four and a half months, and have lost up to half of their body weight. It is a sight to see the well-nourished, sleek, brilliantly feathered, healthy-looking females arrive, and the emaciated°, dirty, tired males leave.

15   How difficult it is for us to understand the emotions involved in these events. Yet it is hard to resist the anthropomorphic urge.

Obviously the male emperor is aware of the loss of what has, after all, been almost a part of his body for two to three months. Is he disappointed, bewildered, relieved, or are his feelings so remote from our own (not inferior, mind you, just different) that we cannot imagine them? We would groan, too, under such circumstances, but the meaning of a penguin's groan is still opaque° to us. Yet we, too, are fathers and mothers with babies to protect and comfort, negotiating meals and absences and other obligations, just like our Antarctic cousins. Sometimes, when we are overwhelmed by an emotion, we are hard-pressed to express ourselves. If penguin fathers could speak about this moment in their lives, perhaps they would be at a similar loss for words. Perhaps the songs and groans of the male penguin are all the expression they need.

Words and Meanings

Paragraph

physiological	having to do with the physical functioning of a living creature	11
emaciated	thin, starved	14
opaque	not transparent; difficult to figure out	15

Structure and Strategy

1. What kind of attention-getter does Masson use in the INTRODUCTION (paragraphs 1 and 2)?
2. What is Masson's THESIS? Is it implied or stated in the essay?
3. Which paragraphs are developed primarily by means of numerical facts and statistics? Why is this a useful strategy for explaining the KEY IDEAS of these paragraphs? Are there any factual details the essay doesn't provide that you would have been interested to learn about?
4. How is the key idea of paragraph 13 developed?
5. The DICTION of this essay combines scientific terms with words and phrases more commonly associated with human emotion, such as "happy couple" in paragraph 6 and "increasingly irritated" in paragraph 12. Find other examples of diction that Masson uses to support the ANALOGY he draws between penguins and humans. Why do you think he uses the penguin–human analogy to develop his process analysis? Do you find this analogy interesting or off-putting? Explain your answer.

Content and Purpose

1. In two or three sentences, summarize Masson's PURPOSE in this essay.
2. In this process analysis of the emperor penguin reproductive cycle, which parts of the process are described in paragraphs 3 to 8, 9 to 11, and 12 to 14?
3. How do emperor penguins mate? What physical characteristic makes it possible for the male to "experience pregnancy as an intimate matter" (paragraph 2)?
4. Why do the female penguins temporarily abandon their eggs and mates? What happens when the females return?
5. What kind of "male bonding" takes place among the males during the females' absence? What purpose is served by the *tortue*?
6. Identify three reproductive behaviours that penguins have in common with humans. Identify three behaviours that are significantly different.
7. What is the mystery at the core of the essay's CONCLUSION (paragraph 15)? What do you think is the source of "the songs and groans of the male penguin"?
8. What is the author's attitude toward the creatures he writes about? Identify three or four examples to support your opinion.
9. From an evolutionary perspective, how is the emperor penguin's mating and chick-rearing process adaptive? (See Helena Cronin's "The Evolution of Evolution," on page 187, for an explanation of this concept.)

Suggestions for Writing

1. Write an essay about the role of a father in his child's life. What are the essential tasks of fatherhood?
2. Write an essay about being a caregiver. Describe a situation in which you have cared for someone on an ongoing basis. What does this narrative reveal about you, the caregiver?
3. When people attribute human characteristics and feelings to gods, animals, or things, they are engaging in *anthropomorphism*. Write an essay that provides one or more examples of anthropomorphism. Why do you suppose people anthropomorphize? Are there any dangers in attributing human feelings to animal behaviours? If so, what are they?

A Tree-Planting Primer

DANNY IRVINE

Born in Toronto, Danny Irvine (b. 1980) lives in Hamilton, Ontario, and is completing an honours undergraduate degree in English and theatre. He won third prize in the 2002 Conference on Christianity and Literature Non-fiction Contest.

INTRODUCTION

Welcome to the wonderful world of tree planting. You are about to embark on an adventure of awesome proportions, fending for yourself in the coniferous° Klondike—the very heartland of Canada. Are you intimidated? Don't be. You can rest assured that any stories you may have heard about the gruelling savagery of the tree-planting experience, about inhospitable landscapes, maimed bodies, and inhuman exhaustion are wild exaggerations, nothing more than hallucinations of former planters who are suffering the residual effects of some obscure psychological trauma.   1

The wilderness is a nurturing, healing place, and it is well known that physical labour can be a contemplative, therapeutic activity. You can see its effects in the euphoria° of the planters at the end of the season. Nevertheless, you may still be a little apprehensive about the planting contract and may feel somewhat alien in your new environment, so far away from the familiar comfort of the city, with its paved roads and snowless summers, its docile elements and herbivorous° wildlife. We encourage you to think of the North as your "home away from home": the trees and rocks your walls and floors, the darkening clouds your vaulted ceiling, the bears and wolves your friendly neighbours. What's more, you have this primer, which is designed to help you to survive and to profit from your silvicultural° experience.   2

EQUIPMENT

By this time, you will have been given your tree-planting equipment. Your planting bags—three pouches of high-tensile nylon, suspended from a padded, ergonomic belt and adjustable shoulder straps—are the first order of business. You will wear this set of bags all day, every day, for the duration of the contract. They will be your uniform, the armour of the noble tree planter; they will adorn and distinguish you; they will soak up your sweat and bear your scent. Think of them as indispensable articles of clothing, a sort of "second underwear," which you put on as soon as you awake and   3 without which you never leave home. Do not get caught without your planting bags. Since this second underwear will be weighted with more than 20 kg of trees, you will want to adjust the belt and shoulder straps to the position most closely approximating comfort. Ignore any uncomfortable chafing you may experience; this abrasion will soon become too familiar to be troublesome.

4   The second piece of equipment: your shovel. Hold it in your hand. Grip it. Swing it. Can you feel the earth part before you? No? Swing it again. Hit something with it. This is no ordinary shovel; this is your livelihood. This is your weapon. This steel-spaded, wood-shafted, D-handled shovel is the instrument with which you will split the earth and subdue the forests. It will be your trusty machete when you encounter obstructive branches and brush. It will be your means of carving yourself bathroom facilities when you are miles from civilization. It will be your sure defence in the event of an encounter with squirrels, raccoons, or small, sickly black bears. For these reasons, it is important that you respect your shovel. Never let it out of your sight. Take care of it. Name it. Talk to it. It will be your best and only friend in the long days of solitude out on the clear cut. At first, your shovel may feel awkward and heavy, but after several weeks of continuously gripping it, you will feel as if it were a fifth limb. You and your shovel will form such a bond that you will find it almost unbearably painful to unclench your grip at night.

GETTING STARTED

5   Once you have familiarized yourself with your equipment, you are ready to plant. To begin, put your planting bags around your waist. If the belt slips, readjust it. If it continues to slip, duct-tape the straps together. If even duct tape fails to maintain a fit, the problem is probably faulty belt buckles. Find a fellow planter with undamaged bags and inconspicuously swap your bag for hers. Write your name on your new bag with a waterproof magic-marker and avoid that planter for a few days.

6   Next, decide how many trees you are willing to carry in one trip, and load up your bags. This is not a casual decision. On the one hand, since you are being paid per tree, there is financial reward in carrying as many trees as you can squeeze into your bags. On the other hand, a heavy load will weigh and slow you down. You will tire quickly, and you will not be able to stop for a rest until your bags are fully unloaded. What's that? You don't plan on taking any breaks? That's the attitude! Heavy or light: you must find a middle road. Forestry is, after all, fundamentally a matter of balance: harvesting lumber without decimating° the sustainable forests, planting

new growth without destabilizing the ecosystem, working harder than a machine without destroying your body, keeping the bugs away without developing cancer from insect repellent.

Once you have packed up your trees, scan the area and pick up   7
any trees you may have inadvertently dropped. The forestry company has paid a good deal of money for these trees, and you will find that they become a little testy if they discover any lying on the ground. Throw any fallen trees into your bag, or, alternatively, onto the ground where another planter has been working.

Packing up your trees, or "bagging up," as you will become   8
conditioned to call it, can, admittedly, be a time-consuming procedure. Having to sit in one place to perform it can be particularly irritating if it happens to be raining or snowing; if it happens to be in the frigid early months or the scorching later months of the season; or if the blackflies, mosquitoes, horseflies, or deerflies happen to be out. But never mind. Having packed up your bags, knowing precisely how many trees you are carrying, you are ready to go. What? You didn't keep track of how many you put in? Well, you'd better take them all out and count again.

Once you have confirmed your count, take your shovel in your   9
right or left hand, whichever is the stronger. This will be your "shovel hand"; your weaker hand will be your "bag hand." Your bag hand is the hand that will pick up and plant each tree; that is why you have put the trees into the pouch on that same side. What? You didn't know this, and put the trees into the pouch on the side of your stronger hand? Well, you'd better take them all out and start again.

Your bags strapped and loaded, your shovel firmly gripped,   10
you are at long last ready to plant your first tree. Make your way to the piece of land, "the block," that has been allotted to you. The block may be a short, convenient distance from your tree depot. More often, however, you will have a long hike to get to the entrance to your land. You may be compensated if this travel time is unusually lengthy or particularly gruelling. But don't count on it. Your employer is more likely to consider this trek an opportunity for you to explore the untamed wilderness and reflect on your contribution to the development of our country's sustainable resources.

PLANTING A TREE

Planting a tree is an art that requires control and precision and, for   11
many individuals, takes years to learn. In Japan, for instance, bonsai-tree planters are chosen while they are still infants and taken to mountain pagodas, where they spend their youth in rigorous training under the tutelage of revered masters. Each day

they spend hours in the forest, learning respect for the trees; they participate in disciplined physical exercises, developing scrupulous control of their bodies; and only after seven years of barehanded labour in the stony Japanese soil are they permitted to handle a shovel.

12   You, on the other hand, have the good fortune to live in a much less demanding culture. With this guide to help you, you can easily learn to plant a tree without years of arduous training. To be a successful tree planter, you need to learn two things. First, you must understand and accept the essential, organic, and spiritual union of body and land—a dynamic, beautiful marriage of arms, legs, back, and shovel with tree and soil. Second, you must learn to harness and relentlessly exploit this union for your own purposes.

13   Begin by retrieving a tree from your bag with (you guessed it) your bag hand. At the same time, step forward with the corresponding leg, pinpoint the spot where you wish to plant a tree, and, with your shovel hand, raise your shovel.

14   This is probably a good point at which to discuss generating and maintaining motivation and morale while out on the clear cut. As everyone knows, a certain degree of mental fortitude is helpful when you are repeatedly performing even the simplest of tasks. The oppressive, dark, and forbidding clouds that perpetually crowd the skies this far north may already have suggested to you that not every planting day will be a sunny outing in the woods. Some planters have even experienced moments of mild discouragement at their work.

15   If ever you should feel a twinge of despair over your ability to fulfill the planting contract, to meet the quota of trees that you have set as a standard for yourself; if ever you are worried that you will not earn enough money to pay off your student debts and will have to sell the family heirlooms to pay your tuition; if you have been planting in a swamp for three weeks and have not spoken to another soul for days; if you notice the extremities of your body turning numb from the cold, from insect bites, or from the pesticides on the trees; if the zipper on your tent has torn and your boots have holes in them and your leg is broken and infected and your girlfriend or boyfriend has stopped writing letters and your mother has forgotten about you and rented out your room to a new son or daughter and you are on the verge of impaling yourself on your own planting shovel, do not be dismayed. Stop. Look about you at the miles of muddied and overturned land, at the endless expanse of barren clear cut, at the infinitely distant and uncompromising sky, and reflect on your relative insignificance. Remember that compared to the immensity and mysterious purposefulness of the universe, your life and

worries are inconsequential. Then, your mind cleared and reinvigorated, take a deep breath, and get back to work.

So, with your shovel aloft in your shovel hand, and with a tree in your tree hand, take a second step forward—this time with your other leg, the one that corresponds to your shovel hand. Bring down your shovel with a swift, heavy stroke, stabbing the blade into the earth as deeply as possible. If your shovel doesn't penetrate the surface, it is likely that you have struck a rock or some sort of impervious sun-fired clay. Nevertheless, you must plant a tree as close to this spot as you can. Move to the next nearest planting spot. If the soil in this location visibly leeches water when you step on it, it is too wet and will drown your tree. Move to the next closest location. If this one is within two metres of a tree that has somehow miraculously survived the clear-cutting, bulldozing, and chemical spraying that has otherwise sterilized the land, keep moving. Eventually, you will find a patch of acceptable soil, a sufficiently rotten stump, or a sizable pile of bear droppings in which to plant your tree. **16**

With your shovel plunged in the earth, take the third and final step, again with the leg that corresponds to your bag hand. Twist the D-handle of your shovel away from you in a wide outward arc, laying open a hole in the ground, and, with the tree still in your bag hand, bend down over your shovel. Poke the roots of the tree into the freshly dug hole and hold the seedling in place while pulling your shovel from the soil. As you straighten your back, slide your fingers up the length of the tree until they gently grip the tip. Remember, the needles of the trees are laced with pesticides, so avoid pricking your fingers. Once you are upright, close the hole by lightly stomping on the ground immediately beside the tree. Finally, give the seedling a small tug to ensure that it is snug in the soil. **17**

Congratulations! You have planted your first tree. Know that you are following in a great human tradition, one that began when agricultural man first informed the flora and fauna° of the world that he knew better than they did how and where they should grow. Since then, humankind has been proudly asserting its place in the natural world and now you, too, are a part of this noble history. Your father and mother are every farmer who ever pressed a seed into the soil, every gardener who ever ripped a weed from its bed, every farm hand who ever forced a bit into a horse's mouth. **18**

All that stands between you and fortune are three easy steps, a swift bend, and a few fluid motions with your shovel—repeated three or four thousand times a day. You have planted your standard. Eventually, one tree at a time, you will own the North. **19**

Unless, of course, your tree is not within the two- or three-millimetre margin of depth; unless it is leaning; unless it is crooked, **20** or its roots are not straight; unless it is less or more than the permitted distance from any other tree, natural or planted; unless the tree is unhealthy, diseased, smothered by loose dirt or missing its tip; or if, as you filled the hole, it got stepped on, or . . .

Words and Meanings

Paragraph		
1	coniferous	relating to cone-bearing evergreen trees
2	euphoria	a feeling of extreme happiness, ecstasy
	herbivorous	plant-eating
	silvicultural	adjective form of *silviculture*, the branch of forestry dealing with the growing and cultivation of trees
6	decimating	destroying
18	flora and fauna	plant and animal life

Structure and Strategy

1. What is a "primer"? Is this essay a good example of a primer? Why or why not?
2. List, in order, the steps in planting a tree.
3. Identify at least three places in the essay that make it clear the author is addressing a specific listener. Who is this imagined listener? Do you think that this person is the actual AUDIENCE for the essay? If not, what audience did Irvine really have in mind when he wrote "A Tree-Planting Primer"?
4. Consider the DICTION of the essay. The author frequently uses sophisticated vocabulary in long sentences. (See, for example, paragraph 2: "docile elements . . . herbivorous wildlife . . . vaulted ceiling . . . silvicultural experience.") What is the effect of the contrast between the stated topic—a simple process—and the formal, complex style in which the topic is explained?
5. The first sentence in paragraph 15 is a monster run-on that goes on for many lines. The author stops punctuating the clauses about two-thirds of the way through the sentence. How does the structure of the sentence reflect its meaning?
6. Consider the last two paragraphs of this essay. Identify Irvine's SUMMARY of his KEY IDEAS. In the final paragraph, he presents no real CONCLUSION; the last sentence just trails off into silence. Why? Is this ending effective? Why or why not?
7. How does the TONE of the essay communicate Irvine's attitude toward tree planting and the companies that sponsor it? (See especially paragraphs 6, 16, and 18.)

Content and Purpose

1. Is this essay a directional process analysis? In other words, does Irvine set out to teach readers how to succeed as tree planters? If not, what is his real PURPOSE? (See IRONY.)
2. What are the two required pieces of tree-planting equipment? According to the author, how should a tree planter regard this equipment?
3. Paragraphs 11 and 12 are based on a contrast between two cultures. What are the two cultures, and what are the differences between them? What is the point of this contrast? Is Irvine serious about the point he makes here?
4. After thirteen paragraphs of instruction that bring us to the point of actually planting a tree, the author suddenly breaks off and begins discussing how to maintain "motivation and morale while out on the clear cut." Why? What are the effects of this digression?
5. In one or two sentences, summarize the message that Irvine communicates to the intended (not the pretend) AUDIENCE in this essay.

Suggestions for Writing

1. Write a directional process analysis about an outdoor task that you know well, such as fishing, camping, skiing, gardening, or jogging. Use the second-person POINT OF VIEW, as Irvine does in his essay.
2. Write a directional process analysis that is ostensibly about a particular job or task, but use the ironic tone that Irvine and Mitford ("Behind the Formaldehyde Curtain") use in their essays. In other words, tell someone how to do something that you really think they shouldn't be doing.

Behind the Formaldehyde° Curtain

JESSICA MITFORD

Essayist Jessica Mitford (1917–1996) was born to a prominent family at Batsford Mansion, England, and settled in the United States in 1939. Mitford began her writing career in the 1950s. Among her best-known works are *Hons and Rebels, The Trial of Dr. Spock,* and *The American Way of Death.*

1   The drama begins to unfold with the arrival of the corpse at the mortuary.

2   Alas, poor Yorick°! How surprised he would be to see how his counterpart of today is whisked off to a funeral parlor and is in short order sprayed, sliced, pierced, pickled, trussed, trimmed, creamed, waxed, painted, rouged and neatly dressed—transformed from a common corpse into a Beautiful Memory Picture. This process is known in the trade as embalming and restorative art, and is so universally employed in the United States and Canada that the funeral director does it routinely, without consulting corpse or kin. He regards as eccentric those few who are hardy enough to suggest that it might be dispensed with. Yet no law requires embalming, no religious doctrine commends it, nor is it dictated by considerations of health, sanitation, or even of personal daintiness. In no part of the world but in North America is it widely used. The purpose of embalming is to make the corpse presentable for viewing in a suitably costly container; and here too the funeral director routinely, without first consulting the family, prepares the body for public display.

3   Is all this legal? The processes to which a dead body may be subjected are after all to some extent circumscribed by law. In most states, for instance, the signature of next of kin must be obtained before an autopsy may be performed, before the deceased may be cremated, before the body may be turned over to a medical school for research purposes; or such provision must be made in the decedent's° will. In the case of embalming, no such permission is required nor is it ever sought. A textbook, *The Principles and Practices of Embalming*, comments on this: "There is some question regarding the legality of much that is done within the preparation room." The author points out that it would be most unusual for a responsible member of a bereaved family to instruct the mortician, in so many words, to "*embalm*" the body of a deceased relative. The very term "embalming" is so seldom used that the mortician must rely upon custom in the matter. The author concludes that unless the family specifies otherwise, the act of entrusting the body to the care of a funeral establishment carries with it an implied permission to go ahead and embalm.

4   Embalming is indeed a most extraordinary procedure, and one must wonder at the docility° of Americans who each year pay hundreds of millions of dollars for its perpetuation, blissfully ignorant of what it is all about, what is done, how it is done. Not one in ten thousand has any idea of what actually takes place. Books on the subject are extremely hard to come by. They are not to be found in most libraries or bookshops.

In an era when huge television audiences watch surgical opera- 5
tions in the comfort of their living rooms, when, thanks to the ani-
mated cartoon, the geography of the digestive system has become
familiar territory even to the nursery school set, in a land where the
satisfaction of curiosity about almost all matters is a national pas-
time, the secrecy surrounding embalming can, surely, hardly be
attributed to the inherent gruesomeness of the subject. Custom in
this regard has within this century suffered a complete reversal. In
the early days of American embalming, when it was performed in
the home of the deceased, it was almost mandatory° for some relative to stay by the embalmer's side and witness the procedure.
Today, family members who might wish to be in attendance would
certainly be dissuaded° by the funeral director. All others, except
apprentices, are excluded by law from the preparation room.

A close look at what does actually take place may explain in 6
large measure the undertaker's intractable reticence° concerning a
procedure that has become his major *raison d'être*°. Is it possible he
fears that public information about embalming might lead patrons to
wonder if they really want this service? If the funeral men are loath
to discuss the subject outside the trade, the reader may, understandably, be equally loath to go on reading at this point. For those who
have the stomach for it, let us part the formaldehyde curtain. . . .

The body is first laid out in the undertaker's morgue—or 7
rather, Mr. Jones is reposing in the preparation room—to be readied
to bid the world farewell.

The preparation room in any of the better funeral establish- 8
ments has the tiled and sterile look of a surgery, and indeed the
embalmer-restorative artist who does his chores there is beginning
to adopt the term "dermasurgeon" (appropriately corrupted by
some mortician-writers as "demi-surgeon") to describe his calling.
His equipment, consisting of scalpels, scissors, augers, forceps,
clamps, needles, pumps, tubes, bowls and basins, is crudely imita-
tive of the surgeon's, as is his technique, acquired in a nine- or
twelve-month post-high-school course in an embalming school. He
is supplied by an advanced chemical industry with a bewildering
array of fluids, sprays, pastes, oils, powders, creams, to fix or soften
tissue, shrink or distend it as needed, dry it here, restore the moisture there. There are cosmetics, waxes and paints to fill and cover
features, even plaster of Paris to replace entire limbs. There are
ingenious aids to prop and stabilize the cadaver: a Vari-Pose Head
Rest, the Edwards Arm and Hand Positioner, the Repose Block (to
support the shoulders during the embalming), and the Throop Foot
Positioner, which resembles an old-fashioned stocks°.

9   Mr. John H. Eckels, president of the Eckels College of Mortuary Science, thus describes the first part of the embalming procedure: "In the hands of a skilled practitioner, this work may be done in a comparatively short time and without mutilating the body other than by slight incision—so slight that it scarcely would cause serious inconvenience if made upon a living person. It is necessary to remove the blood, and doing this not only helps in the disinfecting, but removes the principal cause of disfigurements due to discoloration."

10   Another textbook discusses the all-important time element: "The earlier this is done, the better, for every hour that elapses between death and embalming will add to the problems and complications encountered. . . ." Just how soon should one get going on the embalming? The author tells us, "On the basis of such scanty information made available to this profession through its rudimentary and haphazard system of technical research, we must conclude that the best results are to be obtained if the subject is embalmed before life is completely extinct—that is, before cellular death has occurred. In the average case, this would mean within an hour after somatic° death." For those who feel that there is something a little rudimentary°, not to say haphazard, about his advice, a comforting thought is offered by another writer. Speaking of fears entertained in early days of premature burial, he points out, "One of the effects of embalming by chemical injection, however, has been to dispel fears of live burial." How true; once the blood is removed, chances of live burial are indeed remote.

11   To return to Mr. Jones, the blood is drained out through the veins and replaced by embalming fluid pumped in through the arteries. As noted in *The Principles and Practices of Embalming*, "every operator has a favorite injection and drainage point—a fact which becomes a handicap only if he fails or refuses to forsake his favorites when conditions demand it." Typical favorites are the carotid artery, femoral artery, jugular vein, subclavian vein. There are various choices of embalming fluid. If Flextone is used, it will produce "mild, flexible rigidity. The skin retains a velvety softness, the tissues are rubbery and pliable. Ideal for women and children." It may be blended with B. and G. Products Company's Lyf-Lyk tint, which is guaranteed to reproduce "nature's own skin texture . . . the velvety appearance of living tissue." Suntone comes in three separate tints: Suntan; Special Cosmetic Tint, a pink shade "especially indicated for young female subjects"; and Regular Cosmetic Tint, moderately pink.

12   About three to six gallons of a dyed and perfumed solution of formaldehyde, glycerin, borax, phenol, alcohol and water is soon

circulating through Mr. Jones, whose mouth has been sewn together with a "needle directed upward between the upper lip and gum and brought out through the left nostril," with the corners raised slightly "for a more pleasant expression." If he should be buck-toothed, his teeth are cleaned with Bon Ami and coated with colorless nail polish. His eyes, meanwhile, are closed with flesh-tinted eye caps and eye cement.

The next step is to have at Mr. Jones with a thing called a trocar.   13 This is a long, hollow needle attached to a tube. It is jabbed into the abdomen, poked around the entrails and chest cavity, the contents of which are pumped out and replaced with "cavity fluid." This done, and the hole in the abdomen sewn up, Mr. Jones's face is heavily creamed (to protect the skin from burns which may be caused by leakage of the chemicals), and he is covered with a sheet and left unmolested for a while. But not for long—there is more, much more, in store for him. He has been embalmed, but not yet restored, and the best time to start the restorative work is eight to ten hours after embalming, when the tissues have become firm and dry.

The object of all this attention to the corpse, it must be remem-   14 bered, is to make it presentable for viewing in an attitude of healthy repose. "Our customs require the presentation of our dead in the semblance of normality . . . unmarred by the ravages of illness, disease or mutilation," says Mr. J. Sheridan Mayer in his *Restorative Art*. This is rather a large order since few people die in the full bloom of health, unravaged by illness and unmarked by some disfigurement. The funeral industry is equal to the challenge: "In some cases the gruesome appearance of a mutilated or disease-ridden subject may be quite discouraging. The task of restoration may seem impossible and shake the confidence of the embalmer. This is the time for intestinal fortitude° and determination. Once the formative work is begun and affected tissues are cleaned or removed, all doubts of success vanish. It is surprising and gratifying to discover the results which may be obtained."

The embalmer, having allowed an appropriate interval to   15 elapse, returns to the attack, but now he brings into play the skill and equipment of sculptor and cosmetician. Is a hand missing? Casting one in plaster of Paris is a simple matter. "For replacement purposes, only a cast of the back of the hand is necessary; this is within the ability of the average operator and is quite adequate." If a lip or two, a nose or an ear should be missing, the embalmer has at hand a variety of restorative waxes with which to model replacements. Pores and skin texture are simulated by stippling with a little brush, and over this cosmetics are laid on. Head off? Decapitation cases are rather routinely handled. Ragged edges are trimmed, and head joined to torso with a series of splints, wires and sutures. It is a good idea to have a little something at the neck—a scarf or a high collar—when time for viewing comes. Swollen mouth? Cut out tissue as needed from inside the lips. If too much is removed, the surface contour can easily be restored by padding with cotton. Swollen necks and cheeks are reduced by removing tissue through vertical incisions made down each side of the neck. "When the deceased is casketed, the pillow will hide the suture incisions . . . as an extra precaution against leakage, the suture may be painted with liquid sealer."

16   The opposite condition is more likely to present itself—that of emaciation. His hypodermic syringe now loaded with massage cream, the embalmer seeks out and fills the hollowed and sunken areas by injection. In this procedure the backs of the hands and fingers and the under-chin area should not be neglected.

17   Positioning the lips is a problem that recurrently challenges the ingenuity of the embalmer. Closed too tightly, they tend to give a stern, even disapproving expression. Ideally, embalmers feel, the lips should give the impression of being ever so slightly parted, the upper lip protruding slightly for a more youthful appearance. This takes some engineering, however, as the lips tend to drift apart. Lip drift can sometimes be remedied by pushing one or two straight pins through the inner margin of the lower lip and then inserting them between the two front upper teeth. If Mr. Jones happens to have no teeth, the pins can just as easily be anchored in his Armstrong Face Former and Denture Replacer. Another method to maintain lip closure is to dislocate the lower jaw, which is then held in its new position by a wire run through holes which have been drilled through the upper and lower jaws at the midline. As the French are fond of saying, *il faut souffrir pour être belle°*.

18   If Mr. Jones has died of jaundice, the embalming fluid will very likely turn him green. Does this deter the embalmer? Not if he has intestinal fortitude. Masking pastes and cosmetics are heavily laid on, burial garments and casket interiors are color-correlated with particular care, and Jones is displayed beneath rose-colored lights. Friends will say "How *well* he looks." Death by carbon monoxide, on the other hand, can be rather a good thing from the embalmer's viewpoint: "One advantage is the fact that this type of discoloration is an exaggerated form of a natural pink coloration." This is nice because the healthy glow is already present and needs but little attention.

19   The patching and filling completed, Mr. Jones is now shaved, washed and dressed. Cream-based cosmetic, available in pink, flesh, suntan, brunette and blond, is applied to his hands and face,

his hair is shampooed and combed (and, in the case of Mrs. Jones, set), his hands manicured. For the horny-handed son of toil° special care must be taken; cream should be applied to remove ingrained grime, and the nails cleaned. "If he were not in the habit of having them manicured in life, trimming and shaping is advised for better appearance—never questioned by kin."

Jones is now ready for casketing (this is the present participle of the verb "to casket"). In this operation his right shoulder should be depressed slightly "to turn the body a bit to the right and soften the appearance of lying flat on the back." Positioning the hands is a matter of importance, and special rubber positioning blocks may be used. The hands should be cupped slightly for a more lifelike, relaxed appearance. Proper placement of the body requires a deli- cate sense of balance. It should lie as high as possible in the casket, yet not so high that the lid, when lowered, will hit the nose. On the other hand, we are cautioned, placing the body too low "creates the impression that the body is in a box." 20

Jones is next wheeled into the appointed slumber room where a few last touches may be added—his favorite pipe placed in his hand or, if he was a great reader, a book propped into position. (In the case of little Master Jones a Teddy bear may be clutched.) Here he will hold open house for a few days, visiting hours 10 a.m. to 9 p.m. 21

All now being in readiness, the funeral director calls a staff con- ference to make sure that each assistant knows his precise duties. Mr. Wilber Kriege writes: "This makes your staff feel that they are a part of the team, with a definite assignment that must be properly carried out if the whole plan is to succeed. You never heard of a football coach who failed to talk to his entire team before they go on the field. They have drilled on the plays they are to execute for hours and days, and yet the successful coach knows the importance of making even the bench-warming third-string substitute feel that he is important if the game is to be won." The winning of *this* game is predicated upon glass-smooth handling of the logistics°. The funeral director has notified the pallbearers whose names were fur- nished by the family, has arranged for the presence of clergyman, organist, and soloist, has provided transportation for everybody, has organized and listed the flowers sent by friends. In *Psychology of Funeral Service* Mr. Edward A. Martin points out: "He may not always do as much as the family thinks he is doing, but it is his helpful guidance that they appreciate in knowing they are pro- ceeding as they should. . . . The important thing is how well his ser- vices can be used to make the family believe they are giving unlimited expression to their own sentiment." 22

23   The religious service may be held in a church or in the chapel of
the funeral home; the funeral director vastly prefers the latter arrangement, for not only is it more convenient for him but it affords
him the opportunity to show off his beautiful facilities to the gathered mourners. After the clergyman has had his say, the mourners
queue up to file past the casket for a last look at the deceased. The
family is *never* asked whether they want an open-casket ceremony; in
the absence of their instruction to the contrary, this is taken for
granted. Consequently well over 90 per cent of all American funerals
feature the open casket—a custom unknown in other parts of the
world. Foreigners are astonished by it. An English woman living in
San Francisco described her reaction in a letter to the writer:

> I myself have attended only one funeral here—that of an
> elderly fellow worker of mine. After the service I could not
> understand why everyone was walking towards the coffin
> (sorry, I mean casket), but thought I had better follow the
> crowd. It shook me rigid to get there and find the casket open
> and poor old Oscar lying there in his brown tweed suit,
> wearing a suntan makeup and just the wrong shade of lipstick.
> If I had not been extremely fond of the old boy, I have a hor-
> rible feeling that I might have giggled. Then and there I
> decided that I could never face another American funeral—
> even dead.

24   The casket (which has been resting throughout the service on a
Classic Beauty Ultra Metal Casket Bier) is now transferred by a
hydraulically operated device called Porto-Lift to a balloon-tired,
Glide Easy casket carriage which will wheel it to yet another con-
veyance, the Cadillac Funeral Coach. This may be lavender, cream,
light green—anything but black. Interiors, of course, are color-
correlated, "for the man who cannot stop short of perfection."

25   At graveside, the casket is lowered into the earth. This office,
once the prerogative° of friends of the deceased, is now performed
by a patented mechanical lowering device. A "Lifetime Green" artificial grass mat is at the ready to conceal the sere° earth, and overhead, to conceal the sky, is a portable Steril Chapel Tent ("resists the
intense heat and humidity of summer and the terrific storms of
winter . . . available in Silver Grey, Rose or Evergreen"). Now is the
time for the ritual scattering of earth over the coffin, as the solemn
words "earth to earth, ashes to ashes, dust to dust" are pronounced
by the officiating cleric. This can today be accomplished "with a
mere flick of the wrist with the Gordon Leak-Proof Earth Dispenser.
No grasping of a handful of dirt, no soiled fingers. Simple, digni-

fied, beautiful, reverent! The modern way!" The Gordon Earth Dispenser (at $45) is of nickel-plated brass construction. It is not only "attractive to the eye and long wearing"; it is also "one of the 'tools' for building better public relations" if presented as "an appropriate non-commercial gift" to the clergyman. It is shaped something like a saltshaker.

Untouched by human hand, the coffin and the earth are now united.   26

It is in the function of directing the participants through this maze of gadgetry that the funeral director has assigned to himself his relatively new role of "grief therapist." He has relieved the family of every detail, he has revamped° the corpse to look like a living doll, he has arranged for it to nap for a few days in a slumber room, he has put on a well-oiled performance in which the concept of *death* has played no part whatsoever—unless it was inconsiderately mentioned by the clergyman who conducted the religious service. He has done everything in his power to make the funeral a real pleasure for everybody concerned. He and his team have given their all to score an upset victory over death.   27

Words and Meanings

		Paragraph
formaldehyde	chemical used to embalm bodies	
Alas, poor Yorick	famous line from Shakespeare's *Hamlet*, addressed to a skull	2
decedent	dead person	3
docility	lamblike trust and willingness	4
mandatory	necessary	5
dissuaded	persuaded against	
intractable reticence	stubborn unwillingness to discuss	6
raison d'être	reason for existing [French]	
stocks	wooden shackles used to punish offenders	8
somatic	bodily	10
rudimentary	basic	
intestinal fortitude	"guts," courage	14
il faut souffrir pour être belle	"you have to suffer to be beautiful" [French]	17
horny-handed son of toil	cliché for a labourer	19

22	logistics	complex arrangements
25	prerogative	privilege
	sere	dry
27	revamped	altered

Structure and Strategy

1. Consider the title and first paragraph of this essay. What ANALOGY is introduced? How does the analogy help establish Mitford's TONE?
2. Look at the last paragraph. How is the analogy introduced in paragraph 1 reinforced in the CONCLUSION? What words specifically contribute to the analogy?
3. The process of preparing a corpse for burial involves two main procedures: embalming and restoration. Identify the paragraphs in which Mitford explains these two procedures.
4. Identify the substeps that make up the final stage in the burial process (paragraphs 20 to 25).

Content and Purpose

1. In paragraphs 2 and 8, without saying so directly, how does Mitford imply that she disapproves of embalming? Can you find other examples of her implied disapproval?
2. What justification for embalming is offered in paragraph 10? How does Mitford undercut this argument?
3. Why does Mitford refer to the corpse as "Mr. Jones"?
4. What reason does Mitford suggest is behind the "secrecy surrounding embalming"? If the details of the procedure were common knowledge, what do you think the effect would be on the mortuary business?
5. What was your reaction to Mitford's essay? Do you think your response was what the author intended?

Suggestions for Writing

1. Mitford's essay explains the funeral director's job as a process. Write an informational process analysis explaining a task or procedure with which you are familiar.
2. Research another means of disposing of the dead, such as cremation (burning a dead body) or cryonics (freezing a dead, diseased body in the hope of restoring it to life when a cure has been found). Write an informational process paper explaining it.
3. Write an informational process analysis explaining the ceremony or ritual behaviour associated with the birth of a baby, a

child's birthday, or the initiation of a child into the religious community (such as a bar mitzvah or confirmation).

Additional Suggestions for Writing: Process Analysis

I. Choose one of the topics below and develop it into an informational process analysis.
   1. How a cellphone (or any other electronic device) works
   2. How an animal is born or hatched
   3. How a particular rock group, sports personality, or political figure appeals to the crowd
   4. How to save Canada's universal health-care system (medicare)
   5. How a company plans the marketing of a new product
   6. How alcohol (or any other drug) affects the body
   7. How a star is born
   8. How the Internet has changed dating
   9. How a particular process in nature occurs— for example, how coral grows, a spider spins a web, salmon spawn, lightning happens, a snowflake forms, a specific crop is grown and harvested

II. Choose one of the topics below and develop it into a directional process analysis.
   1. How to buy (or sell) something—for example, a used car, a home, a piece of sports equipment, a computer, a DVD player, or a work of art
   2. How to perform a particular life-saving technique—for example, mouth-to-mouth resuscitation or the Heimlich manoeuvre
   3. How to play roulette, blackjack, poker, or some other game of chance
   4. How to get your driver's licence
   5. How to create an online slide show commemorating a family celebration
   6. How to use a search engine
   7. How to make or build something—for example, beer, bread, a kite, or a radio transmitter
   8. How to survive English (or any other subject that you are studying)
   9. How to get your own way
   10. How to talk your way out of a traffic ticket, a failing grade, a date, a conversation with a bore, a threatened punishment, or keeping a promise

3

Classification and Division

WHAT ARE CLASSIFICATION AND DIVISION?

ANALYSIS is the process of separating something into its parts in order to understand the whole better. In Unit 2, we used the term "process analysis" to refer to a writing pattern in which a process (planting a tree, for example) is described in terms of the steps or stages involved in accomplishing it. All forms of analysis involve sorting or dividing—breaking a complex whole into its stages, parts, or categories in order to understand it better.

In the rhetorical pattern called *classification,* the writer sorts a group of things or people into classes or categories on the basis of some shared characteristic. For example, in "Caught in the Net," Eva Tihanyi classifies Internet users into three categories according to the time they spend online: dabblers, regulars, and addicts. Dennis Dermody, in "Sit Down and Shut Up or Don't Sit by Me," classifies moviegoers on the basis of their behaviour in the movie theatre.

In *division,* on the other hand, a single thing (not a group of things) is divided into its component parts. For example, the model essay "Listen Up" divides the skill of listening into its three separate parts. In "Toothpaste," David Bodanis breaks down the everyday substance of toothpaste into its constituent ingredients and surprises us with the odd stuff that we put into our mouths every morning.

WHY DO WE USE CLASSIFICATION AND DIVISION?

Classification and division answer the lead-in question *what*. (What are the different kinds? What are the various parts?) Classifying or dividing a topic organizes it into logically related units that a reader can understand. These two strategies are essential ways of making sense of the world around us.

A **classification essay** uses a sorting mechanism to examine a group of similar things that have meaningful differences between them. A **division essay** looks at a topic in terms of its constituent parts; it examines each part to discover its distinctive features and its function within the whole. Sometimes writers use both strategies. For example, in "What I Have Lived For," Bertrand Russell divides his life's purpose—his reason for living—into what he calls "three passions": the longing for love, the search for knowledge, and pity for the suffering of mankind. Then he classifies his search for knowledge into the three kinds of knowledge he sought: the social sciences, the natural sciences, and mathematics.

Besides giving form and focus to shapeless chunks of information, division and classification are useful for evaluation purposes. When a writer's purpose is to evaluate the relative merits of several items or ideas, classification and division can help to ensure a clear, coherent piece of communication.

HOW DO WE WRITE CLASSIFICATION AND DIVISION?

Here are three guidelines for writing a good classification paper:

1. Be sure that your classifying principle is logical and consistent. For example, Eva Tihanyi classifies Internet users into categories according to the amount of time they spend online. Therefore, it would not be logical to include the purpose (such as shopping or game playing) as a classification of user.

2. Make sure that your categories do not overlap. Dennis Dermody's humorous classification of annoying moviegoers includes *latecomers, chatterers, krinklers,* and *popcorn people.* The addition of the category *talkers* would overlap with "the *chatterers* [who] comment blithely on everything that is happening on the screen."

3. Include a clear classification thesis statement. For example: "Generally, Internet users fall into one of three categories: dabblers, regulars, or addicts." (Eva Tihanyi, "Caught in the Net")

Here are three guidelines for writing a good division paper:

1. Identify the principle of division. Bertrand Russell's division essay, "What I Have Lived For," divides the complex idea of his reasons for living into three passions that have ruled his life.

2. Clearly explain the KEY IDEAS of your topic. Judy Brady's "Why I Want a Wife" is a satirical essay that divides the role of wife into its various parts: financial support, child care, physical care, entertaining, and sexual gratification. Each part of the role is developed with numerous examples.

3. Construct a clear division thesis statement. For example: "Active listening results from the interaction of three related components: questioning, paraphrasing, and empathizing." (Model Essay, "Listen Up")

Classification and division are two of the most effective strategies you can use to explain a complex topic to your readers. The ability to analyze through classification and division is a valuable skill that every writer should acquire.

The model essay that follows divides the skill of *listening* into its component parts.

Listen Up

Introduction (a striking fact)

As surprising as it is to most of us, listening—not reading, not writing, not speaking—is the communication skill we use most frequently. Perhaps equally surprising is that listening is a skill that can be learned and improved. In other words, we can all become better, more effective listeners: *active* listeners, listeners who not only "hear" but also "understand."

Thesis statement

Active listening results from the interaction of three related components: questioning, paraphrasing, and empathizing.

First component of listening process (developed with an illustration)

One of the easiest ways to check whether you've "heard right" is to ask. By asking questions, you not only show interest, but also get additional details and clarification. For example, if your friend Cindy says she has to cancel the plans the two of you had made for Saturday night, you would be wise to ask why she is cancelling before you assume that she is angry with you.

Second component (supported by definition and example)

Paraphrasing is another way to ensure that you "got it right." It is actually a form of feedback: restating in your own words in a summarized form what you think the speaker said. Perhaps Cindy cancelled by saying, "I've had a terrible week at work, and I don't think I'll be good company on Saturday. I'm really not in much of a mood to sit in a crowded theatre and watch a three-hour movie I haven't heard anything good about." It would be in both your and Cindy's best interests if you "checked" her message by paraphrasing it to make sure you understood her correctly; for example, "You're tired, so you don't feel up to the movie on Saturday. Would you like to get together for a movie or a game of tennis on Sunday?"

Third component (defines term and further develops the example)

Empathizing—putting yourself in the other person's shoes, so to speak—involves a sincere interest in the speaker and his or her perceptions. If you empathize with Cindy, you will respect her feelings although you may not necessarily agree with what she says. You may think that Cindy doesn't have a particularly exhausting job, and you may know that the movie you had planned to see got rave reviews. But what matters is that Cindy isn't feeling up to going out on Saturday night as the two of you had originally planned. Whether you share Cindy's perspective or not isn't the point. The point is to understand what Cindy is saying. Empathizing means listening to the story through the speaker's ears.

Conclusion (restates thesis and asks a rhetorical question)

As you can see, in any conversation, questioning, paraphrasing, and empathizing are intertwined. It is not easy to separate them because they all stem from the same motive: a genuine concern for the speaker that inspires the listener to *want* to hear the message the way it was intended. Active listening improves not only your communication skills but also your ability to get along with the people around you. Are you listening?

Caught in the Net

EVA TIHANYI

Writer, editor, and reviewer Eva Tihanyi (b. 1956) has taught English at the postsecondary level for more than twenty years. Her most recent book, *Restoring the Wickedness*, was published in 2000.

Fueled by ever-lower computer prices and faster connections, Internet use is growing at an astonishing rate. The Net appeals to more and more people for various reasons: as a way to conduct business, learn, socialize, play. For some, the Net is a reliable companion, twenty-four hours a day, seven days a week—one that never sleeps. For others, it simply provides easy access to a vast array of data.

Today, for instance, when I logged on to the home page of my Internet server, I was, as I am every day, treated to a long list of available topics from which I could select simply by clicking on the appropriate heading. I could learn the weather forecast, the latest sports scores, the newest movie releases, and the morning's stock market quotes. I could shop on-line, read about the benefits of a fat-free lifestyle, and get tips on helping my car survive the winter. However, although most of us are becoming increasingly familiar with the Internet as a data source and a communication tool, we don't all use it in the same way or to the same extent. Generally, Internet users fall into one of three categories: dabblers, regulars, or addicts.

The dabblers are the occasional users who go to the Net for several hours a week, usually to look up something specific, such as a Web site for a video game company or references to the Olympics for their son's school project. They might send an e-mail or two to friends across the country, explore tourist attractions in Florida, order concert tickets, or print out next week's train schedule. They might look up a site recommended by a co-worker, check a postal code, find a recipe, read a book review, or learn how to make a perfect martini. In other words, dabblers approach their computers with a particular task in mind. Once the task is accomplished, they log off and do something else. They see the Net as a tool, not a necessity. You know you're a dabbler if you'd rather watch TV, talk on the phone with a friend, or meet your sister for dinner than spend time in a chat room°.

The regulars visit the Internet more frequently and more routinely, eight to ten hours a week. They use it for work-related business; to keep up-to-date on world events, trends, and political developments; check out daily horoscopes or lottery numbers; purchase books, CDs, or unique clothing. There is no end to the variety of items from basic to bizarre for sale on the Net, and the regulars make a regular habit of buying them. You can buy a map of Zimbabwe, jewellery designed by singer Sarah McLachlan, an expandable briefcase, even special gifts for your cat—Kitty Baseball, perhaps, an amusing exercise game in which your cat can chase a ball around a circular outfield track. Or, if you're looking for an up-to-the-minute fashion statement, a "Pink Flamingo" shirt with bamboo buttons, you can contact the Banana Jack Hawaiian Shirt Company directly on the Net.

5   Some regulars are hobbyists with special interests that run the gamut° from apple cider to zebra migration and almost everything in between. Any topic you can imagine, the chances are that there's at least one site devoted to it on the Net. Other regulars are researchers, often students, who rely on the Net not only for quick access to current information but also to help them find specific passages in lengthy, complex works such as the Bible or the plays of William Shakespeare.

6   Even those with more esoteric° or narrowly defined interests— Jennifer Tilley's film career, the holdings of the Louvre, or B.C.'s wine industry, for instance—can find sites that cater to them. They can also cross cyber paths with others who have the same interests—people who sometimes develop into valuable contacts, giving the term "networking" a whole new spin. Unlike the dabblers, the regulars visit the Net not just to gain information but to interact with others who share their interests. Chances are you're a regular if you enter your favourite chat room, and—just as in your favourite bar—everybody knows your name, or "handle," as your chat room pseudonym is called.

7   What distinguishes the addicts from the dabblers and the regulars is that they don't surf the Net; they drown in it. They don't need a reason for spending hours at their computers; in fact, they often need one to shut them off. Addicts spend as much time as they can (an average of 38 hours per week) logged on. They browse sites, follow one trail of links to the next, send numerous e-mails, and converse in chat rooms where they often re-create themselves by pretending to be something more or other than what they really are—often to the point where their computer-based interactions interfere with and sometimes even replace their real-life interactions. Addicts frequently form on-line relationships with people they've never met (and are not ever likely to meet) and live out virtual lives. In all too many cases, the result is divorce, job loss, alienation from friends—in short, personal

havoc. The American Psychological Association has even coined a term for Internet addiction: Pathological Internet Use (PIU), which has the dubious distinction of being the first official mental health disorder associated with computers.

How do you know if you're an addict? The symptoms are similar to those of any other form of addiction. If you habitually stay on the Net for longer than you intend, feel irritable if for some reason you can't get on or your access is curtailed°, and forgo social, occupational, or recreational activities in favour of the Net, chances are you have a problem.   8

Fortunately, most of us have not yet given up the experience of munching on an actual pizza in favour of viewing a virtual one or the intimacy of face-to-face interaction for anonymous words on an otherwise empty screen. Nevertheless, regardless of which category we see ourselves in—dabblers, regulars, or addicts—the fact is that the Net is here to stay, and we're all caught in it. It's just a matter of degree.   9

Words and Meanings

Paragraph

chat room	a virtual café in cyberspace where people can get together in real time to discuss whatever interests them	3
gamut	the whole range, from *a* to *z*	5
esoteric	appealing to a small group of people	6
curtailed	cut short	8

Structure and Strategy

1. What introductory strategy does Tihanyi use in paragraph 2?
2. Identify the thesis statement.
3. Which paragraphs focus on each of the three categories of Internet user as described in the essay?
4. What strategies does Tihanyi use to develop her first category, the "dabblers"?
5. Which category is developed primarily by means of discussing its effects?
6. What FIGURE OF SPEECH does Tihanyi use to introduce the addict in paragraph 7?

Content and Purpose

1. What are the Internet uses that the essay describes in paragraph 1?

2. On average, how many hours a week does each category of Internet user spend online?
3. In addition to the number of hours spent online, what distinguishes the dabbler from the regular user? What distinguishes addicts from both dabblers and regular users?
4. What symptoms does the Internet addict share with drug or alcohol addicts?

Suggestions for Writing

1. Do you use the Internet? Are you a dabbler, a regular, or an addict? Write an essay explaining what you find particularly useful or fun about the Internet.
2. Write an essay classifying people according to their choice of music, comedians, television shows, movies, reading material, leisure pursuits, or any other basis of classification that interests you. (You may want to treat this as a humorous exercise.)

Sit Down and Shut Up or Don't Sit by Me

DENNIS DERMODY

Early in his career, in Provincetown, Massachusetts, Dennis Dermody managed a movie theatre that burned to the ground. He moved to New York where he works as a journalist, editor, and film critic.

1   All right, I admit it: I'm a tad neurotic when it comes to making it to the movies on time. I have to be there at least a half hour before the feature begins. Not that I'm worried about long lines at the box office, either. The movies I rush off to see are generally so sparsely attended you can hear crickets in the audience. It's just a thing I do.

2   Of course, sitting for 30 minutes watching a theater fill up is pretty boring, but through the years I've amused myself with a Margaret Mead°–like study of the way people come in and take their seats and their antics during a movie. I felt I should share my impressions lest you find yourself succumbing to these annoying traits.

3   Right off the bat: Leave the kids at home. We're not talking about *Aladdin* or *Home Alone 2*—that I understand—but recently I

went to see *Body of Evidence*, and it looked like a day-care center in the theater. Strollers were flying down the aisle, children were whining for candy, restless and audibly bored (especially during the hot-wax-dripping sequence), and eventually the day-care atmosphere caused fights among the adults. "Shut your kid up!" prompted a proud parent to slug a fellow patron, and before you knew it there were angry skirmishes all over the theater and the police had to be brought in. So either leave them at home with a sitter or tie them up to a fire hydrant outside the theater.

For some people, choosing a seat takes on moral and philo-   4
sophical implications. Sometimes they stand in the middle of the aisle juggling coats, popcorn, and Cokes, seemingly overwhelmed by the prospect of choice. Should I sit down front, or will that be too close? Is this too far back? That man seems awfully tall, I bet I couldn't see the movie if I sat behind him. I'd love to sit somewhere in the middle but would I be too close to that group of teenagers shooting heroin into their necks? If I sit on this side, will the angle be too weird to watch the movie? Is that seat unoccupied because it's broken? Good Lord, the lights are dimming and I haven't made up my mind and now I won't be able to see where I'm going.

Many, upon choosing their seats, find they are unsatisfied and   5
have to move. I've watched many couples go from one spot to another more than a dozen times before settling down—it's like watching a bird testing different spots to build a nest.

As the lights begin to dim and the annoying theater-chain logo   6
streaks across the screen, lo and behold, here come the *latecomers!* Their eyes unaccustomed to the dark, in a panic they search for friends, for assistance, for a lonely seat. Just the other day, I watched an elderly woman come into the darkened theater 10 minutes after the movie had begun and say out loud, "I can't see anything!" She then proceeded to inch her way down the aisle, grabbing onto what she thought were seats but were actually people's heads. I saw her sit down right in the lap of someone who shrieked in shock. After the woman stumbled back into the aisle, chattering wildly, someone mercifully directed her to an empty seat. Then, after a great flourish of getting out of her bulky coat, she asked spiritedly of the grumbling souls around her, "What did I miss?"

I also must address the behavior of people *during* the movie.   7
The *chatterers* comment blithely on everything that is happening on the screen. Like Tourette's syndrome° sufferers unable to control what they blurt out, these people say anything that comes into their heads. "What a cute puppy," they say when they spy an animal

ambling off to the side of the frame. "I have that lamp at home," they exclaim. And add, five minutes later, "But mine is red."

8   The *krinklers* wander down the aisle with a million shopping bags and wait for a key sequence, then begin to forage° in their bags for the perfect and most annoying plastic wrap, which they use to make noise with sadistic relish. You try to focus on the screen but the racket starts up again with a wild flourish. I've seen grown men leap to their feet with tears streaming down their face and scream, "Will you stop shaking that motherfucking bag!"

9   The *unending box of popcorn* people sit directly behind you and start masticating during the opening credits. It's bad enough having the smell of cooked corn wafting around you, but the sound is enough to drive you mad. You tell yourself that eventually they'll finish, but they never do. They keep chewing and chewing and chewing and you're deathly afraid that next they'll start on a four-pound box of malted milk balls.

10   So in summary: Get to the movie theater early and scout out the territory. It's a jungle in there, filled with a lot of really stupid animals. Know the telltale signs and act accordingly. And then sit down and shut up.

Words and Meanings

Paragraph		
2	Margaret Mead	U.S. anthropologist famous for her studies of people's behaviour in various "exotic" cultures
7	Tourette's syndrome	hereditary disease that causes uncontrollable physical twitching and bursts of speech in its sufferers
8	forage	search for food

Structure and Strategy

1. What is the function of paragraph 3? After all, not all moviegoers bring their children to the theatre.
2. Identify three SIMILES in paragraphs 3, 5, and 7. How would the impact of this essay be lessened if the author had not included these figures of speech?
3. When Dermody uses phrases such as "tie them up to a fire hydrant" (paragraph 3) or "teenagers shooting heroin into their necks" (paragraph 4), he obviously does not mean to be taken seriously. Identify two or three other examples of this kind of exaggeration and consider how it affects the TONE of the essay.
4. What METAPHOR does Dermody use in the CONCLUSION of this piece? How does it contribute to the UNITY of the essay?

Content and Purpose

1. What does Dermody mean when he admits, in his opening sentence, that he is a "tad neurotic"? How does this confession affect the reader's response to the judgments that follow?
2. What is the author's PURPOSE (see paragraph 2)? Do you think he achieves it?
3. This essay classifies moviegoers according to their pre-movie and during-movie behaviours. Identify the six categories of the author's classification system.
4. Would you like to go to a movie with the author? Why or why not?

Suggestions for Writing

1. Write an essay in which you classify partygoers, friends, relatives, neighbours, children, workers, bosses, students, or any other group of people you choose. Be sure your classification is logical and consistent, and that the purpose of your classification is clear to your reader.
2. How do you spend your time? Write an essay identifying the categories into which you divide your time each week. What do you learn about yourself from this exercise?

Toothpaste

DAVID BODANIS

David Bodanis is a science writer who publishes in newspapers both in the United States and in England, where he now lives. He is the author of *The Body Book: A Fantastic Voyage to the World Within* and *The Secret House: 24 Hours in the Strange and Unexpected World in which We Spend Our Nights and Days*. His most recent book, $E=mc^2$: *A Biography of the World's Most Famous Equation*, was published in 2001.

Into the bathroom [we go], and after the most pressing need is satisfied it's time to brush the teeth. The tube of toothpaste is squeezed, its pinched metal seams are splayed, pressure waves are generated inside, and the paste begins to flow. But what's in this toothpaste, so carefully being extruded° out? 1

Water mostly, 30 to 45 per cent in most brands: ordinary, everyday simple tap water. It's there because people like to have a 2 big gob of toothpaste to spread on the brush, and water is the cheapest stuff there is when it comes to making big gobs. Dripping a bit from the tap onto your brush would cost virtually nothing; whipped in with the rest of the toothpaste the manufacturers can sell it at a neat and accountant-pleasing $2 per pound equivalent. Toothpaste manufacture is a very lucrative occupation.

3   Second to water in quantity is chalk: exactly the same material that schoolteachers use to write on blackboards. It is collected from the crushed remains of long-dead ocean creatures. In the Cretaceous° seas chalk particles served as part of the wickedly sharp outer skeleton that these creatures had to wrap around themselves to keep from getting chomped by all the slightly larger other ocean creatures they met. Their massed graves are our present chalk deposits.

4   The individual chalk particles—the size of the smallest mud particles in your garden—have kept their toughness over the aeons°, and now on the toothbrush they'll need it. The enamel outer coating of the tooth they'll have to face is the hardest substance in the body—tougher than skull, or bone, or nail. Only the chalk particles in toothpaste can successfully grind into the teeth during brushing, ripping off the surface layers like an abrading wheel grinding down a boulder in a quarry.

5   The craters, slashes, and channels that the chalk tears into the teeth will also remove a certain amount of built-up yellow in the carnage, and it is for that polishing function that it's there. A certain amount of unduly enlarged extra-abrasive chalk fragments tear such cavernous pits into the teeth that future decay bacteria will be able to bunker down there and thrive; the quality control people find it almost impossible to screen out these errant super-chalk pieces, and government regulations allow them to stay in.

6   In case even the gouging doesn't get all the yellow off, another substance is worked into the toothpaste cream. This is titanium dioxide. It comes in tiny spheres, and it's the stuff bobbing around in white wall paint to make it come out white. Splashed around onto your teeth during the brushing it coats much of the yellow that remains. Being water soluble it leaks off in the next few hours and is swallowed, but at least for the quick glance up in the mirror after finishing it will make the user think his teeth are truly white. Some manufacturers add optical whitening dyes—the stuff more commonly found in washing machine bleach—to make extra sure that the glance in the mirror shows reassuring white.

7   These ingredients alone would not make a very attractive concoction°. They would stick in the tube like a sloppy white plastic

lump, hard to squeeze out as well as revolting to the touch. Few consumers would savor rubbing in a mixture of water, ground-up blackboard chalk and the whitener from latex paint first thing in the morning. To get around that finicky distaste the manufacturers have mixed in a host of other goodies.

To keep the glop from drying out, a mixture including glyc-   8
erine glycol—related to the most common car anti-freeze ingre-dient—is whipped in with the chalk and water, and to give *that* concoction a bit of substance (all we really have so far is wet col-ored chalk) a large helping is added of gummy molecules from the seaweed *Chondrus crispus*. This seaweed ooze spreads in among the chalk, paint and anti-freeze, then stretches itself in all directions to hold the whole mass together. A bit of paraffin oil (the fuel that flickers in camping lamps) is pumped in with it to help the moss ooze keep the whole substance smooth.

With the glycol, ooze and paraffin we're almost there. Only two   9
major chemicals are left to make the refreshing, cleansing substance we know as toothpaste. The ingredients so far are fine for cleaning, but they wouldn't make much of the satisfying foam we have come to expect in the morning brushing.

To remedy that, every toothpaste on the market has a big   10
dollop of detergent added, too. You've seen the suds detergent will make in a washing machine. The same substance added here will duplicate that inside the mouth. It's not particularly necessary, but it sells.

The only problem is that by itself this ingredient tastes, well,   11
too like detergent. It's horribly bitter and harsh. The chalk put in toothpaste is pretty foul-tasting too for that matter. It's to get around that gustatory° discomfort that the manufacturers put in the ingredient they tout° perhaps the most of all. This is the flavoring, and it has to be strong. Double rectified peppermint oil is used—a flavorer so powerful that chemists know better than to sniff it in the raw state in the laboratory. Menthol crystals and saccharin or other sugar simulators are added to complete the camouflage operation.

Is that it? Chalk, water, paint, seaweed, anti-freeze, paraffin oil,   12
detergent and peppermint? Not quite. A mix like that would be irresistible to the hundreds of thousands of individual bacteria lying on the surface of even an immaculately cleaned bathroom sink. They would get in, float in the water bubbles, ingest the ooze and paraffin, maybe even spray out enzymes to break down the chalk. The result would be an uninviting mess. The way manufac-turers avoid that final obstacle is by putting something in to kill the bacteria. Something good and strong is needed, something that will

zap any accidentally intrudant bacteria into oblivion. And that something is formaldehyde—the disinfectant used in anatomy labs.

13   So it's chalk, water, paint, seaweed, anti-freeze, paraffin oil, detergent, peppermint, formaldehyde and fluoride (which can go some way towards preserving children's teeth)—that's the usual mixture raised to the mouth on the toothbrush for a fresh morning's clean. If it sounds too unfortunate, take heart. Studies show that thorough brushing with just plain water will often do as good a job.

Words and Meanings

Paragraph

1	extruded	pushed
3	Cretaceous	relating to the last period of the Mesozoic era (135 million to 65 million years ago)
4	aeons	ages, an immensely long time
7	concoction	mixture
11	gustatory	having to do with taste
	tout	advertise; promote aggressively in order to attract customers

Structure and Strategy

1. This essay analyzes toothpaste by dividing it into its component parts. Identify each ingredient and the paragraph(s) in which it is described.
2. What is the function of paragraph 7? Paragraph 9? Paragraph 13?
3. Underline six or seven examples of the author's use of vivid DESCRIPTION to help communicate KEY IDEAS.
4. Part of the effect of this essay depends on Bodanis's description of toothpaste. He uses words that are very different from those we are familiar with in television commercials to describe the same product. For example, in paragraph 8 we read, "seaweed ooze spreads in among the chalk, paint and anti-freeze." Find other examples of Bodanis's use of language that you would never hear in a product advertisement. What effect does his DICTION have on the reader?

Content and Purpose

1. What is toothpaste's main ingredient and what is its primary function? What is the purpose of the SIMILE used in paragraph 4 to describe this function?

2. What's the function of glycol in toothpaste? The seaweed and paraffin? The detergent? The formaldehyde?
3. Explain the IRONY in the last paragraph.
4. Did you have any idea what toothpaste was made of before you read this essay? Did any of the ingredients surprise you? Revolt you? Why?

Suggestions for Writing

1. Does Bodanis's ANALYSIS of toothpaste make you wonder about the composition of other familiar products? Do you know what goes into margarine? Lipstick? Kraft Dinner? A hot dog? Write an essay that identifies the surprising elements of a common substance.
2. Write an essay in which you classify the different kinds of grooming aids available to assist us in making ourselves irresistible (or at least attractive) to others.

Why I Want a Wife

JUDY BRADY

Judy Brady (b. 1937) first published this article under her married name, Syfers, in *Ms. Magazine*. "Why I Want a Wife" is one of the best-known feminist essays written in the last twenty years. Now divorced, Brady is a feminist and activist who writes on such topics as union organizing, abortion, breast cancer, and women's role in society.

I belong to that classification of people known as wives. I am A Wife. And, not altogether incidentally, I am a mother.   1

Not too long ago a male friend of mine appeared on the scene   2
fresh from a recent divorce. He had one child, who is, of course, with his ex-wife. He is looking for another wife. As I thought about him while I was ironing one evening, it suddenly occurred to me that I, too, would like to have a wife. Why do I want a wife?

I would like to go back to school so that I can become economi-   3
cally independent, support myself, and, if need be, support those dependent upon me. I want a wife who will work and send me to school. And while I am going to school I want a wife to take care of my children. I want a wife to keep track of the children's doctor and

dentist appointments. And to keep track of mine, too. I want a wife to make sure my children eat properly and are kept clean. I want a wife who will wash the children's clothes and keep them mended. I want a wife who is a good nurturant° attendant to my children, who arranges for their schooling, makes sure that they have an adequate social life with their peers, takes them to the park, the zoo, etc. I want a wife who takes care of the children when they are sick, a wife who arranges to be around when the children need special care, because, of course, I cannot miss classes at school. My wife must arrange to lose time at work and not lose the job. It may mean a small cut in my wife's income from time to time, but I guess I can tolerate that. Needless to say, my wife will arrange and pay for the care of the children while my wife is working.

4   I want a wife who will take care of *my* physical needs. I want a wife who will keep my house clean. A wife who will pick up after my children, a wife who will pick up after me. I want a wife who will keep my clothes clean, ironed, mended, replaced when need be, and who will see to it that my personal things are kept in their proper place so that I can find what I need the minute I need it. I want a wife who cooks the meals, a wife who is a *good* cook. I want a wife who will plan the menus, do the necessary grocery shopping, prepare the meals, serve them pleasantly, and then do the cleaning up while I do my studying. I want a wife who will care for me when I am sick and sympathize with my pain and loss of time from school. I want a wife to go along when our family takes a vacation so that someone can continue to care for me and my children when I need a rest and change of scene.

5   I want a wife who will not bother me with rambling complaints about a wife's duties. But I want a wife who will listen to me when I feel the need to explain a rather difficult point I have come across in my course of studies. And I want a wife who will type my papers for me when I have written them.

6   I want a wife who will take care of the details of my social life. When my wife and I are invited out by my friends, I want a wife who will take care of the babysitting arrangements. When I meet people at school that I like and want to entertain, I want a wife who will have the house clean, will prepare a special meal, serve it to me and my friends, and not interrupt when I talk about things that interest me and my friends. I want a wife who will have arranged that the children are fed and ready for bed before my guests arrive so that the children do not bother us. I want a wife who takes care of the needs of my guests so that they feel comfortable, who makes sure that they have an ashtray, that they are passed the hors d'oeuvres, that they are offered a second helping of the food, that their

wine glasses are replenished° when necessary, that their coffee is served to them as they like it. And I want a wife who knows that sometimes I need a night out by myself.

I want a wife who is sensitive to my sexual needs, a wife who makes love passionately and eagerly when I feel like it, a wife who makes sure that I am satisfied. And, of course, I want a wife who will not demand sexual attention when I am not in the mood for it. I want a wife who assumes the complete responsibility for birth control, because I do not want more children. I want a wife who will remain sexually faithful to me so that I do not have to clutter up my intellectual life with jealousies. And I want a wife who understands that *my* sexual needs may entail more than strict adherence° to monogamy°. I must, after all, be able to relate to people as fully as possible. 7

If, by chance, I find another person more suitable as a wife than the wife I already have, I want the liberty to replace my present wife with another one. Naturally, I will expect a fresh, new life; my wife will take the children and be solely responsible for them so that I am left free. 8

When I am through with school and have a job, I want my wife to quit working and remain at home so that my wife can more fully and completely take care of a wife's duties. 9

My God, who *wouldn't* want a wife? 10

Words and Meanings

Paragraph

nurturant	providing care, food, and training	3
replenished	filled again	6
adherence	constancy, sticking to [something]	7
monogamy	custom of marrying, being faithful to only one mate	

Structure and Strategy

1. What is the function of the first two paragraphs? What TONE do they establish?
2. Into what main functions does Brady divide the role of a wife? Identify the paragraph(s) that focus on each. Then write a thesis statement for this essay.
3. Why does Brady never use the pronouns "she" or "her" to refer to a wife? Is the frequent repetition of the word "wife" awkward? Or does it serve a particular purpose?

4. What is the effect of having so many sentences begin with the words "I want"?

Content and Purpose

1. What is Brady's attitude to the roles traditionally assigned to men and to women in our society? Identify two or three passages that clearly convey her feelings.
2. Consider the degree to which Brady's portrayal of male and female roles is an accurate reflection of our society's expectations. Who or what is responsible for these expectations?
3. What would be the effect of this essay if it had been written by a man? How would the readers respond?

Suggestions for Writing

1. Write an essay organized, like Brady's, on the principle of division. Your first paragraph should contain the sentence "I want a husband."
2. Write an essay in which you classify types of wives or husbands (or mothers, or fathers, or children).
3. In a short paper, analyze the role of the ideal parent in the twenty-first century.

What I Have Lived For

BERTRAND RUSSELL

Bertrand Russell (1872–1970), philosopher, mathematician, and social reformer, was awarded the Nobel Prize for Literature in 1950. His progressive views on the liberalization of sexual attitudes and the role of women led to his dismissal from the University of California at Los Angeles in the 1920s. Russell was a leading pacifist and proponent of nuclear disarmament. Among his many books are *Principia Mathematica*, *Why I Am Not a Christian*, and *History of Western Philosophy*.

1   Three passions, simple but overwhelmingly strong, have governed my life: the longing for love, the search for knowledge, and unbearable pity for the suffering of mankind. These passions, like great winds, have blown me hither and thither, in a way-

ward° course, over a deep ocean of anguish, reaching to the very verge° of despair.

I have sought love, first, because it brings ecstasy°—ecstasy so great that I would often have sacrificed all the rest of life for a few hours of this joy. I have sought it, next, because it relieves loneliness—that terrible loneliness in which one shivering consciousness looks over the rim of the world into the cold unfathomable lifeless abyss°. I have sought it, finally, because in the union of love I have seen, in a mystic miniature, the prefiguring° vision of the heaven that saints and poets have imagined. This is what I sought, and though it might seem too good for human life, this is what—at last—I have found.   2

With equal passion I have sought knowledge. I have wished to understand the hearts of men. I have wished to know why the stars shine. And I have tried to apprehend the Pythagorean° power by which number holds sway above the flux°. A little of this, but not much, I have achieved.   3

Love and knowledge, so far as they were possible, led upward toward the heavens. But always pity brought me back to earth. Echoes of cries of pain reverberate° in my heart. Children in famine, victims tortured by oppressors, helpless old people a hated burden to their sons, and the whole world of loneliness, poverty, and pain make a mockery of what human life should be. I long to alleviate° the evil, but I cannot, and I too suffer.   4

This has been my life. I have found it worth living, and would gladly live it again if the chance were offered me.   5

Words and Meanings

		Paragraph
wayward	unpredictable, wandering	1
verge	edge, brink	
ecstasy	supreme joy	2
abyss	bottomless pit, hell	
prefiguring	picturing to oneself beforehand	
Pythagorean	relating to the Greek philosopher Pythagoras and his theory that through mathematics one can understand the relationship between all things and the principle of harmony in the universe	3
flux	continual motion, change	
reverberate	echo	4
alleviate	relieve, lessen	

Structure and Strategy

1. Identify Russell's thesis statement and the TOPIC SENTENCES of paragraphs 2, 3, and 4.
2. How does the structure of the second sentence in paragraph 1 reinforce its meaning?
3. The number three is the basis for the structure of Russell's essay. Three is an ancient symbol for unity and completeness and for the human life cycle: birth, life, death. Find as many examples as you can of Russell's effective use of threes. (Look at paragraph and sentence structure as well as content.)
4. What is the function of the first sentence of paragraph 4?
5. How does Russell's concluding paragraph contribute to the UNITY of the essay?
6. Refer to the introduction to this unit and show how paragraph 1 sets up a division essay and how paragraph 4 is actually a classification.
7. Analyze the ORDER in which Russell explains his three passions. Do you think the order is chronological, logical, climactic, or random? Does the order reflect the relative importance or value that Russell ascribes to each passion? How?

Content and Purpose

1. For Bertrand Russell, love means more than physical passion. What else does he include in his meaning of love (paragraph 2)?
2. What are the three kinds of knowledge Russell has spent his life seeking?
3. Which of Russell's three "passions" has he been least successful in achieving? Why?

Suggestions for Writing

1. What goals have you set for yourself for the next ten years? Write a short paper in which you identify and explain two or three of your goals.
2. In what ways are you different from other people? Write a short paper in which you identify and explain some of the qualities and characteristics that make you a unique human being.
3. Imagine that you are seventy-five years old. Write a short paper explaining what you have lived for.

Principled Uncertainty

RICHARD FEYNMAN

American physicist Richard Feynman (1918–1988) studied at the Massachusetts Institute of Technology and Princeton University before becoming a professor at Cornell University (1945–50) and the California Institute of Technology, where he remained for the rest of his career. He was a joint winner of the 1965 Nobel Prize in physics for his work on quantum electrodynamics.

From time to time, people suggest to me that scientists ought to give more consideration to social problems—especially ... the impact of science upon society. It seems to be generally believed that if scientists would only look at these very difficult social problems and not spend so much time fooling with the less vital scientific ones, great success would come of it. Most scientists do think about these problems from time to time, but we don't put full-time effort into them—because we know that social problems are very much harder than scientific ones, and that we usually don't get anywhere when we do think about them. I believe that a scientist looking at non-scientific problems is just as dumb as the next guy—and when he talks about a non-scientific matter, he will sound as naive as anyone untrained in the matter. Since the question of the value of science is not a scientific subject, this discussion is dedicated to proving my point by example.   1

The first way in which science is of value is familiar to everyone.   2
Scientific knowledge enables us to do and to make all kinds of things. Of course if we make good things, it is to the credit not only of science but also of the moral choice that led us to do good work. The applied sciences should free men from material problems. Medicine controls diseases, for example, and the record here seems to be good. Yet there are also men patiently working to create great plagues and poisons. Scientific knowledge is an enabling power to do either good or bad; it does not carry instructions on how to use it.

I learned a way of expressing this common human problem on   3
a trip to Honolulu. In a Buddhist temple there, the man in charge explained a little bit about the Buddhist religion and then ended his talk with a proverb: "To every man is given the key to the gates of heaven; the same key opens the gates to hell." What, then, is the value of the key to heaven? It is true that the key may be a dangerous object if we lack clear instructions that help to distinguish between the gate to heaven and the gate to hell, but it obviously has value. How can we enter heaven without it?

*   *   *

4   Intellectual enjoyment, which some people get from reading and learning and thinking about science and which others get from working in science, is clearly valuable as well. Science has led us to imagine all sorts of things that are infinitely more marvelous than the imaginings of the poets and dreamers of the past. Science teaches us that the imagination of nature is far, far greater than the imagination of man. Consider how much more remarkable it is for us all to be stuck—half of us upside down—by a mysterious attraction to a spinning ball that has been swinging in space for billions of years than to be carried on the back of an elephant supported on a tortoise swimming in a bottomless sea°.

5   We find that thrill of discovery whenever we look deeply into any scientific problem. Knowledge serves only to deepen the mysteries of nature, which lure us onward to more discoveries. It is true that few unscientific people have this particular type of religious experience. Our poets do not write about it; our artists do not try to portray it. I don't know why. Is nobody inspired by our present picture of the universe? The value of science remains unsung; ours is not yet a scientific age.

6   Perhaps one reason for this is that you have to know how to read the music. A scientific article, for instance, might say something like this: "The radioactive phosphorus content of the cerebrum of the rat decreases to one-half in a period of two weeks." Now, what does that mean? It means that the phosphorus in the brain of a rat (and also in mine and yours) is not the same phosphorus that was there two weeks ago. All the atoms that are in the brain are being replaced, and the ones that were there before have gone away. So what is this mind? What are these atoms with consciousness? Last week's potatoes! Which now can remember what was going on in your mind a year ago—a mind that was long ago replaced. When we discover how long it takes for the atoms of the brain to be replaced by other atoms, we come to realize that the thing I call my individuality is only a pattern or dance. The atoms come into my brain, dance a dance, and then go out, always new atoms but always performing the same dance, remembering what the dance was yesterday.

7   Ultimately, however, the real value of science may lie in uncertainty. The scientist has a lot of experience with ignorance and doubt and uncertainty, and this experience is very important. Scientific knowledge is a body of statements of varying degrees of certainty—about some of them we are mostly unsure, some are nearly certain, none are *absolutely* certain. We scientists are used to this, and we take it for granted that it is perfectly consistent to be unsure, that it is pos-

sible to live and not to know. But I don't know whether everyone realizes that this is true.

This is not a new idea; it is the central idea of the Age of Reason° and of the philosophy that guided the men who made the democracy under which we live. The idea that no one really knew how to run a government led to the notion that we should arrange a system in which new ideas could be developed, tried, and tossed out—a system of trial and error inspired by the scientific advances of the eighteenth century. Even then it was clear to socially minded people that openness was an opportunity and that doubt and discussion were essential to progress. If we want to solve the problems that face us, we must leave the door to the unknown ajar.

Words and Meanings

Paragraph

on the back . . . sea	an allusion to an ancient image of the world, which was rendered obsolete by the advent of modern science	4
Age of Reason	the eighteenth century as the period when rationalism challenged traditional European political, religious, social, and philosophical beliefs; also called the Enlightenment	8

Structure and Strategy

1. The author begins his essay with a premise that he then argues against. Summarize the premise in one sentence. Why does Feynman reject it?
2. Identify the THESIS of the essay. Underline the three key ideas Feynman explores in this piece. In what ORDER has he arranged these ideas?
3. In paragraph 2, what is the TOPIC SENTENCE? What example does the author use to develop it? Summarize in one sentence the point he makes with this example.
4. What is the function of paragraph 3? How does it support Feynman's first key idea?
5. What words or phrases in paragraphs 4 and 7 are used to show the transition from one point to the next?
6. Explain the METAPHOR with which Feynman opens and concludes paragraph 6.

Content and Purpose

1. According to Feynman, how valuable is a scientist's view of social or other non-scientific problems? (See paragraph 1.)

2. What is the "mysterious attraction to a spinning ball" described in paragraph 4? What point of Feynman's ARGUMENT does this example support?

3. Summarize the process Feynman describes in paragraph 6. Why do you think he chose the brain of a rat to illustrate this process? How does this paragraph support the second point of his argument?

4. According to Feynman, what may be the most important value of science? (See paragraph 7.) How does he suggest that non-scientists view this particular value?

5. In paragraph 8, what form of government is used to exemplify the value of scientific uncertainty? How does this example support the author's point?

6. After reading this essay, are you more persuaded than you were before about the value of science in the postmodern age? Why or why not?

Suggestion for Writing

Write an essay about a significant concept or lesson that you have learned from science.

Additional Suggestions for Writing: Classification and Division

Use classification or division, whichever is appropriate, to analyze one of the topics below into its component parts, or characteristics, or kinds. Write a thesis statement based on your analysis and then develop it into an essay that will interest a reader who doesn't necessarily share your point of view.

1. part-time jobs
2. marriage
3. films
4. movie stars (actors, celebrities)
5. computer games
6. popular novels
7. sitcoms
8. a family or families
9. dreams
10. college students
11. commercials
12. drivers
13. activists
14. friendship or friends

15. an unforgettable event
16. websites
17. reality TV shows
18. a short story, poem, or play
19. shoppers
20. a religious or social ritual (such as a wedding, funeral, baptism, bar/bat mitzvah, birthday celebration)

4

Comparison and Contrast

WHAT ARE COMPARISON AND CONTRAST?

Technically, to *compare* two things is to point out the similarities between them, and to *contrast* them is to point out their differences. When we look at both similarities and differences, we are engaging in *comparison and contrast*. Often, however, people use the term "comparison" to describe all three processes. "Comparison shopping," for example, means to discover significant differences among similar items. Therefore, while the purpose of the model essay "She Said, He Said" is to explore the differences between men's and women's conversation, few people would notice or object if you called the essay a comparison.

WHY DO WE USE COMPARISON AND CONTRAST?

Comparison and contrast answer the lead-in question *what*. In what ways are two things alike? In what ways are they different? Comparing and contrasting things is a common mental process; it's something we do, consciously or unconsciously, all the time. Using such a pattern in written communication can be useful in two specific ways.

First, an essay or report structured to compare various items can provide a reader with helpful information. It can offer new insight into two topics by looking at them side by side. For example, Jay Teitel's "Shorter, Slower, Weaker: And That's a Good Thing" contrasts men's and women's performances in a number of sports in order to make an interesting point about the changing physical characteristics of athletes and their games.

Second, a comparison paper can evaluate as well as inform. It can assess the relative merits of two topics and explain the writer's preference for one over the other. In "Ottawa vs. New York," for example, Germaine Greer not only contrasts the two cities but also argues strongly for the quality of life in Canada versus that in the United States.

HOW DO WE WRITE COMPARISON AND CONTRAST?

Here are four guidelines for organizing a paper according to the principles of comparison and contrast:

1. Make sure that your two topics are in fact comparable; they must have something significant in common even if you want to focus on differences.

2. Select terms of comparison that apply to both topics. For example, don't compare the hair, eyes, and figure of one person with the intelligence, ambition, and personality of another. Use the same terms of comparison for both topics.

3. Decide on the most appropriate pattern of organization to use: block or point-by-point (see below).

4. Write a thesis statement that clearly identifies your topic, states or implies your lead-in question, and indicates your organizational pattern.

Organizing a comparison according to the **block pattern** involves separating the two topics and discussing them one at a time, under the headings or categories you've chosen as your KEY IDEAS. If you were asked, for example, to compare the play and the movie versions of William Shakespeare's *Romeo and Juliet,* you might decide to focus your analysis on the characters, the setting, and the plot of the two versions. You would first discuss the play in terms of these three key ideas, and then you would do the same for the film. Here is a sample block outline for such an essay:

Paragraph 1   Introduction and thesis statement
Paragraph 2   The play

      a. characters in the play

      b. setting of the play

      c. plot of the play

Paragraph 3   The film

           a. characters in the film

           b. setting of the film

           c. plot of the film

Paragraph 4   Conclusion summarizing the similarities and differences and possibly stating your preference

The block pattern does not rule out discussing the two topics in the same paragraph. In this example, particularly in your analysis of the film, some mention of the play might be necessary. However, the overall structure of a block comparison should communicate the essentials about Topic 1 and then communicate the essentials about Topic 2. The block style works best with fairly short papers (essay questions on exams, for instance) in which the reader does not have to remember many intricate details about Topic 1 while trying to understand the details of Topic 2.

Structuring a comparison according to the **point-by-point pattern** involves setting out the terms or categories of comparison, then discussing both topics under each category heading. Organized by points, the *Romeo and Juliet* essay could communicate the same information as it does in the block pattern, yet its shape and outline would be quite different:

Paragraph 1   Introduction and thesis statement

Paragraph 2   Characters

           a. in the play

           b. in the film

Paragraph 3   Setting

           a. in the play

           b. in the film

Paragraph 4   Plot

           a. in the play

           b. in the film

Paragraph 5   Conclusion summarizing the similarities and differences and possibly stating your preference

A point-by-point structure makes the resemblances and differences between your two topics more readily apparent to the reader. This structure is ideally suited to longer reports and papers in which the terms of comparison are complex and demand high reader recall.

The model essay that follows illustrates the point-by-point pattern of organization.

She Said, He Said

Introduction
(a scenario)

It's Friday night. You and some friends have met at your favourite bar for a little relaxation. You all place your orders, and the conversation begins. If you watch and listen carefully, you'll notice patterns in this conversation, and, depending on whether you are a male in an all-male group or a female in an all-female one,

Thesis
statement

the patterns you observe will not be the same. When men and women engage in that intrinsically human activity called "talking," there is much that is different in why they talk, the way they talk, and what they talk about.

First key idea
(specific
details
highlight
differences)

Men talk mainly to exchange information, accomplish a task, offer advice, or enhance their status. In other words, they see conversation as a tool and consequently tend to talk for a reason, often with a specific purpose in mind. Women, on the other hand, talk in order to nurture and support and empathize. Sometimes accused of "talking for the sake of talking," women in fact talk to establish and maintain relationships. Because conversation is a human connection, women perceive talking as an end in itself rather than as the means to an end.

Second key
idea (developed
by facts and
examples)

The way men and women talk also differs. Men more readily take charge of a conversation, and they are more assertive in expressing their opinions. They are more likely to interrupt another speaker or to argue with what someone else says. Men tend to make declarative statements—unlike women, who inject their conversation with numerous questions, often ending even their assertions with an uplift of the voice as if their statements were questions. Men tend to state their opinions straight out: "The problem is . . ." Women tend to soften their opinion statements with "I think that . . ." Women also tend to preface their opinions with an apology: "Perhaps I don't understand what's at issue here, but I think that . . ." The pronouns men use most often are *I* and *he;* the pronouns that occur most often in women's speech are *you* and *we.* Men tend to listen in silence, giving non-verbal signals of consent or disagreement; women tend to make positive sounds of encouragement as they listen ("Uh-huh," "Mm-hm"), even when they disagree with the speaker. Women are more willing to defer, are more emotional in their speech, and are more interested in keeping a conversation going than in controlling it.

Note transitional phrase

Given the differences in why and how men and women talk, it should come as no surprise that what they talk about differs too. If you're a male in a group of males, you'll probably hear discussion of such

Third key idea (supported with examples)

things as the latest advance in DVD technology, last night's hockey game, the price of gas, a proposed fishing trip, why Japanese cars continue to outsell North American ones, and who drank the most beer the last time you were all together. The conversation tends to focus on things more than on people. If you're a female in a group of females, chances are you'll hear about quite different topics: a new boyfriend, the latest advance in weight-loss theory, or someone's argument with her mother, fiancé, husband, child, neighbour, boss, or any combination of the above. Female conversations tend to focus less on things than they do on relationships and people.

Conclusion restates the thesis and issues a challenge

Although it is dangerous to stereotype according to gender, research has shown that there are differences in the way men and women converse. Part of what makes male and female relationships so intriguing, if sometimes frustrating, is the divergence in their speech patterns. You're still not convinced? Then conduct your own research. Just listen to your friends: why, how, and what they're saying.

Ottawa vs. New York

GERMAINE GREER

Australian feminist, author, and lecturer Germaine Greer (b. 1939) holds degrees from the universities of Melbourne, Sydney, and Cambridge. A regular contributor to periodicals and newspapers, she earned international recognition for her first book, *The Female Eunuch* (1970). Her later works include *The Obstacle Race* (1979), *Sex and Destiny* (1984), and *The Whole Woman* (1999).

1   Waking up in Ottawa is not something I expect to do more than two or three times in this lifetime, and two of those times have already happened. This is not solely because Ottawa coffee is perhaps the worst in Canada and Canadian coffee on the whole the bitterest and weakest you will ever encounter, though these truths have some bearing. The badness of the coffee could be directly related to the current weakness of the currency; there was certainly an air of poverty-strickenness about the once great hotel I woke up in. My room was huge; as long as it was lit only by the forty-watt bulbs in the four lamps that cowered by the walls I could not see the dispiriting dun colour of the quarter-acre or so of carpet, but I could smell its depressing cocktail of sixty years of food, drink, smoking, cosmetics and sex, overlaid by a choking amalgam of air-freshener, carpet-deodoriser, -dry cleaner and -shampoo. I slept with the window open as the first line of defence, and then leapt out of bed and into a shower that could not be regulated heatwise or pressurewise, and scooted off to an equally dun, dispiriting and malodorous dining room for breakfast, to wit, one bran muffin and juice made from concentrate. It is sybaritism°, rather than self-discipline, that has reduced me to the semi-sylph-like proportions that I at present display. Mind you, giving interviews and making speeches "over lunch" effectively prevents ingestion of anything solid. The Women of Influence lunches I spoke at in Canada featured cold noodle salad and poly-styrene chicken thighs, suggesting more plainly than words could that Canadian businesswomen have at their command small influ-ence and less money.

2   To escape from Ottawa . . . to New York and the Pierpont Morgan Library, I took a plane to LaGuardia. Air Canada, as des-perate to penny-pinch as all other Canadian operations, was sneakily folding the Newark flight into mine, which made me forty-five minutes late, and all the good people who needed to travel to New Jersey a great deal later. In that forty-five minutes the best-run hotel on the planet, or on Fifth Avenue, which comes to the same thing, let some interloper have my room.

3   The yingling at reception was so very, very sorry. Would I endure a night in a suite at the room rate instead of the statutory $3,000 a night, and let them move me to my own room tomorrow? I hummed and hawed and sighed for as long as I thought decent, then leapt at the chance. The yingling took me up himself, and threw open the door. I strode past him into a forty-foot mirrored salon hung with yellow silk damask; through the French windows a terrace hedged with clipped yew offered a spectacular view of aerial New York, as well as serried ranks of terracotta planters in

which green and rose parrot tulips exhibited themselves. The east end of my salon was crowded with sofas and armchairs, all paying homage to a state-of-the-art music centre which, if I'd come equipped, I could have programmed for the whole evening. The west end featured a baronial fireplace and a ten-seater dining table. The yingling showed me my kitchen, my two bathrooms, and my seven-foot-square bed in my twenty-foot bedroom, and swept out before I could decide whether he should be tipped or not.

The only way to bring such magnificence into perspective was   4
to take off all my clothes and skip about as naked as a jaybird, opening and shutting my closets, cupboards and drawers, turning all my appliances off and on, my phones, my faxes, my safe. If I had been anything more substantial than a nude scholar, I could have invited forty friends for cocktails, nine friends for dinner and a hundred for after-dinner drinks, and scribbled my signature on a room service check somewhere in the high six figures.

The salon soon felt less welcoming than vast, so I took a   5
Roederer from the fridge and a salad into the bedroom, where, perched amid piles of pillows and bolsters stuffed with goosedown, I watched the fag-end of the Florida Marlins' batting order knock the Atlanta Braves' relief pitcher all over the park. The bed was meant for better things; under the television there was a VCR player. I could have ordered a selection of video-porn from room service, and had a cute somebody sent up to watch them with me.

Which is the great thing about New York. Anything, but any-   6
thing, can be had for money, from huge diamonds of the finest water°, furs of lynx and sable, wines of vintages long said to have been exhausted, important works of art and rock cocaine, to toy-boys of the most spontaneous, entertaining and beautifully made, of any sexual orientation and all colours. Every day, planes land at JFK freighted with orchids from Malaysia, roses from Istanbul, mangos gathered that morning from trees in Karnataka, passion-fruit from Townsville, limes from Barbados, truffles from Perigord, lobsters brought live from the coldest seas on the planet. Within twenty-four hours all will have been put on sale and consumed. The huge prices are no deterrent. The New York elite likes to be seen to pay them with nonchalance°, on the J. P. Morgan principle that if you need to know how much something costs you can't afford it. Nobody looks at the tab; the platinum credit card is thrown down for the obsequious salesperson to do his worst with.

That is what I don't like about New York. Below the thin upper   7
crust of high rollers there is a dense layer of struggling aspirants° to elite status, and below them dead-end poverty, which no longer aspires, if it ever did. The vast mass of urban New Yorkers are

struggling to get by, in conditions that are truly unbearable, from the helots° who open the hair salons at six in the morning and lock them up at eight at night to the dry-cleaners who have worked twelve hours a day in the steam and fumes ever since they stepped off a boat from Europe sixty or even seventy years ago. It's great that I can get my hair washed at any hour of day or night and my clothes altered or invisibly mended within four hours of dropping them off, but it is also terrible. If I ask these people about their working lives they display no rancour°; they tell me that they cannot afford to retire and are amused at my consternation°. They would rather keep on working, they say. What else would they do? The pain in the hair-dresser's feet and back, the listlessness and pallor of the dry-cleaner, can't be complained of. Everybody has to be up.

8   The power of positive thinking is to persuade people that the narrative of their grim existence is a success story. Though New Yorkers have been telling themselves that story for so long that they have stopped believing it, they cannot permit themselves to stop telling it. Everywhere in New York, wizened ancients are drudging. The lift-driver who takes me up to my hotel room looks ninety if a day. Her bird-body balances on grossly distorted feet; the hands in her white gloves are knobby with arthritis; her skeletal face is gaily painted and her few remaining hairs coloured bright auburn and brushed up into a transparent crest. She opens and shuts the doors of her lift as if her only ambition had ever been to do just that. I want to howl with rage on her behalf. The covers of the bolsters I frolic on have all been laundered, lightly starched and pressed by hand; as I play at being a nabob°, I imagine the terribleness of the hotel laundry-room, all day, every day.

9   Though I love New York, I disapprove of it. Dreary as Ottawa was, it was in the end a better place than New York. Canadians believe that happiness is living in a just society; they will not sing the Yankee song that capitalism is happiness, capitalism is freedom. Canadians have a lively sense of decency and human dignity. Though no Canadian can afford freshly squeezed orange juice, every Canadian can have juice made from concentrate. The lack of luxury is meant to coincide with the absence of misery. It doesn't work altogether, but the idea is worth defending.

Words and Meanings

Paragraph

1   sybaritism   devotion to luxury

6   water   quality
     nonchalance   casual lack of concern or indifference

aspirants	people who seek or hope to attain something (in this case, status)	7
helots	serfs or enslaved people	
rancour	bitter, deep-seated resentment	
consternation	bewilderment and dismay	
nabob	a rich and powerful person	8

Structure and Strategy

1. Greer bases her contrast primarily on DESCRIPTION. Identify details that appeal to four physical senses in paragraph 1. What is the dominant impression created by these details? Now consider Greer's description of her second hotel room, in paragraph 3. What is the dominant impression created by these details?
2. In paragraphs 2 and 3, Greer tells an ANECDOTE to explain her sudden change of surroundings. Where does she go? What happens? Summarize the events.
3. The topic of paragraph 6 is developed by examples. Identify the TOPIC SENTENCE. Which of the examples do you recognize? Which are unfamiliar to you? Do these examples effectively support Greer's key idea?
4. The THESIS of this essay appears in the CONCLUSION. Summarize it in your own words.

Content and Purpose

1. Why is Greer in Ottawa as the essay begins? How does she feel about the city?
2. Who is "the yingling" in paragraph 3? What does he do? Why do you think she refers to him as a yingling? Define the term in your own words.
3. According to the author, what is "the great thing about New York"?
4. What doesn't Greer like about New York? What contrast is the basis of this dislike? (See paragraph 7.)
5. Summarize Greer's DESCRIPTION of the woman who operates the hotel elevator (paragraph 8). Why do you think this description is so detailed? How does it affect you?
6. How does Greer feel about life in Canada? In New York? Where do you think she would rather live? Do you agree with her? Why or why not?

Suggestions for Writing

1. Write an essay comparing or contrasting two cities that you are familiar with.

2. The contrast Greer draws between Ottawa and New York is based on her assessment of the attitudes toward wealth implicit in those cities. Write an essay that contrasts life in a wealthy family, city, or country with life in a less wealthy counterpart.

Adam and Eve Redux

RITA KLEIN-GELTINK

Rita Klein-Geltink (b. 1960) attends Redeemer University College in Ancaster, Ontario. She lives in Cambridge, Ontario, with her husband and their four sons. "Adam and Eve Redux" is her first published work.

1   "I don't know why you told them we'd come," complained my husband as we drove home from one of those excruciatingly boring visits. We'd been in such situations before— the well-intentioned hosts regale° you with a full synopsis of their family history while you spend most of the time trying to devise plausible reasons as to why you have to be on your way. "And why didn't you tell them sooner that we had to get going?" he continued. I sighed as I reminded him that he, too, has a tongue in his head and that it was unfair to hold me totally responsible for the fact that the better part of our precious Sunday afternoon had been spent in a way neither of us had really wanted.

2   This pattern of the man's inaction, coupled with blame for an undesired consequence being placed upon the woman, plays itself out frequently. Men have devised a tidy little exercise whereby they absolve themselves from all responsibility: they adopt a helpless expression, turn their palms out slightly, and shrug their shoulders.

3   Rewind the tape, if you will, to the scene in the church parking lot where the invitation to visit over coffee is first extended. The woman reminds us that we haven't been by to visit for three weeks, and why don't we come over now? I try to explain to her that the kids are having friends over—"Bring them all along!" she insists. I tell her that we have company coming later in the afternoon— "You'll be home in plenty of time!" she assures me. "I really don't want to put you out. . . ." "Nonsense," she says. I glance over my shoulder for support from my husband, and cast him an exasperated look that screams, "Say something!" And what does he do? He

looks at me with that dazed expression and simply shrugs his shoulders. I turn back to the woman and with a sweet smile say, "We'd love to come."

Who made the decision to accept the invitation? My husband   4
insists that I did, and therefore I am to be held responsible for putting both of us through two hours of weak coffee and family photos.

Now rewind the tape back even further, to another couple, to   5
another conversation. The serpent asks the woman about God's instructions concerning the fruit trees in the garden. "Did God really say, 'You must not eat from any tree in the garden'?" The woman responds by recalling that God had given them permission to eat from any tree with the exception of the tree in the middle of the garden. "If we eat from that tree, or even if we touch it, we will die," replies the woman, and she looks at her husband, who nods in agreement. "Nonsense," says the serpent. "You will surely not die, for God knows that when you eat of it your eyes will be opened, and you will be like God, knowing good and evil. Just try it." The woman glances over her shoulder for her husband's reaction and casts him a questioning look, "Should we?" In response, her husband looks at her with that dazed expression and simply shrugs his shoulders. She turns back to the serpent and with an uncertain little smile says, "Okay, I'll try it."

Who made the decision to accept the fruit? Many men, and   6
women too, have been led to believe that the woman is to be held solely responsible for the decision. They are convinced that the woman chose this course of action in a hasty moment of weakness and then, having eaten the fruit, went off to find her husband to offer it to him. Somehow they skim over the last sentence of Genesis 3:6: "She also gave some to her husband, *who was with her, and he ate it*" [italics added]. He was with her. They both heard the arguments presented by the serpent. They both had ample opportunity to decline the offer. The man's inaction has not absolved° him from the responsibility God had entrusted to him. Rather, both the man and the woman must bear the consequences of their action/inaction.

The pattern of man's inaction was established centuries ago.   7
Women would do well to be conscious of his strategy and to insist that he bear his share of the responsibility in decision-making, whether in accepting the unsolicited invitation or eating the forbidden fruit.

Words and Meanings

Paragraph		
1	regale	entertain
6	absolved	set free from an obligation

Structure and Strategy

1. What is the function of paragraph 1? If the essay had opened with paragraph 2, how would the overall effect have changed?
2. Identify the points of comparison between the scenes described in paragraphs 3 and 5. Consider the author's DICTION and SYNTAX as well as the content of the scenes.
3. Who is the intended AUDIENCE for this essay? Explain.

Content and Purpose

1. What does the word "redux" mean? Is Klein-Geltink's title appropriate? Why or why not?
2. In your own words, explain the comparison on which the essay is based.
3. What is the author's main PURPOSE? Does her essay achieve it? Why or why not?
4. What is the author's attitude toward her topic? Do you agree with her? Why or why not?

Suggestions for Writing

1. Should both partners in a relationship be equally responsible for such things as child care and social obligations? Write an essay that explores the idea of shared responsibility.
2. The decisions we make—even those that seem insignificant at the time—can have an unexpectedly big impact on our lives. Write an essay about a decision you made and how it changed your life. How would your life have differed had you not made that decision?

The View from Italy: Puritans 'R Us

ANTANAS SILEIKA

Writer and freelance broadcaster Antanas Sileika teaches English at Toronto's Humber College. He has contributed to a wide range of newspapers and magazines, including *The Globe and Mail, The Toronto Star, Saturday Night,* and *Cottage Life.* His last book, *Buying on Time* (1997), was short-listed for the Stephen Leacock Medal for Humour and for the Toronto Book Award.

I'd forgotten my disposable lighter in Toronto, and so, when the taxi dropped me in the heart of Rome, I bought a new one at a tobacco shop. In the Campo di Fiori open-air market, I tried to figure out where the childproofing device was hidden. Each brand puts this safety device in a different place, and they are devilishly hard to find. An inquisitive *caribinieri°* noticed my confusion, lit my cigarette and returned the lighter with a flourish. No wonder I'd been confused. There was no childproofing device.   1

Far too much has been written about cigarettes and even lighters for me to want to add to the debate. But this difference between Italy and Canada was only one of a series. Rebecca West° once wrote that people in the East try to make the world a better place by adding things to it, while we in the West try to make the world a better place by taking bad things away.   2

She must have had Canada in mind. Puritans 'R us.   3

I wandered around the medieval marketplace admiring the raw-milk cheeses (soon to be forbidden by law here) and admiring as well the Roman women who walked with assurance across the streets and through herds of motor scooters. No crosswalks for the pedestrians. No helmets on the drivers. All of them should have been ashamed of themselves, and probably they would have been if they lived in Canada.   4

In Toronto, speed bumps multiply faster than mushrooms after a rain, and they are joined by other related fungi, such as all-way stop signs. At several intersections where I live, conscientious drivers even stop at all corners when there are not four-way stops. Just in case. Through their windshields I can almost hear their thoughts. "You can never be too safe. No one ever got a ticket for being too careful." This high civic concern is received telepathically° by the bureaucrats who live to make our lives better, saner, safer and more just.   5

6   This Canadian concern for safety covers linguistic dangers as well. At my first meal in Rome, I noticed that *spaghetti putanesca* was on the menu—"whore's spaghetti," a salty, even earthy mix of anchovies and olive oil. Could we have such a name in Canada? Not at all. We'd call it, "Not a Love Story Spaghetti," and add a warning that high salt intake leads to hypertension°. And speaking of warning signs, I saw none that warned pregnant mothers against the dangers of drinking.

7   Are Roman women less forgetful than their Canadian counterparts? Not at all. The signs exist in Canada not to warn pregnant women against drinking so much as to proclaim publicly our commitment to public health. Somewhere in our hearts we are like the reedy farm couple with pitchfork in the painting, *American Gothic*— self-righteous and armed, albeit° discreetly.

8   There seemed to be a women's club in the Roman café where I took my morning coffee. Almost 15 of them, aged from 20 to 80, chatted and laughed together. When a scruffy young man in jeans, leather jacket and Mohawk haircut stopped his scooter on the street outside, the women called out to him. He smiled back and came in to chat over a thick black coffee that I am sure was not decaffeinated. There was no disapproval on the women's faces. Similarly, there was none on the faces of the older men who stopped to chat with punks lounging in the city streets. Live and let live, their attitude seemed to say. No need to "improve" lost youth.

9   On our Vatican tour, my wife and I fell into a hot debate spurred by the massive buildings and ornate decoration, and magnified by the rain outside, which prevented us from walking off our hardened positions. In the Sistine Chapel, we and thousands of other tourists strained our necks to stare up at the intense colours of Michelangelo's restored ceiling. Was it too much? Was it too rich? Perhaps, but the world would not be a better place without it. In Toronto, we seem to have decided that we will be better off without an opera house and without any more subways.

10   Many more Italians have come to Canada than the other way around, so there must be something superior [about] this country. In a nutshell, I'd say we have more space and more money, yet as a society we are always crying poor and trying to eliminate the dangers in everyday life. This country feels like a childproofed room; the safety latches are on, and all the sharp objects have been put away. Like the cuckolded husband° in the . . . *Bridges of Madison County*, the best that can be said about us is that we are clean.

And yet, I am not immune to self-improvement. On our final   11
evening in Rome, we had intended to go to a Pentecost festival
where the Pope carries an icon across the river to St. Peter's
Basilica. Yet another pair of aging boomers in a quest for a little
spirituality. But as we stepped out on the Campo di Fiori, we found
it crammed with tents and people. What was going on?

It was a festival, too, but one very different from the religious   12
event we had planned to attend. It was a festival of spaghetti and
music. High-school bands played music, the likes of which I haven't
heard since seeing some of Fellini's° older films. Dozens of chefs
served plates heaping with spaghetti covered in a rich brown bacon
and Parmesan sauce. Only three dollars a plate! I ate two. I could
always worry about the fat content after I returned to Canada.

What about improving ourselves spiritually? The spaghetti was   13
very good and the music was charming. We decided to stick
around where the fun was. After all, heaven can wait.

Words and Meanings

		Paragraph
inquisitive *caribinieri*	curious soldier	1
Rebecca West	novelist, biographer, and journalist (1892–1983)	2
telepathically	communicated without words	5
hypertension	high blood pressure	6
albeit	although	7
cuckolded husband	man whose wife is unfaithful	10
Fellini	Federico (1920–1993), Italian filmmaker whose works include *La Dolce Vita*	12

Structure and Strategy

1. Sileika introduces and concludes the essay with ANECDOTES. How do they connect to the point he is making about life in Italy?
2. What points of contrast between Italy and Canada does the author explore? What organizational pattern does he use— block or point-by-point?
3. Why do you think that paragraph 3 is so short?
4. How would you describe the TONE of this essay? Find three or four examples of Sileika's use of IRONY that contribute to the tone.

5. Are you familiar with Grant Wood's painting *American Gothic* (see paragraph 7)? If so, how would you describe the couple in the painting? How does this ALLUSION support the point the essay is making?

Content and Purpose

1. In paragraph 2, the author paraphrases Rebecca West's contrast between the Eastern and Western approaches to life. In Sileika's essay, which country represents the "East," and which represents the "West"? Do you agree with Rebecca West's— and, by extension, Sileika's—opinion?
2. How does the essay contrast the pedestrian and motor traffic in Italy with that in Canada? Which details support the notion that Canadians are the "safer" drivers? Find two other examples of Canadians' more conservative and cautious approach to life.
3. Do you think that Sileika would support the repeal of traffic regulations in Canada, the abolition of cigarette-lighter safety devices, or public signs warning of the dangers of drinking? Would these changes in the laws make Canada a more interesting place in which to live? Why or why not?
4. How does the essay explain the fact that so many people— including large numbers of Italians—have immigrated to Canada (see paragraph 10)? What does it suggest are the best features of Canada?
5. How does the author actually feel about his home country, Canada? Support your answer by referring to specific details in the essay.

Suggestions for Writing

1. Write an essay contrasting two different ways of life with which you are familiar. The two ways of life may differ because of generation, gender, religion, and so on.
2. Should we be free to live with risk and assume responsibility for the consequences? Or is it better for the government to try to protect us from risk by regulating such things as smoking, drinking alcohol, owning guns, not wearing seatbelts, biking without a helmet, or other "unhealthy" pastimes? Write an essay that argues for or against regulating risk in people's lives.

Shorter, Slower, Weaker: And That's a Good Thing

JAY TEITEL

Jay Teitel (b. 1949), an award-winning writer and editor, graduated from the University of Toronto in 1973. A frequent contributor to magazines, he writes non-fiction, fiction, humour, and screenplays and is co-inventor of the board game Therapy. His most recent book is *From Here to Paternity* (1993).

Three years ago I was channel-surfing on a Sunday afternoon   1
in December, bouncing between NFL offerings that were even
deadlier than usual, when I flicked to a hockey game that
stopped me cold. There was something about the game that was
both strange and naggingly familiar. For starters, the play on the ice
was shapely and unbroken; teams moved out of their zones in creative wholes, the patterns unclogged by so much of the frantic fluk-
iness of modern NHL play. On top of that, passes were being
completed at a rate that wouldn't have been out of place on a basketball court, and that I hadn't seen on a rink since I watched a
sixteen-year-old Wayne Gretzky play for the Sault Ste. Marie
Greyhounds. In fact I assumed for a second that I was watching a
junior game, maybe an all-star match. But a younger age group
couldn't possibly have explained the style of play I was seeing. And
then it came to me: I was watching something not younger, but
older—something historical. I'd stumbled onto a weirdly faithful
recreation of the old grainy kinetypes of NHL games from the thirties and forties. I was watching a memory.

At which point one of the more boisterous anachronisms° got a   2
penalty for slashing. A helmet was pulled off in chagrin, and I saw
exactly who the creators of this lost and perfect game were: women.

A quick glance through recent issues of *Sports Illustrated*, or   3
TSN's weekend listings, is enough to suggest that there is a small
but unprecedented explosion in the popularity of women's sports,
both amateur and professional. Part of this movement is probably
linked to an increased female fan-base (women are buying more
cars than ever, for instance, and car companies traditionally
sponsor sports events), but just as significant is the phenomenon I
witnessed that afternoon three years ago on my TV screen: what
you might call the Law of the Intersecting Gender Gap. . . . Men
have out-grown many of the traditional sports, while women have
been growing into them.

4   For anyone who's spent a couple of introspective hours watching TV sports lately, the evidence is tangible. While it's undeniable that male athletes today have elevated the skill level in most of the popular sports—football, basketball, hockey, tennis, golf, even track and field—to a dazzling level, in virtually all these sports the same male players have outstripped in size and speed the confines of the standard playing spaces that define their games. Whether it's on rinks, fields, or courts, they just don't seem to fit any more. Pro football, with 250-pound guided missiles capable of running four-second forty-yard dashes on a 100-yard postage stamp of a field, has turned into a kind of mesomorphic pinball; NHL hockey, as much a game of space as speed, is too often more of the same. NBA basketball, half the time a breathtaking nightly highlight package, for the other half is a pituitary, one-dimensional jamboree, with as many field goals being released above the rim as below, with jump shots clanging off rims, and two guys playing one-on-one the rest of the game. In men's golf, prodigal *Übermenschen*° like Tiger Woods have made the notion of par fives, and even fours, obsolete with 350-yard drives, and in tennis the 120-mile serve-and-volley game has turned the sport into a live-action Super Mario game that ends every seven seconds.

5   At the same time the female version of every one of the above-mentioned sports has quietly become an oasis of form. Women's hockey is even more fun to watch now than it was [before body-checking was outlawed]; women's tennis features long rallies and good net play; the women's golf tour continues to boast better putters and fine short-iron players, if less monstrous drivers; and as far as round-ball goes, the legendary John Wooden, coach of ten NCAA men's champion teams at UCLA, recently noted that "Some of the best pure basketball I see lately is being played by women." There seems to be a confluence° between playing surface and game in women's sports that is harmonious and satisfying. The men amaze you, you jump out of your chair crying "All right!" at the same time knowing that something is half wrong. The women let you sink back into the sofa with a quieter delight, and reach for the chips. They have the space to play; you have the space to watch.

6   If this yearning seems nostalgic, it's no accident. The fact is that nearly all modern sports were either invented or codified into their present-day form at the same time—[just over 100 years ago]. More critically, they were designed to be played by men at the turn of the century. And it turns out that men 100 years ago were closer to the women athletes of today, in both size and performance, than they were remotely close to their modern male counterparts. In women's

sports today we see not only the original sports recreated, but the original athletes.

Basketball is a classic example. The average height of the [1990s] Toronto Raptors, an "average" NBA team, [was] 6'6⅓"—about nine inches taller than the average for the male population at large. In 1898, though, just seven years after the transplanted Canadian James Naismith nailed his peach baskets ten feet above the floor at a Springfield, Massachusetts, Y, the average height of the Buffalo Germans, one of the first pro teams, was only marginally taller than the lay-population average of the day. "From 1898 to 1915," notes Bill Himmelman, President/Owner of Sports Nostalgia Research in New Jersey and league historian for the NBA, "the 'big men' on pro teams, the centres, were anywhere from 6' to 6'3". The first exceptional big man, John Wendelken of Columbia University, was all of 6'2". The guards of the day, defensive specialists, were in the 5'10" range, while the forwards, the speedy shooters, were about 5'7"." Assuming equal distribution among the players, the average height of a team like the Buffalo Germans would have been in the 5'11" range—precisely the average height of the women playing in one of today's new professional leagues, the ABL.

But maybe more important than the numerical match was the style of the turn-of-the-century game. "The set-shot was the big weapon then, a 24–40 foot shot, compared to a 21-foot three-point shot today," adds Bill Himmelman, "and the only way a short guy could get it off was to back up on the taller players. Your forwards were your best shooters and your best drivers. Coaches actually avoided recruiting tall players; height was considered a handicap, it was thought to make you uncoordinated. As far as dunking went, coaches wouldn't let you do it; it was considered an absolute sham." No dunking, precision outside shooting, an emphasis on the fast break, a foul shooting percentage consistently higher than the NBA's—all these are hallmarks of topflight women's basketball today. Again, the individual manoeuvres aren't nearly as awe-inspiring as in the NBA, but the gestalt° is a whole level higher. The acting's less prodigious, but the story's better. . . .

The pattern in hockey is the same. Although size statistics don't exist from 1893, the year Baron Stanley of Preston donated a cup to the winners of collegiate hockey in Canada (rink size had been standardized by McGill University students about fifteen years earlier), they are available from 1940. In an NHL guide from that year, the first two pages alone list eighteen players under 5'10" in height, including seven at 5'7" and four at 5'6", with an average weight of

166 lbs (compared to the 6'1", 198-pound average in the NHL today). Using historical growth rates, it's reasonable to posit° a men's pro hockey team at the turn of the century with an average height in the 5'6½" range, and an average weight of about 150 lbs. The averages for the first six position players on the 1996/97 Canadian Women's National Hockey team list? 5'6½", 150 lbs.

10   It could be argued that such coincidences still deal mainly with size, and size doesn't necessarily translate to performance. A 150-pound man, for instance, will probably be stronger and faster than a 150-pound woman. (Tiger Woods, at 160 pounds, regularly outdrives not only 160-pound women but 260-pound men.) But it's in the one sport where we have hard historical comparative performance records that the similarity between today's female athletes and males at the dawn of the century is at its eeriest. It turns out that nearly every major track and field record held by women today is almost identical to the records held by men seventy to ninety years ago. . . .

11   Aside from a couple of intriguing future speculations—in about 2085 someone's great-granddaughter should be matching Donovan Bailey's current record time in the 100 metres—the most important implication of all the above is philosophical as opposed to logistic. The match between today's women and yesterday's men is significant because it gives us a seat at an unexpected remake of a "golden age" of athletics, when sport was less about spectacle and entertainment and more about the game itself. The argument one large camp of veteran sports fans will make in response, that if men's sports were so proportionally deficient today they wouldn't also be so unprecedentedly popular, is as flawed as any cultural argument from popularity. Droves of people go to see pro wrestling and [bad] movies—is that convincing proof of their quality? No, the radical, "dated" notion is that there might be an ideal in sport that actually diverges from the TV ratings. No one denies that male pro sports can be exciting (with the possible exception of NFL football, which without the point spread would be like watching paint dry), but they are a new universe unto themselves that lacks the satisfaction of the conventions, the old verities° of shapeliness.

12   As far as shapeliness of "fit" goes, for that matter, the solution for men's sports seems obvious: if the shoe crimps, stretch it. If male athletes have outgrown the physical spaces they play on, enlarge the spaces. Only a combination of greed (having fewer exorbitantly priced seats to sell) and timidity (having to listen to Don Cherry bray) has prevented the NHL from widening its rinks fifteen feet to Olympic size, and returning the game to its skill players, halting the clutch and grab movement in mid-hook. If the Canadian Football League can produce a superior game with inferior players by dint of a field ten yards longer and fifteen yards

wider than the NFL gridiron, how much more superior would the American game be if it stretched its boundaries? As for basketball, if James Naismith had known that a 7'7" Romanian redwood named Gheorghe Muresan would someday bestride his wooden court, would he not have raised the basket a foot or so?

But juggling dimensions is only half the fix, one that on its own   13
evades the deeper lesson that women's sports have to teach us. In a socio-economic coincidence as unerring as the physical one, women athletes today, particularly team sport athletes, are crossing precisely the same threshold between amateurism and professionalism their male counterparts did at the turn of the century. Love of the game is far more likely to be burning in them than love of money or fame, because the latter simply aren't there. Women's pro leagues are in their infancy; big crowds are still largely wishful thinking. Unless they're tennis players or golfers, most female athletes can only dream about six-figure salaries, let alone the millions doled out regularly to journeyman male athletes. As a result they're still refreshingly free of the arrogance that permeates so many pro male locker-rooms these days. . . . Aside from their physical gifts, the ways and means of women athletes tend to be modest. Which is to say, like ours.

And this is the most delicate message of women's sports today: 14
it isn't necessary that our athletic heroes have our physical limitations, but it helps if their aspirations are scaled close enough to ours that the rhythm of our dreams coincides. Size in this context may be just a handy metaphor. In their rudeness, their ego, the unseemly magnitude of their contracts, and their substitution of contempt for sportsmanship, a large percentage of male pro athletes today have become not just physical but emotional misfits. They have burst not just the dimensions of sport, but its spirit. Conversely, in their relative sincerity, their humility, their lack of affect, their newness to professionalism in many cases, women athletes go a long way towards restoring the balance. This too may change, but for the moment they have about them a forgotten scent of something eternally ancient and eternally new, a sense of proportion, an old-fashioned passion for the game well played.

Words and Meanings

		Paragraph
anachronisms	persons, things, ideas, or customs that are attributed to a historical period to which they do not belong	2
Übermenschen	supermen [German]	4
confluence	a coming together	5

8	gestalt	an integrated set of elements or experiences which is perceived as a whole that is more than the sum of its parts [German]
9	posit	assume or propose as a fact
11	verities	truths

Structure and Strategy

1. What strategy does Teitel use in his INTRODUCTION? Why is paragraph 2 so short?
2. In paragraph 4, what KEY IDEA is supported by examples? Have any significant examples been omitted?
3. To develop his THESIS, does Teitel rely on comparison or contrast—or a combination of the two? Why do you think he chose this pattern of development to explore his topic?

Content and Purpose

1. What is your opinion of the essay's title? Did it appeal to you? What did it lead you to expect from the essay?
2. What is the "Law of the Intersecting Gender Gap" as Teitel explains it in paragraph 3?
3. While men's sports have been outgrowing their playing surfaces, women's sports have "quietly become an oasis of form." Study the examples Teitel provides in paragraph 5 to explain the phrase "oasis of form." Then define this phrase in your own words.
4. What does the comparative record of men's and women's performance in track and field for the past seventy to ninety years suggest about the validity of Teitel's ARGUMENT? (See paragraph 10.)
5. Teitel would like to see playing fields, courts, rinks, and golf courses enlarged to accommodate the increased size and strength of today's male athletes. Do you agree with him? Why or why not?
6. Why does Teitel think that male professional athletes have become "emotional misfits" (paragraph 14)? Do you agree with him? Why or why not?
7. According to Teitel, who is more likely to harbour a "love of the game": professional male athletes or professional female athletes? What are the reasons behind Teitel's position? Summarize his argument.

Suggestions for Writing

1. Are professional athletes overpaid? How do multimillion-dollar salaries affect the performances of individual athletes and their teams? Write an essay on the dramatic growth in professional sports salaries in recent years.
2. Should male and female athletes play together on the same teams? Why or why not?

Should Morality Be a Struggle? Ancient vs. Modern Ideas about Ethics

THOMAS HURKA

Thomas Hurka (b. 1952) has taught philosophy at the University of Calgary and now teaches at the University of Toronto. From 1989 to 1992, he wrote a weekly column for *The Globe and Mail* through which he introduced many Canadians to the relevance of ethics to everyday life. In 1994, Professor Hurka published *Principles: Short Essays on Ethics*, a collection of his columns organized around such topics as abortion, war, capital punishment, and the environment. His most recent book, *Vice, Virtue and Value*, was published in 2001.

I magine that two accountants do similar jobs for similar companies. One day they make the same discovery: with almost no chance of getting caught, they can embezzle a large sum from their employers. They can both use the money, to pay off debts or buy a new car. 1

The first accountant right away says to himself, "It's wrong to steal," and never considers the matter again. But the second accountant is torn. She, too, knows stealing is wrong, but she's tempted and at first decides to go ahead. Then she decides she won't, and then that she will. Finally, after weeks of agonizing, she decides not to embezzle. Who is the morally better person? 2

My fellow students and I were asked this at the start of an undergraduate seminar on Aristotle. The point wasn't that there 3 was a single right answer we had to give; it was to highlight differences between ancient and modern views of ethics.

4   Aristotle and most other Greek philosophers would have said the first accountant is better, because he has a harmonious personality. He has correct beliefs about what's right and no appetites or impulses that conflict with them. He's integrated, stable, at one with his moral convictions.

5   Aristotle thought this kind of harmony was essential to true virtue. The virtuous person would, for example, be moderate about sensual pleasures, but he wouldn't find this difficult. He would dislike the taste of rich or unhealthy foods; he'd get no enjoyment from adultery even if he happened to try it.

6   The Greeks could value inner harmony because they assumed that morality and self-interest go hand in hand. The second accountant is tempted to embezzle the money because she thinks this will benefit her. But Aristotle would say this is a mistake. What's really in your interest is leading the best life, which is a life of virtue and excludes stealing. To be tempted is to be confused.

7   Modern ethics is more sympathetic to the second accountant. We doubt whether virtue in Aristotle's sense is attainable; we think of morality as a struggle against evil or selfish impulses that we can't get rid of but can only restrain. (Think of dieting as portrayed in the "Cathy" comic strip. It's a battle against cravings for chocolate, ice cream, and the like. Wrongdoing strikes us as similarly delicious.)

8   This modern picture has partly religious origins. The Christian doctrine of original sin says that, after the fall in the Garden of Eden, all humans are corrupted. We have within us tendencies to evil that cannot be eliminated ("the old Adam") and against which we must constantly struggle. As St. Paul said, "The flesh lusteth against the spirit," and the best we can do is lust back against it.

9   But there are secular° versions of the same idea. Our twentieth-century psychologies teach us that we have inborn tendencies, the products now of biology rather than divinity, to pleasure, aggression, or dominance. They're the nasty, uncivilized part of our nature, and though they can be diverted, sublimated, or restrained, they can't be eliminated. The moral life, again, is a struggle against oneself.

10   Like the Greek picture, this modern one is tied to beliefs about morality and self-interest. But where the Greeks assume that doing what's right is the same as benefiting yourself, we think the two clash. Morality involves a sacrifice of your interests for other people's, and that's what makes it hard.

This makes us suspicious of the first accountant. Doesn't his easy   11
virtue look like a mindless following of rules whose costs he doesn't
really understand? Morality does require giving up your interests,
and the second accountant's struggle reflects this. But the first
accountant seems to ignore this, or to be missing some basic drives.

Our modern picture of morality is grim, in contrast with the   12
light, harmonious picture Aristotle paints. But sometimes reality is
more hard than beautiful. The German philosopher G. W. F. Hegel
said that Greek civilization expressed a beautiful naïveté°, treating
as in simple harmony what we see as opposed. You can see this in
Greek ethics. There virtue is effortless because it's good for you—
but we find it a struggle.

Words and Meanings

		Paragraph
secular	worldly, not religious or sacred	9
naïveté	simplicity, lack of sophistication	12

Structure and Strategy

1. What introductory strategy does Hurka use to set up his THESIS?
2. What is the principal contrast on which this essay is based?
   What other contrasts are presented, and what is their function
   in the piece?
3. Which paragraphs explore the ancient view of morality? Which
   deal with the modern?
4. What functions do the two accountants serve in this essay?
5. What example does paragraph 7 use to illustrate the modern
   view? Do you think the example is effective?

Content and Purpose

1. Summarize what Hurka means by the ancient and modern
   views of morality. Identify three essential differences between
   them. What similarity is there between the ancient Greeks and
   ourselves?
2. According to the author, what major influences have shaped the
   modern view of morality? Can you think of others that have
   contributed to our contemporary notions of ethical behaviour?
3. Which view of morality—ancient or modern—do you think
   Hurka adheres to? What details in the essay led you to this
   conclusion?

Suggestions for Writing

1. Write an essay that answers the dilemma posed by the ANEC-DOTE of the two accountants. Who is the more "moral" person: the one who would never consider stealing or the one who rejects the idea after considerable soul-searching?
2. Are there any circumstances under which it is permissible to steal? Write an essay in which you contrast "ethical" and "unethical" situations in which one might take what belongs to someone else.
3. Think of another moral dilemma (one that has nothing to do with stealing). Introduce the dilemma, outline two different courses of action to deal with it, and indicate what you think is the ethical response to the dilemma.

Additional Suggestions for Writing: Comparison and Contrast

Write a comparison and/or contrast paper based on one of the topics below. Make sure that your thesis statement identifies the basis of your comparison or contrast, then develop it by providing relevant examples and details.

1. Contrast two people of your acquaintance whose lifestyles reveal different attitudes toward life.
2. Compare and/or contrast living in Canada with living in another country.
3. Compare and/or contrast two sports, teams, or players.
4. Compare and/or contrast men and women as consumers (or voters, employees, supervisors, friends, roommates, students, etc.).
5. Compare and/or contrast two artists—painters, poets, film directors, musicians, or actors—with whose work you are familiar.
6. Contrast your present career goals with those you dreamed of as a child. How do you account for the differences between the two sets of goals?
7. Compare and/or contrast two types of contemporary music, such as hip-hop or punk rock.
8. Compare and/or contrast the way in which you and your parents view a particular issue: premarital sex, postsecondary education, raising children, children's obligations to their parents.
9. Compare and/or contrast men's and women's attitudes toward love, children, and family responsibilities.
10. "All happy families resemble one another, but each unhappy family is unhappy in its own way." (Leo Tolstoy)

U N I T

5

Causal Analysis

WHAT IS CAUSAL ANALYSIS?

In Unit 3, we defined ANALYSIS as the process of separating something into its parts in order to understand the whole better. The word "causal" (not to be confused with "casual," which means something else entirely) refers to "causes," so *causal analysis* means identifying out the causes or reasons for something; the term also refers to analyzing effects.

Causal analysis is a rhetorical pattern based on this kind of thinking. A writer may explain *causes*, the reasons for something. For example, the model essay in this unit, "The Trouble with Readers," explains the reasons for breakdowns in written communication. (Actually, the "cause" isn't readers at all—it's writers.) Or a writer may analyze the *effects* of something. In his funny and sad essay "The Telephone," Anwar Accawi describes the effects of the arrival of the first telephone in his small village in Lebanon. Sometimes, a writer explores both causes and effects, which is often a longer, more complex process. Brent Staples's "Just Walk On By" looks at the causes of a particular kind of racism and movingly charts its effects on the author.

WHY DO WE USE CAUSAL ANALYSIS?

Causal analysis answers the lead-in question *what*. Our natural human curiosity leads us to ask, "What made this happen?" and "What were the results?" We look for causes and examine effects in an attempt to make sense of the flow of events around us.

Causal analysis can be used to explain complicated connections between ideas. Often, complex historical, political, or scientific phenomena are best understood by looking at their causes. For example, in "The Evolution of Evolution," Helena Cronin makes the difficult concept of Darwinian evolution accessible to readers by asking simple questions about the causes of sexual attraction and our craving for fast food.

Causal analysis is also used to get readers to think about new ideas and to argue the merits of a particular point of view. For instance, in "Saving the Songs of Innocence," John Dixon refers to the devastating effects that humans have had on the environment to support his argument that we must respect the natural world.

HOW DO WE WRITE CAUSAL ANALYSIS?

Causal analysis is a challenging pattern of EXPOSITION. It is not easy to write because the thinking behind it must be rigorously logical. During the research and preparation stage, take the time to sort out your ideas before you begin to write. Here are six guidelines for writing a good causal analysis:

1. Be objective in your research. Don't oversimplify. Recognize that an event can be triggered by a number of causes.

2. Don't mistake coincidence for cause. The fact that one event happened before another does not mean the first event caused the second.

3. Analyze complex ideas carefully in order to sort out the *remote* (more distant, not immediately apparent) causes or effects and the *immediate* (direct, readily apparent) causes or effects.

4. Choose your focus and scope with care. In a short essay, you may have to focus on several immediate reasons, while omitting more remote or complicated causes.

5. Write a clear thesis statement. Usually, it will contain a preview of the causes or effects you intend to explain as KEY IDEAS.

6. Support your causal analysis with sufficient, interesting, and well-chosen evidence (e.g., statistical data, examples, facts, definitions where required, and "expert witness" quotations). This supporting material should make the logic of your analysis clear to the reader.

The model essay that follows is a causal analysis of some of the causes of miscommunication between writers and readers.

The Trouble with Readers

Introduction
(a set of
questions)

Thesis
statement

First cause
(developed by
definition and
examples)

Second cause
(developed by
examples)

Have you ever wondered why a letter you spent a long time composing was misunderstood by the recipient? Or why a report you submitted after careful research didn't have the impact you intended? Written language is vulnerable to misinterpretation, and the trouble with readers is that they read what you write, not what you mean. Clarity gives way to confusion if the writer fails to pay attention to the ambiguity of words, the mechanics of writing, or the organization of ideas.

English is notorious for its ambiguity—many English words have more than one meaning. The word *fan,* for instance, means a cooling device, an avid sports enthusiast, and a bird's tail. A *bank* may be a place to deposit money, the edge of a river, or the side-to-side slope of a racetrack. In addition to their dictionary meanings, words are subject to personal interpretation, and the more abstract the word, the more personal the interpretation becomes. Most readers can agree on what *cat* means but have different emotional reactions to words such as *abortion* or *euthanasia*, whose meanings resonate more deeply than their dictionary definitions imply. Even *cat* can stir feelings if used in one of its many slang senses or if the reader is allergic to cats.

If a writer has a shaky grasp of the mechanics of writing and cannot spell, punctuate, or construct grammatical sentences, clarity will be further eroded. Correctness goes beyond avoiding such obvious errors as "We could of done better." Even a single punctuation mark can dramatically alter meaning. Leave out the apostrophe in "The instructor called the students' names," and your reader will assume you have a provocateur, not a professor, in the classroom. Sometimes misunderstanding results from faulty word order: "Under the proposed plan, the elderly who now receive free prescription drugs will be abolished." Few readers will make the mistake of thinking that the writer of this sentence intended its dire implications, but most readers will smile. Of all the possible misunderstandings between writer and reader, perhaps the most painful is being laughed at when you didn't intend to be funny.

Third cause
(developed by
division and
examples)

Finally, there is the matter of content: what to include and in what order. You need to include enough detail to give your reader the complete picture—in other words, all the information he or she requires. But different readers require different amounts of information. For example, if you are a computer programmer writing

Note
transition
words finally,
For example,
Alternatively

a report, you will not waste your supervisor's time by defining terms such as OOP, MIME, or URL. Alternatively, if your report is destined for someone who has little familiarity with computers, you will need to explain these terms and probably many more. You don't want to include anything irrelevant or redundant. If you do, you will create confusion, boredom, frustration—or all three. The order in which you present your points makes a difference, too. In writing, as in life, humans need to perceive a sequence to events. When no order is apparent, readers become confused. If you're describing a process, for example, you will probably arrange your points chronologically. But if you are writing to convince, you will want to build to a strong conclusion and will likely arrange your points in climactic order. Never underestimate the importance of logic to writing!

Conclusion
(highlights
significance of
topic; refers
back to
introduction)

Communicating clearly is not easy, and writing is the most demanding of all forms of communication. As a writer, you must pay close attention to words, mechanics, and organization. If you ignore even one of these obligations, your message may well be misinterpreted—because your readers will read what you wrote, not what you meant.

Bound to Bicker°

LAURENCE STEINBERG

An internationally recognized expert on adolescent psychological development, Dr. Laurence Steinberg (b. 1952) is a professor of child and family studies at Temple University. He is the author or co-author of numerous articles and fifteen books, including *Adolescence* (1985), *When Teenagers Work* (1986), and *You and Your Adolescent* (1991). His most recent book,

Beyond the Classroom (1996), has been acclaimed as one of the most important books on education written during the last decade.

It's like being bitten to death by ducks. That's how one mother described her constant squabbles with her eleven-year-old daughter. And she's hardly alone in the experience. The arguments almost always involve mundane° matters—taking out the garbage, coming home on time, cleaning up the bedroom. But despite its banality°, this relentless bickering takes its toll on the average parent's mental health. Studies indicate that parents of adolescents—particularly mothers—report lower levels of life satisfaction, less marital happiness, and more general distress than parents of younger children. Is this continual arguing necessary? 1

For the past two years, my students and I have been examining the day-to-day relationships of parents and young teenagers to learn how and why family ties change during the transition from childhood into adolescence. Repeatedly, I am struck by the fact that, despite considerable love between most teens and their parents, they can't help sparring. Even in the closest of families, parents and teenagers squabble and bicker surprisingly often—so often, in fact, that we hear impassioned recountings of these arguments in virtually every discussion we have with parents or teenagers. One of the most frequently heard phrases on our interview tapes is, "We usually get along but . . ." 2

As psychologist Anne Petersen notes, the subject of parent–adolescent conflict has generated considerable controversy among researchers and clinicians. Until about twenty years ago, our views of such conflict were shaped by psychoanalytic clinicians and theorists, who argued that spite and revenge, passive aggressiveness and rebelliousness toward parents are all normal, even healthy, aspects of adolescence. But studies conducted during the 1970s on samples of average teenagers and their parents (rather than those who spent Wednesday afternoons on analysts' couches) challenged the view that family storm and stress was inevitable or pervasive°. These surveys consistently showed that three-fourths of all teenagers and parents, here and abroad, feel quite close to each other and report getting along very well. Family relations appeared far more pacific° than professionals and the public had believed. 3

Had clinicians overstated the case for widespread storm and stress, or were social scientists simply off the mark? The answer, just now beginning to emerge, seems to be somewhere between the two extremes. 4

The bad news for parents is that conflict, in the form of nagging, squabbling, and bickering, is more common during adolescence 5 than during any other period of development, except, perhaps, the "terrible twos." But the good news is that arguments between parents and teenagers rarely undo close emotional bonds or lead adolescents and their parents to reject one another. And, although most families with adolescents go through a period of heightened tension, the phase is usually temporary, typically ending by age fifteen or sixteen.

6 My own studies point to early adolescence—the years from ten to thirteen—as a period of special strain between parents and children. But more intriguing, perhaps, is that these studies reveal that puberty plays a central role in triggering parent–adolescent conflict. Specifically, as youngsters develop toward physical maturity, bickering and squabbling with parents increase. If puberty comes early, so does the arguing and bickering; if it is late, the period of heightened tension is delayed. Although many other aspects of adolescent behavior reflect the intertwined influences of biological and social factors, this aspect seems to be directly connected to the biological event of puberty; something about normal physical maturation sets off parent–adolescent fighting. It's no surprise that they argue about overflowing trash cans, trails of dirty laundry, and blaring stereos. But why should teenagers going through puberty fight with their parents more often than youngsters of the same age whose physical development is slower? More to the point: if puberty is inevitable, does this mean that parent–child conflict is, too?

7 It often helps to look closely at our evolutionary relatives when we are puzzled by aspects of human behavior, especially when the puzzle includes biological pieces. We are only now beginning to understand how family relations among monkeys and apes are transformed in adolescence, but one fact is clear: it is common, at puberty, for primates living in the wild to leave their "natal group," the group into which they were born. Among chimpanzees, who are our close biological relatives, but whose family structure differs greatly from ours, emigration is restricted to adolescent females. Shortly after puberty, the adolescent voluntarily leaves her natal group and travels on her own—often a rather treacherous journey—to find another community in which to mate.

8 In species whose family organization is more analogous to ours, such as gibbons°, who live in small, monogamous family groups, both adolescent males and females emigrate. And if they don't leave voluntarily soon after puberty begins, they are thrown out. In both cases, adolescent emigration helps to increase reproductive fitness, since it minimizes inbreeding and increases genetic diversity.

Studies of monkeys and apes living in captivity show just what   9
happens when such adolescent emigration is impeded°. For many
nonhuman primates, the consequences can be dire°: among many
species of monkeys, pubertal development is inhibited° so long as
youngsters remain in their natal group. Recent studies of monogamous or polyandrous° monkeys, such as tamarins and marmosets,
have shown that the sexual development of young females is inhibited specifically by their mothers' presence. When the mother is
removed, so is her inhibitory effect, and the daughter's maturation
can begin in a matter of a few days.

Taken together, these studies suggest that it is evolutionarily   10
adaptive° of most offspring to leave their family early in adolescence. The pressure on adolescents to leave their parents is most
severe among primates such as gibbons, whose evolution occurred
within the context of small family groups, because opportunities for
mating within the natal group are limited and such mating may
threaten the species' gene pool. It should come as no surprise,
therefore, to find social and biological mechanisms that encourage
the departure of adolescent primates—including, I think, humans—
from the family group around puberty.

One such mechanism is conflict, which, if intense enough,   11
drives the adolescent away. Squabbling between teenagers and
their parents today may be a vestige° of our evolutionary past,
when prolonged proximity° between parent and offspring threatened the species' genetic integrity°.

According to psychologist Raymond Montemayor of Ohio State   12
University, who studies the relationships of teenagers and their parents, accounts of conflict between adolescents and their elders date
back virtually as far as recorded history. But our predecessors
enjoyed an important advantage over today's parents: adolescents
rarely lived at home much beyond puberty. Prior to industrialization in this country, high-school-aged youngsters often lived in a
state of semiautonomy° in which they were allowed to work and
earn money but lived under the authority of adults other than their
parents. Indeed, as historian Michael Katz of the University of
Pennsylvania notes, many adolescents actually were "placed out"
at puberty—sent to live away from their parent's household—a
practice that strikingly resembles the forced emigration seen among
our primate relatives living in the wild.

Most historians of adolescence have interpreted the practice of   13
placing out in terms of its implications for youngsters' educational
and vocational development. But did adolescents have to leave
home to learn their trade? And is it just coincidental that this practice

was synchronized with puberty? Historian Alan Macfarlane notes that placing out may have developed to provide a "mechanism for separating the generations at a time when there might otherwise have been considerable difficulty" in the family.

14   Dozens of nonindustrialized societies continue to send adolescents away at puberty. Separating children from their parents, known as "extrusion," has a great deal in common with the behavior of many nonhuman primates. In societies that practice extrusion, youngsters in late childhood are expected to begin sleeping in households other than their parents'. They may see their parents during the day but are required to spend the night with friends of the family, with relatives, or in a separate residence reserved for preadolescents. Even in traditional societies that do not practice extrusion formally, the rite of passage at puberty nevertheless includes rituals symbolizing the separation of the young person from his or her family. The widespread existence of these rituals suggests that adolescent emigration from the family at puberty may have been common in many human societies at some earlier time.

15   Conflict between parents and teenagers is not limited to [North American] family life. . . . Generally, parent–child conflict is thought to exist at about the same rate in virtually all highly developed, industrialized Western societies. The sociological explanation for such intergenerational tension in modern society is that the rapid social change accompanying industrialization creates irreconcilable and conflict-provoking differences in parents' and children's values and attitudes. But modernization may well have increased the degree and pervasiveness of conflict between young people and their parents for other reasons.

16   Industrialization hastened the onset of puberty, due to improvements in health, sanitation, and nutrition. (Youngsters in the United States go through puberty about four years earlier today than their counterparts did a hundred years ago.) Industrialization also has brought extended schooling, which has prolonged youngsters' economic dependence on their parents and delayed their entrance into full-time work roles. The net result has been a dramatic increase over the past century in the amount of time that physically mature youngsters and their parents must live in close contact.

17   A century ago, the adolescent's departure from home coincided with physical maturation. Today, sexually mature adolescents may spend seven or eight years in the company of their parents. Put a different way, industrialization has impeded the emigration of physically mature adolescents from their family of origin—the prescription for parent–adolescent conflict.

Puberty, of course, is just one of many factors that can exacer-   18
bate° the level of tension in an adolescent's household. Inconsistent
parenting, blocked communication channels, and extremes of strict-
ness or permissiveness can all make a strained situation worse than
it need be. An adolescent's family should seek professional help
whenever fighting and arguing become pervasive or violent or
when they disrupt family functioning, no matter what the adolescent's stage of physical development.

Given our evolutionary history, however, and the increasingly   19
prolonged dependence of adolescents on their parents, some degree
of conflict during early adolescence is probably inevitable, even
within families that had been close before puberty began. Telling
parents that fighting over taking out the garbage is related to the
reproductive fitness of the species provides little solace°—and
doesn't help get the garbage out of the house, either. But parents
need to recognize that quarreling with a teenager over mundane
matters may be a normal—if, thankfully, temporary—part of family
life during adolescence. Such squabbling is an atavism° that
ensures that adolescents grow up. If teenagers didn't argue with
their parents, they might never leave at all.

Words and Meanings

Paragraph

bicker	quarrel, argue	
mundane	ordinary, everyday (see also paragraph 19)	1
banality	commonplaceness	
pervasive	widespread (see also paragraphs 15 and 18)	3
pacific	peaceful	
gibbons	small, long-armed apes	8
impeded	hindered, obstructed (see also paragraph 17)	9
dire	extremely serious	
inhibited	delayed	
polyandrous	relationship involving one female and several males	
evolutionarily adaptive	good for the species as a whole	10
vestige	a remnant, something left over	11
proximity	closeness	
genetic integrity	the health of the gene pool, which would be contaminated by incest (here, the mating of parent and offspring)	
semiautonomy	partial independence	12

18	exacerbate	increase, aggravate
19	solace	comfort
	atavism	behaviour that comes from our ancestors

Structure and Strategy

1. What strategy does Steinberg use in his INTRODUCTION? What makes it effective?
2. What two main functions are served by paragraph 5?
3. What ANALOGY does the author develop in paragraphs 7 to 9?
4. What kind of support for the THESIS is presented in paragraph 12?
5. What definition is developed in paragraph 14?
6. How does the CONCLUSION (paragraphs 18 and 19) both summarize the KEY IDEAS of the essay as well as offer practical advice?

Content and Purpose

1. Is Steinberg's title a PUN? What meaning(s) do you think he intended?
2. Paragraphs 3 and 4 present three different theories about the sources of adolescent–parent conflict. What are they?
3. According to Steinberg's studies, what biological phenomenon plays a central role in intergenerational conflict?
4. Paragraph 9 focuses on what "unnatural" group? What happens to the young within this group?
5. Why is it "evolutionarily adaptive" (paragraph 10) for adolescents to leave their families at an early age?
6. How do the practices of "extrusion" and rites of passage reduce or even eliminate adolescent–parent conflict in traditional societies?
7. What effects of "industrialization" have increased the potential for adolescent–parent conflict (paragraph 16)?
8. How do you feel about the traditional practice of extrusion (see paragraph 14)? Do you think it could be effectively practised in Canada?

Suggestions for Writing

1. Do you remember bickering with your family during adolescence? Write an essay that explains the causes or the effects of this conflict on you and your family.

2. Does your culture practise a "rite of passage," a ceremony or ritual that marks the transition from childhood to adulthood? If so, describe its effects on the person who goes through this initiation. If not, do you think such a ritual would be beneficial to those in your cultural community? Write an essay outlining the need for this sort of ritual and describing a ceremony that would appropriately mark the transition from childhood to adulthood.

Just Walk On By: A Black Man Ponders His Power to Alter Public Space

BRENT STAPLES

Brent Staples (b. 1951) holds a Ph.D. in psychology from the University of Chicago. An editorial writer for *The New York Times*, he wrote the award-winning memoir *Parallel Time: Growing Up in Black and White* (1994). His current project is a history of black-owned newspapers during the nineteenth and early twentieth centuries.

My first victim was a woman—white, well dressed, probably in her early twenties. I came upon her late one evening on a deserted street in Hyde Park, a relatively affluent neighborhood in an otherwise mean, impoverished section of Chicago. As I swung onto the avenue behind her, there seemed to be a discreet, uninflammatory distance between us. Not so. She cast back a worried glance. To her, the youngish black man—a broad six feet two inches with a beard and billowing hair, both hands shoved into the pockets of a bulky military jacket—seemed menacingly close. After a few more quick glimpses, she picked up her pace and was soon running in earnest. Within seconds she disappeared into a cross street.   1

That was more than a decade ago. I was 22 years old, a graduate student newly arrived at the University of Chicago. It was in the echo of that terrified woman's footfalls that I first began to know the unwieldy inheritance I'd come into—the ability to alter public space in ugly ways. It was clear that she thought herself the   2 quarry of a mugger, a rapist, or worse. Suffering a bout of insomnia, however, I was stalking sleep, not defenseless wayfarers. As a softy who is scarcely able to take a knife to a raw chicken—let alone hold it to a person's throat—I was surprised, embarrassed, and dismayed all at once. Her flight made me feel like an accomplice in tyranny. It also made it clear that I was indistinguishable from the muggers who occasionally seeped into the area from the surrounding ghetto. That first encounter, and those that followed, signified that a vast, unnerving gulf lay between nighttime pedestrians—particularly women—and me. And I soon gathered that being perceived as dangerous is a hazard in itself. I only needed to turn a corner into a dicey situation, or crowd some frightened, armed person in a foyer somewhere, or make an errant° move after being pulled over by a policeman. Where fear and weapons meet—and they often do in urban America—there is always the possibility of death.

3   In that first year, my first away from my hometown, I was to become thoroughly familiar with the language of fear. At dark, shadowy intersections in Chicago, I could cross in front of a car stopped at a traffic light and elicit° the *thunk, thunk, thunk, thunk* of the driver—black, white, male, or female—hammering down the door locks. On less traveled streets after dark, I grew accustomed to but never comfortable with people who crossed to the other side of the street rather than pass me. Then there were the standard unpleasantries with police, doormen, bouncers, cab drivers, and others whose business it is to screen out troublesome individuals *before* there is any nastiness.

4   I moved to New York nearly two years ago and I have remained an avid° night walker. In central Manhattan, the near-constant crowd cover minimizes tense one-on-one street encounters. Elsewhere—visiting friends in SoHo, where sidewalks are narrow and tightly spaced buildings shut out the sky—things can get very taut indeed.

5   Black men have a firm place in New York mugging literature. Norman Podhoretz in his famed (or infamous) . . . essay, "My Negro Problem—And Ours," recalls growing up in terror of black males; they "were tougher than we were, more ruthless," he writes—and as an adult on the Upper West Side of Manhattan, he continues, he cannot constrain his nervousness when he meets black men on certain streets. Similarly, a decade later, the essayist and novelist Edward Hoagland extols° a New York where once "Negro bitterness bore down mainly on other Negroes." Where

some see mere panhandlers, Hoagland sees "a mugger who is clearly screwing up his nerve to do more than just *ask* for money." But Hoagland has "the New Yorker's quick-hunch posture for broken-field maneuvering," and the bad guy swerves away.

I often witness that "hunch posture," from women after dark on the warrenlike° streets of Brooklyn where I live. They seem to set their faces on neutral and, with their purse straps strung across their chests bandolier style, they forge ahead as though bracing themselves against being tackled. I understand, of course, that the danger they perceive is not a hallucination. Women are particularly vulnerable to street violence, and young black males are drastically overrepresented among the perpetrators° of that violence. Yet these truths are no solace against the kind of alienation that comes of being ever the suspect, against being set apart, a fearsome entity with whom pedestrians avoid making eye contact.

It is not altogether clear to me how I reached the ripe old age of 22 without being conscious of the lethality° nighttime pedestrians attributed to me. Perhaps it was because in Chester, Pennsylvania, the small, angry industrial town where I came of age in the 1960s, I was scarcely noticeable against a backdrop of gang warfare, street knifings, and murders. I grew up one of the good boys, had perhaps a half-dozen fist fights. In retrospect°, my shyness of combat has clear sources.

Many things go into the making of a young thug. One of those things is the consummation° of the male romance with the power to intimidate. An infant discovers that random flailings send the baby bottle flying out of the crib and crashing to the floor. Delighted, the joyful babe repeats those motions again and again, seeking to duplicate the feat. Just so, I recall the points at which some of my boyhood friends were finally seduced by the perception of themselves as tough guys. When a mark cowered and surrendered his money without resistance, myth and reality merged—and paid off. It is, after all, only manly to embrace the power to frighten and intimidate. We, as men, are not supposed to give an inch of our lane on the highway; we are to seize the fighter's edge in work and in play and even in love; we are to be valiant in the face of hostile forces.

Unfortunately, poor and powerless young men seem to take all this nonsense literally. As a boy, I saw countless tough guys locked away; I have since buried several, too. They were babies, really—a teenage cousin, a brother of 22, a childhood friend in his mid-twenties—all gone down in episodes of bravado played out in the streets. I came to doubt the virtues of intimidation early on. I chose, perhaps even unconsciously, to remain a shadow—timid, but a survivor.

10   The fearsomeness mistakenly attributed to me in public places often has a perilous flavor. The most frightening of these confusions occurred in the late 1970s and early 1980s when I worked as a journalist in Chicago. One day, rushing into the office of a magazine I was writing for with a deadline story in hand, I was mistaken for a burglar. The office manager called security and, with an ad hoc posse°, pursued me through the labyrinthine halls, nearly to my editor's door. I had no way of proving who I was. I could only move briskly toward the company of someone who knew me.

11   Another time I was on assignment for a local paper and killing time before an interview. I entered a jewelry store on the city's affluent Near North Side. The proprietor excused herself and returned with an enormous red Doberman pinscher straining at the end of a leash. She stood, the dog extended toward me, silent to my questions, her eyes bulging nearly out of her head. I took a cursory° look around, nodded, and bade her good night. Relatively speaking, however, I never fared as badly as another black male journalist. He went to nearby Waukegan, Illinois, a couple of summers ago to work on a story about a murderer who was born there. Mistaking the reporter for the killer, police hauled him from his car at gunpoint and but for his press credentials would probably have tried to book him. Such episodes are not uncommon. Black men trade tales like this all the time.

12   In "My Negro Problem—And Ours," Podhoretz writes that the hatred he feels for blacks makes itself known to him through a variety of avenues—one being his discomfort with that "special brand of paranoid touchiness" to which he says blacks are prone. No doubt he is speaking here of black men. In time, I learned to smother the rage I felt at so often being taken for a criminal. Not to do so would surely have led to madness—via that special "paranoid touchiness" that so annoyed Podhoretz at the time he wrote the essay.

13   I began to take precautions to make myself less threatening. I move about with care, particularly late in the evening. I give a wide berth to nervous people on subway platforms during the wee hours, particularly when I have exchanged business clothes for jeans. If I happen to be entering a building behind some people who appear skittish°, I may walk by, letting them clear the lobby before I return, so as not to seem to be following them. I have been calm and extremely congenial° on those rare occasions when I've been pulled over by the police.

14   And on late-evening constitutionals° along streets less traveled by, I employ what has proved to be an excellent tension-reducing

measure: I whistle melodies from Beethoven and Vivaldi and the more popular classical composers. Even steely New Yorkers hunching toward nighttime destinations seem to relax, and occasionally they even join in the tune. Virtually everybody seems to sense that a mugger wouldn't be warbling bright, sunny selections from Vivaldi's *Four Seasons*. It is my equivalent of the cowbell that hikers wear when they know they are in bear country.

Words and Meanings

		Paragraph
errant	unexpected	2
elicit	cause to happen	3
avid	keen, enthusiastic	4
extols	praises highly	5
warrenlike	crowded, narrow, dark—like a rabbit warren	6
perpetrators	those who perform or commit a criminal action	
lethality	deadliness	7
retrospect	hindsight, thinking about the past	
consummation	completion, fulfillment	8
ad hoc posse	group of people quickly assembled to catch a criminal	10
cursory	hasty, superficial	11
skittish	nervous	13
congenial	pleasant, friendly	
constitutionals	walks	14

Structure and Strategy

1. What strategy does Staples use in his INTRODUCTION? Identify the details that help the reader picture the scene described. Explain the IRONY in the first sentence.
2. What is the function of the paragraphs that include quotations from writers Norman Podhoretz and Edward Hoagland (paragraphs 5 and 12)? How would the impact of the essay differ if Staples had not included these supporting examples of racist thinking?
3. How is the TOPIC SENTENCE of paragraph 10 developed?
4. What is the TONE of this essay?

Content and Purpose

1. This essay reflects on the effects that the author, a black man, has on people in the street, merely by his presence. It also deals with the effects that this phenomenon has on him. What are they?

2. Explain what Staples means by his "unwieldy inheritance" and his feeling like "an accomplice in tyranny" (paragraph 2).
3. What does Staples acknowledge in paragraph 6? How does this acknowledgment prepare the reader for the next point he makes about street violence (in paragraphs 7 to 9)?
4. What measures does the author take to minimize his effects on other pedestrians as he walks at night?
5. In paragraph 7, the author observes that his own "shyness of combat has clear sources." What causes does he identify for his dislike of violence?
6. Paragraph 8 deals with the causes of another social tragedy, "the making of a young thug." What are these causes, as Staples sees them? How has this sad reality affected his own life?

Suggestions for Writing

1. It is often suggested that our society is much more violent than it was a few decades ago. Others argue that we are simply more fearful, and that the incidence of violent crimes has actually decreased. Write an essay that explores the causes either for the increase or for the perception of an increase in violence.
2. Write an essay that explores the causes or effects of being an "outsider," someone who is seen not to "belong." Support your thesis from personal experience. How did your experience(s) affect you?

The Telephone

ANWAR F. ACCAWI

Anwar F. Accawi was born in the middle of World War II in a small village in the hills of south Lebanon. He moved to the United States in 1965 when he won a scholarship. In 1985, he started writing stories for his children about his childhood home. His most recent book, *The Boy from the Tower of the Moon* (1999), is a personal narrative of his boyhood in Lebanon.

1   When I was growing up in Magdaluna, a small Lebanese village in the terraced, rocky mountains east of Sidon, time didn't mean much to anybody, except maybe to those who were dying, or those waiting to appear in court because

they had tampered with the boundary markers on their land. In those days, there was no real need for a calendar or a watch to keep track of the hours, days, months, and years. We knew what to do and when to do it, just as the Iraqi geese knew when to fly north, driven by the hot wind that blew in from the desert, and the ewes knew when to give birth to wet lambs that stood on long, shaky legs in the chilly March wind and baaed hesitantly, because they were small and cold and did not know where they were or what to do now that they were here. The only timepiece we had need of then was the sun. It rose and set, and the seasons rolled by, and we sowed seed and harvested and ate and played and married our cousins and had babies who got whooping cough and chickenpox—and those children who survived grew up and married *their* cousins and had babies who got whooping cough and chickenpox. We lived and loved and toiled and died without ever needing to know what year it was, or even the time of day.

It wasn't that we had no system for keeping track of time and of the important events in our lives. But ours was a natural—or, rather, a divine—calendar, because it was framed by acts of God. Allah himself set down the milestones with earthquakes and droughts and floods and locusts and pestilences°. Simple as our calendar was, it worked just fine for us. 2

Take, for example, the birth date of Teta Im Khalil, the oldest woman in Magdaluna and all the surrounding villages. When I first met her, we had just returned home from Syria at the end of the Big War° and were living with Grandma Mariam. Im Khalil came by to welcome my father home and to take a long, myopic° look at his foreign-born wife, my mother. Im Khalil was so old that the skin of her cheeks looked like my father's grimy tobacco pouch, and when I kissed her (because Grandma insisted that I show her old friend affection), it was like kissing a soft suede glove that had been soaked with sweat and then left in a dark closet for a season. Im Khalil's face got me to wondering how old one had to be to look and taste the way she did. So, as soon as she had hobbled off on her cane, I asked Grandma, "How old is Teta Im Khalil?" 3

Grandma had to think for a moment; then she said, "I've been told that Teta was born shortly after the big snow that caused the roof on the mayor's house to cave in." 4

"And when was that?" I asked. 5

"Oh, about the time we had the big earthquake that cracked the wall in the east room." 6

Well, that was enough for me. You couldn't be more accurate than that, now, could you? Satisfied with her answer, I went back to 7 playing with a ball made from an old sock stuffed with other, much older socks.

8   And that's the way it was in our little village for as far back as anybody could remember: people were born so many years before or after an earthquake or a flood; they got married or died so many years before or after a long drought or a big snow or some other disaster. One of the most unusual of these dates was when Antoinette the seamstress and Saeed the barber (and tooth puller) got married. That was the year of the whirlwind during which fish and oranges fell from the sky. Incredible as it may sound, the story of the fish and oranges was true, because men—respectable men, like Abu George the blacksmith and Abu Asaad the mule skinner, men who would not lie even to save their own souls—told and retold that story until it was incorporated° into Magdaluna's calendar, just like the year of the black moon and the year of the locusts before it. My father, too, confirmed the story for me. He told me that he had been a small boy himself when it rained fish and oranges from heaven. He'd gotten up one morning after a stormy night and walked out into the yard to find fish as long as his forearm still flopping here and there among the wet navel oranges.

9   The year of the fish-bearing twister, however, was not the last remarkable year. Many others followed in which strange and wonderful things happened: milestones added by the hand of Allah to Magdaluna's calendar. There was, for instance, the year of the drought, when the heavens were shut for months and the spring from which the entire village got its drinking water slowed to a trickle. The spring was about a mile from the village, in a ravine that opened at one end into a small, flat clearing covered with fine gray dust and hard, marble-sized goat droppings, because every afternoon the goatherds brought their flocks there to water them. In the year of the drought, that little clearing was always packed full of noisy kids with big brown eyes and sticky hands, and their mothers—sinewy°, overworked young women with protruding collarbones and cracked, callused brown heels. The children ran around playing tag or hide-and-seek while the women talked, shooed flies, and awaited their turns to fill up their jars with drinking water to bring home to their napping men and wet babies. There were days when we had to wait from sunup until late afternoon just to fill a small clay jar with precious, cool water.

10   Sometimes, amid the long wait and the heat and the flies and the smell of goat dung, tempers flared, and the younger women, anxious about their babies, argued over whose turn it was to fill up her jar. And sometimes the arguments escalated into full-blown, knockdown-dragout fights; the women would grab each other by

the hair and curse and scream and spit and call each other names that made my ears tingle. We little brown boys who went with our mothers to fetch water loved these fights, because we got to see the women's legs and their colored panties as they grappled and rolled around in the dust. Once in a while, we got lucky and saw much more, because some of the women wore nothing at all under their long dresses. God, how I used to look forward to those fights. I remember the rush, the excitement, the sun dancing on the dust clouds as a dress ripped and a young white breast was revealed, then quickly hidden. In my calendar, that year of drought will always be one of the best years of my childhood, because it was then, in a dusty clearing by a trickling mountain spring, I got my first glimpses of the wonders, the mysteries, and the promises hidden beneath the folds of a woman's dress. Fish and oranges from heaven . . . you can get over that.

But, in another way, the year of the drought was also one of the worst of my life, because that was the year that Abu Raja, the retired cook who used to entertain us kids by cracking walnuts on his forehead, decided it was time Magdaluna got its own telephone. Every civilized village needed a telephone, he said, and Magdaluna was not going to get anywhere until it had one. A telephone would link us with the outside world. At the time, I was too young to understand the debate, but a few men—like Shukri, the retired Turkish-army drill sergeant, and Abu Hanna the vineyard keeper— did all they could to talk Abu Raja out of having a telephone brought to the village. But they were outshouted and ignored and finally shunned by the other villagers for resisting progress and trying to keep a good thing from coming to Magdaluna. 11

One warm day in early fall, many of the villagers were out in their fields repairing walls or gathering wood for the winter when the shout went out that the telephone-company truck had arrived at Abu Raja's *dikkun*, or country store. There were no roads in those days, only footpaths and dry streambeds, so it took the telephone-company truck almost a day to work its way up the rocky terrain from Sidon—about the same time it took to walk. When the truck came into view, Abu George, who had a huge voice, and, before the telephone, was Magdaluna's only long-distance communication system, bellowed the news from his front porch. Everybody dropped what they were doing and ran to Abu Raja's house to see what was happening. Some of the more dignified villagers, however, like Abu Habeeb and Abu Nazim, who had been to big cities like Beirut and Damascus and had seen things like telephones and telegraphs, did not run the way the rest did; they walked with their canes hanging from the crooks of their arms, as if on a Sunday afternoon stroll. 12

13   It did not take long for the whole village to assemble at Abu
Raja's *dikkan*. Some of the rich villagers, like the widow Farha and the
gendarme° Abu Nadeem, walked right into the store and stood at the
elbows of the two important-looking men from the telephone company, who proceeded with utmost gravity, like priests at Communion, to wire up the telephone. The poorer villagers stood outside
and listened carefully to the details relayed to them by the not-so-
poor people who stood in the doorway and could see inside.

14   "The bald man is cutting the blue wire," someone said.

15   "He is sticking the wire into the hole in the bottom of the black
box," someone else added.

16   "The telephone man with the mustache is connecting two
pieces of wire. Now he is twisting the ends together," a third voice
chimed in.

17   Because I was small and unaware that I should have stood outside with the other poor folk to give the rich people inside more
room (they seemed to need more of it than poor people did), I wrig-
gled my way through the dense forest of legs to get a first-hand
look at the action. I felt like the barefoot Moses, sandals in hand,
staring at the burning bush on Mount Sinai. Breathless, I watched
as the men in blue, their shirt pockets adorned with fancy lettering
in a foreign language, put together a black machine that supposedly would make it possible to talk with uncles, aunts, and cousins
who lived more than two days' ride away.

18   It was shortly after sunset when the man with the mustache
announced that the telephone was ready to use. He explained that
all Abu Raja had to do was lift the receiver, turn the crank on the
black box a few times, and wait for an operator to take his call. Abu
Raja, who had once lived and worked in Sidon, was impatient with
the telephone man for assuming that he was ignorant. He grabbed
the receiver and turned the crank forcefully, as if trying to start a
Model T Ford. Everybody was impressed that he knew what to do.
He even called the operator by her first name: "Centralist." Within
moments, Abu Raja was talking with his brother, a concierge° in
Beirut. He didn't even have to raise his voice or shout to be heard.

19   If I hadn't seen it with my own two eyes and heard it with my
own two ears, I would not have believed it—and my friend Kameel
didn't. He was away that day watching his father's goats, and
when he came back to the village that evening, his cousin Habeeb
and I told him about the telephone and how Abu Raja had used it
to speak with his brother in Beirut. After he heard our report,
Kameel made the sign of the cross, kissed his thumbnail, and
warned us that lying was a bad sin and would surely land us in
purgatory. Kameel believed in Jesus and Mary, and wanted to be a

priest when he grew up. He always crossed himself when Habeeb, who was irreverent, and I, who was Presbyterian, were around, even when we were not bearing bad news.

And the telephone, as it turned out, was bad news. With its coming, the face of the village began to change. One of the first effects was the shifting of the village's center. Before the telephone's arrival, the men of the village used to gather regularly at the house of Im Kaleem, a short, middle-aged widow with jet-black hair and a raspy voice that could be heard all over the village, even when she was only whispering. She was a devout Catholic and also the village *shlikki*—whore. The men met at her house to argue about politics and drink coffee and play cards or backgammon. Im Kaleem was not a true prostitute, however, because she did not charge for her services—not even for the coffee and tea (and, occasionally, the strong liquor called arrack) that she served the men. She did not need the money; her son, who was overseas in Africa, sent her money regularly. (I knew this because my father used to read her son's letters to her and take down her replies, as Im Kaleem could not read and write.) Im Kaleem was no slut either—unlike some women in the village—because she loved all the men she entertained, and they loved her, every one of them. In a way, she was married to all the men in the village. Everybody knew it—the wives knew it; the itinerant° Catholic priest knew it; the Presbyterian minister knew it—but nobody objected. Actually, I suspect the women (my mother included) did not mind their husbands' visits to Im Kaleem. Oh, they wrung their hands and complained to one another about their men's unfaithfulness, but secretly they were relieved, because Im Kaleem took some of the pressure off them and kept the men out of their hair while they attended to their endless chores. Im Kaleem was also a kind of confessor and troubleshooter, talking sense to those men who were having family problems, especially the younger ones.

Before the telephone came to Magdaluna, Im Kaleem's house was bustling at just about any time of day, especially at night, when its windows were brightly lit with three large oil lamps, and the loud voices of the men talking, laughing, and arguing could be heard in the street below—a reassuring, homey sound. Her house was an island of comfort, an oasis for the weary village men, exhausted from having so little to do.

But it wasn't long before many of those men—the younger ones especially—started spending more of their days and evenings at Abu Raja's *dikkan*. There, they would eat and drink and talk and play checkers and backgammon, and then lean their chairs back against the wall—the signal that they were ready to

20

21

22

toss back and forth, like a ball, the latest rumors going around the village. And they were always looking up from their games and drinks and talk to glance at the phone in the corner, as if expecting it to ring any minute and bring news that would change their lives and deliver them from their aimless existence. In the meantime, they smoked cheap, hand-rolled cigarettes, dug dirt out from under their fingernails with big pocketknives, and drank lukewarm sodas that they called Kacula, Seffen-Ub, and Bebsi. Sometimes, especially when it was hot, the days dragged on so slowly that the men turned on Abu Saeed, a confirmed bachelor who practically lived in Abu Raja's *dikkan*, and teased him for going around barefoot and unshaven since the Virgin had appeared to him behind the olive press.

23   The telephone was also bad news for me personally. It took away my lucrative° business—a source of much-needed income. Before the telephone came to Magdaluna, I used to hang around Im Kaleem's courtyard and play marbles with the other kids, waiting for some man to call down from a window and ask me to run to the store for cigarettes or arrack, or to deliver a message to his wife, such as what he wanted for supper. There was always something in it for me: a ten- or even a twenty-five-piaster piece. On a good day, I ran nine or ten of those errands, which assured a steady supply of marbles that I usually lost to Sami or his cousin Hani, the basket weaver's boy. But as the days went by, fewer and fewer men came to Im Kaleem's, and more and more congregated at Abu Raja's to wait by the telephone. In the evenings, no light fell from her window onto the street below, and the laughter and noise of the men trailed off and finally stopped. Only Shukri, the retired Turkish-army drill sergeant, remained faithful to Im Kaleem after all the other men had deserted her; he was still seen going into or leaving her house from time to time. Early that winter, Im Kaleem's hair suddenly turned gray, and she got sick and old. Her legs started giving her trouble, making it hard for her to walk. By spring she hardly left her house anymore.

24   At Abu Raja's *dikkan*, the calls did eventually come, as expected, and men and women started leaving the village the way a hailstorm begins: first one, then two, then bunches. The army took them. Jobs in the cities lured them. And ships and airplanes carried them to such faraway places as Australia and Brazil and New Zealand. My friend Kameel, his cousin Habeeb, and their cousins and my cousins all went away to become ditch diggers and mechanics and butcher-shop boys and deli owners who wore dirty aprons sixteen hours a day, all looking for a better life than the one they had left behind. Within a year, only the sick, the old, and the maimed were left in the

village. Magdaluna became a skeleton of its former self, desolate and forsaken, like the tombs, a place to get away from.

Finally, the telephone took my family away, too. My father got a call from an old army buddy who told him that an oil company in southern Lebanon was hiring interpreters and instructors. My father applied for a job and got it, and we moved to Sidon, where I went to a Presbyterian missionary school and graduated in 1962. Three years later, having won a scholarship, I left Lebanon for the United States. Like the others who left Magdaluna before me, I am still looking for that better life.   25

Words and Meanings

		Paragraph
pestilences	disease epidemics	2
Big War	World War II	3
myopic	near-sighted	
incorporated	merged with, became part of	8
sinewy	lean, muscular	9
gendarme	police officer	13
concierge	hotel attendant	18
itinerant	moving from place to place, not resident	20
lucrative	profitable	23

Structure and Strategy

1. Does this essay focus primarily on cause or on effect? Of what?
2. This essay is divided into two parts: paragraphs 1 to 10 and 11 to 25. Summarize the content of the two halves of the piece.
3. What IRONY is there in paragraph 11, the turning point of the essay?
4. Identify two or three ANECDOTES in the essay that make it clear that the story is being told from the POINT OF VIEW of a child.
5. Identify three descriptive details in paragraph 1 that you think are particularly effective. How do these descriptive elements help support the topic of the paragraph?
6. The ILLUSTRATION developed in paragraphs 3 to 7 contains more dialogue than any other anecdote in the essay. What point is Accawi making here, and why do you think that he uses dialogue to support it?
7. Identify two SIMILES in paragraphs 13 and 17 that are specifically religious in meaning. Are they appropriate in an account of the introduction of technology into a village? Why or why not?

8. What are "Kacula, Seffen-Ub, and Bebsi" (paragraph 22)? Is Accawi's description of the villagers' pronunciation humorous? What is his attitude toward the speakers? How do details such as these influence the TONE of the essay?

Content and Purpose

1. According to Accawi, how did the villagers of Magdaluna mark time before the coming of the telephone? How did they "keep track of the hours, days, months, and years" (paragraph 1)?
2. Identify three memorable people among the villagers that Accawi describes. What descriptive and narrative details does he provide to help you "know" each of these people? How do they come alive to you? How do you think the author feels about each of these characters?
3. Who works harder in Magdaluna, the women or the men? Support your answer with specific references to the essay.
4. The first effect of the telephone on the village community is told through the story of Im Kaleem, "the village *shlikki*" (paragraphs 20 to 22). What is this consequence, and why do you think Accawi chooses Im Kaleem's story to communicate it?
5. The effects of the telephone on two specific people are detailed in paragraph 23. Who are the people, and what happens to them?
6. In paragraph 24, we are told that the "calls did eventually come." What happens then? Where do people go? What happens to Magdaluna itself? Do you think that these effects are all due to the arrival of the telephone in the village?
7. In your own words, describe how Accawi feels about the changes that swept through his world. Refer to specific details from paragraphs 24 and 25.

Suggestions for Writing

1. How do technologies such as the Internet, computerized slot machines, cellphones, or video games change people and their environment? Write an essay describing the effects of a new technology on a person or place you know.
2. Write an essay describing a neighbourhood, town, or village that you know (perhaps one that you or your family came from). What has happened to this place over time? What caused the changes? Your essay should both describe the transformation and communicate your feelings about it.

Saving the Songs of Innocence

JOHN DIXON

A philosophy instructor at Capilano College, John Dixon (b. 1943) has been a guest lecturer at Harvard's Kennedy School of Government, special policy adviser to the Minister of National Defence in Ottawa, senior policy adviser to the Attorney General of Canada, and president of the B.C. Civil Liberties Association. He is the author of numerous articles; *Catastrophic Rights* (1990); and co-author of *Kiddie Porn: Sexual Representation, Free Speech, and the Robin Sharpe Case* (2001), which was short-listed for the Donner Prize.

When I was a little boy, we called them Blackfish. My father 1 and I would sometimes see them when we strip-cast for coho° at the mouth of the Big Qualicum River. We never got very close to them in that shallow bay, and I don't remember much more than the big dorsal fins coming up and going down in the distance—except that the fishing always seemed to go off then. Dad said that it was because the salmon hugged the bottom, dodging the hunting sonar° of the killer-whale pack. I still don't know if that's true.

Last summer, with my own 7-year-old son, it was different. We 2 were spinning for cutthroat° at the mouth of a stream that flows into Pryce Channel, in the Desolation Sound area of British Columbia. It was hot, the deer flies were getting very tough, and we were starting to think more fondly of swimming than catching big trout.

"Puuuff," it sounded far away. But loud enough that we stood 3 still in our little aluminum boat, watching in the direction of the Brem River.

In less than a minute, the black fin of a killer slowly appeared 4 about a quarter of a mile away. Edge on, it looked for all the world like a dock piling slowly wavering out of the water and then falling back in, except that pilings don't spout steamy breath. He was moving along the shore, coming out of Toba Inlet on a course that would bring him right up to us. His dorsal was so tall that its tip drooped over in the way that (we say) means it's a big bull. Excitement! I started our old Evinrude and began idling along the shore waiting for him to catch up.

The next time he surfaced he was beside us, about 30 feet away 5 on the open water side. I speeded up a bit to match his pace, and we held our course, staying about 50 feet off the steep shore. With not a ripple of wind on the water, we could see all of him as he angled into us a bit, coming up 10 feet closer after his next shore dive.

6   To say what is seen then is easier than to say what is felt or known. He looked like a huge rubbery thing that had been molded out of six or seven elephants. And I say "thing" because on one level he didn't appear, deliberately swimming at such profound ease, to be alive. Beside the obvious matter of the scale being all wrong, there was none of the fuss or business we associate with life, even when it is quietly on the move. But on another level, you didn't have to know that he ate seals like buttered popcorn in order to feel the near world humming with his predatory° purpose. And we were alone with him—primates on a tin half shell.

7   He went down again, shallow, and angled in another 10 feet. When he came up we saw his eye, and Matthew said, simply and emphatically: "I'm scared now." "Smart," I said to myself: "You've just been spotted by one who prefers dining as high up the food chain as possible." But out loud I did my father stuff: "We're okay. Let's just go along like this."

8   The tip of his dorsal slowly slid under again, and I watched it closely for any change of course. "Look!" Matthew yelled: "Look at the herring!" Under the boat I saw two things at once. We had shallowed up so much that I could see the ground about 20 feet down, and the boat was over a big school of herring packed against the shore. And then there was a different "Puuuuff!" as the killer surged up and dived, turning directly under the boat into the feed.

9   I saw white and black under us and hit the gas. We squirted away, and turned around to look just as, about 25 yards behind us, the whale erupted out of our wake. He came out completely, but so slowly that it was hard to believe, from about the point he was halfway, that he could possibly go any further. And when he fell back into the light smoke of our exhaust, it seemed to take as long as the collapse of a dynamited skyscraper.

10   I tend to think of Job whenever I'm whacked over the head with a strong experience of nature. The story of his peek into God's wild portfolio and subsequent attitude-adjustment reminds us of one of the rudiments° of human wisdom: we are out of our depth in this world. In this respect, nothing has changed. What has changed, sadly and urgently, is the gap between our relatively unimproved powers of understanding and the monstrous development of our capacity to despoil. I cannot really know the oceans that Homer called "the whale road," but I can effortlessly reach their deepest regions with a neoprene gumboot° that has a half-life of about a million years.

11   Looking that whale in the eye with Matthew has produced at least one point of clarity in me. I don't know how I made my chil-

dren, but I know that—in a way that has nothing to do with posses-sion—they are mine and I must try to find the strength and wisdom to care for them. Now we know that we have mixed ourselves so completely with the world that not even the mercury and cad-mium-laced flesh of the whales has been spared our touch. We have made ourselves so thoroughly immanent° in the world that we have taken it away from nature and hence made it—if only through default—our own.

As is the case with God, when the wilderness no longer exists it 12 cannot be invented, no matter how appealing the idea or powerful the human will to realize it. Because an invented God or an invented wilderness lacks the autonomous power that is at the core of its reality. Once innocence is lost, its songs can still be sung but it can never be genuinely restored.

This means that the pious path of Job, leaving the running of 13 the world to some separate and autonomous competence such as Spinoza°'s *deus sive natura* . . . God or nature, is now forever closed to us. We never understood the significance of that path (the next best thing to not getting kicked out of the Garden of Eden in the first place) until it was too late, and now must search out a future of which the only thing certainly known is that it will require inestimably more from us than patient restraint. We face responsibilities, and obstacles in the way of their being met, of unfathomable° profundity°. The good news—and it didn't have to turn out this way—is that when the world chooses to reveal itself to us, as it does from time to time in Desolation Sound, we continue to fall in love with it as deeply and inevitably as with our children.

Words and Meanings

		Paragraph
coho	salmon	1
sonar	underwater sound waves whales use to find fish	
spinning for cutthroat	fishing for trout	2
predatory	hunting for prey	6
rudiments	the basics	10
neoprene gumboot	synthetic rubber boot	
immanent	indwelling; we have permeated the environ-ment and all life forms with chemicals	11

13	Spinoza	seventeenth-century Dutch philosopher who believed that God and Nature were not two different things, but different aspects of one substance
	unfathomable	so deep we cannot get to the bottom of it
	profundity	idea that is deep, complex, extremely difficult to understand

Structure and Strategy

1. This essay combines all four RHETORICAL MODES. Identify passages that are primarily narrative, descriptive, expository, and persuasive in nature.
2. Identify five or six descriptive details involving the whale that you find particularly effective.
3. Paragraph 10 contains two ALLUSIONS (Job and Homer). Who were they? Why does Dixon include them to develop his THESIS?
4. How does the CONCLUSION contribute to the UNITY of the essay?

Content and Purpose

1. What is the connection between the brief narrative in paragraph 1 and that which begins in paragraph 2? What is the purpose of the contrast between these two stories?
2. What is Dixon's THESIS?
3. What does the author mean by "primates on a tin half shell" in paragraph 6?
4. Where in the essay does the author move from relating the experience to interpreting it? How does he interpret the encounter with the killer whale?
5. Summarize the point of paragraphs 10 and 11. What is the connection between "God's wild portfolio" and the "neoprene gumboot that has a half-life of about a million years" (paragraph 10)?
6. To what does Dixon compare the loss of the wilderness in paragraph 12? Paraphrase the meaning of the last sentence in this paragraph. What is the effect of this loss?
7. What human impulse does Dixon see as positive in its implications for the possible re-establishment of a healthy link between humankind and nature? (See paragraph 13.)

Suggestions for Writing

1. Write an essay recounting an experience you have had in nature (hiking, camping, fishing, kayaking, skiing, etc.) that had a profound effect on you. Using NARRATION, DESCRIPTION, and

example to develop your THESIS, explain the causal relationship between your experience and its effects.

2. Write an essay exploring the causes or the effects of a particular kind of damage that you, your community, or an industry you are familiar with inflicts on the natural environment.

--- ❦ ---

The Evolution of Evolution

HELENA CRONIN

A philosopher and natural scientist, Helena Cronin (b. 1942) divides her time between the Centre for Philosophy of Natural and Social Science at the London School of Economics and the Department of Zoology at Oxford University. She is the author of the award-winning *The Ant and the Peacock*, an account of the debates that have surrounded evolutionary theory since Darwin published *The Origin of Species*.

In one of my favorite cartoons, a hopeful patient asks his doctor, "Have you got something for the human condition?" One cannot but sympathize with the hapless physician. Or so I used to feel. Now my urge is to leap into action crying, "I'm a Darwinian°; perhaps I can help." For in the past decade or so evolutionary theory has yielded a mind-blowing discovery: it has pried open the neatly-arrayed toolbox that is our mind. Just as *Gray's Anatomy*° laid bare the human frame, so Darwinian scientists are beginning to write the owner-occupier's manual to that hitherto most recondite° of mysteries: human nature. Yes, human nature does exist and it is universal. Our minds and brains, just like our bodies, have been honed° by natural selection to solve the problems faced by our ancestors over the past two million years. Just as every normal human hand has a precision-engineered opposable thumb for plucking, so every normal human mind enters the world bristling with highly specialized problem-solving equipment. And these capacities come on stream during development as surely as the toddler's first faltering steps or the adolescent's acne and ecstasy.

This mind-and-body-building is orchestrated by genes. But we're not merely their slavish puppets. Certainly, genes can do their work single-mindedly. However, genes—responding to different environments—also underpin the flexibility and variety that typify human behavior. All this apparent design has come about without a designer. No purpose, no goals, no blueprints. Natural selection is simply about genes replicating° themselves down the generations. Genes that build bodies that do what's needed—seeing, running, digesting, mating—get replicated; and those that don't, don't. All the more wondrous, then, to discover what natural selection has achieved with human nature. The Darwinian exploration is still a fledgling science. But already it is yielding answers that we didn't even know had questions: What's the winning figure for ratio of waist to hips? Why are mother and fetus locked in irresolvable conflict? Why is fast food so addictive?

3   New though this science is, researchers are already pretty confident about some things. Fortunately, one of them is sex. Consider a familiar sex difference that emerged in a study of American college students. Asked by a stranger for a date, 50% of both women and men agreed. But asked "Have sex with me tonight?" not one woman agreed—whereas men shot to 75%. And when students were asked "How long would you have to know someone before having sex?" the questionnaire had to be rescaled for males requiring only minutes or seconds. Not only are men willing to have sex with a perfect stranger; they're more than willing with an imperfect one too. Another American study found that, for brief encounters, men (but not women) were willing to drop their standards as low as their trousers, ready to dispense with intelligence, humor, charm, honesty and emotional stability.

4   Why this difference between men and women? When natural selection shaped male–female differences, it didn't stop at muscles and naughty bits. It also shaped differences in our psychologies. Evolution made men's and women's minds as unalike as it made their bodies. Why? Think of it this way. Give a man 50 wives and he could have children galore. But a woman with 50 husbands? Huh! Generation after generation, down evolutionary time, natural selection favored the men who strove most mightily for mates—the most competitive, risk-taking, opportunistic. We are all the descendants of those winners. Females, meanwhile, faced nine months hard labor, breast feeding, rearing. A woman had to be far more picky about whose genes ended up partnering hers. Faced with the prospect of highly dependent offspring, she'd be on the lookout for someone who was not only fit and healthy but also had access to resources. Nowadays a Rolex or designer trainers provide cues. But for our hunter-gatherer ancestors roving the Pleistocene° plains, what mattered were social resources—status, reputation, respect. Genes that built brains with tools for making these shrewd decisions were the ones that got themselves replicated.

Of course, natural selection doesn't download its strategic   5
plans straight into our consciousness. Its instruments are emotions,
priorities, desires. Behind each of these everyday human feelings
are the calculations of natural selection, millions of careful years in
the making. So, for example, men, without knowing it, tend to
prefer women with a waist-to-hip ratio (WHR) of 0.7—a waist that
is 70% of the hips. Twiggy's skeletal form and Rubens' hefty muses
share a 0.7 WHR; so do dumpy Paleolithic "Venuses," figurines
shaped by our ancestors 28 000 years ago. Why? It's an ingenious
fertility-detection mechanism. Waists and hips are shaped by sex
hormones, estrogen in particular. And the optimal hormonal mix
for fertility also sculpts that desired ratio.

Both sexes have a predilection° for symmetry. A body with   6
matching right and left sides is an honest signal (because it is hard
to fake) that the genes that built it are robust against invading
pathogens°. As for women's breasts, the larger they are, the more
symmetrical they're likely to be. Why? Breast-building requires
estrogen; the larger the breasts the more the developing body must
have been awash with it. But estrogen suppresses immunity,
making the woman vulnerable to pathogens. So breasts that are
large and yet manage to be symmetrical signal that their owner's
immune system is reliably robust. Facial symmetry, too, is highly
attractive; beauty, far from being skin deep, is a Stone Age body
scan, brimming with information about health and fertility. It's no
surprise, then, that there's cross-cultural agreement on what constitutes a beautiful face; even two-month old babies concur.

Sherlock Holmes° read the personal column "because it is   7
always instructive." Yes, the instructions come straight from the
Darwinian textbook. Turn to lonely hearts listings: man seeks
young, good-looking woman; woman seeks older, financially stable
man. Study sexual fantasies: men—anonymous multiple partners,
thoughts of bare skin; women—someone familiar, tender emotions.
Consider adultery (what Darwinians politely call "extra-pair copu-
lations"): males go for quantity; females, having established
resources within monogamy°, go for quality, particularly high-
quality genes. Across all its manifestations, human sexuality bears
the stamp of evolved sex differences: always preferences diverge°
and always predictably. But it's not just sexuality. A funny thing
happened on the way to divergent mating strategies. Natural selection created males and females so unalike that the differences don't
stop at how fast you'll jump into bed; they pervade our psychology,
shaping our interests, our values, our ambitions, our skills.

It's often said, for example, that men lack social skills. Don't   8
believe it. It's just that their skills are, all too understandably, not

what we call sociable. They are masters at status-seeking, face-saving, assessing reputation, detecting slights, retaliating against insults and showing off. They are more persistent and competitive than females, more disposed to take risks. Who causes most road accidents, climbs Everest, flies to the moon, commits suicide? Who are the alcoholics, motor-bike riders, scientists, child-abusers, CEOs, gamblers, smokers, bungee jumpers, murderers and computer nerds? Men, of course. Men outstrip women in deaths from smoking, homicide and accidents. Social scientists view these causes of death as "life-style" as opposed to "biology." But, in the light of evolutionary theory, speeding to death in a flashy car is enmeshed in men's biology.

9   Put males and females in the same environment and their evolved psychologies trigger hugely different responses. Boys thrive in competitive exams; girls could do without. Boys play competitive games, big on rules and winners; girls play co-operative games with consensual° endings. Men buy records to complete the set, women to enjoy the music. Rich, successful men go for ever-younger "trophy" wives; top women go for men even richer, more successful—and older—than themselves.

10   After the enlightenment of the personal column, Sherlock Holmes would turn dutifully to the criminal news. This, he felt, was not instructive. Darwinian detectives do better. Consider the family. Criminologists° are fond of remarking that it is the most dangerous place to be. If this were true, it would be a Darwinian scandal. Why? Remember that evolution is about genes getting themselves replicated. Sex is one way. Another is for genes to help copies of themselves in other bodies. One reliable way is to help kin—the closer the relationship, the more help is given. From this genetic reckoning, calculated by the blind forces of natural selection over millions of years, spring some of our most cherished human values. Whenever a mother braves hazards to save her child from drowning, whenever a brother donates a kidney for his sibling, "kin selection" is at work. We are evolved to lavish altruism on our kin, not to abuse or kill them. So it's no surprise to find that the criminologists are wrong.

11   Take murder. For a start, most family victims are spouses—not genetically related at all. But what about infanticide°? Children are cargoes of their parents' genes, 50% each, sallying forth into future generations. Infanticide is therefore a profound challenge to evolutionists—so profound that it sent intrepid Darwinians trawling through the statistics in Britain and North America to find out what proportion of murdered children died at the hands of their genetic parents. The researchers discovered that step-children are about 100

times more likely to be killed than genetic children. It's true what they say about Cinderella: having a step-parent puts a child at greater risk than any other known cause.

But where there is sharing, there also lies competition. When your children insist indignantly that your decision is not fair; when they squabble over a toy; when mother's keen to wean and baby resists—then bear in mind the following calculus of kin selection. A child's life is its sole bid for genetic immortality; and it values itself more than it values its brothers and sisters. Indeed, it is 100% related to itself but has only a 50% chance of sharing genes with siblings. But for a parent each child has the same value, a 50% relationship. The child will therefore always value itself, relative to its siblings, more than its parents do. The result is conflict. A child is evolved to want more than parents are evolved to give.   12

Pregnancy puts its own peculiar twist on this conflict because, at this point in the child's life, even the parents' interests diverge. Indeed, the womb harbors strife between mother and father that would make a divorce court look peaceable. "He only wants me for my body," women have cried down the ages. Darwinian analysis is now revealing that this is even more true after conception than before it. Fifty per cent of a fetus' genes come from its father. Our species cannot boast a history of reliable monogamy; so genes from that father might never borrow that womb again. Therefore paternal genes in the fetus have evolved to exploit the mother's body more than is optimal for her. The battleground is the placenta°, an invasive network of plumbing that seizes control of the mother's blood supply, enabling the fetus to grab more than its (maternally calculated) fair share of nutrients. This has set off a maternal–fetal arms race, escalating wildly over evolutionary time. Occasionally, a mother succumbs to one of the typical illnesses of pregnancy, such as diabetes. Only in the light of Darwinian analysis have we at last been able to understand these recurrent pathologies; they are glitches in an irresolvable conflict.   13

Darwinian science is also beginning to discover how our ancient tool kit fares in the modern world. For 99% of human existence we lived as hunter-gatherers. Ten thousand years ago agriculture arrived. Our evolved bodies and minds were unchanged; but, placed in novel environments, triggered by cues they were not designed to cope with, how would they respond? For an inkling°, go no further than your local fast-food joint. It is a monument to ancient tastes, to our evolved preferences for sugar, fat and salt. In our past, these finds were so scarce that we couldn't eat too much. Now our instincts are misled, resulting in the first epidemic of obesity that humans have ever known.   14

15 And we are processing not only food but also information that we weren't designed to digest. We have initiated a huge inadvertent° experiment on human nature. Think of our devices for choosing mates—exquisitely fine-tuned but not, perhaps, to some of today's challenges. A recent study found that, when people were shown pictures of beautiful and high status people of the opposite sex, both women and men became more dissatisfied with their own partners. We were evolved to assess beauty and status, and to calibrate° our satisfaction against a few hundred people at most. Yet we are all now exposed daily to images of the world's most beautiful women and richest and most powerful men, more beguiling than any our ancestors ever saw. Global communications amplify these invidious° messages across the world.

16 Our species has been faced with unprecedented inequalities ever since agriculture enabled us to hoard resources. But in recent years the game has increasingly become winner-take-all. From the world's chess champion to the leading libel lawyer, the few places at the top command almost all the status; and, as rewards rise, the gap between top and bottom grows. Caught in this game are males who are evolved to value status. What impact might these novel inequalities be making on them? Might it be significant that throughout the developed world, countries with the greatest inequalities in income have the poorest health and earliest death?

17 What of the future? It is often claimed that human evolution has ended because technology cushions us from disease and death; and, equally often, it is claimed that human evolution is accelerating because technology favors balloon brains on puny bodies. Neither is true. Natural selection's pace is slow; genes are plodding on with building bodies and minds in much the same way as they were for a million or so years, and that's how they'll continue for a long time to come. The adaptations that we bear tell us about long-lost worlds in which our ancestors dwelt. But those same adaptations tell us about our future. For it is not to human nature that we should look for change but to the intriguing new responses, the innovative behavior, that changing environments will elicit from that nature. And this enduring thread of humanity reminds us that, however novel our environments, their most salient° feature—for us and our descendants, as for our ancestors—is other human beings like ourselves, a meeting of evolved minds.

Words and Meanings

Darwinian	someone who supports the theory of natural selection originated by Charles Darwin (1809–82), which states that all species arise and develop through genetic variations that increase the individual's ability to survive and reproduce	1
Gray's Anatomy	medical text first published in 1858 and still in use today	
recondite	profound, hidden	
honed	shaped, perfected	
replicating	reproducing, copying	2
Pleistocene	era that began about two million years ago	4
predilection	preference	6
pathogens	disease-carrying agents	
Sherlock Holmes	famous fictional detective, protagonist of Sir Arthur Conan Doyle's mystery novels	7
monogamy	practice of having only one mate at a time	
diverge	differ, go in different directions	
consensual	based on the agreement of all participants	9
criminologists	social scientists who study crime and criminals	10
infanticide	murder of a child	11
placenta	organ in womb connecting mother and fetus	13
inkling	hint or suggestion	14
inadvertent	unplanned, accidental	15
calibrate	measure	
invidious	causing resentment, ill will	17
salient	noticeable, prominent	

Structure and Strategy

1. What strategy does Cronin use in her INTRODUCTION? Does the essay focus primarily on causes or on effects?
2. In paragraph 1, Cronin introduces an ANALOGY, comparing the human mind to a toolbox. Where else in the essay does she use this same analogy? Can you find other instances where the author explains an ABSTRACT idea by comparing it to a CONCRETE example?

3. Paragraph 2 ends with three questions. Where are these questions answered in the essay? What three KEY IDEAS do these questions represent? Rephrase the last sentence of paragraph 2 as a traditional thesis statement.
4. What is the TOPIC SENTENCE of paragraph 3? What strategy does Cronin use to develop it?
5. Find three or four examples of Cronin's use of question-and-answer to develop her points (see, for instance, the first sentence of paragraph 4). Is this informal, conversational style effective, given the seriousness of Cronin's topic?
6. Why are Cronin's ALLUSIONS to the literary figure Sherlock Holmes (paragraphs 7 and 10) appropriate in a causal analysis essay?

Content and Purpose

1. Cronin proposes that human nature is genetically determined. According to paragraphs 1 and 2, how do "our minds and brains" come to share certain characteristics?
2. What fundamental difference between men and women is explored in paragraph 3? How does the theory of natural selection explain this difference (see paragraph 4)?
3. According to the author, what physical characteristic do both men and women find attractive in the opposite sex? How do Darwinians explain the attractiveness of this characteristic?
4. Sex is one way that genes produce copies of themselves. What is another way for genes to promote their survival? How does Darwinian theory alter our traditional notions of the family and of altruism? (See paragraph 10.)
5. Cronin states that criminologists are wrong in their thinking that the family "is the most dangerous place to be." How does she defend the Darwinian point of view against that of the criminologists? Who does Cronin say is most likely to be murdered within a family? Why?
6. According to evolutionary theory, what is the source of sibling rivalry?
7. In your own words, explain why Darwinians think mother and fetus are locked in "irresolvable conflict" (see paragraph 13).
8. According to Cronin, why do we like junk food? What effect is our taste for junk food having on us in a world where we no longer have to hunt to survive?
9. Cronin suggests that the media, like junk food, adversely affect us because they feed us "information that we weren't designed to digest" (paragraph 15). What two negative effects of global communication does Cronin cite to support her point?

Suggestions for Writing

1. Write an essay in which you argue that perception of beauty, sibling conflict, and addiction to fast food are culturally rather than genetically determined.
2. Write an essay that explains a possible evolutionary cause of some aspect of human nature not discussed in Cronin's essay: for example, our religious impulse, inherent curiosity, fear of the dark, consumerism, fondness for jokes, tendency to break promises, xenophobia.
3. Does the theory that humans are creatures of evolution, designed simply to "replicate genes" (in other words, to get our own personal genetic material into the gene pool) appeal to you? Write an essay that details your response and argues either for or against the Darwinian point of view.

Additional Suggestions for Writing: Causal Analysis

Choose one of the topics below and write a paper that explores its causes *or* effects. Write a clear thesis statement and plan the development of each key idea before you begin to write the paper.

1. sibling rivalry
2. cuts in health care
3. the popularity of a current television series
4. corporal punishment of children
5. Native land claims
6. compulsive shopping
7. the pressure on women to be thin
8. vegetarianism
9. peer pressure among adolescents
10. mental illness
11. obesity
12. the trend to postpone childbearing until a couple is in their thirties or even forties
13. a specific phobia that affects someone you know
14. the attraction of religious cults
15. marriage breakdown
16. lying
17. Internet addiction
18. the demand among employers for ever-increasing levels of literacy
19. shyness
20. our tendency to distrust or dislike people who are different from ourselves

U   N   I   T

6

Definition

WHAT IS DEFINITION?

All communication depends on shared understanding. In writing, the writer and the reader must have a common understanding of what the words mean. Sometimes a definition is required to ensure this common understanding. Knowing when and how to define terms clearly is one of the most useful skills a writer can learn. Through definition, a writer creates shared meaning.

There are two basic ways to define terms: the short way and the long way. The short way is sometimes called **formal definition.** The writer explains in one sentence a word that may be unclear to the reader. In the model essay "Talking Pidgin," the second paragraph begins with a formal definition: "A pidgin is a simplified language that evolves between groups of people who have no language in common." A fuller, more elaborate definition of "pidgin languages" follows. The essay as a whole is an example of the long way of definition, known as **extended definition.** Extended definition is a form of expository writing in which the word or idea being defined is the topic of the essay. Extended definition is required when the nature of the thing to be defined is complex, and explaining *what it is* in detail is the writer's goal.

WHY DO WE WRITE DEFINITION?

Definition answers the lead-in question *what.* It is a key way to provide information about a topic. A short, formal definition is often used to introduce an unfamiliar word or technical term. It may also be used to explain an unusual meaning of a word that is normally understood in another way. For instance, in the first paragraph of "Altruism," Lewis Thomas defines the word "survival" as follows:

"Survival, in the cool economics of biology, means simply the persistence of one's own genes in the generations to follow." This unusual definition—and the shared understanding between writer and reader that it ensures—is crucial to the ideas Thomas presents in the essay.

An extended definition is useful to explain ABSTRACT ideas. "The Approaching Age of Virtual Nations," for example, defines what the authors see as a powerful emerging political force: virtual nations that are bound by ideology and the Internet, rather than by geography, ethnicity, or history. Extended definition can also be used to show how the meaning of a given term has changed over time. For example, in "Beauty," Susan Sontag explains how our culture's definition of "beauty" differs from that of the ancient Greeks. Tracking the evolution of a word's meaning can be an interesting way to define the word for readers.

Definition is not restricted to a purely informative or expository function. Defining something in a particular way sometimes involves persuading other people to accept and even act on the definition. Neil Bissoondath's definition of the term "racism" in "I'm Not Racist But . . ." is an integral part of his controversial THESIS, as is Stanley Fish's definition of "relativism" in "Condemnation Without Absolutes." Extended definition is a powerful rhetorical strategy that can engage and influence readers.

HOW DO WE WRITE DEFINITION?

There is no single rhetorical pattern that applies to extended definition. Its development relies instead on one or more of the other patterns explained in this text. In other words, depending on the topic and the AUDIENCE, an extended definition can employ any of a number of organizational patterns, or even a combination of strategies.

It is often helpful to begin your extended definition with a formal definition. To write a formal definition, first put the term being defined into the general class of things to which it belongs; then identify the qualities that set it apart or distinguish it from the others in that class. Here are some examples of formal definitions:

TERM		CLASS	DISTINGUISHING FEATURES
A turtle	is	a shelled reptile	that lives in water.
A tortoise	is	a shelled reptile	that lives on land.
Misogyny	is	the hatred	of women.
Misanthropy	is	the hatred	of people in general.

Constructing a formal definition is a logical way to begin the task of definition. It prevents vague formulations such as "a turtle lives in water" (so does a tuna), or "misanthropy is when you don't like people." Here are two pitfalls to avoid when writing definitions:

1. Do not begin your essay with a word-for-word definition copied from the dictionary. When you're staring at a piece of blank paper, it's hard to resist the temptation to resort to this strategy. But you should resist, because a dictionary definition is boring and often not directly relevant to your own topic.

2. Don't chase your own tail by using a form of the word you're defining in your definition. Stating that "adolescence is the state of being an adolescent" doesn't clarify anything for readers.

A good definition establishes clearly, logically, and precisely the boundaries of meaning. It communicates the meaning in an organizational pattern appropriate to the term and to the reader. To define is, in many ways, to create, and doing this well shows respect for both the ideas you're explaining and the readers you're addressing.

The following model essay—an extended definition of the term "pidgin language"—illustrates definition by example, etymology, and distinctive characteristics.

Talking Pidgin

Introduction (quotation and question to intrigue the reader)

Thesis is a question

Begins with formal definition and adds examples

Pren, man bolong Rom, Wantok, harim nau. Mi kam tasol long plantim Kaesar. Mi noken beiten longen. Can you translate these words? Not likely, unless you are familiar with Tok Pisin, a pidgin language spoken by about a million people in Papua New Guinea. What is a pidgin language?

A pidgin is a simplified language that evolves between groups of people who have no language in common. It is a new "hybrid" language made up of elements derived from its source languages: English and Chinese, for example, or Spanish and Tagalog. Most pidgin languages developed to permit groups to trade with each other. For example, when the Nootka and Chinook peoples living on the West Coast came in contact with French and English traders in the nineteenth century, they developed a pidgin language so they could talk and do business with each other. Like all pidgins, this language—Chinook Jargon—combined elements of its source languages: Nootka,

Chinook, English, and French. From the 1830s to the 1920s, from California to Alaska, Chinook Jargon was spoken by people from widely varying language backgrounds who came together to hunt, log, or look for gold. Chinook Jargon expressions are still used on the West Coast today: *mucketymuck* is a slang term for an important person, and *saltchuck* means the sea.

Definition by example

There are hundreds, perhaps thousands, of pidgin languages around the world. Many are based on European languages such as Portuguese, Spanish, French, Dutch, and English, and they reflect the extent of European colonization over the past 500 years. Probably the best-known example is Pidgin English, the language used by British and Chinese traders in ports such as Canton. But pidgins can develop wherever different languages collide. Mogilian is a Choctaw-based pidgin formerly used by Amerindian tribes along the Gulf of Mexico. Pachuco, or "Spanglish," is an English–Spanish hybrid used in Latino communities in the United States. Bazaar Malay is a pidgin derived from Malaysian and Chinese that is widely used in Malaysia and Indonesia.

Definition by etymology

Pidgins are so widespread and so multilingual in origin that linguists (scholars who study the nature of language) are not certain where the word *pidgin* comes from. Some suggest that it derives from the Portuguese word for business, *ocupacao;* others think the source is a Chinese-inflected pronunciation of the English word *business*. Some etymologists (linguists who specialize in word origins) theorize that the word comes from the Hebrew *pid yom,* which means *barter.*

Definition by distinctive characteristics

All pidgin languages are characterized by a small vocabulary (a few hundred or thousand words), a simplified grammatical structure, and a narrower range of use than the languages they are based on. Pidgins are unique in that they are the native languages of no one. Speakers use them for a few restricted purposes—usually work and trade—and they use their native tongues for more diverse and complex communications.

Conclusion (highlights significance and provides translation of opening quotation)

Pidgins cease to exist when the contact between the source-language groups diminishes, or when one

group adopts the language of the other. In their adapt-
ability and transience, pidgins are excellent examples
of the processes of linguistic change. More than any
other kind of verbal communication, pidgins demonstrate how resourceful and ingenious humans can be
in adapting language to fit their needs.

So what does the opening quotation actually say?
It is none other than Shakespeare's famous words
from *Julius Caesar:* "Friends, Romans, countrymen,
lend me your ears; I come to bury Caesar, not to
praise him."

Blush, Cringe, Fidget

MARGARET VISSER

Margaret Visser (b. 1940) describes herself as "an anthropologer of
everyday life." A former contributing editor at *Saturday Night* magazine and
professor of classics at York University, she now devotes her time to writing
and giving public lectures in Canada, the United States, and Britain. Her
books include *Much Depends on Dinner* (1986), *The Rituals of Dinner*
(1991), *The Way We Are* (1994), *The Geometry of Love* (2001), and
Beyond Fate (2002).

The reactions are physical all right: face turning red and some-   1
times white, voice switching to falsetto or to bass°, stuttering,
throat contracting, inhibited breath, dry mouth, stomach contractions, blinking, lowered head and eyes, shaking, fumbling, fid-
geting, plucking at the clothes, hands cold and twisting together or
held behind the back, smile fixed, feet frozen. These are symptoms
of embarrassment, or dis-ease. They are brought on by entirely
social and mental conditions, and they constitute proof positive
that the human body reacts directly to the mind, even without reference to willpower or design.

To be embarrassed is to be disclosed, in public. Both factors are   2
important: you must have something to hide first, and you must have
an audience. Fall over your shoes as you get out of your solitary bed
in the morning, and you may curse but you will not blush: embarrassment is about how you look in *other people's* eyes. (Extremely sensitive

people might blush in private—but only when imagining that audience, which remains indispensable to the experience.)

3   The revelation of something we wanted to keep hidden explains the fingering of our clothes: we touch, tighten, and arrange, reassuring ourselves that the shell is still in place. Clothes cover what society has decreed shall be concealed, and a good many embarrassing moments involve clothes: lacking them, popping out of them, or wearing the wrong ones.

4   What we would like to hide is most often the truth about ourselves: the inexperience, incompetence, and ignorance that lie behind the bombastic° or slick facade°. To step forward before the expectant crowd with every sign of cool control, and then to fall flat on your face, is to produce embarrassment at nightmare level. The slip on the banana peel, the rug sliding out from under are concrete shorthand for the public fall from grandeur that everyone who is sane can recognize and remember. Failure to live up to expectations is another cause for embarrassment, both for you (provided you understand the extent of your inadequacy) and for everybody watching. . . .

5   The word *embarrass* is from the Spanish *embarazar*, "to hinder by placing a bar or impediment in the way." It creates confusion, as when the march of a column of ants is broken up by a sudden interference—someone "putting their foot in it," perhaps. (In dialects of French and Spanish the equivalents of this word are coarse terms for "to get someone pregnant [*embarazada*].") . . .

6   The specific meaning of *embarrassment* in English arrives fairly late in the language. The term once meant merely "not knowing what to do" in a specific situation, for instance when confronted by a dilemma (as in the French *embarras de choix*), or when there is a superfluity of good things (an *embarras de richesses*). The narrowing of the sense till we get "an inability to respond where a response is due," approaches the modern English meaning of the word. One can still feel "financially embarrassed," or unable to pay. The sense of inadequacy that having no money can arouse in the breasts of upright citizens was then further honed° and differentiated until we get the naming of the precise phenomenon we now call "embarrassment." It still includes occasions where we have to respond, but the role we must play is one we have not learned. Examples are finding yourself honoured by a surprise party, or having suddenly to dance in public (if you are not in the habit of dancing, of course).

7   If, on the other hand, what your image *requires* is a crowd of spectators, then, if no one takes any notice of you, that absence will constitute your shame. If you set yourself up to give a speech and no one comes, the lack will hurt as much as being howled down. But

even here, embarrassment comes about only if there are *some* people around: the three members who make up the audience, or the idle ticket sellers who watch you arrive, are needed in order for you to cringe. (Cringing is making yourself small, which is why embarrassment causes the hanging of heads, the shrinking back: these physically express the belittlement you see in the eyes of others.)

There is often complicity° in the watching crowd; embarrassment is contagious. So when you step out on stage, or before the TV cameras, and start to sing, only to hear yourself warbling way out of tune, the audience will start to squirm and blush on your behalf. They imagine what it must be like to be you—and they can do it because somewhere in their lives they too have experienced your fate. It is far worse, of course, for members of the crowd who are your friends and relatives, for, as allies, their reputations are vested in° your behaving "properly." **8**

The only way socially to pass muster° is to "fit in," as we say: to do what is proper, or "fitting." Impropriety°, then, is the very stuff of embarrassment. Once again the body comes into play: exposure that is deemed "indecent" evokes embarrassment, and so do flatulence, snores, dribbles, burps, and sniffing. You should not be caught talking to yourself either, or picking your nose, or being smelly. To have committed such misdemeanours in public means the death of your reputation—and it is important to remember that in such cases whether you are to blame or not is of no significance. Your only hope is that the crowd, who usually have an interest in not interrupting the official agenda of the meeting and in not being contaminated by an impropriety through drawing attention to it, will behave—at least for the moment—as though nothing has happened. **9**

Incompetence is what impropriety of the embarrassing kind most often demonstrates. I once said to an important gentleman who arrived to visit my French landlady, "*Madame est sur le téléphone*," and he answered gravely, "*Cela ne doit pas être très confortable.*" The stories travellers bring home from foreign countries often concern the embarrassing results of not knowing the language well enough, or not knowing what the social norms are: what you should on no account do or say. You bumble ahead with the best intentions, yet commit the offence—and the horror or the amusement you evoke cannot subsequently be put back into the bottle. **10**

Involuntary impropriety is, of course, most acutely embarrassing when you cannot explain away what you have done. What you want more than anything else on earth is an escape from your predicament, and there is none. You are caught and helpless (which is why you wring or hide your hands in reaction to embarrassment). You haven't the vocabulary in the foreign language; or your situation **11** is compromised° in such a way that no one would believe your explanation if you gave it, the clues pointing so much more plausibly° to what the audience believes they can see. Into this category fall many of the cases of mistaken identity. You hug your husband, whisper extremely private endearments into his ear, then discover to your horror that you have made a mistake: this is not your husband at all. And immediately you know exactly what this total stranger must be thinking: sympathy is essential to embarrassment.

12   [Ironically,] the embarrassed reaction itself shows not that you lack social adjustment but that you have it, in spades. You *care* what society thinks, and really that is what it wants most. If we look at who most often gets embarrassed, we see that it is sensitive people, people who are trying hard to succeed, who are prepared to mend their ways, who never forget the lesson learned—and what more could society ask? On the whole, people who are never embarrassed (the "shameless") are the most antisocial of us, the least considerate and most uncaring.

13   The most exquisite kind of embarrassment, and the one that helps us see that the reaction need not merely mean a blind bowing to the pressures of convention, is the horrible realization that you might have hurt someone without intending to do so, or that your own arrogance has made you behave condescendingly° where respect was due. Again you have demonstrated incompetence, but here the lesson learned has ethical implications.

14   Two women discuss, in Norwegian, the handicap of a man with one leg who is sitting opposite them on a Paris subway train. What would it be like to sleep with a one-legged man? The man gets up and says, in faultless Norwegian, "If you would care for a demonstration, Madam, I would be happy to oblige." . . .

15   My favourite example of this kind of embarrassment happened to John Fraser, the [former] editor of *Saturday Night* magazine. Visiting one of Jean Vanier's l'Arche communities, he saw a man struggling with a carpentry chore, and spoke to him in a slow clear voice, with the nervously careful solicitude° that we all reserve for the mentally retarded. He discovered later that the man was a Sorbonne professor who had taken time off to care for and learn from the handicapped. The way John tells this story, all those listening imagine themselves in the same position, being kind. Then the punch line is delivered, to all of us. Embarrassment, when it is in working order, can produce enlightenment as well as shock.

16   Precisely because embarrassment often arises from unawareness of important factors in the social environment, and because it is a powerful aid to learning and never forgetting, it most commonly occurs in adolescence. Almost all the good embarrassment

stories happened when we were young, and just discovering the mines and traps laid for those who want desperately to find a place among their peers. Very small children know fear and shyness, but they never blush because of social faux pas°.

Adults become surer and surer of themselves as well as less and less sensitive, largely through knowing the rules, and through practice and general wear and tear. It often requires decades of experience and self-assurance before the worst of our blunders can be told to people. Yet even then, what is laughing publicly at ourselves but further social complicity? We have found out not only that everybody else knows what it's like to look a fool, but that a very good way to defuse and rise above a crowd's contempt is to make an even larger crowd laugh *with* you, even if it's at yourself.   17

Words and Meanings

		Paragraph
falsetto or bass	very high or very low	1
bombastic	pompous, inflated	4
facade	surface appearance	
honed	refined	6
complicity	participation, involvement	8
vested in	personally connected to	
pass muster	be found acceptable	9
impropriety	behaviour that is improper, not "fitting"	
compromised	made to look bad	11
plausibly	believably	
condescendingly	"talking down" to your audience	13
solicitude	concern	15
faux pas	blunders, mistakes	16

Structure and Strategy

1. The title and long first sentence of this essay describe symptoms of the topic before telling the reader what the topic is. What, specifically, is being defined here? Do you think this indirect approach is an effective INTRODUCTION? Why or why not?
2. Which sentences in the introduction of this essay contain a broad statement of its THESIS?
3. What techniques does the author use in paragraphs 5 and 6 to define the word "embarrass"? How has the meaning of the word in English changed over time?

4. What strategy does Visser use to develop the topic of paragraph 9?
5. What contrast does Visser use in paragraph 12 to help develop her definition?

Content and Purpose

1. According to Visser, what two factors must be present for a person to suffer embarrassment?
2. Why do people sometimes feel uncomfortable, even cringe or fidget, when they watch someone else embarrass himself or herself? Where in the essay is this phenomenon described?
3. According to Visser, we are embarrassed by improprieties because they reveal our inexperience or incompetence, but "the most exquisite kind of embarrassment" (paragraph 13) has "ethical implications." What do you think she means by this, and how does she support the point? Do you agree or disagree? Why?
4. According to the author, at what age is a person most likely to suffer from embarrassment? Do you think people this age suffer from personal embarrassment only, or does their heightened sensitivity extend to include the "social faux pas" (paragraph 16) of other people? Why?
5. Visser suggests that suffering through an embarrassing incident can have a positive outcome. Where in the essay do you find this suggestion?

Suggestion for Writing

Tell the story of your most embarrassing moment. What happened? How did you feel? How did you deal with the situation? What did you learn from the incident?

Being Canadian

DENISE CHONG

Vancouver-born Denise Chong (b. 1953) trained as an economist and worked as an economic adviser to Pierre Elliott Trudeau before pursuing her interest in writing. She edited *The Penguin Book of Canadian Women's Short Stories* (1997) and is the author of *The Concubine's Children* (1994), which chronicles the experiences of Chinese immigrants and their families.

Her most recent work, *The Girl in the Picture* (1999), is built around the horrific photograph—taken during the Vietnam War—of a severely burned Kim Phuc fleeing her napalmed village.

I ask myself what it means to be a Canadian. I was lucky enough to be born in Canada [, so] I look back at the price paid by those who made the choice that brought me such luck.   1

South China at the turn of the century became the spout of the teapot that was China. It poured out middle-class peasants like my grandfather, who couldn't earn a living at home. He left behind a wife and child. My grandfather was 36 when exclusion° came. Lonely and living a penurious existence, he worked at a sawmill on the mud flats of the Fraser River, where the Chinese were third on the pay scale behind "Whites" and "Hindus." With the door to Chinese immigration slammed shut, men like him didn't dare even go home for a visit, for fear Canada might bar their re-entry. With neither savings enough to go home for good, nor the means once in China to put rice in the mouths of his wife and child there, my grandfather wondered when, if ever, he could return to the bosom of a family. He decided to purchase a concubine, a second wife, to join him in Canada.   2

The concubine, at age 17, got into Canada on a lie. She got around the exclusion law in the only way possible: she presented the authorities with a Canadian birth certificate. It had belonged to a woman born in Ladner, British Columbia, and a middleman sold it to my grandfather at many times the price of the old head tax. Some years later, the concubine and my grandfather went back to China with their two Vancouver-born daughters. They lived for a time under the same roof as my grandfather's first wife. The concubine became pregnant. Eight months into her pregnancy, she decided to brave the long sea voyage back so that her third child could be born in Canada. [Her] false Canadian birth certificate would get her in. Accompanied by only my grandfather, she left China. Three days after the boat docked, on the second floor of a tenement on a back alley in Vancouver's Chinatown, she gave birth to my mother.   3

Canada remained inhospitable. Yet my grandparents *chose* to keep Canada in their future. Both gambled a heritage and family ties to take what they thought were better odds in the lottery of life. . . .   4

My own sense, four generations on, of being Canadian is one of belonging. I belong to a family. I belong to a community of values. I didn't get to choose my ancestors, but I can try to leave the world a better place for the generations that follow. The life I lead begins before and lingers after my time.   5

6   I am now the mother of two young children. I want to pass on a sense of what it means to be a Canadian. But what worries me as a parent, and as a Canadian, is whether we can fashion an enduring concept of citizenship that will be the glue that holds us together as a society. Curiously, Canadian citizenship elicits the most heartfelt response outside Canada. Any Canadian who has lived or travelled abroad quickly discovers that Canadian citizenship is a coveted possession. In the eyes of the rest of the world, it stands for an enlightened and gentle society.

7   Can we find a strong concept of citizenship that could be shared by all Canadians when we stand on our own soil? Some would say it is unrealistic to expect a symbol to rise out of a rather pragmatic° past. We spilled no revolutionary blood, as did France— where the word *citoyen*° was brought into popular usage—or America. Some lament the absence of a founding myth; we don't have the equivalent of a Boston Tea Party. Others long for Canadian versions of heroes to compete with the likes of American images that occupy our living rooms and our playgrounds. The one Canadian symbol with universal recognition is the flag. But where does the maple leaf strike a chord? Outside Canada. On the back packs of Canadian travellers. . . .

8   Some say Canadian citizenship is devalued because it is too easy to come here. But what sets Canadian society apart from others is that ours is an inclusive society. Canada's citizenship act remains more progressive than [the immigration laws of] many countries. Canadians by immigration have equal status with Canadians by birth. In contrast, in western Europe, guest workers, even if they descended from those who originally came, can be sent "home" any time. In Japan, Koreans and Filipinos have no claim to the citizenship of their birth. The plight of the Palestinians in Kuwait after the Gulf War gave the lie to a "free Kuwait."

9   Canadian citizenship recognizes differences. It praises diversity. It is what we as Canadians *choose* to have in common with each other. It is a bridge between those who left something to make a new home here and those born here. What keeps the bridge strong is tolerance, fairness, understanding, and compassion. Citizenship has rights and responsibilities. I believe one responsibility of citizenship is to use that tolerance, fairness, understanding, and compassion to leaf through the Canadian family album together. . . .

10   How we tell our stories is the work of citizenship. The motive of the storyteller should be to put the story first. To speak with authenticity and veracity° is to choose narrative over commentary. It is not to glorify or sentimentalize the past. It is not to sanitize our differences. Nor [is it] to rail against or to seek compensation today

for injustices of bygone times. In my opinion, to try to rewrite history leads to a sense of victimization. It marginalizes Canadians. It backs away from equality in our society, for which we have worked hard to find expression.

I believe our stories ultimately tell the story of Canada itself. In all our pasts are an immigrant beginning, a settler's accomplishments and setbacks, and the confidence of a common future. We all know the struggle for victory, the dreams and the lost hopes, the pride and the shame. When we tell our stories, we look in the mirror. I believe what we will see is that Canada is not lacking in heroes. Rather, the heroes are to be found within.   11

The work of citizenship is not something just for the week that we celebrate citizenship every year. It is part of every breath we take. It is the work of our lifetimes. . . .   12

If we do some of this work of citizenship, we will stand on firmer ground. Sharing experience will help build strength of character. It will explain our differences, yet make them less divisive. We will yell at each other less, and understand each other more. We will find a sense of identity and a common purpose. We will have something to hand down to the next generation.   13

My grandfather's act of immigration to the new world and the determination of my grandmother, the girl who first came here as a *kay toi neu°*, to chance a journey from China back to Canada so that my mother could be born here, will stand as a gift to all future generations of my family. Knowing they came hoping for a better life makes it easy to love both them and this country.   14

In the late 1980s, I [found] myself in China, on a two-year stint living in Peking and working as a writer. In a letter to my mother in Prince George, I confessed that, despite the predictions of friends back in Canada, I was finding it difficult to feel any "Chineseness." My mother wrote back: "You're Canadian, not Chinese. Stop trying to feel anything." She was right. I stopped such contrivances. I was Canadian; it was that which embodied the values of my life.   15

Words and Meanings

		Paragraph
exclusion	the closing off of Chinese immigration to Canada	2
pragmatic	practical as opposed to idealistic	7
citoyen	citizen [French]	
authenticity and veracity	genuineness and truthfulness	10
kay toi neu	serving girl [Cantonese]	14

Structure and Strategy

1. Identify the METAPHOR at the beginning of paragraph 2. Is it an effective image or a CLICHÉ? Explain.
2. Paragraph 8 is developed mainly by use of examples. What are these examples, and what KEY IDEA do they support?
3. How does Chong support her definition of Canadian citizenship in paragraph 9?
4. What kind of CONCLUSION does the essay use? Is it effective? Why or why not?

Content and Purpose

1. Summarize the experience of the people whose story is told in paragraphs 2, 3, and 4. What is the relationship between them and the author? What is her attitude toward them?
2. What is the question that "worries" Chong as she defines what being Canadian means to her? (See paragraphs 6 to 8.)
3. According to Chong, how do people outside Canada view this country? Do you agree with her? Why or why not?
4. What are some of the obstacles Chong sees to a "concept of citizenship that could be shared by all Canadians" (paragraph 7)?
5. What are the "rights and responsibilities" (paragraph 9) of citizenship expressed in the essay?
6. Paragraph 10 discusses the role of narrative—"how we tell our stories"—as an important element of the "work of citizenship." How does Chong feel about stories that condemn past injustices as a way of demanding compensation? Do you agree with her? Why or why not?
7. According to the essay, how will all Canadians benefit from telling our stories as part of the "work of citizenship" (paragraph 13)?
8. In two or three sentences, summarize Chong's definition of "being Canadian." How does her definition compare with your own understanding of what it means to be Canadian?

Suggestions for Writing

1. Chong maintains, "How we tell our stories is the work of citizenship." Write an essay that tells the story of someone you know who has become a Canadian citizen.
2. Chong argues that seeking compensation for past injustice "leads to a sense of victimization [and] marginalizes Canadians." Do you agree? Why or why not?

"I'm Not Racist But . . ."

NEIL BISSOONDATH

Neil Bissoondath (b. 1955) is a Trinidad-born Canadian novelist, short-story writer, and essayist. His works include *Digging Up the Mountains* (1985), *A Casual Brutality* (1988), *The Innocence of Age* (1992), *Selling Illusions: The Cult of Multiculturalism in Canada* (1994), *The Worlds Within Her* (1998), and *Doing the Heart Good* (2002).

Someone recently said that racism is as Canadian as maple syrup. 1 I have no argument with that. History provides us with ample proof. But, for proper perspective, let us remember that it is also as American as apple pie, as French as croissants, as Jamaican as ackee, as Indian as aloo, as Chinese as chow mein, as . . . Well, there's an entire menu to be written. This is not by way of excusing it. Murder and rape, too, are international, multicultural, as innate° to the darker side of the human experience. But we must be careful that the inevitable rage evoked does not blind us to the larger context.

The word "racism" is a discomforting one: It is so vulnerable to 2 manipulation. We can, if we so wish, apply it to any incident involving people of different colour. And therein lies the danger. During the heat of altercation°, we seize, as terms of abuse, on whatever is most obvious about the person. It is, often, a question of unfortunate convenience. A woman, because of her sex, easily becomes a female dog or an intimate part of her anatomy. A large person might be dubbed "a stupid ox," a small person "a little" whatever. And so a black might become "a nigger," a white "a honky," an Asian "a paki," a Chinese "a chink," an Italian "a wop," a French-Canadian "a frog."

There is nothing pleasant about these terms; they assault every 3 decent sensibility°. Even so, I once met someone who, in a stunning surge of naiveté°, used them as simple descriptives and not as terms of racial abuse. She was horrified to learn the truth. While this may have been an extreme case, the point is that the use of such patently abusive words may not always indicate racial or cultural distaste. They may indicate ignorance or stupidity or insensitivity, but pure racial hatred—such as the Nazis held for Jews, or the Ku Klux Klan for blacks—is a thankfully rare commodity.

Ignorance, not the willful kind but that which comes from lack 4 of experience, is often indicated by that wonderful phrase, "I'm not racist but . . ." I think of the mover, a friendly man, who said, "I'm not racist, but the Chinese are the worst drivers on the road." He was convinced this was so because the shape of their eyes, as far as he could surmise°, denied them peripheral° vision.

5   Or the oil company executive, an equally warm and friendly man, who, looking for an apartment in Toronto, rejected buildings with East Indian tenants not because of their race—he was telling me this, after all—but because he was given to understand that cockroaches were symbols of good luck in their culture and that, when they moved into a new home, friends came by with gift-wrapped cockroaches.

6   Neither of these men thought of himself as racist, and I believe they were not, deep down. (The oil company executive made it clear he would not hesitate to have me as a neighbour; my East Indian descent was of no consequence to him, my horror of cockroaches was.) Yet their comments, so innocently delivered, would open them to the accusation, justifiably so if this were all one knew about them. But it is a charge which would undoubtedly be wounding to them. It is difficult to recognize one's own misconceptions°.

7   True racism is based, more often than not, on willful° ignorance, and an acceptance of—and comfort with—stereotype. We like to think, in this country, that our multicultural mosaic will help nudge us into a greater openness. But multiculturalism as we know it indulges in stereotype, depends on it for a dash of colour and the flash of dance. It fails to address the most basic questions people have about each other. Do those men doing the Dragon Dance really all belong to secret criminal societies? Do those women dressed in saris really coddle cockroaches for luck? Do those people in dreadlocks all smoke marijuana and live on welfare? Such questions do not seem to be the concern of the government's multicultural programs, superficial and exhibitionistic as they have become.

8   So the struggle against stereotype, the basis of all racism, becomes a purely personal one. We must beware of the impressions we create. A friend of mine once commented that, from talking to West Indians, she has the impression that their one great cultural contribution to the world is in the oft-repeated boast that "We (unlike everyone else) know how to party."

9   There are dangers, too, in community response. We must be wary of the self-appointed activists who seem to pop up in the media at every given opportunity spouting the rhetoric of retribution°, mining distress for personal, political and professional gain. We must be skeptical about those who depend on conflict for their sense of self, the non-whites who need to feel themselves victims of racism, the whites who need to feel themselves purveyors° of it.

And we must be sure that, in addressing the problem, we do not end up creating it. Does the *Miss Black Canada Beauty Contest* still exist? I hope not. Not only do I find beauty contests offensive, but a racially segregated one even more so. What would the public reaction be, I wonder, if every year CTV broadcast the *Miss White Canada Beauty Pageant?* We give community-service awards only to blacks. Would we be comfortable with such awards only for whites? In Quebec, there are The Association of Black Nurses, The Association of Black Artists, The Congress of Black Jurists. Play tit for tat: The Association of White Nurses, White Artists, White Jurists: visions of apartheid. Let us be frank, racism for one is racism for others.

Finally, and perhaps most important, let us beware of abusing   10
the word itself.

Words and Meanings

Paragraph

innate	natural, inborn	1
altercation	quarrel, dispute	2
sensibility	feeling	3
naiveté	simplicity; lack of sophistication	
surmise	figure out, guess	4
peripheral	side	
misconceptions	mistaken beliefs	6
willful	deliberate	7
rhetoric of retribution	language of revenge, of retaliation	9
purveyors	providers	

Structure and Strategy

1. With what ANALOGY does Bissoondath introduce this essay? Why is it effective?
2. This essay is divided into three parts. Identify the KEY IDEAS in paragraphs 2 to 6, 7 to 8, and 9 to 10.
3. Identify the sentence that most clearly defines what Bissoondath thinks racism is.
4. Do you think the CONCLUSION of this essay is effective? Explain.

Content and Purpose

1. In paragraph 3, Bissoondath draws a distinction between "ignorance or stupidity or insensitivity" and "pure racial hatred." Into which category does he place the kind of racial epithets cited in paragraph 2?
2. What is the difference between the kind of ignorance represented by the examples in paragraphs 4 and 5 and "true racism" as Bissoondath sees it?
3. What does Bissoondath think of Canada's multicultural policies and programs? Do you agree with him? Why or why not?
4. In paragraph 8, Bissoondath maintains that we "must beware of the impressions we create" in the struggle against racism. Do you agree that ethnic groups are to some extent responsible for their own stereotyping? Is it reasonable to make an ethnic group responsible for counteracting the stereotypical image other groups have of them?
5. What does Bissoondath think of beauty contests, clubs, or organizations that limit participation to a particular ethnic group? Do you think he would be in favour of or opposed to affirmative action programs? Explain.

Suggestions for Writing

1. Have you ever experienced the kind of racist stereotyping that Bissoondath describes in this essay? Write a paper explaining the incident, or series of incidents, and its effects on you.
2. Write an essay in which you agree or disagree with Bissoondath's opinion that awards, associations, and competitions that are restricted to people of colour are racist.
3. Read Brent Staples's "Just Walk On By" (page 169) and compare his view of racism with Bissoondath's.

Beauty

SUSAN SONTAG

Susan Sontag (b. 1933) is an American cultural analyst who writes novels, essays, and screenplays. Her works include *Against Interpretation, and Other Essays* (1966), *Illness as Metaphor* (1977), *AIDS and Its Metaphors* (1988), *In America: A Novel* (2000), and *Where the Stress Falls* (2001).

For the Greeks, beauty was a virtue: a kind of excellence. Persons then were assumed to be what we now have to call— lamely, enviously—*whole* persons. If it did occur to the Greeks to distinguish between a person's "inside" and "outside," they still expected that inner beauty would be matched by beauty of the other kind. The well-born young Athenians who gathered around Socrates° found it quite paradoxical° that their hero was so intelligent, so brave, so honorable, so seductive—and so ugly. One of Socrates' main pedagogical° acts was to be ugly—and teach those innocent, no doubt splendid-looking disciples of his how full of paradoxes life really was. 1

They may have resisted Socrates' lesson. We do not. Several thousand years later, we are more wary° of the enchantments of beauty. We not only split off . . . the "inside" (character, intellect) from the "outside" (looks); but we are actually surprised when someone who is beautiful is also intelligent, talented, good. 2

It was principally the influence of Christianity that deprived beauty of the central place it had in classical ideals of human excellence. By limiting excellence (*virtus* in Latin) to *moral* virtue only, Christianity set beauty adrift—as an alienated, arbitrary, superficial enchantment. And beauty has continued to lose prestige. For close to two centuries it has become a convention to attribute beauty to only one of the two sexes: the sex which, however Fair, is always Second. Associating beauty with women has put beauty even further on the defensive, morally. 3

A beautiful woman, we say in English. But a handsome man. "Handsome" is the masculine equivalent of—and refusal of—a compliment which has accumulated certain demeaning overtones, by being reserved for women only. That one can call a man "beautiful" in French and in Italian suggests that Catholic countries—unlike those countries shaped by the Protestant version of Christianity— still retain some vestiges° of the pagan admiration for beauty. But the difference, if one exists, is of degree only. In every modern country that is Christian or post-Christian, women *are* the beautiful sex—to the detriment° of the notion of beauty as well as of women. 4

To be called beautiful is thought to name something essential to women's character and concerns. (In contrast to men—whose essence is to be strong, or effective, or competent.) It does not take someone in the throes of advanced feminist awareness to perceive that the way women are taught to be involved with beauty encourages narcissism°, reinforces dependence and immaturity. Everybody (women and men) knows that. For it is "everybody," a whole society, that has identified being feminine with caring about 5 how one *looks*. (In contrast to being masculine—which is identified with caring about what one *is* and *does* and only secondarily, if at all, about how one looks.) Given these stereotypes, it is no wonder that beauty enjoys, at best, a rather mixed reputation.

6   It is not, of course, the desire to be beautiful that is wrong but the obligation° to be—or to try. What is accepted by most women as a flattering idealization of their sex is a way of making women feel inferior to what they actually are—or normally grow to be. For the ideal of beauty is administered as a form of self-oppression. Women are taught to see their bodies in *parts*, and to evaluate each part separately. Breasts, feet, hips, waistline, neck, eyes, nose, complexion, hair, and so on—each in turn is submitted to an anxious, fretful, often despairing scrutiny°. Even if some pass muster°, some will always be found wanting. Nothing less than perfection will do.

7   In men, good looks is a whole, something taken in at a glance. It does not need to be confirmed by giving measurements of different regions of the body, nobody encourages a man to dissect his appearance, feature by feature. As for perfection, that is considered trivial—almost unmanly. Indeed, in the ideally good-looking man a small imperfection or blemish is considered positively desirable. According to one movie critic (a woman) who is a declared Robert Redford fan, it is having that cluster of skin-colored moles on one cheek that saves Redford from being merely a "pretty face." Think of the depreciation of women—as well as of beauty—that is implied in that judgment.

8   "The privileges of beauty are immense," said Cocteau°. To be sure, beauty is a form of power. And deservedly so. What is lamentable is that it is the only form of power that most women are encouraged to seek. This power is always conceived in relation to men; it is not the power to do but the power to attract. It is a power that negates itself. For this power is not one that can be chosen freely—at least, not by women—or renounced° without social censure°.

9   To preen°, for a woman, can never be just a pleasure. It is also a duty. It is her work. If a woman does real work—and even if she has clambered up to a leading position in politics, law, medicine, business, or whatever—she is always under pressure to confess that she still works at being attractive. But in so far as she is keeping up as one of the Fair Sex, she brings under suspicion her very capacity to be objective, professional, authoritative, thoughtful. Damned if they do—women are. And damned if they don't.

One could hardly ask for more important evidence of the dan-   10
gers of considering persons as split between what is "inside" and
what is "outside" than that interminable half-comic half-tragic tale,
the oppression of women. How easy it is to start off by defining
women as caretakers of their surfaces, and then to disparage° them
(or find them adorable) for being "superficial." It is a crude trap,
and it has worked for too long. But to get out of the trap requires
that women get some critical distance to see how much beauty
itself has been abridged° in order to prop up the mythology of the
"feminine." There should be a way of saving beauty *from* women—
and *for* them.

Words and Meanings

		Paragraph
Socrates	Greek philosopher and teacher (469–399 B.C.) who believed the highest meaning of life is attained through self-knowledge	1
paradoxical	contradictory, even absurd	
pedagogical	having to do with teaching	
wary	cautious, on guard against	2
vestiges	traces, remains	4
detriment	loss, harm, disadvantage	
narcissism	obsessive self-love	5
obligation	responsibility	6
scrutiny	close examination	
pass muster	be accepted as adequate	
Cocteau	Jean (1889–1963), French writer and film director	8
renounced	rejected, given up	
censure	disapproval	
preen	groom oneself, make oneself attractive	9
disparage	belittle, criticize	10
abridged	diminished, reduced	

Structure and Strategy

1. Sontag defines beauty partly through a series of contrasts. Identify two sets of contrasts that are explained in the first seven paragraphs of the essay.
2. What is the THESIS of "Beauty"? State it in your own words.
3. Study the examples Sontag uses in paragraphs 7 and 9. Do they provide effective support for her points? Why?
4. Explain the paradoxes with which Sontag introduces and concludes her essay. How do they contribute to the UNITY of the piece?

Content and Purpose

1. How did the ancient Greeks define beauty? How do we define it today?
2. According to Sontag, how did Christianity change the classical view of beauty?
3. What difference does Sontag identify in the ways in which men and women define themselves? How has this difference affected our culture's perception of physical attractiveness?
4. How does the "obligation" to be beautiful affect the way women see their bodies?
5. What relationship does Sontag identify between a woman's beauty and power? Do you agree with her?
6. According to this essay, physical beauty puts women in a double bind: they are "damned if they do" and "damned if they don't." What does Sontag mean by this? Do you agree? Why or why not?

Suggestions for Writing

1. Define your own idea of beauty. Is it an internal or an external quality?
2. Do you agree or disagree with Sontag that our culture's emphasis on the physical beauty of women is a "crude trap"? Explore the relationship between physical attractiveness and power.
3. More men than ever before are working out, using cosmetics, and having plastic surgery to improve the appearance of their faces and bodies. Are men today more obliged to be physically attractive than they were twenty-five years ago when Sontag wrote her essay? Do men now have to be "beautiful"? Why?

Altruism

LEWIS THOMAS

Dr. Lewis Thomas (1913–1993) combined the careers of research scientist, physician, teacher, and writer. The recipient of many scientific and academic awards, he strove in his essays to humanize science and to remind us that medicine is an art. A recurring theme in books such as *The Lives of a Cell* (1974), *The Medusa and the Snail* (1979), and *The Youngest Science* (1983) is the interrelatedness of all life forms.

A ltruism has always been one of biology's deep mysteries. 1 Why should any animal, off on its own, specified and labeled by all sorts of signals as its individual self, choose to give up its life in aid of someone else? Nature, long viewed as a wild, chaotic battlefield swarmed across by more than ten million different species, comprising unnumbered billions of competing selves locked in endless combat, offers only one sure measure of success: survival. Survival, in the cool economics of biology, means simply the persistence of one's own genes in the generations to follow.

At first glance, it seems an unnatural act, a violation of nature, 2 to give away one's life, or even one's possessions, to another. And yet, in the face of improbability, examples of altruism abound. When a worker bee, patrolling the frontiers of the hive, senses the nearness of a human intruder, the bee's attack is pure, unqualified suicide; the sting is barbed, and in the act of pulling away the insect is fatally injured. Other varieties of social insects, most spectacularly the ants and higher termites, contain castes of soldiers for whom self-sacrifice is an everyday chore.

It is easy to dismiss the problem by saying that "altruism" is 3 the wrong technical term for behavior of this kind. The word is a human word, pieced together to describe an unusual aspect of human behavior, and we should not be using it for the behavior of mindless automata°. A honeybee has no connection to creatures like us, no brain for figuring out the future, no way of predicting the inevitable outcome of that sting.

But the meditation of the 50,000 or so connected minds of a 4 whole hive is not so easy to dismiss. A multitude of bees can tell the time of day, calculate the geometry of the sun's position, argue about the best location for the next swarm. Bees do a lot of close observing of other bees; maybe they know what follows stinging and do it anyway.

Altruism is not restricted to the social insects, in any case. Birds 5 risk their lives, sometimes lose them, in efforts to distract the attention of predators from the nest. Among baboons, zebras, moose, wildebeests, and wild dogs there are always stubbornly fated guardians, prepared to be done in first in order to buy time for the herd to escape.

6   It is genetically determined behavior, no doubt about it. Animals have genes for altruism, and those genes have been selected in the evolution of many creatures because of the advantage they confer for the continuing survival of the species. It is, looked at in this way, not the emotion-laden problem that we feel when we try to put ourselves in the animal's place; it is just another plain fact of life, perhaps not as hard a fact as some others, something rather nice, in fact, to think about.

7   J. B. S. Haldane, the eminent British geneticist, summarized the chilly arithmetic of the problem by announcing, "I would give up my life for two brothers or eight cousins." This calculates the requirement for ultimate self-interest: the preservation and survival of an individual's complement of genes. Trivers, Hamilton, and others have constructed mathematical models to account nicely for the altruistic behavior of social insects, quantifying the self-serving profit for the genes of the defending bee in the act of tearing its abdomen apart. The hive is filled with siblings, ready to carry the *persona* of the dying bee through all the hive's succeeding generations. Altruism is based on kinship; by preserving kin, one preserves one's self. In a sense.

8   Haldane's prediction has the sound of a beginning sequence: two brothers, eight (presumably) first cousins, and then another series of much larger numbers of more distant relatives. Where does the influence tail off? At what point does the sharing of the putative° altruist's genes become so diluted as to be meaningless? Would the line on a graph charting altruism plummet to zero soon after those eight cousins, or is it a long, gradual slope? When the combat marine throws himself belly-down on the live grenade in order to preserve the rest of the platoon, is this the same sort of altruism, or is this an act without any technically biological meaning? Surely the marine's genes, most of them, will be blown away forever; the statistical likelihood of having two brothers or eight cousins in that platoon is extremely small. And yet there he is, belly-down as if by instinct, and the same kind of event has been recorded often enough in wartime to make it seem a natural human act, normal enough, even though rare, to warrant the stocking of medals by the armed services.

9   At what point do our genetic ties to each other become so remote that we feel no instinctual urge to help? I can imagine an

argument about this, with two sides, but it would be a highly speculative discussion, not by any means pointless but still impossible to settle one way or the other. One side might assert, with total justification, that altruistic behavior among human beings has nothing at all to do with genetics, that there is no such thing as a gene for self-sacrifice, not even a gene for helpfulness, or concern, or even affection. These are attributes that must be learned from society, acquired by cultures, taught by example. The other side could maintain, with equal justification, since the facts are not known, precisely the opposite position: we get along together in human society because we are genetically designed to be social animals, and we are obliged, by instructions from our genes, to be useful to each other. This side would argue further that when we behave badly, killing or maiming or snatching, we are acting on misleading information learned from the wrong kinds of society we put together; if our cultures were not deformed, we would be better company, paying attention to what our genes are telling us.

For the purposes of the moment I shall take the side of the   10
sociobiologists because I wish to carry their side of the argument a certain distance afield, beyond the human realm. I have no difficulty in imagining a close enough resemblance among the genomes° of all human beings, of all races and geographic origins, to warrant a biological mandate° for all of us to do whatever we can to keep the rest of us, the species, alive. I maintain, despite the moment's evidence against the claim, that we are born and grow up with a fondness for each other, and we have genes for that. We can be talked out of it, for the genetic message is like a distant music and some of us are hard-of-hearing. Societies are noisy affairs, drowning out the sound of ourselves and our connection. Hard-of-hearing, we go to war. Stone-deaf, we make thermonuclear missiles. Nonetheless, the music is there, waiting for more listeners.

But the matter does not end with our species. If we are to take   11
seriously the notion that the sharing of similar genes imposes a responsibility on the sharers to sustain each other, and if I am right in guessing that even very distant cousins carry at least traces of this responsibility and will act on it whenever they can, then the whole world becomes something to be concerned about on solidly scientific, reductionist, genetic grounds. For we have cousins more than we can count, and they are all over the place, run by genes so similar to ours that the differences are minor technicalities. All of us, men, women, children, fish, sea grass, sandworms, dolphins, hamsters, and soil bacteria, everything alive on the planet, roll ourselves along through all our generations by replicating DNA° and

RNA°, and although the alignments of nucleotides within these molecules are different in different species, the molecules themselves are fundamentally the same substance. We make our proteins in the same old way, and many of the enzymes most needed for cellular life are everywhere identical.

12   This is, in fact, the way it should be. If cousins are defined by common descent, the human family is only one small and very recent addition to a much larger family in a tree extending back at least 3.5 billion years. Our common ancestor was a single cell from which all subsequent cells derived, most likely a cell resembling one of today's bacteria in today's soil. For almost three-fourths of the earth's life, cells of that first kind were the whole biosphere°. It was less than a billion years ago that cells like ours appeared in the first marine invertebrates, and these were somehow pieced together by the joining up and fusion of the earlier primitive cells, retaining the same blood lines. Some of the joiners, bacteria that had learned how to use oxygen, are with us still, part of our flesh, lodged inside the cells of all animals, all plants, moving us from place to place and doing our breathing for us. Now there's a set of cousins!

13   Even if I try to discount the other genetic similarities linking human beings to all other creatures by common descent, the existence of these beings in my cells is enough, in itself, to relate me to the chestnut tree in my backyard and to the squirrel in that tree.

14   There ought to be a mathematics for connections like this before claiming any kinship function, but the numbers are too big. At the same time, even if we wanted to, we cannot think the sense of obligation away. It is there, maybe in our genes for the recognition of cousins, or, if not, it ought to be there in our intellects for having learned about the matter. Altruism, in its biological sense, is required of us. We have an enormous family to look after, or perhaps that assumes too much, making us sound like official gardeners and zookeepers for the planet, responsibilities for which we are probably not yet grown-up enough. We may need new technical terms for concern, respect, affection, substitutes for altruism. But at least we should acknowledge the family ties and, with them, the obligations. If we do it wrong, scattering pollutants, clouding the atmosphere with too much carbon dioxide, extinguishing the thin carapace° of ozone, burning up the forests, dropping the bombs, rampaging at large through nature as though we owned the place, there will be a lot of paying back to do and, at the end, nothing to pay back with.

Words and Meanings

automata	unthinking, machinelike organisms	3
putative	supposed	8
genomes	chromosomal structures	10
mandate	contract, requirement	
DNA	deoxyribonucleic acid; the molecule that carries genetic information	11
RNA	ribonucleic acid; the substance that transmits genetic information from the nucleus to the surrounding cellular material	
biosphere	earth's zone of life—from crust to atmosphere—encompassing all living organisms	12
carapace	protective outer shell or covering	14

Structure and Strategy

1. What two ABSTRACT terms does Thomas define in his introductory paragraph? How does he do so?
2. The BODY of this essay can be divided into sections, as follows: paragraphs 2 to 5, 6 to 8, 9 and 10, and 11 to 13. Identify the KEY IDEA Thomas develops in each of these four sections, and list some of the expository techniques he uses in his development.
3. In paragraphs 1 to 8, Thomas writes in the third person. Why does he shift to the first person in paragraph 9 and continue in first person until the end? To understand the different effects of the two POINTS OF VIEW, try rewriting some of the sentences in paragraph 14 in the third person.
4. In paragraph 10, Thomas introduces and develops a SIMILE to explain his faith in the "genetic message." Identify the simile and explain how it helps prepare the reader for the conclusion.
5. What concluding strategy does Thomas use in paragraph 14? How does his CONCLUSION contribute to the UNITY of the essay?

Content and Purpose

1. What is Thomas's THESIS? Summarize it in a single sentence.
2. In paragraph 1, Thomas introduces the fundamental IRONY on which this essay is based. Explain in your own words the ironic connection between altruism and survival.

3. Identify six or seven specific examples of animals that, according to Thomas, display altruistic behaviour. What ILLUSTRATION does Thomas use to show the altruistic behaviour of human beings?

4. Explain in your own words Thomas's claim that altruism is not an "emotion-laden problem," but rather a behaviour that is based on self-interest. (See paragraph 7.)

5. In paragraph 9, Thomas identifies two opposing explanations for altruistic behaviour: the cultural and the sociobiological. Summarize these in your own words. Which side does Thomas take, and why? (See paragraphs 10 to 13.)

Suggestions for Writing

1. Write an extended definition of the term "parenthood." Explain the reasons why people choose to have children, an act that involves a considerable amount of self-sacrifice.

2. Define another ABSTRACT term such as "wisdom," "integrity," "freedom," "evil," or "success." Attempt to define this term as clearly and concretely as Thomas does "altruism."

3. Write an essay exploring how a particular word has changed in meaning over time. Words such as "gay," "cool," "black," or even "grammar" reveal interesting changes in denotation and connotation.

4. Scores of people died on September 11, 2001, trying to save the lives of others. Why are certain people attracted to careers in which they risk their lives in altruistic pursuits?

The Approaching Age of Virtual Nations

MIKE DILLARD AND JANET HENNARD

Mike Dillard has over thirty years' experience in executive technology management. Janet Hennard is the founder of Strategic Marketing Services, a firm that specializes in business intelligence and strategic directions.

1   One of the most significant sociopolitical evolutions since the formation of cities and states may begin soon: the emergence of virtual nations. Individuals bound by a common,

passionate cause or set of beliefs form virtual nations (v-nations). Bridging time and space, the Internet provides fertile ground for members across the globe to fine-tune their ideologies and develop plans for their community's future. Ultimately, they strive to achieve all the elements of a nation, including leadership, governance, power, security, control, action, and loyalty. V-nations may also claim ownership of landmasses to increase their presence.

Posing a direct challenge to the world's existing nations, v-   2
nations will be both the cause and [the] effect of a monumental shift in global economic, political, and social structures. These new nations will at once threaten and stimulate hope for worldwide cooperation, security, and use of resources. Using the openness and relative freedom of online networks, v-nations will transcend simple online communities° or user groups that typically band together for common needs and interests. They will be far more ambitious, coalescing° individuals to create power and influence. A v-nation will seek to defend and protect its people, to provide for their health and well-being, and to implement a monetary system in support of its economic, social, political, and/or religious goals.

As v-nations emerge, interlinked societies will form in an over-   3
arching space above the current "real" nations. V-nation citizens will give their allegiance to a new kind of organization whose people are united by common ideals, goals, ambitions, or needs, and where one is as likely to share loyalty with acquaintances thousands of miles away as with a next-door neighbor. The potential outcomes range from noble to sinister, from order to chaos.

The hope is that the formation of v-nations will lead to a higher   4
level of human understanding and cooperation. The risk is that this evolution will tumble out of control, forever changing ordered societies as we know them. Free and democratic nations will need to prepare now for ways to combat the potential threats and to embrace the potential benefits that v-nations will bring. . . .

THE NECESSARY CONDITIONS—AND THE CATALYST

A potential virtual nation needs two basic conditions to surface: 5
reliable communications access and a significant cause. But the v-nation will need more than that—a catalyst—to truly take hold. Just as any nation or coalition requires inspirational leadership to survive, a compelling leader must either be present at the onset of the v-nation or emerge quickly to ensure its sustainability. A powerful and charismatic leader who captures the hearts and minds of the fledgling members becomes the catalytic agent with the authority to demand unquestioning loyalty, inspire action, get people to

change direction, and shape the future of the v-nation. Only then will the v-nation truly come to life.

6   A disturbing example of a rudimentary but menacing virtual nation exists today—one with all the required conditions. On September 11, 2001, we witnessed the power and force of that virtual nation, borne out of the combination of easy access to sophisticated communications, a fervent cause (the overthrow of "heretic governments" in their respective countries and the establishment of Islamic governments), and a charismatic leader.

7   Al Qaeda, a worldwide network of fundamentalist Islamic organizations, was formed in 1998 with a handful of members, no homeland, no army, no ongoing revenues, and only a few leaders operating from remote areas of the world. The Internet enabled al Qaeda to become a formidable virtual nation, gaining strength as Internet access spread globally and especially as its primary leader-catalyst, Osama bin Laden, earned the unquestioning loyalty of its members. In Afghanistan, al Qaeda demonstrated how a v-nation can further its causes by taking an entire country hostage and even dictating the actions of that country's ruling army.

8   The al Qaeda v-nation now operates in some 40 countries and is organized into hundreds of cells. Its economic power is believed to come from worldwide business enterprises, charities, international stock manipulation, and, at least until the fall of Afghanistan's ruling Taliban, from large, indirect profits of Afghanistan's production of an estimated 70% of the world's heroin cash crop according to the U.S. Drug Enforcement Administration. With little physical structure, the al Qaeda v-nation has been able to wreak horrific havoc on the world.

EVOLUTION AT A TRANSITION POINT

9   The emergence of v-nations can be seen as a natural evolutionary phenomenon. We know that human organization evolved from bands of people to hunting and agrarian societies to city-state governments to our current nations. During its first 50 years, the computer industry has been following or mimicking this same societal evolution, never challenging the future of our societies, but rather supporting societies as we know them. The fact that man communicates with others led to the development of the computer network. That man is not linked directly to another person via a wire led to the wireless age of computing. That societies evolved to hunt led to the modern-day equivalent of hunting parties—the business-to-business buying portals. And now we know that the need to com-

municate and bond among groups across geographical and national divides was a predicator of the burgeoning online communities. Throughout, the technology networking evolution has continued to shadow the evolutionary march of human behavior.

But today we are at a unique point, where society and technology are intrinsically drawn together into a web of evolution and collusion°, each driving the other. Unblocked by the natural geography that limited us in the past, and unbounded by the ideological trenches of our modern world, networked societies are driving the next societal transformation—the development of societies without geographical borders, with new ways of bonding, new concepts of nations, and new paradigms° of societal organizations. This societal evolution, driven by larger and more sophisticated online communities with their common needs and goals, will use the efficiencies and advantages of the next-generation networked society, regardless of location, geography, or historical functions. The question is to what degree virtual nations and traditional nations should and can coexist.

THE EMERGENCE OF VIRTUAL NATIONS

Nations and societies have always been somewhat insulated by distance, ideas, culture, resources, and time. Earlier in history, societies and nations were formed around the distance one could walk, then by geographical or natural boundaries. Today, geography, history, inertia, patriotism, resources, and economic structure define them. But increasingly, loyalty, needs, goals, and fears will define them.

Nations as we know them will continue to exist. But among new societies we will see new reasons for existing and a synergy among entities that is likely to transcend the relationships among traditional nations. As this happens, people will not tolerate the current boundaries that cause inefficiencies in the use of the world's assets. They will use the world's online network to optimize the allocation of those assets or to promote their own agendas. The result will be societies with new methods of protecting people, new monetary systems, and new hierarchies—virtual nations that capitalize on online connectedness.

As a virtual nation emerges, its citizens can be from anywhere, but they will have a common bond based on one or more principles or needs. It will be as easy to start in Bangalore as it is in Sunnyvale, as easy in rich countries as in those with less wealth. Just as with a traditional nation, a virtual nation runs the risk of being captured by those with sinister or misguided goals. It will also have the same foibles° and challenges as any other government

10

11

12

13

or organization. And it will have to struggle with such questions as, Who will lead it? What will be its laws? Who will be a member? Who will govern and how?

CHALLENGES TO OUR CURRENT NATIONS

14   As virtual nations arise—whether they have the best intent for their members, or are sinister in nature, or even act as rogue nations°— they will begin to . . . challenge our current nations, their way of life, and the security that we perceive in those nations. Especially critical will be challenges in areas of citizenship, loyalty, security, and quality of life. Innovative monetary systems will likely emerge to address bartering among v-nations.

15   Current concepts of national loyalty and citizenship are likely to change dramatically and will be severely challenged as virtual nations become prevalent. People will inherit a citizenship based on place of birth, but they may elect to participate in a virtual nation or nations where loyalty brings them more health, wealth, safety, support, or religious approval. At the most basic level, citizens will want to protect themselves and be able to make a living for their families. Their allegiance will be to those nations, virtual or physical, that can best guarantee the right to a better education, better medical care, better income, opportunity to own land and property, religious freedom, or better jobs.

16   Eventually, individuals will want citizenship in numerous nations and organizations, moving in and out as particular benefits are needed or desired. The concept of citizenship is likely to evolve into one of dual or even multiple citizenships and loyalties, and individuals will be torn between their land of ancestry and the lure of the virtual nations. In the end, the tug of the virtual nations will become too powerful for many to resist, and loyalty will shift to this form of organizational control.

DEFENDING AGAINST VIRTUAL ENEMIES

17   With the rise of virtual nations, society's enemies will not be geographically based nations, but rather organizations of people linked by information and commitment. Threats to society will come on all levels, from global to local, physical to psychological. The most abominable threats will come from virtual nations of terrorists or jingoists° who use networked societies and weapons within targeted nations to advance their causes.

18   We have already witnessed how a group can be called to action via a global network. The events of September 11 are a sobering example of the tremendous power a worldwide terror nation can wield. Imagine an equally sinister opponent that calls for a partic-

ular movement to control research or that calls for oppressive treatment of a particular group or population.

The mechanisms for traditional nations to control the threat of   19
terrorist nations are limited today. If this continues to be true, we may imagine a period of sustained anarchy [in which] threats continue on a regular basis with no way for nations or individuals to fully protect themselves.

POSSIBLE BENEFITS

In seeking the best in health and life quality, people will go outside   20
of their current national umbrellas. No longer will quality of life be tied to an employer or government, but rather to similar demographic groups linked by a virtual bond. The traditional inefficiencies of remoteness or national laws will no longer prevent people from seeking proper medical attention, education, food, shelter, and opportunity for income. Virtual nations will open vistas never before available to many people.

Intrinsic to virtual nations is the need to trade. Although not   21
mandatory, it is highly likely that an "Internet barter dollar" will emerge to overcome the inefficiencies that will arise as v-nations attempt to exchange goods across old boundaries. Processes to complete a transaction, which require many steps, several currency conversions, and multiple tax calculations, will be considered absurd and unrealistic.

To meet these challenges, a new currency will emerge that will   22
have the same value no matter where it is used. It might initially be something as simple as airline miles. It is easy to imagine a person offering 2,000 frequent flyer miles for a carpet from the Andes. But whatever form it takes, this new currency will likely begin on the black markets before gaining acceptance as a legal tender.

A TIME TO ACT

Virtual nations will occur. The basic infrastructure is in place to   23
enable them to emerge. Already we are seeing the first stages and examples, some good and some bad. It is unfortunate that our most visible example of the approaching age of v-nations was one with such sinister goals and actions—the al Qaeda v-nation. But it clearly lays out the challenges that mankind faces. As virtual nations arise, they offer untold opportunities for the advancement of society. However, we must understand that they don't change the attitudes of people; they only mirror those attitudes. There will be those with positive ambitions, and there will be those with sinister intent. We must develop strategies that deal with both, just as we develop strategies to deal with our nations of today. We must

24   begin to consider whether to include virtual nations into the family of nations. If we do not plan for the reality of v-nations, we will find ourselves in a period of sustained and continuous turmoil.

Perhaps the most we can do at this point is to acknowledge the emergence of v-nations and, as much as possible, guide them in a direction that benefits mankind or legitimate businesses. We do have the potential to make this the best societal evolution yet—one led by the human spirit of survival, kindness, and free markets. We can create v-nations for research, pulling together the world's best minds. We can create nations for distributing the world's resources to benefit all humanity. We can create nations that specialize in providing educational benefits for all those around the world. We can use these nations to break down religious bigotry and persecution. We can help [establish] the long-called-for world order, where everyone is treated equally and where all people have the best education, shelter, and respect for their common value.

25   The great nations of the current world must help shape the world to come—a world of coexistence between nations and virtual nations, where well-meaning virtual nations are fostered, encouraged, and guided for the true causes that benefit mankind and free economies. Virtual nations will challenge our world as we know it—a breathtaking change. Now is the time to build a world that embodies the best of both natural and virtual nations.

Words and Meanings

Paragraph		
2	online communities	groups of people with common interests who come together on the World Wide Web
	coalescing	coming together; combining to form a coalition
10	collusion	a secret agreement or pact
	paradigms	examples or patterns
13	foibles	minor weaknesses
14	rogue nations	countries that refuse to comply with the principles of international law
17	jingoists	extreme nationalists or patriots who support an aggressive foreign policy

Structure and Strategy

1. In their INTRODUCTION, the authors provide a definition of "virtual nations." Summarize it in your own words.

2. What is the function of paragraphs 2, 3, and 4? Would removing these paragraphs diminish the effectiveness of the essay? Explain.
3. Where in the essay do the authors provide an extended example of an existing v-nation? Explain why this example is (or is not) effective in illustrating their definition of a v-nation.
4. In paragraphs 9 and 10, the authors draw an ANALOGY between five thousand years of social evolution and the first fifty years in the development of the computer industry. Explain the analogy in your own words. Do you think it is valid? Why or why not?
5. How would you describe the TONE of this essay? Do the authors support, applaud, oppose, or fear the rise of virtual nations?
6. What kind of CONCLUSION have the authors provided? Is it effective? Why or why not?

Content and Purpose

1. How does the authors' definition of virtual nations change the traditional meaning of the word "nation"?
2. Which of the characteristics of a v-nation described in paragraph 2 does al Qaeda exhibit? Not exhibit?
3. What three fundamental factors do the authors claim are necessary for the emergence of a virtual nation? (See paragraph 5.)
4. According to the authors, what problems and challenges will v-nations and traditional nations have in common?
5. What are some of the potential threats and benefits posed by the rise of virtual nations? (See paragraphs 17 to 19, 20 to 22, and 24.)
6. How do the authors suggest that the obstacles to trade among v-nations might be resolved?
7. Do you belong to one or more online communities? If so, does your online community exhibit any of the characteristics of a virtual nation as defined by the authors? Explain.

Suggestions for Writing

1. How do you think the Internet has changed (or will change) the world? Write an essay that explores Internet-driven changes and their consequences for our culture and way of life.
2. Write an essay that defines your own concept of a nation.

Condemnation Without Absolutes

STANLEY FISH

Stanley Fish (b. 1938) is dean of the College of Liberal Arts and Sciences and professor of English and criminal justice at the University of Illinois at Chicago. A renowned literary critic and cultural theorist, he has written extensively for a wide range of international periodicals. His recent books include *Professional Correctness: Literary Studies and Political Change* (1995), *The Trouble with Principle* (1999), and *How Milton Works* (2001).

1   During the interval between the terrorist attacks and the United States' response, a reporter called to ask me if the events of Sept. 11 meant the end of postmodernist relativism°. It seemed bizarre that events so serious would be linked causally with a rarefied form of academic talk. But in the days that followed, a growing number of commentators played serious variations on the same theme: that the ideas foisted° upon us by postmodern intellectuals have weakened the country's resolve. The problem, according to the critics, is that since postmodernists deny the possibility of describing matters of fact objectively, they leave us with no firm basis for either condemning the terrorist attacks or fighting back.

2   Not so. Postmodernism maintains only that there can be no independent standard for determining which of many rival interpretations of an event is the true one. The only thing postmodern thought argues against is the hope of justifying our response to the attacks in universal terms that would be persuasive to everyone, including our enemies. Invoking the abstract notions of justice and truth to support our cause wouldn't be effective anyway because our adversaries lay claim to the same language. (No one declares himself to be an apostle° of injustice.) Instead, we can and should invoke the particular lived values that unite us and inform the institutions we cherish and wish to defend.

3   [At such times], the nation rightly falls back on the record of aspiration and accomplishment that makes up our collective understanding of what we live for. That understanding is sufficient, and far from undermining its sufficiency, postmodern thought tells us that we have grounds enough for action and justified condemnation in the democratic ideals we embrace, without grasping for the empty rhetoric of universal absolutes to which all subscribe but which all define differently.

4   But of course it's not really postmodernism that people are bothered by. It's the idea that our adversaries have emerged not

from some primordial° darkness, but from a history that has equipped them with reasons and motives and even with a perverted version of some virtues. Bill Maher, Dinesh D'Souza and Susan Sontag have gotten into trouble by pointing out that "cowardly" is not the word to describe men who sacrifice themselves for a cause they believe in. Ms. Sontag grants them courage, which she is careful to say is a "morally neutral" term, a quality someone can display in the performance of a bad act. (Milton's Satan is the best literary example.) You don't condone° that act because you describe it accurately. In fact, you put yourself in a better position to respond to it by taking its true measure. Making the enemy smaller than he is blinds us to the danger he presents and gives him the advantage that comes along with having been underestimated.

That is why what Edward Said has called "false universals"   5
should be rejected: they stand in the way of useful thinking. How many times have we heard these new mantras: "We have seen the face of evil"; "these are irrational madmen"; "we are at war against international terrorism." Each is at once inaccurate and unhelpful. We have not seen the face of evil; we have seen the face of an enemy who comes at us with a full roster° of grievances, goals and strategies. If we reduce that enemy to "evil," we conjure up a shape-shifting demon, a wild-card moral anarchist° beyond our comprehension and therefore beyond the reach of any counterstrategies.

The same reduction occurs when we imagine the enemy as   6
"irrational." Irrational actors are by definition without rhyme or reason, and there's no point in reasoning about them on the way to fighting them. The better course is to think of these men as bearers of a rationality we reject because its goal is our destruction. If we take the trouble to understand that rationality, we might have a better chance of figuring out what its adherents will do next and preventing it.

And "international terrorism" does not adequately describe   7
what we are up against. Terrorism is the name of a style of warfare in service of a cause. It is the cause, and the passions informing it, that confront us. Focusing on something called international terrorism—detached from any specific purposeful agenda—only confuses matters. This should have been evident when President Vladimir Putin of Russia insisted that any war against international terrorism must have as one of its objectives victory against the rebels in Chechnya.

When Reuters° decided to be careful about using the word "ter-   8
rorism" because, according to its news director, one man's terrorist

is another man's freedom fighter, Martin Kaplan, associate dean of the Annenberg School for Communication at the University of Southern California, castigated° what he saw as one more instance of cultural relativism. But Reuters is simply recognizing how unhelpful the word is, because it prevents us from making distinctions that would allow us to get a better picture of where we are and what we might do. If you think of yourself as the target of terrorism with a capital T, your opponent is everywhere and nowhere. But if you think of yourself as the target of a terrorist who comes from somewhere, even if he operates internationally, you can at least try to anticipate his future assaults.

9   Is this the end of relativism? If by relativism one means a cast of mind that renders you unable to prefer your own convictions to those of your adversary, then relativism could hardly end because it never began. Our convictions are by definition preferred; that's what makes them our convictions. Relativizing them is neither an option nor a danger. But if by relativism one means the practice of putting yourself in your adversary's shoes, not in order to wear them as your own but in order to have some understanding (far short of approval) of why someone else might want to wear them, then relativism will not and should not end, because it is simply another name for serious thought.

Words and Meanings

Paragraph

1	postmodernist relativism	the belief that concepts such as right and wrong, good and evil, or truth and falsehood change from culture to culture and situation to situation
	foisted	forced or imposed
2	apostle	an ardent supporter (of a cause or principle)
4	primordial	existing at the beginning of time
	condone	to overlook or disregard an offence or wrongdoing
5	roster	list
	moral anarchist	a person who challenges society's values or beliefs
8	Reuters	a major international news agency
	castigated	criticized or rebuked harshly

Structure and Strategy

1. For what AUDIENCE did Fish write this piece? Identify in as much detail as you can four or five significant characteristics of these readers (for example, age, education, profession, interests, politics).
2. How would you describe the TONE of this piece? How do the author's DICTION and SYNTAX contribute to the tone?
3. In paragraphs 4 and 5, Fish illustrates his THESIS by drawing on the ideas of people who are considered to be authorities in their respective fields. Identify each source and the field he or she represents. Why do you think Fish includes these people in his essay?
4. Identify the ALLUSION in paragraph 4. How does it support Fish's ARGUMENT?
5. What are the "new mantras" (paragraph 5) Fish objects to? How do these topics influence the structure and development of paragraphs 5 to 7?

Content and Purpose

1. In paragraph 1, a reporter asks Fish a question shortly after the attacks of September 11, 2001. What is the question, and why would the reporter ask it of Fish? (See biographical note.)
2. The first two paragraphs explain one of the major tenets of postmodernism. Summarize this idea in your own words.
3. What are the "universal terms" (paragraph 2) postmodernists argue should not be used to justify a response to the events of 9/11? Explain the reasoning behind their position.
4. Does Fish think that postmodern thought is able to justify a response to the 9/11 attacks? If so, what are the grounds that would validate "either condemning the terrorist attacks or fighting back" (paragraph 1)?
5. Why does Fish think that it is unhelpful, even dangerous, to define one's enemies as "evil"?
6. How does Fish define "irrational" in paragraph 6? According to the essay, how does defining one's enemies as lacking in reason diminish our ability to deal with them?
7. Why do Reuters and Fish have concerns about the way we use the word "terrorism"? Do you agree with their assumption that language influences thought? Why or why not?
8. The concluding paragraph provides two definitions of the term "relativism"—one of which, according to Fish, is irrelevant. PARAPHRASE both definitions.

Suggestions for Writing

1. Write an essay in which you define "evil" and the kinds of acts you consider evil. Are the people who carry out evil acts by definition evil themselves? What standards would you use in order to label an act or a person "evil"?
2. Choose a well-known recent (or not so recent) event and provide an interpretation of it. Define your standard for determining the truth of your interpretation. Do you regard this standard as independent or absolute? Or do you agree with Fish and the postmodernists that "there can be no independent standard for determining which of many rival interpretations of an event is the true one"?

Additional Suggestions for Writing: Definition

Write an extended definition of one of the topics below.

1. Canadian humour
2. superstition
3. anxiety (or depression)
4. status symbol
5. wisdom
6. terrorism
7. creativity
8. pop culture
9. a typical Canadian
10. success

U N I T

7

Argument and Persuasion

WHAT ARE ARGUMENT AND PERSUASION?

In Unit 6, we pointed out that some words have specific meanings that are different from their generally accepted meanings. The word ARGUMENT is commonly defined as a disagreement or quarrel, while PERSUASION usually refers to the act of trying to bring someone over to our side. In the context of writing, however, argument and persuasion refer to specific kinds of writing that have a special PURPOSE— one that is a bit different from the purpose of expository prose.

The introductions to Units 2 through 6 of this text have explained organizational patterns commonly found in EXPOSITION—writing intended primarily to explain. It is true that a number of the essays in these units contain strong elements of argument or persuasion: consider Jessica Mitford's indictment of embalming in Unit 2, for instance, or Lewis Thomas's plea for altruism in Unit 6. Nevertheless, the primary purpose of expository writing is to *inform* the reader—to explain a topic clearly.

Argument and persuasion have a different primary purpose. They attempt to lead the reader to share the writer's beliefs and perhaps even to act on these beliefs. For example, in "The Talent Myth," Malcolm Gladwell attempts to convince readers that intelligence is an overrated virtue in the corporate world; in "What Is the Good Life?" Mark Kingwell presents a thoughtful and compelling argument that "the good life" is not achieved through material comforts alone. Of course, readers are not likely to be persuaded of anything without clear explanation, so there is nearly always some overlap between exposition and argument. Nonetheless, in this unit, we consider argument and persuasion as writing strategies intended mainly to *convince* the reader of an opinion, judgment, or course of action.

WHY DO WE WRITE ARGUMENT AND PERSUASION?

Argument and persuasion answer the lead-in question *why.* Why is this idea or action a good (or bad) idea? There are two fundamental ways to appeal to readers: through their minds and through their hearts. *Argument* is the term applied to the logical approach, convincing a person by way of the mind. "The Case for Marriage," which uses statistics and logic to support the authors' pro-marriage thesis, is a clear example of argument. *Persuasion* is the term often applied to the emotional approach, convincing a person by way of the heart. Hal Niedzviecki's "Stupid Jobs Are Good to Relax With" is a provocative piece of persuasion that appeals to the emotions—mostly resentment—of well-educated people in their twenties who are stuck in dead-end jobs. Often, writers use both strategies. For example, in "The Great Democracy Drop Out," Gregory Boyd Bell uses the techniques of logical argument as well as emotional appeals to encourage young Canadians to participate in the political process. We decide which approach to use—logical, emotional, or a combination of the two—depending on the issue we are discussing.

HOW DO WE WRITE ARGUMENT AND PERSUASION?

While exposition tends to focus on objective topics, argument and persuasion focus on issues. An **issue** is an opinion or belief that not all people agree on. It is always *controversial,* which literally means "having two sides." To begin to argue an issue, clearly and concisely state your opinion about it. This is your statement of THESIS. Here are two theses from essays in this unit:

> Stupid jobs can be good for you. (Hal Niedzviecki, "Stupid Jobs Are Good to Relax With")

> Today's young activists should get involved in mainstream political parties. (Gregory Boyd Bell, "The Great Democracy Drop Out")

The test of a good thesis for an argument or persuasion paper is that someone could plausibly argue the opposite POINT OF VIEW: "Stupid jobs are depressing and demeaning"; "Young activists have no hope of influencing the direction of mainstream political parties."

Once your opinion about an issue is clearly stated, you need to identify reasons to support it. The lead-in question to ask is *why*. Why do you believe what you do about your issue? The reasons you identify are the KEY IDEAS you will explore and support in your essay.

Persuasive papers can be developed in a variety of ways. It is possible, as the readings in this unit indicate, to use a number of different structural patterns to convince your readers. For example, the model essay "Why Write?" relies on the familiar thesis statement structure. Rex Murphy's "September 11, 2001: A Wake-Up More Than a Nightmare" is based on a contrast of different views of world history. Most of the expository patterns can be adapted to persuasive purposes.

One structural pattern is specific to argument and persuasion: the **their side–my side strategy** involves presenting the "con" (or "against") points of the opposing side first, then refuting them with the "pro" (or "for") side of the argument. This technique is particularly useful when you are arguing a contentious position that will provoke serious dispute. For instance, the second paragraph of "The Case for Marriage" offers the negative view of marriage: "Marriage, its detractors contend, can trap women and men in unhealthy relationships." The "their side–my side" strategy tends to neutralize opposition by meeting it head-on.

Here are four guidelines for writing clear argument and persuasion:

1. Write a thesis statement that clearly states your opinion about an issue and, if appropriate, briefly previews your reasons (key ideas).
2. Think through your key ideas carefully and make sure that you can support them with appropriate and convincing details. It is a good idea to do some research to find supporting EVIDENCE.
3. Assemble accurate, relevant, and sufficient evidence to develop your key ideas.
4. Arrange your reasons in the ORDER that will be most convincing to the reader. Usually, you save your strongest reason for the end of the paper.

Bringing readers over to our side through well-chosen words is a challenge. Argument and persuasion are probably the most formidable writing tasks that we undertake, yet they may also be the most important. Armed with logic, feelings, and words, we can persuade others to agree with us and even to act. Effective persuasion is an art that truly deserves to be called civilized.

The model essay that follows takes a light-hearted approach to an old but still timely argument.

Why Write?

Introduction
challenges the
view that
writing skill has
nothing to do
with sex appeal

This may come as a surprise to you, but being able to write well contributes to your sex appeal. Even more surprising is the fact that not being able to write well decreases your attractiveness to prospective mates. Intrigued? Read on! Writing is an essential skill if you want to achieve three vital objectives: communicate effectively and memorably, obtain and hold satisfying employment, and attract worthy sex partners. Once you understand the influence good communication can have on your life, then you will see how skills such as faultless grammar, sound sentence structure, and an appealing style can transform you from road kill on the highway of life to a turbocharged powerhouse.

*Thesis
statement*

*Key idea #1:
the reason is
developed by
contrast and
example*

While spoken communication is, for most of us, easy, natural—almost automatic—it doesn't have the lasting power of written language. Even e-mail, the least permanent form of writing, can be re-read, forwarded, and redirected, attaining a kind of permanence that conversation cannot. Who wants to be the author of a message remembered for its unintended but hilarious grammatical flaws or syntactical blunders ("Sisters reunite after 18 years at checkout counter!")? Writing permits us to organize and present our thoughts effectively. Who hasn't mentally replayed a conversation over and over before finding, when it's too late, just the right comeback to a humiliating put-down? Writing allows the time to ensure that every sentence is precise, memorable, and devastating.

*Note use of
questions to
engage reader*

*Key idea #2:
the reason is
developed by
contrasting old
and new
business
environments*

In business environments, good writing is a predictor of success. People who communicate well, do well. This fact is continually emphasized in executive surveys, recruitment panels, and employer polls. At one time, novices heading for a career on the corporate ladder held the attitude that writing was something secretaries did. In today's climate of instant and incessant electronic communication and networked industries (not to mention downsizing), few people can rely on a subordinate to correct their errors or polish their style before their colleagues or clients see their work. (Besides, many of those secretaries who could write well are now occupying executive suites themselves.) It doesn't matter what career you choose: your effectiveness is going to be judged in part by how well you communicate. Whether you're a health-care worker who must keep comprehensive and accurate notes, an environmental technician who writes reports for both experts and laypeople, or a technologist who must defend her need for a budget increase, good writing enhances both the message and the messenger.

Throughout evolutionary history, men and women have sought mates with the skills and attributes that would enable them to thrive in the environment of the times. Eons ago, female survival depended on choosing a man with a concrete cranium and bulging biceps because he was most likely to repel predators and survive attacks. Prehistoric men selected women for their squat, sturdy bodies and thick fat layer because such females were more likely than their sinewy sisters to survive an Ice Age winter (and even provide warmth). Attraction between the sexes is based on attributes that suggest ability to survive, procreate, and provide. Skills such as spear-hurling and fire-tending are not in much demand anymore. Today's men and women are on the lookout for mates with updated thriving expertise. Your ability to communicate effectively is one of the skills that place you among the twenty-first-century elite, those who will rise to the top of the corporate food chain, claiming the most desirable mates as you ascend. Besides, the ability to write melting love letters or clever, affectionate e-mail is a far more effective turn-on these days than the ability to supply a slab of mastodon or a well-crafted loincloth. Go ahead—flex those writing muscles, flaunt that perfect style!

Why write? Because excellent communication skills are the single most important attribute you can bring to the table, whether you are negotiating for power, profession, prestige, or a partner.

Note use of examples to support key idea

Key idea #3: reason is developed by contrasting the survival skills required in prehistoric times with those required today

Note use of descriptive details

Topic is reinforced in a paraphrase

Conclusion emphasizes significance of the topic

Author answers the question "Why write?" with a carefully constructed sentence fragment designed to linger in the reader's mind

The Case for Marriage

LINDA J. WAITE AND MAGGIE GALLAGHER

Linda J. Waite (b. 1947) is a professor of sociology at the University of Chicago and former president of the Population Association of America. Her most recent research focuses on the family, divorce, and aging. A graduate of Yale University, Maggie Gallagher (b. 1960) is an affiliate scholar at the Institute for American Values and a senior fellow at the Center for Social Thought. She writes a regular opinion column for New York *Newsday* and is the author of *Enemies of Eros* (1989) and *The Abolition of Marriage* (1996). In 2000, she co-authored (with Linda Waite) the book from which this selection is taken.

1   In the 1950s, the rules were clear: first love, next marriage, and only then the baby carriage. Who could have imagined the tsunami° ahead? In a rapid blur came the Pill, the sexual revolution, gay pride, feminism, the mass move of married mothers into the workplace, no-fault divorce, and an unexpected orgy of unmarried child-bearing. Without warning, the one firm understanding that marriage is a cornerstone of our society had all but disappeared.

2   Marriage, its detractors contend, can trap women and men in unhealthy relationships, pressuring them with irrational taboos to live in a way that does nobody any good. Preferences for marriage, special benefits for married couples—once viewed as common-sense supports for a vital social institution—are denounced as discriminatory. Some say marriage is financially unfair to men and frustrates their sexual needs. Others argue that it benefits men at the expense of women's independence, gratification, physical safety, and even sanity. Marriage "protects men from depression and makes women more vulnerable," [contends] Neil Jacobson, University of Washington psychologist and author of the 1998 book *When Men Batter Women.* . . .

3   From this perspective, divorce is perceived as a great social boon. And far from being cause for alarm and reform, the astonishing growth of births out of wedlock—from about five percent of total births in 1960 to a third of all births today—is seen as welcome proof of the emancipation of women from marital restrictions.

4   Even our language betrays the new attitudes toward marriage. A reluctance even to use the word seems to be sweeping the West. The Marriage Guidance Council of Australia recently changed its name to Relationships Australia. Britain's National Marriage Guidance Council metamorphosed into Relate. A popular sex education manual for children does not mention the M-word, although

it acknowledges, vaguely, that "there are kids whose mothers and fathers live together."

But here is the great irony: if you ask the right questions, there is plenty of evidence suggesting that marriage is a vital part of overall well-being. Contrary to what many Americans now believe, getting and staying married is good for men, women, and children. Marriage, it turns out, is by far the best bet for ensuring a healthier, wealthier, and sexier life.

Imagine, for example, a group of men and women all 48 years old and as alike in background as social scientists can make them. How many will be alive at age 65? According to a study we did, of those men who never married or are divorced, only 60 percent will still be around. By contrast, 90 percent of the married [men] will survive. Similarly, 90 percent of married women will reach 65, compared to 80 percent of single and divorced women.

It's not just a matter of mortality. Among men and women nearing retirement age, wives are almost 40 percent less likely than unmarried women to say their health is poor. Even in old age married women are less likely to become disabled, and married people of both sexes are much less likely to enter nursing homes.

How can a mere social contract have such far-reaching effects? For one thing, new research suggests that marriage might improve immune system functioning, as married people are shown to be less susceptible than singles to the common cold. For another, married people tend to pursue healthier lifestyles. The evidence is clear: spousal nagging works. A wife feels licensed to press her husband to get checkups or eat better. And a man responds to a wife's health consciousness in part because he knows that she depends on him as he depends on her. Statistics show that getting married leads to a dramatic reduction in smoking, drinking, and illegal drug use for both men and women, while just moving in together typically does not. And according to Justice Department data, wives are almost four times less likely than single women to fall victim to violent crime.

Then there's the question of domestic violence. Many commentators talk as if the institution of marriage itself is at fault. Two eminent scholars, for example, title their influential essay on rates of domestic violence "The Marriage License as Hitting License." And Jacobson declares flatly that "marriage as an institution is still structured in such a way as to institutionalize male dominance, and such dominance makes high rates of battering inevitable." Even the best researchers tend to use *wife abuse* and *domestic violence* interchangeably, strongly implying that getting married can put women at special risk.

10   But the truth is that women who live with men out of wedlock are in much greater danger. Cohabiting men are almost twice as likely as husbands to engage in domestic violence. To look at it another way, women who have never married are more than four times more likely than wives—and divorced women more than seven times more likely—to be the victims of intimate violence.

11   The kids' health can also benefit from marriage. Children are 50 percent more likely to develop health problems due to a parental separation, and those in female-headed single-parent homes are more likely to be hospitalized or to suffer chronic health conditions such as asthma. And for babies marriage can mean the difference between life and death. Those born to single mothers are much more likely to die in the first year. Even among groups with the lowest risk of infant mortality, marriage makes a big difference: babies born to college-educated single mothers are 50 percent more likely to die than babies born to married couples. What's more, the health advantage of having married parents can be long-lasting.

12   If marriage can benefit health, how about its effect on the pocketbook? Recent research suggests that getting and keeping a wife may be as important to a man's financial portfolio as getting a good education. Depending on which study you cite, husbands earn anywhere from 10 percent to 40 percent more than single men, and the longer men stay married, the greater the gap.

13   Like men, women get an earnings boost from marriage. But children change the picture. One study finds that having a child reduces a woman's earnings by almost four percent and that two or more reduce her pay by almost 12 percent. Women get a marriage premium, but also pay a substantial motherhood penalty.

14   Still, there are countervailing benefits. Married couples manage their money more wisely than singles and are less likely to report signs of economic hardship. And the longer they stay married, the more wealth they build. By retirement, the average married couple has accumulated assets worth about $410,000, compared to $167,000 for those never married and $154,000 for the divorced.

15   Arguably, marriage itself is a form of wealth. Because they can share both the labor and the goods of life, husbands and wives produce more with less effort and cost. And having a partner who promises to care for you in good times and bad is also valuable— equal, according to one recent estimate, to a 12 percent increase in wealth for a 30-year-old spouse, and a whopping 33 percent for 75-year-old married people.

16   In theory, unmarried people who live together might enjoy the same economies. In practice, however, things work out differently.

In *American Couples*, Philip Blumstein and Pepper Schwartz describe how a typical cohabiting couple thinks about money. Jane is a pediatrician living with Morton, a lawyer. "Morton was not particularly thrilled when I took the bonus and traded in the Volvo for the Alfa. Well, too bad. I let him alone and I expect him to let me alone." Morton agrees, somewhat wistfully: "I would not always make the same decisions she does. I would save and invest more. But it's her money, and I don't dare interfere."

By contrast, Lisa, a homemaker married to machinist Al, has no   17
problems interfering with her husband's spending habits, because the money he makes is not "his" but "theirs." "He doesn't control it," Lisa says of her husband's spending, "so we have to stop quite often and discuss our budget and where did all this money go to. Why are you broke? Where did it go to? If it went to good causes, I can find 10 dollars more," she says confidently—the money manager for both of them. "If it didn't, tough."

Some experts try to de-emphasize the apparent benefits of mar-   18
riage as a cover for the "real" problems plaguing children of divorce: poverty, family conflict, and poor parenting. As scholar Arlene Skolnick put it in a recent family studies textbook, "Family structure—the number of parents in the home or the fact of divorce—is not in itself the critical factor in children's well-being. In both intact and other families, what children need most is a warm, concerned relationship with at least one parent."

But three decades of evidence have made it clear that divorce   19
dramatically increases economic hardship and puts new stress on the parent–child bond, thus exacerbating° precisely the problems Skolnick decries. In the face of the hard data, it is almost impossible to argue that having married parents is not a critical factor in a child's well-being.

All right: so marriage trumps being single as far as health,   20
wealth, and the kids' well-being goes. But surely the single person enjoys better sex? Wedding cake, in the old joke, is the best food to curb your sexual appetite. "What is it about marriage," wonders Dalma Heyn in *Marriage Shock*, "that so often puts desire at risk?"

Surprisingly, the truth is just the opposite: married people have   21
better sex lives than singles. Indeed, married people are far more likely to have sex lives in the first place. Married people are about twice as likely as unmarried people to make love at least two or three times a week.

And that's not all: married sex is more fun. Certainly, at least,   22
for men: forty-eight percent of husbands say sex with their partners is extremely satisfying, compared to just 37 percent of cohabiting men.

23   When it comes to creating a lasting sexual union, marriage implies at least a promise of permanence, which may be why cohabiting men are four times more likely to cheat, and cohabiting women eight times more likely, than husbands and wives.

24   That is doubtless one reason why married men and women, on average, tend to be emotionally and mentally healthier—less depressed and anxious or psychologically distressed than single, divorced, or widowed Americans. One study that followed 14,000 adults over a 10-year period found that marital status was one of the single most important predictors of personal happiness.

25   Marriage, we'd like to argue, is not just one of many kinds of relationships that are all "equally valid"—equally likely to advance health and happiness of men, women, and children. Of course we don't suggest that people should be dragooned into marrying against their will, or that some marriages should not end. But we do say that what enables marriage to deliver its powerful life-enhancing benefits is that it is not just a private lifestyle, an arrangement whose success or failure concerns the lover alone.

26   Marriage creates powerful positive changes in couples' lives because it is a public relationship, living proof that interdependence, faithfulness, obligation, responsibility, and union are more fruitful over the long run than choices that may seem more immediately gratifying.

27   Helping people imagine that long run, then making it come true, is what marriage still does best.

Words and Meanings

Paragraph

1 tsunami   a large, destructive ocean wave; also called a tidal wave

19 exacerbating   making worse

Structure and Strategy

1. Find the essay's thesis statement. What three KEY IDEAS does it contain? Identify the paragraphs that develop each key idea.
2. What strategy do the authors use in the INTRODUCTION? Is it effective? Why or why not?
3. What kind of development do the authors use as support for their ideas in paragraphs 6 to 7, 12 to 15, and 22 to 23? Is this development strategy effective? Convincing? Why or why not?
4. How are the topics of paragraphs 16 and 17 developed? Do you find this development strategy more or less convincing than

the one used in the paragraphs identified in question 3? Explain.

5. What is the function of paragraph 20? How does it help the reader to follow the authors' ARGUMENT?
6. Which paragraphs make up the essay's CONCLUSION? What kind of concluding strategy is used? Why do you think the final paragraph is so short?

Content and Purpose

1. What is a tsunami? As a METAPHOR for the change that is the topic of paragraph 1, is it effective? Why or why not?
2. According to the authors, what are some of the factors that have changed our view of marriage over the last fifty years?
3. Identify three ARGUMENTS used by opponents of marriage. (See paragraphs 2 and 3.) Do you agree with any of these arguments? Why or why not?
4. According to the authors, you'll discover the benefits of marriage for men, women, and children "if you ask the right questions" (paragraph 5). What are the "right questions"?
5. What are three health benefits that the authors attribute to marriage?
6. After citing statistics to support their argument that married people are wealthier than unmarried people, the authors suggest that "marriage itself is a form of wealth" (paragraph 15). Explain this statement in your own words.
7. What is "one reason why married men and women, on average, tend to be emotionally and mentally healthier" (paragraph 24) than their unmarried counterparts? Do you find the authors' argument convincing? Why or why not?
8. How do married people benefit from the fact that marriage is a "public relationship" (paragraph 26)? Do you agree with the authors that marriage "creates powerful positive changes in couples' lives"? Why or why not?

Suggestions for Writing

1. Write an essay that either confirms or disproves the arguments presented in "The Case for Marriage." Draw on your own marriage, or that of someone you know, to support your argument.
2. Using some of Waite and Gallagher's argumentation techniques, write an essay in which you argue for or against having children.

September 11, 2001: A Wake-Up More Than a Nightmare

REX MURPHY

Born in Carbonear, Newfoundland, Rex Murphy (b. 1947) graduated from Memorial University and attended Oxford University, as a Rhodes scholar, at the same time as former U.S. president Bill Clinton. Extending a CBC career that began in the early 1970s, Murphy hosts the radio show *Cross Country Checkup* and contributes a weekly opinion piece to *The National*. He writes a regular column for *The Globe and Mail*, and has won several national and provincial broadcasting awards.

1   Everything hasn't changed. There are unalterables, pleasant and unpleasant. . . . Our repertoire of pleasure or annoyance is the same as it's always been. When people portended after the cataclysm of September 2001 that "everything has changed," they weren't thinking of [what Samuel Johnson called] the "public stock of harmless human pleasures." Or for that matter, the equally large common stock of human pains. September 11 did not alter our nature, or the things our nature, with its mixed receptors, responds to.

2   *Everything* never changes. The instant motto in the aftermath of 9/11 was a leap to stamp that day's horrors with some meaning, to provide rhetorical purchase° while people gathered the resources of spirit and intelligence necessary to read its final import. It was never meant to say the whole truth about that day, or to be taken at any time in full literalness.

3   In a curious way, the "everything has changed" message actually carried quite the opposite meaning. Since the close of the Second World War, the West has been, in comparison with most parts of the globe, on something of a holiday. We had begun to think the holiday was "normal." Great wealth, longer lives, technology, the absence of conflict—this side of the globe was saturated with the hubris° of its own exceptionality. We had forgotten the common lot of our kind, which is, sadly, that the world, for all its wonders and beauty, is also and inevitably a place of pain and sorrow and, all too commonly, blood. Uninterrupted peace is always more rare than war. Harmony is the contingent° experience, conflict and tragedy the rule.

4   The "everything" that had changed was a wealth-cocooned dream, the fantasy that the West was past tasting the horrors of history, that on this side of the water history in its cruelty and madness was something we caught up with watching those other places

on TV. That certainly changed. I think New York last year, and Washington and Pennsylvania, shocked us out of a comforting illusion, that we were exempt from the turbulence of the world, that history had two faces—one grim, one meek—and reserved the benign one for us.

The deeper seriousness that was said to follow September 11 was just the old seriousness returned, the realization of every generation that the comfort and shape of everyday life is something most generations must consciously construct and defend. That it doesn't just happen; that everyday life is built on hard-won habits, on structures of tolerance and civility, on forms of self-governance achieved only after much experiment and determination, on values nursed over generations and often articulated° at the price of great sacrifice.

Every previous generation has also understood, or learned the hard way, that the world harbours much menace, that violence is more common than its absence, and that evil men are at least as busy, and considerably more energetic, than good ones. This great line of Yeats has much poetry, more truth: "The best lack all conviction, while the worst / Are full of passionate intensity." Hitler, unchecked, would have placed the planet in an eclipse of pain and tyranny. Stalin yoked the lives of millions to the nightmare of police-state communism. Starvation, prison, torture and execution were "normal" in all the despotisms of the 20th century, from Idi Amin, who still crawls the globe, to Tito, who no longer cumbers° it. There are always giant egos seeking to corral humankind, and a few outsized madmen dreaming of enslaving it.

We had forgotten that bitter lesson until [9/11]. Osama bin Laden may turn out to be a cartoon pygmy of a villain who got "lucky" with one big strike. Saddam Hussein may just be a monstrous buffoon who collapses with the next exhale of determination. Or these men may be signals of even greater portent°.

September 11, in all its vicious suddenness, was a return to business as usual. The world was ever more hostile than tranquil, more threat than succour; this is an ancient, howsoever melancholy, truth. All those pleasant, ordinary experiences that make up our everyday lives are ours, spontaneously to enjoy, only because we have built and maintained systems to house and protect them. The everyday doesn't just happen. It is a precarious achievement.

So everything hasn't changed after all. We're back, alas, to normal.

Words and Meanings

Paragraph

2	rhetorical purchase	the hold or grip on events that language gives us
3	hubris	excessive pride or arrogance
	contingent	chance; accidental
5	articulated	expressed
6	cumbers	burdens
7	portent	a sign (often ominous) of something to come

Structure and Strategy

1. In your own words, state the THESIS of this essay.
2. Paragraph 6 is developed by means of example. How do the examples Murphy uses support his ARGUMENT?
3. "The best lack all conviction, while the worst / Are full of passionate intensity." Explain how this quotation from "The Second Coming," by Irish poet William Butler Yeats, supports the KEY IDEA of paragraph 6.

Content and Purpose

1. Why do you think Murphy begins his ARGUMENT with the assertion that "Everything hasn't changed"?
2. According to Murphy, why did so many commentators use the phrase "everything has changed" after the "cataclysm" of September 11, 2001 (paragraph 1)? What did this "instant motto" (paragraph 2) provide for people in the West?
3. Why does Murphy think that nothing changes in world history? How does he characterize humanity's "common lot"?
4. According to Murphy, before the events of 9/11, how long had people in the West felt exempt from "the horrors of history" (paragraph 4)? What reason does he give for the West's sense of "exceptionality"? Do you agree with his analysis? Why or why not?
5. According to Murphy, what is the basis of "our everyday lives"? Why does he say "the everyday" must be defended? How does he propose we defend it?
6. Summarize Murphy's sense of the experience that most of us endure or enjoy from day to day. Do you agree with Murphy? Why or why not?

Suggestions for Writing

1. Write an essay about your response to 9/11. Discuss where you were when you heard the news, your initial reaction, and how that reaction changed or developed over time.
2. According to Murphy, "Harmony is the contingent experience, conflict and tragedy the rule." Write an essay in which you agree or disagree with this statement. Consider both world events (past and present) and your personal history.

The Great Democracy Drop-Out

GREGORY BOYD BELL

Writer and editor Gregory Boyd Bell (b. 1963) is a media issues columnist at *The Hamilton Spectator*. From 1996 to 2002, he wrote a regular media column for *eye Weekly*, a Toronto arts and opinion magazine. Boyd Bell's essays on media, politics, and culture have appeared in such publications as *This Magazine* and New York *Newsday*. His media column was short-listed for a National Magazine Award in 2000.

When British Columbia's new Liberal government took power [in 2001], one of its priorities was to undo the previous NDP government's work on treaty negotiations with First Nations. The crowbar of choice was a referendum that sought, through eight innuendo-laced° questions, to manufacture a popular mandate to damn legal precedent and revise the constitutional status of treaty rights to somewhere just below the inalienable right to go camping.   1

The B.C. referendum was a horrid bit of mobocracy. It asked voters, though of course not in quite so many words, if they'd like to gang up and turn all those claimed lands into provincial parks and tell the pesky Indians to take a long walk off a short pier.   2

In response, the Union of B.C. Indian Chiefs, supported by union groups and various social justice campaigners, called for an "active boycott" of the vote in which participants would send their mail-in ballots to First Nations governments for ritual burning. On June 10 the Hupacasath First Nation, which lost its attempt to persuade the B.C. Supreme Court to block the referendum, held a ballot-burning party for some of the nearly 13,000 voided ballots they [had] received. They planned to immolate° the rest in Victoria   3 on July 3, when the results of the referendum were to be published. While there's no doubting the newsworthiness of the scheme, it sadly reflects how progressive political groups find themselves drawn to the margins, from the actual practice of power and influence to the mere performance of political theatre.

4   "Don't vote—it only encourages them!" This ancient bumper sticker joke is one of the slogans adopted by the Edible Ballot Society, a small Canadian group that follows the proud tradition of parodic critiques of establishment democracy. The familiar notion is that voting doesn't make a difference because the whole thing is rigged. Candidates only get to be on the ballot by selling out to The Man, so picking one tool over another is but an illusion of democracy. But whether you burn, eat, or quietly scrawl "burn in hell" on your ballot, you are making a statement. And the statement is: Please ignore me.

5   That statement can be made by organized groups, like the B.C. chiefs, or the edible ballotists, or by those who get their jollies from chucking rocks at riot cops. It is certainly being made by a much larger number of younger citizens who are simply withdrawing from politics, if indeed they were ever involved. When Canada's federal Liberals won their third straight majority government in November 2000, only 61% of eligible citizens cast a ballot. The abysmal turnout bumped Canada from its place among high-participation democracies—like Sweden, Germany, France, Italy, Uruguay, Chile, and Brazil—and relegated us to the slough° of apathy that prevails in places like Poland, Guatemala, Egypt and the United States. Post-election surveys confirmed that the sharp drop—down by six percent from the 1997 federal vote—was largely due to an even greater drop in voting by one demographic group: people born after 1970.

6   In recent studies of voter (and non-voter) behaviour, activist critiques of democracy do not register. What studies do show is that the number of people who do not vote is strongly correlated with the number that is clueless. In a 1990 survey carried out for the Royal Commission on Electoral Reform and Party Financing, a dismal five percent of Canadians could not name the prime minister. In 2000, the number in a similar survey was 11%. It gets worse. Since 1965, surveys of voters have been carried out by the Canadian Election Study. In the 1984 study, almost 90% could name their provincial premier. In 1997, it was 77%. The decline in knowledge was greatest among young adults.

7   Luring younger voters into the system is certainly a top priority for the . . . New Democratic Party, whose declining support through

the 1990s follows the falling participation by younger voters like hangover follows the fifth martini. Yet the problem affects all Canadian political parties, and indeed most modern liberal democracies, which have seen declines in voter turnout of varying severity over the past decade. If this Great Democracy Drop-Out continues, we face being ruled by governments whose corroding legitimacy can only fuel a vicious circle of further alienation, still lower turnout, and a spiral into inherently unstable oligarchy°.

Of course, some younger citizens don't vote because they believe the words on another old bumper sticker: "If voting could change anything, it would be illegal." They're too smart to fall for the con. They've exchanged passive voting for an active quest for political or social change, usually within a patchwork of organizations that are often lumped together under the banner of anti-capitalism or anti-globalism.   8

Consider for a moment the key contention by activists that meetings like the Summit of the Americas or the G-8 are "non-democratic." The critique is rather undercut if the critics themselves aren't participating in electoral politics, whether by running as candidates or infiltrating major parties.   9

The alternative to electoral participation is marginalization. That's how democratic electoral politics works. All parties have core supporters, but in order to win a majority they must extend their support by appealing to other groups, usually on an issue-by-issue basis. If one of your group's defining characteristics is that you don't vote, won't vote, or just say screw the vote, then don't look so surprised when vote-seekers demonstrate no sympathy or concern for your priorities.   10

This isn't to dismiss valid concerns about Canadian democracy. It's true that democracy needs to be more than an event that happens every few years in which you mark your X and go home and bar the door. And it's hard to argue with the view that the government appears to be a revolving door of the same business interests and party fat cats. But this criticism doesn't support abandoning the system in order to save it. If you want to fix the government, it's a bit odd to announce that your first step will be to avoid the government. This is like announcing you're going to fix your bicycle by reassembling the toaster oven. If we agree that the baddies are dehumanizing and anti-democratic, doesn't that mean we should humanize democracy?   11

If you want big changes, there are only two approaches open: revolution or peaceful takeover. For a revolution, you need lots of people who aren't squeamish. Or you can make like the Ottawa Committee of the World March of Women who earlier this year   12

launched a "Revolutionary Knitting Action in protest against corporate greed and globalization" by inviting women of the community to knit or crochet one-foot squares to be assembled into a
"gigantic 'social safety net' to symbolize a caring, compassionate
and peaceful society." The project hopes to create "a 'soft' barrier of
knitted yarn as a way to reclaim public spaces from the elite to the
common good."

13   The knitting project, like lobbing teddy bears at riot cops, is
amusing and ingenious but not much of a basis for constitutional
government. In the event that the mass knitters of Ottawa fail to
bring global capitalism to its knees, that leaves the less socially
exciting option of actually trying to change the system. That
requires you to get involved in the practice of politics.

14   Today's younger activists could kick ass in mainstream political
parties. Do they realize how few votes it takes to nominate a candidate? Or perhaps they secretly fear that their commitment, or that
of their fellow-travellers, is so shallow that it could be uprooted by
a few executive meetings or, God forbid, taking a seat in the
Commons.

15   It's vital for the future of Canada, and all Western liberal
democracies, to reintegrate those who are turning or simply falling
away from electoral politics. Activists need to lead their peers, not
like sheep back into the fold of electoral politics, but as a powerful
block of voters and policy makers. The alternative is further
declines in voter turnout and more noisy but marginal activism,
leading to an oligarchy in which a narrowing electorate selects a
largely permanent government. If this seems an exaggeration, consider that in both Canadian and American elections, the lower the
turnout, the better the odds that the incumbent will win. Or that the
next leadership vote for the Liberal Party of Canada, which is
restricted to paid-up members, will have more impact on Canada's
federal government than the last two general elections combined.

16   Burning and eating ballots—organized nonparticipation—is a waste
of effort that might go into actual reform of actual politics. The
better course is to persuade people that, if they fail to exercise their
franchise°, it will get flabby—and it may not be up to much when
they really need it. This kind of mass persuasion is something that
many younger activists are very good at. For example, one project
that needs help is the push for some form of proportional represen-
tation°, which just happens to be a great way to raise voter turnout
because people get a better sense that their individual vote matters.

Activists who stay to the outside are unlikely to get much more   17
than a few headlines unless they dirty their hands with boring
dusty old electoral politics. Taking part in protests like those in
Quebec City or Calgary is, of course, a healthy outdoor activity that
gives young people a chance to make new friends and learn about
the value of co-operation. But it's not going to fix the system.

No matter whether it's apathy or misguided activism, dropping   18
out of mainstream politics is an excellent way to ensure that young
life is circumscribed by a bunch of aging white guys whose primary
ambitions are to pay off their pals, leave their name on a building
and die in the arms of someone less than half their age.

Before you go drop out, remember that democracy is a lot of   19
things, many of them untidy, some of them embarrassing. But it's
not supposed to be the solution; it's just a process by which we try
to grant a government a public mandate. Mainstream politics is a
nasty, dirty, smelly, noisy sort of monkey house. You can stand on
the outside and throw peanuts through the bars. But if you really
want change, you have to go inside and get dirty.

Words and Meanings

		Paragraph
innuendo-laced	biased	1
immolate	burn	3
slough	swamp	5
oligarchy	government by a small group of people who govern for their own purposes	7
franchise	the right to vote	16
proportional representation	an electoral system in which a political party is represented in the legislature in direct proportion to the number of votes it receives	

Structure and Strategy

1. Summarize the details of the political narrative presented in the INTRODUCTION (paragraphs 1 to 3). Why do you think Boyd Bell begins the essay with this narrative? What is his opinion of the action taken by the Union of B.C. Indian Chiefs?
2. What is the example Boyd Bell uses in paragraph 4? What does "parodic" mean?

3. Who is the AUDIENCE for this essay? Identify four or five examples of DICTION and supporting EVIDENCE Boyd Bell uses to appeal to this audience.
4. Identify the SIMILES in paragraph 7 and 11. How does each one reinforce the point Boyd Bell is making?
5. Describe the STYLE of the essay. What is the effect of the author's dramatic shifts from formal to informal? (Compare, for example, paragraphs 15 and 18.)
6. What METAPHOR does Boyd Bell use in paragraph 19? Is it an effective way to conclude the essay? Why or why not?

Content and Purpose

1. According to the essay, what demographic group most consistently ignores or refuses to participate in electoral politics? Why? How does the "clueless" (paragraph 6) factor contribute to this behaviour?
2. Define in your own words the term "oligarchy" (paragraphs 7 and 15). Why does Boyd Bell see oligarchy as a possible result of what he calls the "Great Democracy Drop-Out"?
3. According to Boyd Bell, for people who "want big changes" (paragraph 12), what is the alternative to electoral participation? Why does he include the Revolutionary Knitting Action as an example in this CONTEXT?
4. Do you agree with Boyd Bell that "younger activists could kick ass in mainstream political parties" (paragraph 14)? Why or why not?
5. Summarize Bell's ARGUMENT. Do you find it convincing? Why or why not?
6. Do you follow electoral politics? Belong to a political party? Vote? Why or why not?

Suggestions for Writing

1. Why do many Canadians choose not to vote? What are the consequences of low voter turnout? Write an essay explaining the causes and/or effects of voter apathy.
2. Imagine that you are running for a government office (e.g., school trustee, council member, mayor). What issues do you think would be of special interest to younger voters? What strategies would you use to get them to vote for you?

Stupid Jobs Are Good to Relax With

HAL NIEDZVIECKI

Hal Niedzviecki (b. 1971) is editor of the anthology *Concrete Forest: The New Fiction of Urban Canada* (1998) and *Broken Pencil*, a website (www.brokenpencil.com) and print magazine devoted to underground culture and the independent arts. A correspondent for CBC Radio's *Brave New Waves*, he has contributed to newspapers and periodicals across North America. His books include *Smell It, Lurvy, We Want Some Too*, and *Ditch*.

S pringsteen kicked off his world tour at Toronto's Massey Hall   1
a while back. Along with record company execs and those who could afford the exorbitant° prices scalpers wanted for tickets, I was in attendance. As Bruce rambled on about the plight of the itinerant Mexican workers, I lolled° in the back, my job, as always, to make myself as unapproachable as possible—no easy feat, trapped as I was in paisley vest and bow-tie combo. Nonetheless, the concert was of such soporific° proportions and the crowd so dulled into pseudo-reverence, I was able to achieve the ultimate in ushering—a drooping catatonia° as close as you can get to being asleep while on your feet at a rock concert.

But this ushering nirvana° wouldn't last long. For an usher,   2
danger takes many forms, including vomiting teens and the usher's nemesis°: the disruptive patron. And yes, to my semi-conscious horror, there she was: well-dressed, blond, drunk and doped up, swaying in her seat and . . . clapping. Clapping. In the middle of Springsteen's solo dirge about Pancho or Pedro or Luisa, she was clapping.

Sweat beaded on my forehead. The worst was happening. She   3
was in my section. Her clapping echoed through the hall, renowned for its acoustics. The Boss glared from the stage, his finger-picking folksiness no match for the drunken rhythm of this fan. Then, miracle of miracles, the song ended. The woman slumped back into her seat. Bruce muttered something about how he didn't need a rhythm section. Placated° by the adoring silence of the well-to-do, he launched into an even quieter song about an even more desperate migrant worker.

I lurked in the shadows, relaxed the grip I had on my flashlight   4
(the usher's only weapon). Springsteen crooned. His guitar twanged. It was so quiet you could hear the rats squirrelling around the ushers' subterranean change rooms. The woman roused herself from her slumber. She leaned forward in her seat, as if

suddenly appreciating the import of her hero's message. I wiped the sweat off my brow, relieved. But slowly, almost imperceptibly, she brought her arms up above her head. I stared, disbelieving. Her hands waved around in the air until . . . boom! Another song ruined, New York record execs and L.A. journalists distracted from their calculations of Bruce's net worth, the faint cry of someone calling, "Usher! Do something!"

5   For several years now, I have relied on stupid jobs to pay my way through the world. This isn't because I am a stupid person. On the contrary, stupid jobs are a way to avoid the brain-numbing idiocy of full-time employment. They are the next best thing to having no job at all. They will keep you sane, and smart.

6   I'm lazy sometimes. I don't always feel like working. On the stupid job, you're allowed to be lazy. All you have to do is show up. Hey, that's as much of an imposition on° my life as I'm ready to accept. Does The Boss go to work every day? I don't think so. He's The Boss.

7   Understanding the stupid job is the key to wading your way through the muck of the working week and dealing with such portentous° concepts as The Youth Unemployment Crisis and The Transformation of the Workplace. So sit back and let me explain. Or, as I used to say behind the scowl of my shining grin: "Hi, how are you this evening? Please follow me and I will show you to your seat."

8   "Out of Work: Is There Hope for Canada's Youth?" blurted the October 1997 issue of *Canadian Living*. My answer? There is more hope than ever. I'm not talking about ineffectual governments and their well-intentioned "partners," the beneficent corporations, all banding together to "create" jobs. After all, what kind of jobs do you think these corporations are going to create? Jobs that are interesting, challenging and resplendent° with possibilities? Hardly. These are going to be stupid jobs. Bring me your college graduates, your aspiring business mavens°, your literature lovers and we will find them rote° employment where servility° and docility° are the best things they could have learned at university.

9   But hope, hope is something altogether different. Hope is the process whereby entire generations learn to undervalue their work, squirm out of the trap of meaningless employment, work less, consume less and actually figure out how to enjoy life.

10   I hope I'm right about this, because the reality of the underemployed, overeducated young people of Canada is that the stupid job is their future. As the middle-aged population continues to occupy all the "real" jobs, as the universities continue to hike tuition prices

(forcing students to work and study part time), as the government continues to shore up employment numbers with make-work and "retraining," there will be more stupid jobs than ever. And these stupid jobs won't be reserved for the uneducated and poor. The fertile growth of the stupid job is already reaping a crop of middle-class youngsters whose education and upbringing have, somehow, given way to (supposedly) stalled° prospects and uncertain incomes.

These are your grandchildren, your children, your sisters, your   11
cousins, your neighbours. Hey, that might very well be a multi-coloured bow-tie wrapped around your neck.

I took a few tenuous° steps down the aisle. All around me, luxurious   12
people hissed in annoyance and extended their claws. Clapping woman was bouncing in her seat. She was smiling. Her face was flushed and joyous. The sound of her hands coming together was deafening. I longed for the floor captain, the front-of-house manager, the head of security, somebody to come and take this problem away from me. I hit her with a burst of flashlight. Taking advantage of her momentary blindness, I leaned in: "Excuse me Miss," I said. "You can't do that." "What?" she said. "That clapping," I said. "Listen," she slurred. "I paid $300 to see this. I can do what I want."

My flashlight hand wavered. Correctly interpreting my silence   13
for defeat, she resumed her clapping. Springsteen strummed louder, unsuccessful in his attempt to drown out the beat of luxury, the truth of indulgence. I faded away, the darkness swallowing me up. For a blissful moment, I was invisible.

A lot of young people think their stupid jobs are only temporary.   14
Most of them are right, in a way. Many will move on from being, as I have been, an usher, a security guard, a delivery boy, a data co-ordinator, a publishing intern. They will get marginally better jobs, but what they have learned from their stupid jobs will stay with them forever. Hopefully.

If I'm right, they will learn that the stupid job—and by exten-   15
sion, all jobs—must be approached with willing stupidity. Set your mind free. It isn't necessary, and it can be an impediment°. While your body runs the maze and finds the cheese, let your mind go where it will.

Look at it this way: you're trading material wealth and luxury   16
for freedom and creativity. To simplify this is to say that while you may have less money to buy things, you will have a lot more time to think up ways to achieve your goals without buying things. It is remarkable how quickly one comes to value time to just sit and think. Oddly, many of us seem quite proud of having absolutely no

time to think about anything. The words "I'm so busy" are chanted over and over again like a mantra°, an incantation° against some horrible moment when we realize we're not so busy. In the stupid job universe, time isn't quantifiable. You're making so many dollars an hour, but the on-job perks include daydreams, poems scribbled on napkins, novels read in utility closets and long conversations about the sexual stamina of Barney Rubble. How much is an idea worth? An image? A moment of tranquillity? A bad joke? The key here is to embrace the culture of anti-work.

17   Sometime after the Springsteen debacle°, I was on a delivery job dropping off newspapers at various locales. I started arguing with my co-worker, the van driver, about work ethic. I suggested we skip a drop-off or two, claiming that no one would notice and even if they did, we could deny it and no one would care. He responded by telling me that no matter what job he was doing, if he accepted the work, he was compelled to do it right. I disagreed. Cut corners, I argued. Do less for the same amount of pay. That's what they expect us to do, I said. Why else would they pay us so little? Not that day, but some weeks later, he came to see things my way.

18   What am I trying to tell you? To be lazy? To set fire to the corporation?

19   Maybe. Our options might be limited, but they are still options. Somewhere in the bowels of Massey Hall it has probably been noted in my permanent record that I have a bad attitude. That was a mistake. I wasn't trying to have a bad attitude. I was trying to have no attitude. . . .

20   What I should have told my friend in the delivery van was that when working the stupid job, passivity° is the difference between near slavery and partial freedom. It's a mental distinction. Your body is still in the same place for the same amount of time (unless you're unsupervised), but your mind is figuring things out. Figuring out how many days you need to work to afford things like hard-to-get tickets to concerts by famous American icons. Or figuring out why it is that at the end of the week, most people are too busy or too tired to do anything other than spend their hard-earned dollars on fleeting moments of cotton candy ecstasy as ephemeral° as lunch hour. Personally, I'd take low-level servitude over a promotion that means I'll be working late the rest of my life. You want me to work weekends? You better give me the rest of the week off. . . .

21   Montreal has one of the highest unemployment rates of any city in Canada. Young people in that city are as likely to have full-time jobs as they are to spend their nights arguing about Quebec separa-

tion. Not coincidentally, some of the best Canadian writers, comic artists and underground periodicals are from that city. We're talking about the spoken-word capital of North America here. Creativity plus unemployment equals art.

The burgeoning° stupid job aesthetic° is well documented in another youth culture phenomenon, the vaunted 'zine (photo-copied periodicals published by individuals for fun, not money). Again, it doesn't take a genius to make the connection between the youth culture of stupid jobs and the urgency and creativity 'zine publishers display when writing about their lives. "So why was I dishonest and subversive?" asks Brendan Bartholomew in an article in the popular Wisconsin 'zine *Temp Slave*. "Well, I've been sabo-taging employers for so long, it's become second nature. It's in my blood. I couldn't stop if I wanted to." 22

Slacking off, doing as little as possible, relishing my lack of responsibility, this is what the workplace has taught me to do. This is the stupid job mantra. It isn't about being poor. The stupid job aesthetic is not about going hungry. Canada is a country of excess. You cannot have a stupid job culture when people are genuinely, truly, worried that they are going to starve in the streets. 23

Nevertheless, the tenets° of the stupid job revolution are uni-versal: work is mainly pointless; if you can think of something better to do, you shouldn't have to work; it's better to have a low-paying job and freedom than a high-paying job and a 60-hour workweek. It was Bruce's drunken fan who highlighted the most important aspect of what will one day be known as the stupid job revolution: with money, you think you can do whatever you want, but you rarely can; without money, you can be like Bartholomew— a postmodern rat, a stowaway writing his diaries from the comfort of his berth at the bottom of the sinking ship. 24

My father's plight is a familiar one. He started his working life at 13 in Montreal. He's 55 now. His employer of 12 years forced him to take early retirement. The terms were great, and if he didn't own so much stuff (and want more stuff) he could live comfortably without ever working again. But he feels used, meaningless, rejected. 25

On his last day, I helped him clean out his office. The sight of him stealing staplers, blank disks and Post-it note pads was some-thing I'll never forget. It was a memo he was writing to his own soul (note: they owe me). 26

But the acquisition° of more stuff is not what he needs to put a life of hard work behind him. I wish that he could look back on his years of labour and think fondly of all the hours he decided not to work, those hours he spent reading a good book behind the closed 27 door of his office, or skipping off early to take the piano lessons he never got around to. Instead of stealing office supplies, he should have given his boss the finger as he walked out the door. Ha ha. I don't care what you think of me. And by the way, I never did.

28 Despite his decades of labour and my years of being barely employed (and the five degrees we have between us), we have both ended up at the same place. He feels cheated. I don't.

Paragraph

Words and Meanings

Paragraph		
1	exorbitant	grossly excessive
	lolled	lazily stood or leaned
	soporific	causing sleep
	catatonia	state of semiconsciousness in which one is unable to move
2	nirvana	blissful state
	nemesis	someone who is fated to do you harm
3	placated	soothed
6	imposition on	restriction on, interference with
7	portentous	of tremendous importance or significance (here, ironic)
8	resplendent	bright, shining
	aspiring mavens	ambitious would-be experts
	rote	routine, repetitive
	servility	slavishly doing what you're told
	docility	dutiful obedience, willingness to learn
10	stalled	at a standstill; halted with no hope of advancement
12	tenuous	hesitant
15	impediment	obstacle; something blocking your path to achievement
16	mantra	frequently repeated sound, word, or phrase, often sacred (see also paragraph 23)
	incantation	verbal charm or spell whose purpose is to produce magic effect
17	debacle	disaster
20	passivity	patient acceptance, not resisting
	ephemeral	lasting only a short time

burgeoning	fast-growing	22
aesthetic	theory of what is valid, worthwhile, or beautiful	
tenets	beliefs, principles	24
acquisition	accumulation, piling up	27

Structure and Strategy

1. Identify the paragraphs that tell the story of the author's ushering at a Springsteen concert. What is the point of the paragraphs that he inserts into the middle of the narrative? Why do you think he interrupts his story in this way?
2. What does Niedzviecki's DICTION tell us about his attitude toward the people in the audience, the music, and his job as an usher? See, for example, paragraphs 1, 3, 4, and 12.
3. Which paragraph states the THESIS of the essay?
4. What strategy does the author use in his CONCLUSION (see paragraphs 25 to 28)? Do you think it's effective? Why or why not?
5. Why is the author's use of IRONY appropriate in this essay, given his topic? Identify two or three examples of both verbal and situational irony and explain why you find them effective.
6. What were your expectations of the author when you read the title of the essay? Were you surprised to find words such as "exorbitant," "soporific," and "catatonia" in the first paragraph? What other elements of STYLE and structure tell us that the author is far from "stupid"?
7. Is this essay primarily ARGUMENT or PERSUASION?

Content and Purpose

1. According to Niedzviecki, what kinds of jobs are college graduates most likely to get in the coming years? (See paragraphs 8 to 11.) Why? Even if the author's pessimistic view proves to be correct, do you agree that "servility and docility are the best things [students can learn] at university"?
2. At several points in the essay, the author refers to rats—some literal, some figurative. (See, for example, paragraphs 4, 15, and 24.) What point is he making?
3. Explain what Niedzviecki means by "the culture of anti-work" (paragraph 16). What advantages does he see in being underemployed?
4. What is the basis of the author's argument with the van driver as they're dropping off newspapers? (See paragraphs 17 to 20.) Whom do you agree with? Who has the right attitude toward the job?

5. What proof does Niedzviecki offer to support his point that art and creativity are likely to flourish among people who are unemployed or have "stupid jobs"?
6. What is Niedzviecki's attitude toward consumerism? Does he think we buy too much or not enough? Where in the essay is his attitude most clearly revealed? Do you agree with him? Why or why not?

Suggestions for Writing

1. Most of us have worked in what Niedzviecki calls a "stupid job." Did you learn anything from the experience? Write an essay that details your own experience in a low-paying, routine job in which intelligence and creativity were neither required nor encouraged.
2. Write an essay that argues for or against the "do it right" work ethic: that we should work hard at any or all jobs we do.
3. What should a postsecondary education prepare us for? Do people go to college or university to prepare for work, learn about the world, or pursue personal interests? What reasonable expectations might graduates have after completing their education?
4. Niedzviecki recommends that we "embrace the culture of anti-work." Write an essay in which you argue for or against this proposition.

The Talent Myth: Are Smart People Overrated?

MALCOLM GLADWELL

Malcolm Gladwell (b. 1963) was born in England and grew up in Canada, where he graduated from the University of Toronto in 1984. A former reporter for *The Washington Post* (1987–96), he has been a staff writer at *The New Yorker* since 1996. He is the author of *The Tipping Point: How Little Things Can Make a Big Difference* (2000).

1   [A few] years ago, several executives at McKinsey & Company, America's largest and most prestigious management-consulting firm, launched what they called the War for Talent. Thousands of questionnaires were sent to managers

across the country. Eighteen companies were singled out for special attention, and the consultants spent up to three days at each firm, interviewing everyone from the C.E.O. down to the human-resources staff. McKinsey wanted to document how the top-performing companies in America differed from the other firms in the way they handle matters like hiring and promotion. But, as the consultants sifted through the piles of reports and questionnaires and interview transcripts, they grew convinced that the difference between winners and losers was more profound than they had realized. "We looked at one another and suddenly the light bulb blinked on," the three consultants who headed the project—Ed Michaels, Helen Handfield-Jones, and Beth Axelrod—write in their new book, also called *The War for Talent*. The very best companies, they concluded, had leaders who were obsessed with the talent issue. They recruited ceaselessly, finding and hiring as many top performers as possible. They singled out and segregated their stars, rewarding them disproportionately, and pushing them into ever more senior positions. "Bet on the natural athletes, the ones with the strongest intrinsic skills," the authors approvingly quote one senior General Electric executive as saying. "Don't be afraid to promote stars without specifically relevant experience, seemingly over their heads." Success in the modern economy, according to Michaels, Handfield-Jones, and Axelrod, requires "The talent mind-set": the "deep-seated belief that having better talent at all levels is how you outperform your competitors."

This "talent mind-set" is the new orthodoxy° of American management. It is the intellectual justification for why such a high premium is placed on degrees from first-tier business schools, and why the compensation packages for top executives have become so lavish. In the modern corporation, the system is considered only as strong as its stars, and, in the past few years, this message has been preached by consultants and management gurus all over the world. None, however, have spread the word quite so ardently as McKinsey, and, of all its clients, one firm took the talent mind-set closest to heart. It was a company where McKinsey conducted twenty separate projects, where McKinsey's billings topped ten million dollars a year, where a McKinsey director regularly attended board meetings, and where the C.E.O. himself was a former McKinsey partner. The company, of course, was Enron°. 2

The Enron scandal [came to light in 2001]. The reputations of Jeffrey Skilling and Kenneth Lay, the company's two top executives, have been destroyed. Arthur Andersen, Enron's auditor, has been all but driven out of business, and now investigators have turned their attention to Enron's investment bankers. The one Enron partner that 3 has escaped largely unscathed is McKinsey, which is odd, given that it essentially created the blueprint for the Enron culture. Enron was the ultimate "talent" company. When Skilling started the corporate division known as Enron Capital and Trade, in 1990, he "decided to bring in a steady stream of the very best college and M.B.A. graduates he could find to stock the company with talent," Michaels, Handfield-Jones, and Axelrod tell us. During the nineties, Enron was bringing in two hundred and fifty newly minted M.B.A.s a year. "We had these things called Super Saturdays," one former Enron manager recalls. "I'd interview some of these guys who were fresh out of Harvard, and these kids could blow me out of the water. They knew things I'd never heard of." Once at Enron, the top performers were rewarded inordinately°, and promoted without regard for seniority or experience. Enron was a star system. "The only thing that differentiates Enron from our competitors is our people, our talent," Lay, Enron's former chairman and C.E.O., told the McKinsey consultants when they came to the company's headquarters, in Houston. Or, as another senior Enron executive put it to Richard Foster, a McKinsey partner who celebrated Enron in his 2001 book, *Creative Destruction*, "We hire very smart people and we pay them more than they think they are worth."

4   The management of Enron, in other words, did exactly what the consultants at McKinsey said that companies ought to do in order to succeed in the modern economy. It hired and rewarded the very best and the very brightest—and it is now in bankruptcy. The reasons for its collapse are complex, needless to say. But what if Enron failed not in spite of its talent mind-set but because of it? What if smart people are overrated?

5   At the heart of the McKinsey vision is a process that the War for Talent advocates refer to as "differentiation and affirmation." Employers, they argue, need to sit down once or twice a year and hold a "candid, probing, no-holds-barred debate about each individual," sorting employees into A, B, and C groups. The A's must be challenged and disproportionately rewarded. The B's need to be encouraged and affirmed. The C's need to shape up or be shipped out. Enron followed this advice almost to the letter, setting up internal Performance Review Committees. The members got together twice a year, and graded each person in their section on ten separate criteria, using a scale of one to five. The process was called "rank and yank." Those graded at the top of their unit received bonuses two-thirds higher than those in the next thirty per cent; those who ranked at the bottom received no bonuses and no extra stock options—and in some cases were pushed out.

How should that ranking be done? Unfortunately, the 6
McKinsey consultants spend very little time discussing the matter.
One possibility is simply to hire and reward the smartest people.
But the link between, say, I.Q. and job performance is distinctly
underwhelming. On a scale where 0.1 or below means virtually no
correlation and 0.7 or above implies a strong correlation (your
height, for example, has a 0.7 correlation with your parents' height),
the correlation between I.Q. and occupational success is between
0.2 and 0.3. "What I.Q. doesn't pick up is effectiveness at common-
sense sorts of things, especially working with people," Richard
Wagner, a psychologist at Florida State University, says. "In terms
of how we evaluate schooling, everything is about working by
yourself. If you work with someone else, it's called cheating. Once
you get out in the real world, everything you do involves working
with other people."

Wagner and Robert Sternberg, a psychologist at Yale 7
University, have developed tests of this practical component,
which they call "tacit knowledge." Tacit knowledge involves
things like knowing how to manage yourself and others, and how
to navigate complicated social situations. Here is a question from
one of their tests:

> You have just been promoted to head of an important
> department in your organization. The previous head has
> been transferred to an equivalent position in a less impor-
> tant department. Your understanding of the reason for the
> move is that the performance of the department as a
> whole has been mediocre. There have not been any
> glaring deficiencies, just a perception of the department as
> so-so rather than very good. Your charge is to shape up
> the department. Results are expected quickly. Rate the
> quality of the following strategies for succeeding at your
> new position.
>
> > (a) Always delegate to the most junior person who
> >   can be trusted with the task.
> >
> > (b) Give your superiors frequent progress reports.
> >
> > (c) Announce a major reorganization of the depart-
> >   ment that includes getting rid of whomever you
> >   believe to be "dead wood."
> >
> > (d) Concentrate more on your people than on the
> >   tasks to be done.
> >
> > (e) Make people feel completely responsible for their
> >   work.

Wagner finds that how well people do on a test like this predicts how well they will do in the workplace: good managers pick (b) and (e); bad managers tend to pick (c). Yet there's no clear connection between such tacit knowledge and other forms of knowledge and experience. The process of assessing ability in the workplace is a lot messier than it appears.

8   An employer really wants to assess not potential but performance. Yet that's just as tricky. In *The War for Talent*, the authors talk about how the Royal Air Force used the A, B, and C ranking system for its pilots during the Battle of Britain. But ranking fighter pilots—for whom there are a limited and relatively objective set of performance criteria (enemy kills, for example, and the ability to get their formations safely home)—is a lot easier than assessing how the manager of a new unit is doing at, say, marketing or business development.

9   And whom do you ask to rate the manager's performance? Studies show that there is very little correlation between how someone's peers rate him and how his boss rates him. The only rigorous way to assess performance, according to human-resources specialists, is to use criteria that are as specific as possible. Managers are supposed to take detailed notes on their employees throughout the year, in order to remove subjective personal reactions from the process of assessment. You can grade someone's performance only if you *know* [his or her] performance. And, in the freewheeling culture of Enron, this was all but impossible. People deemed "talented" were constantly being pushed into new jobs and given new challenges. Annual turnover from promotions was close to twenty per cent. . . . How do you evaluate someone's performance in a system where no one is in a job long enough to allow such evaluation?

10   The answer is that you end up doing performance evaluations that aren't based on performance. Among the many glowing books about Enron written before its fall was the best-seller *Leading the Revolution*, by the management consultant Gary Hamel, which tells the story of Lou Pai, who launched Enron's power-trading business. Pai's group began with a disaster: it lost tens of millions of dollars trying to sell electricity to residential consumers in newly deregulated markets. The problem, Hamel explains, is that the markets weren't truly deregulated: "The states that were opening their markets to competition were still setting rules designed to give their traditional utilities big advantages." It doesn't seem to have occurred to anyone that Pai ought to have looked into those rules more carefully before risking millions of dollars. He was promptly given the chance to build the commercial electricity-outsourcing

business, where he ran up several more years of heavy losses before cashing out of Enron last year with two hundred and seventy million dollars. Because Pai had "talent," he was given new opportunities, and when he failed at those new opportunities he was given still more opportunities . . . because he had "talent." "At Enron, failure—even of the type that ends up on the front page of the *Wall Street Journal*—doesn't necessarily sink a career," Hamel writes, as if that were a good thing. Presumably, companies that want to encourage risk-taking must be willing to tolerate mistakes. Yet if talent is defined as something separate from an employee's actual performance, what use is it exactly?

What the War for Talent amounts to is an argument for indulging A
employees, for fawning over them. "You need to do everything you can to keep them engaged and satisfied—even delighted," Michaels, Handfield-Jones, and Axelrod write. "Find out what they would most like to be doing, and shape their career and responsibilities in that direction. Solve any issues that might be pushing them out the door, such as a boss that frustrates them or travel demands that burden them." No company was better at this than Enron. In one oft-told story, Louise Kitchin, a twenty-nine-year-old gas trader in Europe, became convinced that the company ought to develop an online-trading business. She told her boss, and she began working in her spare time on the project, until she had two hundred and fifty people throughout Enron helping her. After six months, Skilling was finally informed. "I was never asked for any capital," Skilling said later. "I was never asked for any people. They had already purchased the servers. They had already started ripping apart the building. They had started legal reviews in twenty-two countries by the time I heard about it." It was, Skilling went on approvingly, "exactly the kind of behavior that will continue to drive this company forward."

Kitchin's qualification for running EnronOnline, it should be
pointed out, was not that she was good at it. It was that she wanted to do it, and Enron was a place where stars did whatever they wanted. "Fluid movement is absolutely necessary in our company. And the type of people we hire enforces that," Skilling told the team from McKinsey. "Not only does this system help the excitement level for each manager, it shapes Enron's business in the direction that its managers find most exciting." Here is Skilling again: "If lots of [employees] are flocking to a new business unit, that's a good sign that the opportunity is a good one. . . . If a business unit can't attract people very easily, that's a good sign that it's a business Enron shouldn't be in." You might expect a C.E.O. to say

11

12

that if a business unit can't attract *customers* very easily that's a good sign it's a business the company shouldn't be in. A company's business is supposed to be shaped in the direction that its managers find most *profitable*. But at Enron the needs of the customers and the shareholders were secondary to the needs of its stars.

13   [In 1990], the psychologists Robert Hogan, Robert Raskin, and Dan Fazzini wrote a brilliant essay called "The Dark Side of Charisma." It argued that flawed managers fall into three types. One is the High Likability Floater, who rises effortlessly in an organization because he never takes any difficult decisions or makes any enemies. Another is the Homme de Ressentiment, who seethes below the surface and plots against his enemies. The most interesting of the three is the Narcissist, whose energy and self-confidence and charm lead him inexorably up the corporate ladder. Narcissists are terrible managers. They resist accepting suggestions, thinking it will make them appear weak, and they don't believe that others have anything useful to tell them. "Narcissists are biased to take more credit for success than is legitimate," Hogan and his co-authors write, and "biased to avoid acknowledging responsibility for their failures and shortcomings for the same reasons that they claim more success than is their due." . . .

14   Tyco° and WorldCom° were the Greedy Corporations: they were purely interested in short-term financial gain. Enron was the Narcissistic Corporation—a company that took more credit for success than was legitimate, that did not acknowledge responsibility for its failures, that shrewdly sold the rest of us on its genius, and that substituted self-nomination for disciplined management. At one point in *Leading the Revolution*, Hamel tracks down a senior Enron executive, and what he breathlessly recounts—the bragadocio°, the self-satisfaction—could be an epitaph° for the talent mind-set:

> "You cannot control the atoms within a nuclear fusion reaction," said Ken Rice when he was head of Enron Capital and Trade Resources (ECT), America's largest marketer of natural gas and largest buyer and seller of electricity. Adorned in a black T-shirt, blue jeans, and cowboy boots, Rice drew a box on an office whiteboard that pictured his business unit as a nuclear reactor. Little circles in the box represented its "contract originators," the gunslingers charged with doing deals and creating new business. Attached to each circle was an arrow. In Rice's diagram the arrows were pointing in all different directions. "We allow people to go in whichever direction that they want to go."

The distinction between the Greedy Corporation and the 15
Narcissistic Corporation matters, because the way we conceive our
attainments helps determine how we behave. Carol Dweck, a psychologist at Columbia University, has found that people generally
hold one of two fairly firm beliefs about their intelligence: they consider it either a fixed trait or something that is malleable and can be
developed over time. Five years ago, Dweck did a study at the
University of Hong Kong, where all classes are conducted in
English. She and her colleagues approached a large group of social-
sciences students, told them their English-proficiency scores, and
asked them if they wanted to take a course to improve their language skills. One would expect all those who scored poorly to sign
up for the remedial course. The University of Hong Kong is a
demanding institution, and it is hard to do well in the social sciences without strong English skills. Curiously, however, only the
ones who believed in malleable intelligence expressed interest in
the class. The students who believed that their intelligence was a
fixed trait were so concerned about appearing to be deficient that
they preferred to stay home. "Students who hold a fixed view of
their intelligence care so much about looking smart that they act
dumb," Dweck writes, "for what could be dumber than giving up a
chance to learn something that is essential for your own success?"

In a similar experiment, Dweck gave a class of preadolescent 16
students a test filled with challenging problems. After they were
finished, one group was praised for its effort and another group
was praised for its intelligence. Those praised for their intelligence
were reluctant to tackle difficult tasks, and their performance on
subsequent tests soon began to suffer. Then Dweck asked the children to write a letter to students at another school, describing their
experience in the study. She discovered something remarkable:
forty per cent of those students who were praised for their intelligence lied about how they had scored on the test, adjusting their
grade upward. They weren't naturally deceptive people, and they
weren't any less intelligent or self-confident than anyone else. They
simply did what people do when they are immersed in an environment that celebrates them solely for their innate "talent." They
begin to define themselves by that description, and when times get
tough and that self-image is threatened they have difficulty with
the consequences. They will not take the remedial course. They will
not stand up to investors and the pubic and admit that they were
wrong. They'd sooner lie.

The broader failing of McKinsey and its acolytes° at Enron is their 17
assumption that an organization's intelligence is simply a function

of the intelligence of its employees. They believe in stars, because they don't believe in systems. In a way, that's understandable, because our lives are so obviously enriched by individual brilliance. Groups don't write great novels, and a committee didn't come up with the theory of relativity. But companies work by different rules. They don't just create; they execute and compete and coördinate the efforts of many different people, and the organizations that are most successful at that task are the ones where the system *is* the star. . . . The talent myth assumes that people make organizations smart. More often than not, it's the other way around.

18   There is ample evidence of this principle among America's most successful companies. Southwest Airlines hires very few M.B.A.s, pays its managers modestly, and gives raises according to seniority, not "rank and yank." Yet it is by far the most successful of all United States airlines, because it has created a vastly more efficient organization than its competitors have. At Southwest, the time it takes to get a plane that has just landed ready for takeoff—a key index of productivity—is, on average, twenty minutes, and requires a ground crew of four, and two people at the gate. (At United Airlines, by contrast, turnaround time is closer to thirty-five minutes, and requires a ground crew of twelve and three agents at the gate.) . . .

19   Procter & Gamble doesn't have a star system, either. How could it? Would the top M.B.A. graduates of Harvard and Stanford move to Cincinnati to work on detergent when they could make three times as much reinventing the world in Houston? Procter & Gamble isn't glamorous. Its C.E.O. is a lifer—a former Navy officer who began his corporate career as an assistant brand manager for Joy dishwashing liquid—and, if Procter & Gamble's best played Enron's best at Trivial Pursuit, no doubt the team from Houston would win handily. But Procter & Gamble has dominated the consumer products field for close to a century, because it has a carefully conceived managerial system, and a rigorous marketing methodology that has allowed it to win battles for brands like Crest and Tide decade after decade. . . .

20   Among the most damning facts about Enron, in the end, was something its managers were proudest of. They had what, in McKinsey terminology, is called an "open market" for hiring. In the open-market system—McKinsey's assault on the very idea of a fixed organization—anyone could apply for any job that he or she wanted, and no manager was allowed to hold anyone back. Poaching° was encouraged. When an Enron executive named Kevin Hannon started the company's global broadband unit, he launched what he

called Project Quick Hire. A hundred top performers from around the company were invited to the Houston Hyatt to hear Hannon give his pitch. Recruiting booths were set up outside the meeting room. "Hannon had his fifty top performers for the broadband unit by the end of the week," Michaels, Handfield-Jones, and Axelrod write, "and his peers had fifty holes to fill." Nobody, not even the consultants who were paid to think about the Enron culture, seemed worried that those fifty holes might disrupt the functioning of the affected departments, that stability in a firm's existing businesses might be a good thing, that the self-fulfillment of Enron's star employees might possibly be in conflict with the best interests of the firm as a whole.

These are the sort of concerns that management consultants 21 ought to raise. But Enron's management consultant was McKinsey, and McKinsey was as much as prisoner of the talent myth as its clients were. In 1998, Enron hired ten Wharton M.B.A.s; that same year, McKinsey hired forty. In 1999, Enron hired twelve from Wharton; McKinsey hired sixty-one. The consultants at McKinsey were preaching at Enron what they believed about themselves. "When we would hire them, it wouldn't just be for a week," one former Enron manager recalls, of the brilliant young men and women from McKinsey who wandered the hallways at the company's headquarters. "It would be for two to four months. They were always around." They were there looking for people who had the talent to think outside the box. It never occurred to them that, if everyone had to think outside the box, maybe it was the box that needed fixing.

Words and Meanings

orthodoxy	commonly accepted belief, theory, or practice	2
Enron	Houston-based energy-trading giant that hid debt and overstated earnings for years as part of a scheme to boost the company's stock price; declared bankruptcy in 2001	
inordinately	excessively	3
Tyco	diversified manufacturing conglomerate whose reputation was tarnished in 2002, when former CEO Dennis Kozlowski was indicted on charges of corruption and grand larceny	14
WorldCom	Telecommunications company that declared bankruptcy in 2002 following revelations of massive accounting fraud	

braggadocio   empty boasting or bragging

epitaph   words in memory of something past (often a dead person)

17   acolytes   devoted followers

20   poaching   taking something unfairly or illegally; here, raiding a fellow manager's staff

Structure and Strategy

1. What strategy does Gladwell use in the INTRODUCTION?
2. Explain the IRONY in the fact that, unlike other Enron partners, McKinsey & Company emerged from the scandal "largely unscathed" (paragraph 3). What is the irony at the heart of paragraph 10?
3. Good journalists use reliable sources to support their ideas. How does Gladwell acknowledge his sources in paragraphs 7, 13, 14, 15, and 16? If this essay had been published as an academic research paper, what additional information would he have needed to provide?
4. What is the function of the questions in the subtitle of the essay and paragraphs 4, 9, 10, and 19? Are these questions effective? Why or why not?
5. Is the THESIS of this essay stated (if so, where) or implied? Summarize it in your own words.
6. How do the examples in paragraphs 18 and 19 support the essay's thesis?
7. What strategy does Gladwell use in the CONCLUSION?

Content and Purpose

1. This essay begins with a long ANECDOTE about how McKinsey & Company arrived at "the talent mind-set," an organizational theory Gladwell calls the "new orthodoxy of American management" (paragraph 2). Where does Gladwell provide a summary of this theory? What is the anecdote's punch line? (See paragraph 2.)
2. What system did Enron, at McKinsey's suggestion, use to hire people? How did the company rank and reward its employees? (See paragraphs 3 and 5.)
3. According to the essay, what is the correlation between intelligence (I.Q.) and job performance (paragraph 6)? What example does Gladwell use to illustrate "correlation" to the general reader?

4. Do you agree with the point Gladwell makes in paragraph 6? Why or why not?
5. Enron's strategy was to hire and promote people based on their presumed intelligence, talent, and potential—not their performance. What were the results of this strategy? (See paragraphs 10, 11, and 12.)
6. What is a narcissist? How does one of Gladwell's sources characterize a flawed managerial type it calls "the Narcissist?" Why is this kind of manager destructive to an organization?
7. What conclusions does the essay draw from two experiments conducted by Carol Dweck of Columbia University? (See paragraphs 15 and 16.) How do Dweck's findings support Gladwell's argument?
8. According to Gladwell, what is the major difference between "systems" and "stars"? (See paragraph 17.) What are the implications of this difference for an organization?
9. What were the consequences of Enron's "open market" for hiring (paragraph 20)?
10. Explain in your own words the phrase "think outside the box." Should a company's employees be encouraged to use this strategy? Why or why not?
11. According to paragraph 21, what did Enron and McKinsey have in common? Summarize Gladwell's CONCLUSION.
12. What do you think about Gladwell's ARGUMENT? Do we overrate smart people? Are talent, intelligence, or potential overvalued in our culture?

Suggestions for Writing

1. Have you ever received a performance evaluation at work or at school? Write an essay on the criteria that should be considered in such evaluations.
2. Do you like working with other people? Write an essay on the differences between completing a task individually and completing it with a team.
3. Imagine that you are a member of the hiring committee at your college or university. What are the characteristics of a good professor? Make a list of interview questions that will help you determine if candidates for a teaching position have those qualities.

With Pens Drawn

MARIO VARGAS LLOSA

Novelist and critic Mario Vargas Llosa was born in Peru in 1936. His works include *Death in the Andes* (1996), *Making Waves* (1997), *The Notebooks of Don Rigoberto* (1998), and *The Feast of the Goat* (2000). Always politically outspoken, Vargas Llosa served as the first Latin American president of PEN, an international group that champions the rights of authors and journalists, and was a presidential candidate in Peru's 1990 elections. He now lives in London.

1   My vocation as a writer grew out of the idea that literature does not exist in a closed artistic sphere but embraces a larger moral and civic° universe. This is what has motivated everything I have written. It is also, alas, now turning me into a dinosaur in trousers, surrounded by computers.

2   Statistics tell us that never before have so many books been sold. The trouble is that hardly anybody I come across believes any longer that literature serves any great purpose beyond alleviating° boredom on the bus or the underground, or has any higher ambition beyond being transformed into television or movie scripts. Literature has gone light. That's why critics such as George Steiner have come to believe literature is already dead, and why novelists such as V. S. Naipaul have come to proclaim that they will not write another novel because the genre now fills them with disgust.

3   But amid this pessimism about literature, we should remember that many people still fear the writer. Look at the criminal clique that governs Nigeria and executed Ogoni author and activist Ken Saro-Wiwa after a trumped-up murder charge; at the imams° who declared a *fatwa°* on novelist Salman Rushdie for criticizing Islamic practices in *The Satanic Verses*; at the Muslim fundamentalists in Algeria who have cut the throats of dozens of journalists, writers, and thespians°; and at all those regimes in North Korea, Cuba, China, Laos, Burma, and elsewhere where censorship prevails and prisons are full of writers.

4   So in countries that are supposed to be cultivated—and are the most free and democratic—literature is becoming a hobby without real value, while in countries where freedom is restricted, literature is considered dangerous, the vehicle of subversive ideas. Novelists and poets in free countries, who view their profession with disillusionment, should open their eyes to this vast part of the globe that is not yet free. It might give them courage.

5   I have an old-fashioned view: I believe that literature must address itself to the problems of its time. Authors must write with

the conviction that what they are writing can help others become more free, more sensitive, more clear-sighted; yet without the self-righteous illusion of many intellectuals that their work helps contain violence, reduce injustice, and promote liberty. I have erred° too often myself, and I have seen too many writers I admired err—even put their talents at the service of ideological° lies and state crimes—to delude° myself. But without ceasing to be entertaining, literature should immerse itself in the life of the streets, in the unraveling of history, as it did in the best of times. This is the only way in which writers can help their contemporaries and save literature from the flimsy state to which it sometimes seems condemned.

If the only point of literature is to entertain, then it cannot compete with the fictions pouring out of screens, large or small. An illusion made of words requires the reader's active participation, an effort of the imagination and sometimes, in modern literature, complex feats° of memory, association, and creativity. Television and cinema audiences are exempt from all this by virtue of the images. This makes them lazy and increasingly allergic to intellectually challenging entertainment.

Screen fiction is intense on account of its immediacy and ephemeral° in terms of effect: it captivates us and then releases us almost instantly. Literary fiction holds us captive for life. To say that the works of authors such as Dostoevsky, Tolstoy, and Proust° are entertaining would be to insult them. For, while they are usually read in a state of high excitement, the most important effect of a good book is in the aftermath, its ability to fire memory over time. The afterglow is still alive within me because without the books I have read, I would not be who I am, for better or worse, nor would I believe what I believe, with all the doubts and certainties that keep me going. Those books shaped me, changed me, made me. And they continue changing me, in step with the life I measure them against. In those books I learned that the world is in bad shape and that it will always be so—which is no reason to refrain from doing whatever we can to keep it from getting worse. They taught me that in all our diversity of culture, races, and beliefs, as fellow actors in the human comedy, we deserve equal respect. They also taught me why we so rarely get it. There is nothing like good literature to help us detect the roots of the cruelty human beings can unleash.

Without a committed° literature it will become even more difficult to contain all those outbreaks of war, genocide°, ethnic and religious strife, refugee displacement, and terrorist activity that threaten to multiply and that have already smashed the hopes raised by the collapse of the Berlin Wall. Removing blindfolds,

6

7

8

expressing indignation° in the face of injustice, and demonstrating that there is room for hope under the most trying circumstances are all things literature has been good at, even though it has occasionally been mistaken in its targets and defended the indefensible.

9   The written word has a special responsibility to do these things because it is better at telling the truth than audiovisual media, which are by their nature condemned to skate over the surface of things and are much more constrained° in their freedom of expression. The phenomenal sophistication with which news bulletins can nowadays transport us to the epicenter° of events on every continent has turned us all into voyeurs° and the whole world into one vast theater, or more precisely into a movie. Audiovisual information—so transient°, so striking, and so superficial—makes us see history as fiction, distancing us by concealing the causes and context behind the sequence of events that are so vividly portrayed. This condemns us to a state of passive acceptance, moral insensibility, and psychological inertia° similar to that inspired by television fiction and other programs whose only purpose is to entertain.

10   We all like to escape from reality; indeed, that is one of the functions of literature. But making the present unreal, turning actual history into fiction, has the effect of demobilizing° citizens, making them feel exempt from civic responsibility, encouraging the conviction that it is beyond anyone's reach to intervene in a history whose screenplay is already written. Along this path we may well slide into a world where there are no citizens, only spectators, a world where, although formal democracy may be preserved, we will be resigned to the kind of lethargy° dictatorships aspire to establish.

Words and Meanings

Paragraph

1   civic — having to do with public life

2   alleviating — bringing relief from

3   imams — Islamic religious leaders
      fatwa — ruling issued by religious leader; in this case, a death sentence

      thespians — actors

5   erred — been wrong, made mistakes
      ideological — having to do with the ideas and beliefs on which a political, economic, or religious system is based

delude	deceive	5
feats	acts, achievements	6
ephemeral	lasting only a short time	7
Dostoevsky, Tolstoy, and Proust	novelists whose works are universally recognized and celebrated	
committed	serious, devoted to the public interest	8
genocide	systematic slaughter of a racial, ethnic, or religious group	
indignation	outrage, anger	
constrained	restricted, limited	9
epicenter	focal point	
voyeurs	people obsessed with watching sensational (usually sexual or sordid) events	
transient	brief, fleeting, short-lived	
inertia	inability or unwillingness to act or move	
demobilizing	discharging from service (as in the military); excusing from duty	10
lethargy	passive acceptance	

Structure and Strategy

1. What is the THESIS of this essay?
2. What FIGURE OF SPEECH does Vargas Llosa use in paragraph 1 to suggest to readers that he is old-fashioned, perhaps out-of-date?
3. What point does the author develop in paragraph 2? How does he support it?
4. What contrast is the topic of paragraph 6?
5. Is this essay primarily ARGUMENT or PERSUASION? Support your answer with specific references to the essay.

Content and Purpose

1. What motivates Vargas Llosa? Why did he become a writer? What does he believe is the purpose of literature?
2. Summarize the political paradox that Vargas Llosa presents in paragraphs 3 and 4. Who "still fear[s] the writer"? Why?
3. According to the author, what has "condemned" literature to its current "flimsy state" (paragraph 5)? Why is he so pessimistic about modern literature?

4. What is the difference between the effect on the imagination of reading and watching television or a movie? (See paragraphs 6 and 9.)
5. According to Vargas Llosa, what is the function of literature in our lives? (See paragraph 7.) What is the function of literature in the social and political realms? (See paragraph 8.) Do you agree or disagree with these opinions? Why?
6. Vargas Llosa maintains that the "written word . . . is better at telling the truth than audiovisual media" (paragraph 9). Yet television and film provide us with a great deal of information about the world, people, and ideas. Do you agree with Vargas Llosa's view of the limitations of television and film? Or do you think Vargas Llosa is a "dinosaur" (paragraph 1)? Explain.
7. What effects does the author predict will occur in a world that expects literature to provide nothing more than an escape from reality? (See paragraph 10.)

Suggestions for Writing

1. Have you ever read a novel that changed the way you see the world? What did you learn from the novel, how did it change you, and why would you recommend that others read it?
2. Many people would argue that great films have influenced our view of the world in complex and meaningful ways. Similarly, television in the era of cable news can make us immediately and intensely aware of the plight of people we would otherwise know little or nothing about. Write an essay arguing that audio-visual media are more powerful than literature as agents of social change.

What Is the Good Life?

MARK KINGWELL

Mark Kingwell (b. 1963) is assistant professor of philosophy at the University of Toronto. He was educated at the universities of Toronto and Edinburgh, and holds a Ph.D. from Yale University. An award-winning political and cultural theorist, he writes a biweekly column for *The National Post* and is a regular contributor to *Saturday Night, This Magazine, Shift, Descant,* and *Harper's Magazine.* His books include *Dreams of Millennium: Report from a Culture on the Brink* (1996) and *Better Living: In Pursuit of Happiness from Plato to Prozac* (1998).

When my first-year philosophy students write their final examination each year they are asked, among other things, to comment on this statement taken from the philosopher Alasdair MacIntyre: "The good life is the life spent seeking the good life." *Discuss. True or false. Agree or disagree.*

Don't worry. I always tell them this beforehand. There isn't much point, after all, in springing something like that on a nineteen-year-old who's sitting in a chilly gym at 9 a.m., probably wondering what she's going to do for a summer job or, maybe more to the point, why he signed up for philosophy in the first place. I try to give them all the breaks I can. On the other hand, I also want to unsettle them as much as possible. What is the good life? MacIntyre's deliberately puzzling formulation is an attempt to rise above the shifting sands of time and fashion. It neatly captures the paradoxical nature of critical reflection on the possibilities of life, because its logic undermines the blithe assurance of those whose knowingness gives them all the answers to our problems, usually doled out during dinner-party debates or in 750-word chunks on the op-ed pages of newspapers. This odd-sounding answer to the basic ethical question constantly reminds us of the disruptive elements in our attempts to make sense of ourselves and our place in the world.

That is an important reminder, even if we are rightly suspicious of philosophers (or anyone else, for that matter) who seem to think that the answer to all our problems lies in further theorizing and more explanation. *Reflection* . . . is conceptually distinct from *theory.* It is much more modest in its aims and aware of the intellect's shortcomings—but also much more searching and powerful in its potential effects. Reflection involves the always incomplete attempt to make sense of who we are and what we are up to, trying all the while to do that most difficult of things, to live better. Theory believes it provides answers. Reflection knows that it merely pursues questions, and does that often enough only tentatively or in the midst of perplexity and sadness.

Even reflection has limits when it must cut so much against the spirit of the age. What constitutes success in living seems always to be changing, and that variation can lead to a judgment of relativism: the ultimately self-defeating notion that there is no fact of the matter about the good life—so knock yourself out in your chosen quest, for power or money or sexual pleasure. You might as well live like a depraved moral lunatic! Why not? What is there to stop you? These days, such judgments even draw a measure of social sanction and become the nihilistic° common sense of the age. In the process they send ethical debate to the bleakly humorous margins so effectively rendered in contemporary films, usually about Los Angeles. The bickering armed robbers of *Reservoir Dogs*, the morally decentred group of bachelor-party buddies in *Very Bad Things*, the nuance-disputing drug dealers of *Go:* they all enact a kind of twisted Platonic dialogue about how to go on. "Sure we'll kill him, but not *that* way. Of *course* I'm going to commit a hit-and-run, but not without leaving the body where it can be discovered." Nobody sane would draw their notions of the good life from such material, of course, but these visions do serve to mark the decline of our reasoning about what Socrates considered the foundational philosophical question, What is the life worth living?

5   That question has lately become more about things than wisdom, more about brand names than the common good. These days, indeed, it is difficult to keep any discussion of "the good life" from sliding, sometimes immediately and sometimes by imperceptible stages, into a seminar on material comforts and lifestyle aids. The phrase "living well" has almost entirely shed its ethical connotations. That is why looking at certain lifestyle magazines can make you feel faintly sick: their lack of shame about materialism is, at one remove, shaming. This is certainly not to say that material goods are irrelevant to happiness, or that the good life involves nothing of what those tasty, coated-paper magazines deliver to us in their backlit visions. Try telling someone without the means to buy a television, or to make a phone call, that they shouldn't long for these double-edged toys of modern life. And anyone who has had the luck to enjoy some luxury now and then must agree with Aristotle that a truly blessed life involves a measure of wealth and the chance to enjoy its fruits. But we seem to have lost our ability to think clearly about these matters, and for fairly precise historical and economic reasons.

6   Today we are not really materialists. We are, rather, fetishists° of the material. If we were truly materialist, as the critic Raymond Williams once pointed out, we would be *satisfied* with the acquisition of material goods; they would make us happy in themselves. We are precisely the opposite of this, ever-conflicted victims of the vice the ancient Greek philosophers called *pleonexia:* wanting more, the more we have. We do not really desire the goods most of the time, only the complicated feelings of pleasure that acquiring the goods makes possible. Strummed by advertisers and marketers, like plummy mandolins, surrendering to our own internalized desires, we are forever in search of the next consumer hit. Well, so what? This is hardly news. Lots of people will tell you that it was ever thus, or that we can't expect anything else. Actually, both claims are false—it was not, and we can. But it is worth wondering

why such argument-ending claims have the cachet° they do, given how weak they are.

Part of the motivation for thinking in that reductive way, maybe   7
a large part, is defensive. Consider an example. There is nothing more common in disputes about the state of the world today than what we might agree to call the Evasive Elision. I mean the way important distinctions, say between art and advertising, or between argument and self-promotion, are these days eagerly rubbed out in a face-saving attempt to suggest that everything is for sale and therefore nothing is untainted. Ironically, the arguments about a lack of purity are most often made by those who would otherwise shrink from the idea that purity matters, and from the idea that engagement with the market signifies impurity. This is a clear sign of the cynicism of the position, which proceeds not from conviction but from self-protection. Levelling charges of hypocrisy is always the fastest, and cheapest, route to the moral high ground. . . . The trouble is, that move doesn't help anybody except the leveller, who now gets to dodge criticism but only at the cost of shutting down debate altogether.

Indeed, such erasures recall Oscar Wilde's definition of the cynic   8
as the person who knows the price of everything but the value of nothing. And that kind of apparently sophisticated attitude, perversely, makes us more comfortable with our weaknesses, not less. If the nihilism of the fastidious professional killer or mildly scrupulous drug dealer is not for all of us, this more general piece of cynical self-protection certainly is. The good life? Nowadays it is the life spent fending off all those naive challenges to one's acquisitiveness, throwing out facile charges of bad faith at those who dare to suggest things might be better, and claiming to find it baffling that anyone really thinks the adventitious° privilege of birth might entail positive duties to the less fortunate. In this weirdly protracted battle for the modern soul, the glossy consumer objects, so ubiquitous° and fetching, are themselves an unanswerable challenge to political awareness, a carapace° of brand-name armour. [German Marxist literary critic Walter] Benjamin . . . circa 1928: "The luxury goods swaggering before us now parade such brazen solidity that all the mind's shafts break harmlessly on their surface."

The real trouble, of course, is that all this acquisition does not   9
seem to make us any happier. In this sense, the Evasive Elision and its cousins are mere window-dressing, the distracting appearance of argument that does not touch the core problem. The renegade economist Robert Frank notes that there is no logical stopping point to acquisition, and yet beyond a certain level there is no correlation between wealth and happiness. "Behavioral scientists," he says,

"have found persuasive evidence that once a threshold level of affluence is achieved, the average life-satisfaction level in any country is essentially independent of its per capita income." Which is one reason why the 39 percent rise in U.S. per capita income between 1972 and 1991, say, left a legacy of lower average happiness levels. At the heart of this apparently bizarre result is the confused nature of our conceptions of happiness. We are competitive and envious creatures, whether by nature or by some complex of natural and social factors, and so our sense of well-being is dangerously dependent on what is going on with others.

10   Thus studies consistently indicate results surprising only in their honesty about human desire. Beyond the levels of basic subsistence, we want to have things and wealth relative to what other people have, not for themselves. Most people, for example, would prefer earning $50,000 while others made $25,000 to earning $100,000 while others made $250,000. This kind of result holds even when it is true that a flatter income-distribution level would be advantageous to everyone. As long as individuals measure themselves against other individuals, we are caught in what Frank calls the "smart for one, dumb for all" trap. Instead of channelling money into cheap and reliable public transit, for example, we all strive to buy sporty convertibles or massive trucks—though they clog the highways, pollute the air, cut us off from one another, and regularly crash. Instead of reflecting on the possibility that need and want may be distinct concepts, we immerse ourselves in the nearly overwhelming pleasures of the unstable material world.

11   These are real pleasures, of course, and there is real joy to be found in the marketplace. That is why merely denunciatory° critics of consumerism are doing nobody but themselves any good. If we want to engage this world of ours with real results, we have to accept and understand the fact that watching a thirty-second television ad can sometimes be an exhilarating experience, that shopping is indeed a form of release and pleasure for many people, that putting on an expensive suit can occasion a liberating and wonderful feeling of well-being. Only then should we even attempt to separate that kind of exhilaration or pleasure from the consumer impulse that seems to accompany it. Why attempt that separation at all, ever? Well, because once we take a first step on the road to luxury, there is little to prevent a kind of consumerist arms race, with small gaps or advantages in material goods closing as fast as they open. Ever in search of a competitive advantage or pocket of enviable happiness, we are now driven to newer and more inventive forms of acquisition. Standard luxury items like Rolexes and ChrisCraft speedboats sell on the basis of their exclusivity, a combination of outrageous cost and artificially

limited supply, in order to make them markers of success in the envy stakes. *I have it —and you don't!*

By the same token, the contemporary branding and narra- 12 tivizing° of consumer products, which compresses desire and expectation into the slick miniature plot of a television commercial, makes all of us into de facto° experts on names and logos and spokespeople. Our overwhelming exposure to these micro-tales of success and beauty transforms acquisition into a kind of hyper-competitive graduate school, with Phil Knight or Bill Gates or Michael Jordan our presumptive professors. All the buying and selling of cool naturally comes down to this: I know more than you do about the available brands, I am more *au courant°* with the latest narrative, I discovered this logo sooner, and therefore I have an advantage over you. You may catch up, finally buying your Kangol golf cap or FUBU shirt—or whatever it now is, for time overtakes a writer's examples as relentlessly as a person's expectations—but I will already be gone. We all know this is true, because marketers and their critics (who are sometimes, in another elision, the very same people) have been telling us this for years. And yet we seem unwilling to act on that knowledge.

It is hard to know whether the sharply unequal distribution of 13 wealth we now observe in the world is a direct result of these aspects of our current notions of the good life, or whether we construct visions to match our situation. I think the relationship is symbiotic°, complex, and hard to analyze with anything like a clarity that would issue in° a course of action. The competitive impulse of all this envy drives a system away from horizontal distributions, even as it sharpens the unhappiness felt by the majority that, of necessity, finds itself unable to scale the pinnacles of the resulting x-y curve. It is certainly the case, for example, as the economist Robert Samuelson has argued persuasively, that most North Americans are far better off in absolute material terms now than during the 1950s. Rare today is the home without running water, a television or two, even a car. North Americans eat out more than twice as often now as they did during the 1950s, and spend vastly more on toys, travel, and entertainment.

There are fewer servants in North America today, it's true, 14 because local wage expectations make them too expensive. Appliances and home shopping alleviate the need for most people, while cheaper foreign labour is once more making the domestic servant a familiar sight, at least in the homes of the very wealthy. Some people still live in abject poverty, but a larger proportion of the population is provably more comfortable than their parents' generation—and yet they think of themselves as poor because, compared with what they see and expect, they are. Visions of luxurious living clearly contribute strongly to this impression, since in the contemporary mediascape it becomes nearly impossible to avoid images of a life more desirable than your own. From Martha Stewart's mad domestic perfectionism to the cool-to-rule kids of the fashion glossies, there's always somebody somewhere who has it better than you. This leads in turn to a sense that life is letting you down, that there is no good reason for relative differences in comfort, and therefore no good reason for the social structures that permit them.

15   Envy may be the basis of democracy, as [the English philosopher] Bertrand Russell once said, but it is also the most common source of unhappiness. By 1995, household debt in the United States had grown to 81 percent of disposable income, not least because going into debt is the only way most people can acquire the things they crave. Those of us in the most prosperous parts of the world now work longer hours, commute farther, and sleep less—all in the service of the good life. People will do anything, apparently even to their own detriment°, to find some manner of what they think constitutes "better living." On the surface, then, we observe more luxury goods, more seductive visions of individual achievement and self-creation, and more subtle comparisons. But we also see more unhappiness, more resentment, and more imminent social unrest. Programs of voluntary simplicity or renewed spirituality, the countertenor° of the era's loud chorus, keen and warble their dissent but don't really affect the dominant melody of getting and spending.

16   Is there a solution to this crazy merry-go-round? Some economists propose a luxury tax to counter our upward spiral of acquisition, a bold attempt to turn individual self-interest away from itself by sharply raising the opportunity costs of indulgence. Individuals would have to decide on and declare a single luxury pursuit, preserving a measure of choice thereby, but would then be bound in their spending by the redistributive constraints of steep marginal tax rates. (The argument is that such a directed tax is fairer than across-the-board progressive income tax, which is indiscriminate in its application of redistributive burdens.)

17   Others would have us return, as if that were possible, to a less rapacious°, fifties-style version of North America. For those who would not actually endorse the social and tax policies of any allegedly simpler era, there is always the costless option of nostalgia. Wander through the high-end home stores of Chelsea or Yorkville or SoHo and you will be struck by the ubiquity of a watered-down modernist style, a generalized and somehow bleakly appealing version of the good life as distributed, in the main, by

cinematic imagery: skyscrapers in cool black and white, silver frames, bullet-headed cocktail shakers. We all want to live on this film set, to inhabit this fantasy. But like all fantasies, it is structurally unstable, important for what it hides more than what it reveals. The more of these literally fantastic goods there are to purchase, the more they, and the well-being they promise, seem to slip through our fingers. Nostalgia cannot aid us here, because its wispy attractions are meretricious°; it leaves everything as it is.

I have a different suggestion. Denunciations of materialism and consumerism so often fall on deaf ears because at a deep level they miss the point. Appearances sometimes to the contrary, we are all struggling, in our different ways, to bestow meaning on the world of our everyday experience. We are trying to forge identities from the play of cultural materials. And the basics of the good life have not really changed, though this became harder and harder to see as we reached the end of the expiring decadent century and sifted through our trunks of mechanically reproduced images, faux° memories, and siren calls° to comfort. The relentless acquisition of goods is just a symptom of a deeper ailment, a lack of secure placement in a world of shared understanding, a failure to be at home. Denouncing the symptom instead of the illness, we would miss the point—and fail in our duty as social critics. 18

The important thing to see here is the currents of desire beneath the pretty surfaces, the wishes and fantasies there facilitated. What do they point to? The sociological studies bear out something that philosophical inquiry can see without taking a survey. We are, finally, happier not with more stuff but with more meaning: more creative leisure time, stronger connections to groups of friends, deeper commitment to common social projects, and a greater opportunity to reflect. In short, the life of the well-rounded person, including crucially the orienting aspect of life associated with virtuous citizenship. Nor is this basic social commitment something we should pursue for ourselves alone, a project simply to promote our personal happiness. At its best, it is an expression of commonality that creates something greater than the sum of its—let us be honest—often self-interested and distracted members. It creates a community. 19

Words and Meanings

		Paragraph
nihilistic	rejecting moral, religious, and other established beliefs	4
fetishists	people with an obsessive attachment (often sexual) to an object, body part, or act	6

	cachet	an indication of approval; prestige
8	adventitious	accidental
	ubiquitous	being or seeming to be everywhere
	carapace	hard, protective shell (of a turtle, lobster, etc.)
11	denunciatory	accusing or condemning (especially publicly)
12	narrativizing	attaching a story to something (for example, a product)
	de facto	existing whether officially recognized or not [Latin]
13	*au courant*	well informed; fully acquainted with [French]
	symbiotic	inseparable and mutually dependent
	issue in	result in
15	detriment	harm or disadvantage
	countertenor	the highest adult male singing voice
17	rapacious	greedy and grasping (especially for wealth)
	meretricious	superficially attractive but without real value
18	faux	false or fake [French]
	siren calls	irresistibly tempting appeals (often destructive in their effects)

Structure and Strategy

1. In his INTRODUCTION (paragraphs 1 and 2), what strategy does Kingwell use to provide a CONTEXT for the major question he poses in the essay? Is it an effective strategy? Why or why not?
2. Paragraph 3 is developed by means of contrast. Of the two terms that are contrasted, which one does Kingwell's essay illustrate?
3. What unfamiliar term does Kingwell define in paragraph 6? Why is an understanding of this term important to his ARGUMENT?
4. In the SIMILE Kingwell uses in paragraph 6, who or what is compared to "plummy mandolins"?
5. In paragraph 9, what is the TOPIC SENTENCE, and what strategies does the author use to develop and support it?
6. Summarize the example Kingwell uses in paragraph 10, and explain how it contributes to his argument.
7. In paragraph 11, Kingwell employs a strategy that is often used in argumentation—acknowledging the validity of an opponent's argument—when he concedes that "there is real joy to be found

in the marketplace." Is his use of this strategy effective? Why or why not?

8. In paragraph 12, what is the common enemy of a "writer's examples" and "a person's expectations"?

9. Identify the symbiotic relationship that Kingwell explores in paragraph 13.

10. Explain the METAPHOR at the end of paragraph 15. According to this metaphor, what is the "dominant melody" of our time? Who are those who "keen and warble their dissent"? What does the metaphor imply about the effectiveness of their dissent?

11. How does Kingwell make the transition to his proposed solution to the problems stemming from consumerism? (See paragraph 18.)

Content and Purpose

1. What is the "deliberately puzzling formulation" that Kingwell uses as an exam question for his first-year philosophy students? Why does he want "to unsettle them as much as possible" (paragraph 2)? If you were one of Kingwell's students, would the question unsettle you? Why or why not?

2. In our society, according to the essay, where does any discussion of "the good life" tend to keep "sliding" (paragraph 5)? What does the notion of "living well" no longer include?

3. Consider the references to poverty in paragraphs 5 and 8. Why does Kingwell describe the "toys of modern life" as "double-edged" (paragraph 5)? What does he think the "adventitious privilege of birth" (paragraph 8) might obligate a person to do? Explain why you agree or disagree with his position.

4. What does Kingwell mean by the argument he calls "the Evasive Elision" (paragraph 7), and what example does he use to support his definition? Why does he characterize the Evasive Elision as defensive and cynical?

5. What does Kingwell see as the "core problem" (paragraph 9) of our relentless pursuit of wealth?

6. According to Kingwell, how is our sense of well-being affected by the fact that we are "competitive and envious creatures" (paragraph 9)? How does the example in paragraph 10 support the statement that we are caught in a "'smart for one, dumb for all' trap"? Do you agree with that statement? Why or why not?

7. How are "standard luxury items" marketed to consumers (paragraph 11)? What is the basis of their appeal?

8. Explain in your own words the "branding and narrativizing of consumer products" (paragraph 12). What do you think will be

the long-term effects of our emphasis "on names and logos and spokespeople"?

9. According to paragraphs 13 and 14, many people see themselves as poor even though they are "more comfortable than their parents' generation." What is the reason for this kind of thinking? Do you share it? Why or why not?

10. According to paragraph 15, what are the social consequences of envy-driven consumerism?

11. In paragraphs 16 and 17, Kingwell describes two solutions to the consumerism problem. What are they, and why does he reject both?

12. In paragraph 18, Kingwell argues that "[t]he relentless acquisition of goods is just a symptom of a deeper ailment." Explain that ailment in your own words.

13. In paragraph 19, Kingwell proposes a solution to the consumerism problem that expresses his concept of the good life. Summarize the main elements of his solution in a sentence or two. What do you think of it? Given our culture, is it a workable solution? Why or why not?

Suggestions for Writing

1. Write an essay that expresses your own concept of the good life, and compare it with Kingwell's.

2. Spend a few days studying the advertisements you encounter in various media (television, billboards, magazines, etc.). Write an essay about some of the ads you studied, focusing on (a) the assumptions they make about the kind of life you should be living, and (b) the strategies they use to persuade you to live your life in a certain way.

Additional Suggestions for Writing: Argument and Persuasion

Choose one of the topics below and write an essay based on it. Think through your position carefully, formulate your opinion, and identify logical reasons for holding that opinion. Construct a clear thesis statement before you begin to write the paper.

1. Violence against an established government is (or is not) justified in certain circumstances.

2. Racial profiling is (or is not) necessary for the police to protect society against criminals.

3. Genetically modified food should (or should not) be labelled.

4. Canada should (or should not) adopt the U.S. dollar.

5. The government of Canada should (or should not) decriminalize the use of marijuana.
6. Music bridges (or widens) the gap between generations.
7. Males and females should (or should not) play on the same sports teams.
8. Parents should (or should not) be legally responsible for property damage (e.g., vandalism, theft) caused by their underage children.
9. Children should (or should not) be responsible for the care of their elderly parents.
10. Private religious schools should (or should not) receive government subsidies.
11. Critically ill patients should (or should not) be permitted to end their lives if and when they choose.
12. A teacher should (or should not) aim most of the course work at the weakest students in the class.
13. Fetal tissue obtained by abortion should (or should not) be made available to legitimate scientists for research.
14. Dishonesty is sometimes (or is never) the best policy.
15. Argue for or against the following statement: "One thing is certain: offering employment—the steady kind, with benefits, holiday pay, a measure of security, and maybe even union representation—has fallen out of economic fashion." (Naomi Klein)

8

Further Reading

Bumping into Mr. Ravioli

ADAM GOPNIK

Born in Philadelphia and raised in Montreal, Adam Gopnik holds degrees from McGill University and the Institute of Fine Arts at New York University. A staff writer at *The New Yorker* since 1986, he spent five years in Paris, as a correspondent for the magazine, writing essays about French life that were gathered in his best-selling collection *Paris to the Moon* (2000). Gopnik's broadcasting credits include appearances on CBC Newsworld's *Hot Type* and CBC Radio's *Cross Country Checkup*. His work for *The New Yorker* has won the National Magazine Award for Essay and Criticism and the George Polk Award for Magazine Reporting.

M y daughter Olivia, who just turned three, has an imaginary friend whose name is Charlie Ravioli. Olivia is growing up in Manhattan, and so Charlie Ravioli has a lot of local traits: he lives in an apartment "on Madison and Lexington," he dines on grilled chicken, fruit, and water, and, having reached the age of seven and a half, he feels, or is thought, "old." But the most peculiarly local thing about Olivia's imaginary playmate is this: he is always too busy to play with her. She holds her toy cell phone up to her ear, and we hear her talk into it: "Ravioli? It's Olivia . . . It's Olivia. Come and play? O.K. Call me. Bye." Then she snaps it shut, and shakes her head. "I always get his machine," she says. Or she will say, "I spoke to Ravioli today." "Did you have fun?" my wife and I ask. "No. He was busy working. On a television" (leaving it up in the air if he repairs electronic devices or has his own talk show). 1

On a good day, she "bumps into" her invisible friend and they go to a coffee shop. "I bumped into Charlie Ravioli," she announces 2 at dinner (after a day when, of course, she stayed home, played, had a nap, had lunch, paid a visit to the Central Park Zoo, and then had another nap). "We had coffee, but then he had to run." She sighs, sometimes, at her inability to make their schedules mesh, but she accepts it as inevitable, just the way life is. "I bumped into Charlie Ravioli today," she says. "He was working." Then she adds brightly, "But we hopped into a taxi." What happened then? we ask. "We grabbed lunch," she says.

3   It seemed obvious that Ravioli was a romantic figure of the big exotic life that went on outside her little limited life of parks and playgrounds—drawn, in particular, from a nearly perfect, mynah-bird-like imitation of the words she hears her mother use when she talks about *her* day with *her* friends. ("How was your day?" Sighing: "Oh, you know. I tried to make a date with Meg, but I couldn't find her, so I left a message on her machine. Then I bumped into Emily after that meeting I had in SoHo, and we had coffee and then she had to run, but by then Meg had reached me on my cell and we arranged . . .") I was concerned, though, that Charlie Ravioli might also be the sign of some "trauma," some loneliness in Olivia's life reflected in imaginary form. "It seems odd to have an imaginary playmate who's always too busy to play with you," Martha, my wife, said to me. "Shouldn't your imaginary playmate be someone you tell secrets to and, I don't know, sing songs with? It shouldn't be someone who's always *hopping* into taxis."

4   We thought, at first, that her older brother Luke might be the original of Charlie Ravioli. (For one thing, he is also seven and a half, though we were fairly sure that this age was merely Olivia's marker for As Old as Man Can Be.) He *is* too busy to play with her much anymore. He has become a true New York child, with the schedule of a Cabinet secretary: chess club on Monday, T-ball on Tuesday, tournament on Saturday, play dates and after-school conferences to fill in the gaps. But Olivia, though she counts days, does not yet really *have* days. She has *a* day, and into this day she has introduced the figure of Charlie Ravioli—in order, it dawned on us, to insist that she does have days, because she is too harried to share them, that she does have an independent social life, by virtue of being too busy to have one.

5   Yet Charlie Ravioli was becoming so constant and oddly discouraging a companion—"He cancelled lunch. Again," Olivia would say—that we thought we ought to look into it. One of my sisters is a developmental psychologist who specializes in close scientific studies of what goes on inside the heads of one- and two- and three-year-olds. Though she grew up in the nervy East, she lives in California now, where she grows basil in her garden and

jars her own organic marmalades. I e-mailed this sister for help with the Ravioli issue—how concerned should we be?—and she sent me back an e-mail, along with an attachment, and, after several failed cell-phone connections, we at last spoke on a land line.

It turned out that there is a recent book on this very subject by the psychologist Marjorie Taylor, called *Imaginary Companions and the Children Who Create Them*, and my sister had just written a review of it. She insisted that Charlie Ravioli was nothing to be worried about. Olivia was right on target, in fact. Most under-sevens (sixty-three per cent, to be scientific) have an invisible friend, and children create their imaginary playmates not out of trauma but out of a serene sense of the possibilities of fiction— sometimes as figures of pure fantasy, sometimes, as Olivia had done, as observations of grownup manners assembled in tranquil-lity and given a name. . . .   6

"An imaginary playmate isn't any kind of trauma-marker," my sister said. "It's just the opposite: it's a sign that the child is now confident enough to begin to understand how to organize her expe-rience into stories." The significant thing about imaginary friends, she went on, is that the kids know they're fictional. In an instant message on AOL, she summed it up: "The children with invisible friends often interrupted the interviewer to remind her, with a cer-tain note of concern for her sanity, that these characters were, after all, just pretend." . . .   7

"Don't worry about it," my sister said in a late-night phone call. "Knowing something's made up while thinking that it matters is what all fiction insists on. She's putting a name on a series of manners."   8

"But he seems so real to her," I objected.   9

"Of course he is. I mean, who's more real to you, Becky Sharp or Gandalf or the guy down the hall? Giving a manner a name makes it real."   10

I paused. "I grasp that it's normal for her to have an imaginary friend," I said, "but have you ever heard of an imaginary friend who's too busy to play with you?"   11

She thought about it. "No," she said. "I'm sure that doesn't occur anywhere in the research literature. That sounds *completely* New York." And then she hung up.   12

The real question, I saw, was not "Why this friend?" but "Why this fiction?" Why, as Olivia had seen so clearly, are grownups in New York so busy, and so obsessed with the language of busyness that it dominates their conversation? Why are New Yorkers always bumping into Charlie Ravioli and grabbing lunch, instead of sitting   13 down with him and exchanging intimacies, as friends should, as people do in Paris and Rome? Why is busyness the stuff our children make their invisible friends from, as country children make theirs from light and sand?

14   This seems like an odd question. New Yorkers are busy for obvious reasons: they have husbands and wives and careers and children, they have the Gauguin show to see and their personal trainers and accountants to visit. But the more I think about this the more I think it is—well, a lot of Ravioli. We are instructed to believe that we are busier because we have to work harder to be more productive, but everybody knows that busyness and productivity have a dubious, arm's-length relationship. Most of our struggle in New York, in fact, is to be less busy in order to do more work.

15   Constant, exhausting, no-time-to-meet-your-friends Charlie Ravioli–style busyness arrived as an affliction in modern life long after the other parts of bourgeois city manners did. Business long predates busyness. In the seventeenth and eighteenth centuries, when bourgeois people were building the institutions of bourgeois life, they seem never to have complained that they were too busy— or, if they did, they left no record of it. Samuel Pepys, who had a Navy to refloat and a burned London to rebuild, often uses the word "busy" but never complains of busyness. For him, the word "busy" is a synonym for "happy," not for "stressed." Not once in his diary does Pepys cancel lunch or struggle to fit someone in for coffee at four-thirty. Pepys works, makes love, and goes to bed, but he does not bump and he does not have to run. Ben Franklin, a half century later, boasts of his industriousness, but he, too, never complains about being busy, and always has time to publish a newspaper or come up with a maxim or swim the ocean or invent the lightning rod.

16   Until sometime in the middle of the nineteenth century, in fact, the normal affliction of the bourgeois was not busyness at all but its apparent opposite: boredom. It has even been argued that the grid of streets and cafés and small engagements in the nineteenth-century city—the whole of social life—was designed self-consciously as an escape from that numbing boredom. (Working people weren't bored, of course, but they were engaged in labor, not work. They were too busy to be busy.) Baudelaire, basically, was so bored that he had to get drunk and run out onto the boulevard in the hope of bumping into somebody.

17   Turn to the last third of the nineteenth century and the beginning of the twentieth, though, and suddenly everybody is busy, and everybody is complaining about it. Pepys, master of His Majesty's Navy, may never have complained of busyness, but Virginia Woolf,

mistress of motionless lull, is continually complaining about how she spends her days racing across London from square to square, just like—well, like Charlie Ravioli. Ronald Firbank is wrung out by his social obligations; Proust is constantly rescheduling rendezvous and apologizing for being overstretched. Henry James, with nothing particular to do save live, complains of being too busy all the time. He could not shake the world of obligation, he said, and he wrote a strange and beautiful story, "The Great Good Place," which begins with an exhausting flood of correspondence, telegrams, and manuscripts that drive the protagonist nearly mad.

What changed? That James story helps supply the key. It was trains and telegrams. The railroads ended isolation, and packed the metropolis with people whose work was defined by a complicated network of social obligations. Pepys's network in 1669 London was, despite his official position, relatively small compared even with that of a minor aesthete like Firbank, two centuries later. Pepys had more time to make love because he had fewer friends to answer. 18

If the train crowded our streets, the telegram crowded our minds. It introduced something into the world which remains with us today: a whole new class of communications that are defined as incomplete in advance of their delivery. A letter, though it may enjoin a response, is meant to be complete in itself. Neither the Apostle Paul nor Horace Walpole ever ends an epistle with "Give me a call and let's discuss." By contrast, it is in the nature of the telegram to be a skeletal version of another thing—a communication that opens more than it closes. The nineteenth century telegram came with those busy-threatening words "Letter follows." 19

Every device that has evolved from the telegram shares the same character. E-mails end with a suggestion for a phone call ("Anyway, let's meet and/or talk soon"), faxes with a request for an e-mail, answering-machine messages with a request for a fax. All are devices of perpetually suspended communication. My wife recalls a moment last fall when she got a telephone message from a friend asking her to check her e-mail apropos a phone call she needed to make vis-à-vis a fax they had both received asking for more information about a bed they were thinking of buying from Ireland online and having sent to America by Federal Express—a grand slam of incomplete communication. 20

In most of the Western world outside New York, the press of trains and of telegraphic communication was alleviated by those other two great transformers: the car and the television. While the train and the telegram (and their love children, subways and commuter trains and e-mail) pushed people together, the car and the television pulled people apart—taking them out to the suburbs and 21 sitting them down in front of a solo spectacle. New York, though, almost uniquely, got hit by a double dose of the first two technologies, and a very limited dose of the second two. Car life—car obsessions, car-defined habits—is more absent here than almost anywhere else in the country, while television, though obviously present, is less fatally prevalent here. New York is still a subject of television, and we compare *Sex and the City* to sex and the city; they are not yet quite the same. Here two grids of busyness remain dominant: the nineteenth- and early-twentieth-century grid of bump and run, and the late-twentieth- and early-twenty-first-century postmodern grid of virtual call and echo. Busyness is felt so intently here because we are both crowded and overloaded. We exit the apartment into a still dense nineteenth-century grid of street corners and restaurants full of people, and come home to the late-twentieth-century grid of faxes and e-mails and overwhelming incompleteness.

22   We walk across the Park on a Sunday morning and bump into our friend the baker and our old acquaintance from graduate school (what the hell is she doing now?) and someone we have been avoiding for three weeks. They all invite us for brunch, and we would love to, but we are too . . . busy. We bump into Charlie Ravioli, and grab a coffee with him—and come home to find three e-mails and a message on our cell phone from him, wondering where we are. The crowding of our space has been reinforced by a crowding of our time, and the only way to protect ourselves is to build structures of perpetual deferral: I'll see you next week, let's talk soon. We build rhetorical baffles around our lives to keep the crowding out, only to find that we have let nobody we love in.

23   Like Charlie Ravioli, we hop into taxis and leave messages on answering machines to avoid our acquaintances, and find that we keep missing our friends. I have one intimate who lives just across the park from me, whom I e-mail often, and whom I am fortunate to see two or three times a year. We are always . . . busy. He has become my Charlie Ravioli, my invisible friend. I am sure that he misses me—just as Charlie Ravioli, I realized, must tell his other friends that he is sorry he does not see Olivia more often.

24   Once I sensed the nature of his predicament, I began to feel more sympathetic toward Charlie Ravioli. I got to know him better, too. We learned more about what Ravioli did in the brief breathing spaces in his busy life when he could sit down with Olivia and dish. "Ravioli read your book," Olivia announced, for instance, one night at dinner. "He didn't like it much." We also found out that

Ravioli had joined a gym, that he was going to the beach in the summer, but he was too busy, and that he was working on a "show." ("It isn't a very good show," she added candidly.) Charlie Ravioli, in other words, was just another New Yorker: fit, opinionated, and trying to break into show business.

I think we would have learned to live happily with Charlie   25
Ravioli had it not been for the appearance of Laurie. She threw us badly. At dinner, Olivia had been mentioning a new personage almost as often as she mentioned Ravioli. "I talked to Laurie today," she would begin. "She says Ravioli is busy." Or she would be closeted with her play phone. "Who are you talking to, darling?" I would ask. "Laurie," she would say. "We're talking about Ravioli." We surmised that Laurie was, so to speak, the Linda Tripp of the Ravioli operation—the person you spoke to for consolation when the big creep was ignoring you.

But a little while later a more ominous side of Laurie's role   26
began to appear. "Laurie, tell Ravioli I'm calling," I heard Olivia say. I pressed her about who, exactly, Laurie was. Olivia shook her head. "She works for Ravioli," she said.

And then it came to us, with sickening clarity: Laurie was not   27
the patient friend who consoled you for Charlie's absence. Laurie was the bright-toned person who answered Ravioli's phone and told you that unfortunately Mr. Ravioli was in a meeting. "Laurie says Ravioli is too busy to play," Olivia announced sadly one morning. Things seemed to be deteriorating; now Ravioli was too busy even to say he was too busy.

I got back on the phone with my sister. "Have you ever heard   28
of an imaginary friend with an assistant?" I asked.

She paused. "Imaginary friends don't have assistants," she   29
said. "That's not only not in the literature. That's just . . . I mean—in California they don't have assistants."

"You think we should look into it?"   30

"I think you should move," she said flatly.   31

Martha was of the same mind. "An imaginary playmate   32
shouldn't have an assistant," she said miserably. "An imaginary playmate shouldn't have an agent. An imaginary playmate shouldn't have a publicist or a personal trainer or a caterer—an imaginary playmate shouldn't have . . . *people*. An imaginary playmate should just *play*. With the child who imagined it." She started leaving on my pillow real-estate brochures picturing quaint houses in New Jersey and Connecticut, unhaunted by busy invisible friends and their entourages.

33   Not long after the appearance of Laurie, though, something remarkable happened. Olivia would begin to tell us tales of her frustrations with Charlie Ravioli, and, after telling us, again, that he was too busy to play, she would tell us what she had done instead. Astounding . . . tall tales poured out of her: she had been to a chess tournament and brought home a trophy; she had gone to a circus and told jokes. Searching for Charlie Ravioli, she had "saved all the animals in the zoo"; heading home in a taxi after a quick coffee with Ravioli, she took over the steering wheel and "got all the moneys." From the stalemate of daily life emerged the fantasy of victory. She had dreamed of a normal life with a few close friends, and had to settle for worldwide fame and the front page of the tabloids. The existence of an imaginary friend had liberated her into a paracosm [a society thought up by a child—an invented universe with a distinctive language, geography, and history], but it was a curiously New York paracosm—it was the unobtainable world outside her window. Charlie Ravioli, prince of busyness, was not an end but a means: a way out onto the street in her head, a declaration of potential independence.

34   Busyness is our art form, our civic ritual, our way of being us. Many friends have said to me that they love New York now in a way they never did before, and their love, I've noticed, takes for its object all the things that used to exasperate them—the curious combination of freedom, self-made fences, and paralyzing preoccupation that the city provides. "How did you spend the day?" Martha and I now ask each other, and then, instead of listing her incidents, she says merely, "Oh, you know . . . just . . . bumping into Charlie Ravioli," meaning, just bouncing from obligation to electronic entreaty, just spotting a friend and snatching a sandwich, just being busy, just living in New York. If everything we've learned in the past year could be summed up in a phrase, it's that we want to go on bumping into Charlie Ravioli for as long as we can.

35   Olivia still hopes to have him to herself someday. As I work late at night in the "study" (an old hallway, an Aalto screen) I keep near the "nursery" (an ancient pantry, a glass-brick wall), I can hear her shift into pre-sleep, still muttering to herself. She is still trying to reach her closest friend. "Ravioli? Ravioli?" she moans as she turns over into her pillow and clutches her blanket, and then she whispers, almost to herself, "Tell him call me. Tell him call me when he comes home."

Immigration: The Hate Stops Here

MICHAEL IGNATIEFF

An award-winning author, historian, and broadcaster, Michael Ignatieff (b. 1947) was educated at the University of Toronto and abroad at Harvard and Cambridge universities. His books include *The Russian Album* (1987), which received the Governor General's Award; *Scar Tissue* (1993); *Isaiah Berlin: A Life* (1998); and *Virtual War: Kosovo and Beyond* (2000), the third in a trilogy of books on ethnic war and nationalism. Ignatieff is Carr Professor of Human Rights Practice and director of the Carr Center for Human Rights Policy at Harvard's Kennedy School of Government.

C anadians tell the story of immigration to our country in 1 terms of two myths: that we are a welcoming people, and that we are welcoming because those we welcome are only too happy to leave their hatreds behind. When the two myths are put together, they allow us to imagine Canada as a haven, a place where people abandon their own hatreds and escape the hatreds that drove them from their homes. This double myth is both self-congratulatory and self-deprecating. A safe haven is not necessarily a very exciting place—but better to be dull than dangerous. Most newcomers have lived our dullness as deliverance.

But now we must ask two other questions. Were we ever as 2 welcoming as the myth made us out to be? And now, in a world transfigured by terror, are we sure that newcomers are leaving their hatreds behind?

A multicultural Canada is a great idea in principle, but in reality 3 it is more like a tacit contract of mutual indifference. Communities share political and geographical space, but not necessarily religious, social or moral space. We have little Hong Kongs, little Kabuls, little Jaffnas, just as we once had little Berdichevs, little Pescaras, little Lisbons. But what must we know about each other in order to be citizens together?

In 1999, a moderate Tamil intellectual I greatly admired was 4 blown to pieces by a car bomb in Colombo by an extremist Tamil group. His offence: seeking a peaceful solution to the Sri Lankan catastrophe through negotiations with the Sinhalese government. After I went to Colombo to denounce the act of terror that had claimed his life, I began receiving Tamil magazines arguing that anyone from the Tamil community who sought non-violent solutions to political problems was a stooge or a fool.

The French call this strategy *la politique du pire:* endorsing 5 strategies to make things worse so that they cannot possibly get better. I came away from these Tamil magazines feeling that I could say nothing to the persons who had written them. The punch line of my story is that the postmarks were Canadian; they had been printed and published on my native soil.

6   The point of the story is not to turn on the Tamil community; most members despise the sort of rhetoric that I, too, despise. The point is that we need to rethink larger Canadian myths about the passage to Canada as a passage from hatred to civility. Is it true now? Was it ever true?

7   In the 1840s, the Irish brought their hatreds with them on the emigrant ships. Emigrants from the Balkans did not forget or forgive the oppression that caused them to flee. After the Second World War, emigrants from territories under Soviet tyranny came to this country with all their hatreds still alive. It is an innocent, liberal assumption to suppose that hatred is always bad. It's a necessity to hate oppression. I think, for example, of the Baltic Canadians who, whenever the Soviet Bolshoi Ballet toured Canada, held up signs outside the theatre protesting Soviet tyranny. These people now seem more morally aware than those, and they included me, who thought it was time to acquiesce in the facts of life, i.e. the permanent Soviet occupation of Eastern Europe.

8   It is not always right for exile and emigration to be accompanied by political forgetting. Remembering a conquered or oppressed home is one of the duties of emigrants. The problem is that exile can freeze conviction at the moment of departure. Once in exile, groups fail to evolve; they return, once their countries are free, speaking and behaving as if it were still 1945. A case in point: Croatian exiles, who escaped to Canada in the 1940s to flee Josip Broz Tito's imposition of Communist rule over Yugoslavia, remained more nationalistic than they would have in Tito's postwar Croatia. In exile, few could bear to learn that the country they had lost was also guilty of atrocities against Jews, Serbs, Roma and other minorities. Facing up to the reality of Ante Pavelic's wartime regime was hard enough in Zagreb; it was harder in Toronto. Indeed, it was often said in Zagreb that the chief support for the most intransigent and aggressive Croatian nationalism after independence was to be found, not in Zagreb, but in Toronto.

9   Dual allegiances are complex: a newly-minted Canadian citizen who would not dream of assassinating a fellow citizen from some oppressor group does not hesitate to fund assassinations in the old country. Sometimes emigration is accompanied by the guilt of departure. This guilt makes diaspora groups more violent and more extreme than those that live in the country where the oppression is taking place. Diaspora nationalism is a dangerous phenomenon

because it is easier to hate from a distance: you don't have to live with the consequences—or the reprisals.

Canadians, new and old, need to think about what role their 10
diasporas play in fanning and financing the hatreds of the outside world. The disturbing possibility is that Canada is not an asylum from hatred but an incubator of hatred. Are we so sure that acts of terror in Kashmir do not originate in apparently innocent funding of charitable and philanthropic appeals in Canadian cities? Are we certain that the financing of a car bomb in Jerusalem did not begin in a Canadian community? Do we know that when people die in Colombo, or Jaffna, there's no Canadian connection?

I don't have answers to these questions and it would be inflam- 11
matory to make allegations without evidence. My point is only to ask us to rethink our myths of immigration, particularly that inno-cent one that portrays us as a refuge from hatred. It is clear that this was never entirely true: many immigrant groups that make their lives here have not been extinguishing, but rather fanning, the hatreds they brought with them.

It would be a good idea to get the rules for a multicultural 12
Canada clear to all. Canada means many things—and in the debate about what it means, new voices are as valuable as older ones—but one meaning is indisputable. We are a political community that has outlawed the practice and advocacy of violence as an instrument of political expression. We have outlawed it within, and we need to outlaw it without. Just as we have laws against racial incitement or the promulgation of ethnic hatred in order to protect our new citizens from bigotry, abuse and violence, so we must have laws for the prose-cution of anyone in Canada who aids, abets, encourages or incites acts of terror. There may be political causes that justify armed resistance, but there are none that justify terrorizing and murdering civilians. 13

The distinction between freedom fighters and terrorists is not the relativist quagmire. There are laws of war governing armed resistance to oppression, as there are laws of war governing the conduct of hostilities between states. Those who break these laws are barbarians, whatever cause they serve. Those who target civil-ians to cause death and create fear are terrorists, no matter how just their armed struggle may be. States that use terror against civilians are as culpable as armed insurgents.

Coming to Canada is not the passage from hatred to civility 14
that we have supposed. And frankly, some hatred—of oppression, cruelty and racial discrimination—is wanted on the voyage. But Canada must keep to one simple rule of the road: we are not a political community that aids, abets, harbours or cultivates terror.

15   So it is appropriate to say to newcomers: You do not have to embrace all our supposed civilities. You can and should keep the memory of the injustice you have left firmly in your heart. But the law is the law. You will have to leave your murderous fantasies of revenge behind.

Growing Up Native

CAROL GEDDES

Carol Geddes is an Indian from the Tlingit Nation in the Yukon. She holds a graduate degree in communications from McGill University and has made several films, including *Doctor, Lawyer, Indian Chief*, a National Film Board production about the struggles of Native women. Geddes serves on the Women's Television Network Foundation Board, as well as a number of Aboriginal and Yukon heritage and arts boards.

1   I remember it was cold. We were walking through a swamp near our home in the Yukon bush. Maybe it was fall and moose-hunting season. I don't know. I think I was about four years old at the time. The muskeg was too springy to walk on, so people were taking turns carrying me—passing me from one set of arms to another. The details about where we were are vague, but the memory of those arms and the feeling of acceptance I had is one of the most vivid memories of my childhood. It didn't matter who was carrying me—there was security in every pair of arms. That response to children is typical of the native community. It's the first thing I think of when I cast my mind back to the Yukon bush, where I was born and lived with my family.

2   I was six years old when we moved out of the bush, first to Teslin, where I had a hint of the problems native people face, then to Whitehorse, where there was unimaginable racism. Eventually I moved to Ottawa and Montreal, where I further discovered that to grow up native in Canada is to feel the sting of humiliation and the boot of discrimination. But it is also to experience the enviable security of an extended family and to learn to appreciate the richness of the heritage and traditions of a culture most North Americans have never been lucky enough to know. As a film-maker, I have tried to explore these contradictions, and our triumph over them, for the half-million aboriginals who are part of the tide of swelling independence of the First Nations today.

But I'm getting ahead of myself. If I'm to tell the story of what   3
it's like to grow up native in northern Canada, I have to go back to
the bush where I was born, because there's more to my story than
the hurtful stereotyping that depicts Indian people as drunken welfare cases. Our area was known as 12-mile (it was 12 miles from
another tiny village). There were about 40 people living there—
including 25 kids, eight of them my brothers and sisters—in a sort
of family compound. Each family had its own timber plank house
for sleeping, and there was one large common kitchen area with
gravel on the ground and a tent frame over it. Everybody would
go there and cook meals together. In summer, my grandmother
always had a smudge fire going to smoke fish and tan moose hides.
I can remember the cosy warmth of the fire, the smell of good food,
and always having someone to talk to. We kids had built-in playmates and would spend hours running in the bush, picking berries,
building rafts on the lake and playing in abandoned mink cages.

One of the people in my village tells a story about the day the   4
old lifestyle began to change. He had been away hunting in the
bush for about a month. On his way back, he heard a strange sound
coming from far away. He ran up the crest of a hill, looked over the
top of it and saw a bulldozer. He had never seen or heard of such a
thing before and he couldn't imagine what it was. We didn't have
magazines or newspapers in our village, and the people didn't
know that the Alaska Highway was being built as a defence against
a presumed Japanese invasion during the Second World War. That
was the beginning of the end of the Teslin Tlingit people's way of
life. From that moment on, nothing turned back to the way it was.
Although there were employment opportunities for my father and
uncles, who were young men at the time, the speed and force with
which the Alaska Highway was rammed through the wilderness
caused tremendous upheaval for Yukon native people.

It wasn't as though we'd never experienced change before. The   5
Tlingit Nation, which I belong to, arrived in the Yukon from the
Alaskan coast around the turn of the century. They were the mid-
dlemen and women between the Russian traders and the Yukon
inland Indians. The Tlingit gained power and prestige by trading
European products such as metal goods and cloth for the rich and
varied furs so much in fashion in Europe. The Tlingit controlled
Yukon trading because they controlled the trading routes through the
high mountain passes. When trading ceased to be an effective means
of survival, my grandparents began raising wild mink in cages. Mink
prices were really high before and during the war, but afterwards the
prices went plunging down. So, although the mink pens were still
there when I was a little girl, my father mainly worked on highway

construction and hunted in the bush. The Yukon was then, and still is in some ways, in a transitional period—from living off the land to getting into a European wage-based economy.

6   As a young child, I didn't see the full extent of the upheaval. I remember a lot of togetherness, a lot of happiness while we lived in the bush. There's a very strong sense of family in the native community, and a fondness for children, especially young children. Even today, it's like a special form of entertainment if someone brings a baby to visit. That sense of family is the one thing that has survived all the incredible difficulties native people have had. Throughout a time of tremendous problems, the extended family system has somehow lasted, providing a strong circle for people to survive in. When parents were struggling with alcoholism or had to go away to find work, when one of the many epidemics swept through the community, or when a marriage broke up and one parent left, aunts, uncles, and grandparents would try to fill those roles. It's been very important to me in terms of emotional support to be able to rely on my extended family. There are still times when such support keeps me going.

7   Life was much simpler when we lived in the bush. Although we were poor and wore the same clothes all year, we were warm enough and had plenty to eat. But even as a youngster, I began to be aware of some of the problems we would face later on. Travelling missionaries would come and impose themselves on us, for example. They'd sit at our campfire and read the bible to us and lecture us about how we had to live a Christian life. I remember being very frightened by stories we heard about parents sending their kids away to live with white people who didn't have any children. We thought those people were mean and that if we were bad, we'd be sent away, too. Of course, that was when social workers were scooping up native children and adopting them out to white families in the south. The consequences were usually disastrous for the children who were taken away—alienation, alcoholism and suicide, among other things. I knew some of those kids. The survivors are still struggling to recover.

8   The residential schools were another source of misery for the kids. Although I didn't have to go, my brothers and sisters were there. They told stories about having their hair cut off in case they were carrying head lice, and of being forced to do hard chores without enough food to eat. They were told that the Indian culture was evil, that Indian people were bad, that their only hope was to be Christian. They had to stand up and say things like "I've found the Lord," when a teacher told them to speak. Sexual abuse was rampant in the residential school system.

By the time we moved to Whitehorse, I was excited about the 9
idea of living in what I thought of as a big town. I'd had a taste of
the outside world from books at school in Teslin (a town of 250
people), and I was tremendously curious about what life was like. I
was hungry for experiences such as going to the circus. In fact, for a
while, I was obsessed with stories and pictures about the circus, but
then when I was 12 and saw my first one, I was put off by the condition and treatment of the animals.

Going to school in Whitehorse was a shock. The clash of native 10
and white values was confusing and frightening. Let me tell you a
story. The older boys in our community were already accomplished
hunters and fishermen, but since they had to trap beaver in the
spring and hunt moose in the fall, and go out trapping in the winter
as well, they missed a lot of school. We were all in one classroom and
some of my very large teenage cousins had to sit squeezed into little
desks. These guys couldn't read very well. We girls had been in
school all along, so, of course, we were better readers. One day the
teacher was trying to get one of the older boys to read. She was typical of the teachers at that time, insensitive and ignorant of cultural
complexities. In an increasingly loud voice, she kept commanding
him to "Read it, read it." He couldn't. He sat there completely still,
but I could see that he was breaking into a sweat. The teacher then
said, "Look, she can read it," and she pointed to me, indicating that I
should stand up and read. For a young child to try to show up an
older boy is wrong and totally contrary to native cultural values, so I
refused. She told me to stand up and I did. My hands were trembling
as I held my reader. She yelled at me to read and when I didn't she
smashed her pointing stick on the desk to frighten me. In terror, I wet
my pants. As I stood there fighting my tears of shame, she said I was
disgusting and sent me home. I remember feeling this tremendous
confusion, on top of my humiliation. We were always told the white
teachers knew best, and so we had to do whatever they said at
school. And yet I had a really strong sense of receiving mixed messages about what I was supposed to do in the community and what I
was supposed to do at school.

Pretty soon I hated school. Moving to a predominantly white 11
high school was even worse. We weren't allowed to join anything
the white kids started. We were the butt of jokes because of our sec-
ondhand clothes and moose meat sandwiches. We were constantly
being rejected. The prevailing attitude was that Indians were
stupid. When it was time to make course choices in class—between
typing and science, for example—they didn't even ask the native
kids, they just put us all in typing. You get a really bad image of
yourself in a situation like that. I bought into it. I thought we were

awful. The whole experience was terribly undermining. Once, my grandmother gave me a pretty little pencil box. I walked into the classroom one day to find the word "squaw" carved on it. That night I burned it in the wood stove. I joined the tough crowd and by the time I was 15 years old, I was more likely to be leaning against the school smoking a cigarette than trying to join in. I was burned out from trying to join the system. The principal told my father there was no point in sending me back to school so, with a Grade 9 education, I started to work at a series of menial jobs.

12   Seven years later something happened to me that would change my life forever. I had moved to Ottawa with a man and was working as a waitress in a restaurant. One day, a friend invited me to her place for coffee. While I was there, she told me she was going to university in the fall and showed me her reading list. I'll never forget the minutes that followed. I was feeling vaguely envious of her and once again, inferior. I remember taking the paper in my hand, seeing the books on it and realizing, Oh, my God, I've read these books! It hit me like a thunderclap. I was stunned that books I had read were being read in university. University was for white kids, not native kids. We were too stupid, we didn't have the kind of mind it took to do those things. My eyes moved down the list, and my heart started beating faster and faster as I suddenly realized I could go to university, too!

13   My partner at the time was a loving supportive man who helped me in every way. I applied to the university immediately as a mature student but when I had to write Grade 9 on the application, I was sure they'd turn me down. They didn't. I graduated five years later, earning a bachelor of arts in English and philosophy (with distinction). . . .

14   Today, there's a glimmer of hope that more of us native people will overcome the obstacles that have tripped us up ever since we began sharing this land. Some say our cultures are going through a renaissance. Maybe that's true. Certainly there's a renewed interest in native dancing, acting and singing, and in other cultural traditions. Even indigenous forms of government are becoming strong again. But we can't forget that the majority of native people live in urban areas and continue to suffer from alcohol and drug abuse and the plagues of a people who have lost their culture and have become lost themselves. And the welfare system is the insidious glue that holds together the machine of oppression of native people.

15   Too many non-native people have refused to try to understand the issues behind our land claims. They make complacent pro-

nouncements such as "Go back to your bows and arrows and fish with spears if you want aboriginal rights. If not, give it up and assimilate into white Canadian culture." I don't agree with that. We need our culture, but there's no reason why we can't preserve it and have an automatic washing machine and a holiday in Mexico, as well.

The time has come for native people to make our own decisions. We need to have self-government. I have no illusions that it will be smooth sailing—there will be trial and error and further struggle. And if that means crawling before we can stand up and walk, so be it. We'll have to learn through experience.   16

While we're learning, we have a lot to teach and give to the world—a holistic philosophy, a way of living with the earth, not disposing of it. It is critical that we all learn from the elders that an individual is not more important than a forest; we know that we're here to live on and with the earth, not to subdue it.   17

The wheels are in motion for a revival, for change in the way native people are taking their place in Canada. I can see that we're equipped, we have the tools to do the work. We have an enormous number of smart, talented, moral Indian people. It's thrilling to be a part of this movement.   18

Someday, when I'm an elder, I'll tell the children the stories: about the bush, about the hard times, about the renaissance, and especially about the importance of knowing your place in your nation.   19

Lost in Translation

EVA HOFFMAN

Eva Hoffman is the author of *Shtetl*, *Exit into History*, and *Lost in Translation*. Born in Cracow, Poland, in 1945, Hoffman immigrated to Canada with her family in 1959. She lived and went to school in Vancouver, then completed her Ph.D. in English at Harvard University. She now lives in London, England.

Every day I learn new words, new expressions. I pick them up from school exercises, from conversations, from the books I take out of Vancouver's well-lit, cheerful public library. There are some turns of phrase to which I develop strange allergies. "You're welcome," for example, strikes me as a gaucherie, and I can   1 hardly bring myself to say it—I suppose because it implies that there's something to be thanked for, which in Polish would be impolite. The very places where the language is at its most conventional, where it should be most taken for granted, are the places where I feel the prick of artifice.

2   Then there are words to which I take an equally irrational liking, for their sound, or just because I'm pleased to have deduced their meaning. Mainly they're words I learn from books, like "enigmatic" or "insolent"—words that have only a literary value, that exist only as signs on the page.

3   But mostly, the problem is that the signifier has become severed from the signified. The words I learn now don't stand for things in the same unquestioned way they did in my native tongue. "River" in Polish was a vital sound, energized with the essence of riverhood, of my rivers, of my being immersed in rivers. "River" in English is cold—a word without an aura. It has no accumulated associations for me, and it does not give off the radiating haze of connotation. It does not evoke.

4   The process, alas, works in reverse as well. When I see a river now, it is not shaped, assimilated by the word that accommodates it to the psyche—a word that makes a body of water a river rather than an uncontained element. The river before me remains a thing, absolutely other, absolutely unbending to the grasp of my mind.

5   When my friend Penny tells me that she's envious, or happy, or disappointed, I try laboriously to translate not from English to Polish but from the word back to its source, to the feeling from which it springs. Already, in that moment of strain, spontaneity of response is lost. And anyway, the translation doesn't work. I don't know how Penny feels when she talks about envy. The word hangs in a Platonic stratosphere, a vague prototype of all envy, so large, so all-encompassing that it might crush me—as might disappointment or happiness.

6   I am becoming a living avatar of structuralist wisdom; I cannot help knowing that words are just themselves. But it's a terrible knowledge, without any of the consolations that wisdom usually brings. It does not mean that I'm free to play with words at my wont; anyway, words in their naked state are surely among the least satisfactory play objects. No, this radical disjoining between word and thing is a desiccating alchemy, draining the world not only of significance but of its colors, striations, nuances—its very existence. It is the loss of a living connection.

7   The worst losses come at night. As I lie down in a strange bed in a strange house—my mother is a sort of housekeeper here, to the

aging Jewish man who has taken us in return for her services—I wait for that spontaneous flow of inner language which used to be my nighttime talk with myself, my way of informing the ego where the id had been. Nothing comes. Polish, in a short time, has atrophied, shriveled from sheer uselessness. Its words don't apply to my new experiences; they're not coeval with any of the objects, or faces, or the very air I breathe in the daytime. In English, words have not penetrated to those layers of my psyche from which a private conversation could proceed. This interval before sleep used to be the time when my mind became both receptive and alert, when images and words rose up to consciousness, reiterating what had happened during the day, adding the day's experiences to those already stored there, spinning out the thread of my personal story.

Now, this picture-and-word show is gone; the thread has been snapped. I have no interior language, and without it, interior images— those images through which we assimilate the external world, through which we take it in, love it, make it our own— become blurred too. My mother and I met a Canadian family who live down the block today. They were working in their garden and engaged us in a conversation of the "Nice weather we're having, isn't it?" variety, which culminated in their inviting us into their house. They sat stiffly on their couch, smiled in the long pauses between the conversation, and seemed at a loss for what to ask. Now my mind gropes for some description of them, but nothing fits. They're a different species from anyone I've met in Poland, and Polish words slip off them without sticking. English words don't hook on to anything. I try, deliberately, to come up with a few. Are these people pleasant or dull? Kindly or silly? The words float in an uncertain space. They come up from a part of my brain in which labels may be manufactured but which has no connection to my instincts, quick reactions, knowledge. Even the simplest adjectives sow confusion in my mind; English kindliness has a whole system of morality behind it, a system that makes "kindness" an entirely positive virtue. Polish kindness has the tiniest element of irony. Besides, I'm beginning to feel the tug of prohibition, in English, against uncharitable words. In Polish, you can call someone an idiot without particularly harsh feelings and with the zest of a strong judgment. Yes, in Polish these people might tend toward "silly" and "dull"—but I force myself toward "kindly" and "pleasant." The cultural unconscious is beginning to exercise its subliminal influence.

The verbal blur covers these people's faces, their gestures with a sort of fog. I can't translate them into my mind's eye. The small event, instead of being added to the mosaic of consciousness and

8

9

memory, falls through some black hole, and I fall with it. What has happened to me in this new world? I don't know. I don't see what I've seen, don't comprehend what's in front of me. I'm not filled with language anymore, and I have only a memory of fullness to anguish me with the knowledge that, in this dark and empty state, I don't really exist. . . .

10   My voice is doing funny things. It does not seem to emerge from the same parts of my body as before. It comes out from somewhere in my throat, tight, thin, and mat—a voice without the modulations, dips, and rises that it had before, when it went from my stomach all the way through my head. There is, of course, the constraint and the self-consciousness of an accent that I hear but cannot control. Some of my high school peers accuse me of putting it on in order to appear more "interesting." In fact, I'd do anything to get rid of it, and when I'm alone, I practice sounds for which my speech organs have no intuitions, such as "th" (I do this by putting my tongue between my teeth) and "a," which is longer and more open in Polish (by shaping my mouth into a sort of arrested grin). It is simple words like "cat" or "tap" that give me the most trouble, because they have no context of other syllables, and so people often misunderstand them. Whenever I can, I do awkward little swerves to avoid them, or pause and try to say them very clearly. Still, when people—like salesladies—hear me speak without being prepared to listen carefully, they often don't understand me the first time around. "Girls' shoes," I say, and the "girls" comes out as a sort of scramble. "Girls' shoes," I repeat, willing the syllable to form itself properly, and the saleslady usually smiles nicely, and sends my mother and me to the right part of the store. I say "Thank you" with a sweet smile, feeling as if I'm both claiming an unfair special privilege and being unfairly patronized.

11   It's as important to me to speak well as to play a piece of music without mistakes. Hearing English distorted grates on me like chalk screeching on a blackboard, like all things botched and badly done, like all forms of gracelessness. The odd thing is that I know what is correct, fluent, good, long before I can execute it. The English spoken by our Polish acquaintances strikes me as jagged and thick, and I know that I shouldn't imitate it. I'm turned off by the intonations I hear on the TV sitcoms—by the expectation of laughter, like a dog's tail wagging in supplication, built into the actors' pauses, and by the curtailed, cutoff rhythms. I like the way Penny speaks, with an easy flow and a pleasure in giving words a fleshly fullness; I like what I hear in some movies; and once the Old Vic comes to Vancouver to perform *Macbeth*, and though I can

hardly understand the particular words, I am riveted by the tones of sureness and command that mold the actors' speech into such majestic periods.

Sociolinguists might say that I receive these language messages 12 as class signals, that I associate the sounds of correctness with the social status of the speaker. In part, this is undoubtedly true. The class-linked notion that I transfer wholesale from Poland is that belonging to a "better" class of people is absolutely dependent on speaking a "better" language. And in my situation especially, I know that language will be a crucial instrument, that I can overcome the stigma of my marginality, the weight of presumption against me, only if the reassuringly right sounds come out of my mouth.

Yes, speech is a class signifier. But I think that in hearing these 13 varieties of speech around me, I'm sensitized to something else as well—something that is a matter of aesthetics, and even of psychological health. Apparently, skilled chefs can tell whether a dish from some foreign cuisine is well cooked even if they have never tasted it and don't know the genre of cooking it belongs to. There seem to be some deep-structure qualities—consistency, proportions of ingredients, smoothness of blending—that indicate culinary achievement to these educated eaters' taste buds. So each language has its own distinctive music, and even if one doesn't know its separate components, one can pretty quickly recognize the propriety of the patterns in which the components are put together, their harmonies and discords. Perhaps the crucial element that strikes the ear in listening to living speech is the degree of the speaker's self-assurance and control.

As I listen to people speaking that foreign tongue, English, I 14 can hear when they stumble or repeat the same phrases too many times, when their sentences trail off aimlessly—or, on the contrary, when their phrases have vigor and roundness, when they have the space and the breath to give a flourish at the end of a sentence, or make just the right pause before coming to a dramatic point. I can tell, in other words, the degree of their ease or disease, the extent of authority that shapes the rhythms of their speech. That authority— in whatever dialect, in whatever variant of the mainstream language—seems to me to be something we all desire. It's not that we all want to speak the King's English, but whether we speak Appalachian or Harlem English, or Cockney, or Jamaican Creole, we want to be at home in our tongue. We want to be able to give voice accurately and fully to ourselves and our sense of the world. John Fowles, in one of his stories in *The Ebony Tower*, has a young man cruelly violate an elderly writer and his manuscripts because the legacy of language has not been passed on to the youthful vandal properly. This seems to me an entirely credible premise.

Linguistic dispossession is a sufficient motive for violence, for it is close to the dispossession of one's self. Blind rage, helpless rage is rage that has no words—rage that overwhelms one with darkness. And if one is perpetually without words, if one exists in the entropy of inarticulateness, that condition itself is bound to be an enraging frustration. In my New York apartment, I listen almost nightly to fights that erupt like brush-fire on the street below—and in their escalating fury of repetitious phrases ("Don't do this to me, man, you fucking bastard, I'll fucking kill you"), I hear not the pleasures of macho toughness but an infuriated beating against wordlessness, against the incapacity to make oneself understood, seen. Anger can be borne—it can even be satisfying—if it can gather into words and explode in a storm, or a rapier-sharp attack. But without this means of ventilation, it only turns back inward, building and swirling like a head of steam—building to an impotent, murderous rage. If all therapy is speaking therapy—a talking cure—then perhaps all neurosis is a speech disease.

Passion Play

LORNE RUBENSTEIN

Lorne Rubenstein (b. 1948) lives in Toronto and travels widely in the world of golf. A regular columnist for *The Globe and Mail* since 1980, he also contributes to a variety of sports publications. His books include *Links: An Insider's Tour through the World of Golf* (1990), *Touring Prose* (1992), *The Swing* (1998, with Nick Price), and *A Season in Dornoch: Golf and Life in the Scottish Highlands* (2002).

1   The squishiness of the green, still sodden ground beneath my spiked feet; the earthy scent of the now-fertile soil and the spray of water as my club head contacts the ball; the flight of the ball towards the green; or, often, its helter-skelter path, windborne, clasped to the welcome breezes blowing spring warmth onto the course. These are some of my impressions of early games of golf each spring. Every year for 30 years I have taken to the game anew, wondering what the season will bring. Still, the passion remains for a game that Winston Churchill once derided as being like "chasing a quinine pill around a cow pasture."

Ah, but Churchill was misguided. What did he know of the energizing feeling that courses through a golfer's body when he contacts the ball on the sweet spot of the club face? How could he even dare to speak so maliciously of a game in which even the most horrible hacker can sink a long putt across the hollows and humps of a tricky green, knowing for a moment that he or she is feeling just like Jack Nicklaus or Nancy Lopez? More golfers than ever are celebrating an illogical love of a game in which even the great Ben Hogan, master of the swing, said that he hits only a few shots each round that come off as he imagines.

Can so little success anywhere, on any field of play or in any walk of life, offer such rewards as a golf ball perfectly struck? Golfers know. And never mind the golfer's standard rueful lament. Asked after a round how he played, a golfer can quite rightly answer: "I didn't play my usual game today. Come to think of it, I never play my usual game."

But who needs "usual" games anyway? Golf, and especially late spring golf, when hope still is writ large in the golfer's mind, is about reaching for the unusual, the outer limits of what the golfer can do. We golfers are exhorted to "extend" the club head, to "swing to the target." Spring golf stretches our vision, pulls us out of our winter selves, huddled for warmth, at last. But winter also propels us forward for golf. The very hibernation it imposes makes the anticipation of a spring round keen indeed. Awakening, sensate again, we believe in ourselves. Against common sense, encouraged by thoughts sharpened over many a winter's night, the golfer believes that he can still play to his potential. That is the promise of the game, the lure that brings the golfer out spring after spring. An odd round down south during the winter does not count. That's a holiday round. Now comes the real thing, in spring.

But what is the real thing? With no apologies to Churchill, or to George Bernard Shaw, who sneered that golf is "a typical capitalist lunacy of upper-class Edwardian England," the fact is that golf is not some backwater foolishness where only the lightweight, the fat cat and the dopey participate. Many golfers are fit, and more than a few read books, attend plays, keep up with the news and even make worthwhile contributions to society beyond advising fellow golfers where to place their elbows on the backswing. There is high art and bizarre science enough in striking the ball to satisfy most anybody, and even to capture the imagination of people who, mistakenly thinking they are politically correct, call golf "an old man's game."

No, no, a thousand scorecards no. Think of something Brendan Gill wrote about his father in his memoir *Here at The New Yorker*. Gill's father was "a brilliant surgeon and physician. . . . He hunted, fished, hiked, chopped wood, planted trees, and painted houses, barns, sheds and every other surface a brush could reach. But his favorite outdoor activity was golf. The game amounted to a passion with him."

7   Passion. Now there's a word often heard in connection with golf. Go figure: "Passion," used to describe a game in which nobody even hits one another, or runs after a ball. The word means "strong emotion; outburst of anger; strong enthusiasm." Roget comes up with such synonyms as "desire, distress, eloquence, fervor, mania, torment, zeal." Golf does inspire these feelings. It might seem crazy, but there's a fellow who shall go unnamed here who has said that his self-esteem rises and falls with his golf. He's an orthopedic surgeon whose family life and career are going beautifully. But he can't figure his golf game out. He can't play his "usual" game.

8   This fellow, and millions like him around the world, know what a gentleman named Douglas Bertram Watson meant when he titled his book *I'll Never Be Cured and I Don't Much Care: The History of an Acute Attack of Golf and Pertinent Remarks Relating to Various Places of Treatment.* Exactly. Who cares? Life is fraught with problems, so why should a golfer not be allowed the simple pleasure of an early evening on the course, alone or in company. How good it feels when a warm drizzling rain tickles one's head. The white flag on the green ahead may be barely discernible as it slaps the air in the dusk, but a shot hit just so will reach the green, and perhaps cuddle up to the flagstick. Is this a dream, only a dream? These spring rounds can make the dream real.

9   But perhaps it does not matter if the shot is good. Maybe the walk is what matters, the opportunity for silence, for reflection. A round of golf can be a communion with oneself and with nature. Truly, though, the game is rarely played this way nowadays. Most public courses are jammed, and buzz with carts. People accuse one another of playing too slowly. Golfers diligently add up their scores as if they are checking stock quotations; they are too concerned with their scores. The game becomes a sombre affair.

10   To care too much about score is to lose the rhythm of the game. Judging our shots, we can miss the essential pliability of golf, the way it bends us every which way. Golf is really not about judgment, but about acceptance. The essence of the game is that a player drives the ball in the middle of the fairway and lands in a deep, ugly scar of a divot left by a golfer ahead. Accept it. This is the game: golf is played outdoors on grass. It is not possible to control the environment. Let the pliability of the game encourage a suppleness within yourself.

This is what the late George Knudson, Canada's deeply intro- 11
spective and mightily gifted golfer, alluded to when he suggested
that the golfer "give up control to gain control." That is, the player
ought to stop thinking about what to do with the golf club at every
segment of its route away from and back to the ball. Said Knudson:
"Let yourself swing."

Perhaps that sounds too much like Zen golf. But we will risk 12
any accusation of limp thinking because we know that we find
almost an altered state when we bounce on the rolling turf, and
when we are aware of the high grass swaying in the rough and
when we wrap our fingers around a velvety grip and when we
swing the club to and fro and when we fall into the grace of the
game, an outing that sends us inward.

If we play sensibly, we can discover the sensuality that lurks 13
everywhere on the course. Thinking about slow play, Knudson
once said: "I don't know what all the concern is about. Slow play
just means that you're going to spend a longer time in a nice place."
Take a book along on the course, then. Read a poem. Chat with
your companions. Swing, swing, swing. Walk in the woods.

Knudson's comment can be a code for the game. Spring has 14
been here for weeks, but the season still feels fresh, and we are
renewed. As for me, I have scratched the itch long enough. I want
grass clippings stuck to the soles of my shoes, mud on my golf ball,
dirt on my club face, the club in my hand while I turn it round and
round until it feels right. Care to join me?

Pornography

MARGARET ATWOOD

One of Canada's best-known writers, Margaret Atwood was born in Ottawa
in 1939. She has published more than twenty books, including novels,
short stories, poetry, and criticism. Among her most recent works are *The
Robber Bride* (1993), *Morning in the Burned House* (1995), and *Alias
Grace* (1996). In 2000, Atwood won the prestigious Booker Prize for her
novel *The Blind Assassin*.

When I was in Finland a few years ago for an international 1
writers' conference, I had occasion to say a few paragraphs in public on the subject of pornography. The context was a discussion of political repression, and I was suggesting

the possibility of a link between the two. The immediate result was that a male journalist took several large bites out of me. Prudery and pornography are two halves of the same coin, said he, and I was clearly a prude. What could you expect from an Anglo-Canadian? Afterward, a couple of pleasant Scandinavian men asked me what I had been so worked up about. All "pornography" means, they said, is graphic depictions of whores, and what was the harm in that?

2   Not until then did it strike me that the male journalist and I had two entirely different things in mind. By "pornography," he meant naked bodies and sex. I, on the other hand, had recently been doing the research for my novel *Bodily Harm*, and was still in a state of shock from some of the material I had seen, including the Ontario Board of Film Censors' "outtakes." By "pornography," I meant women getting their nipples snipped off with garden shears, having meat hooks stuck into their vaginas, being disemboweled; little girls being raped; men (yes, there are some men) being smashed to a pulp and forcibly sodomized. The cutting edge of pornography, as far as I could see, was no longer simple old copulation, hanging from the chandelier or otherwise: it was death, messy, explicit and highly sadistic. I explained this to the nice Scandinavian men. "Oh, but that's just the United States," they said. "Everyone knows they're sick." In their country, they said, violent "pornography" of that kind was not permitted on television or in movies; indeed, excessive violence of any kind was not permitted. They had drawn a clear line between erotica, which earlier studies had shown did not incite men to more aggressive and brutal behavior toward women, and violence, which later studies indicated did.

3   Some time after that I was in Saskatchewan, where, because of the scenes in *Bodily Harm*, I found myself on an open-line radio show answering questions about "pornography." Almost no one who phoned in was in favor of it, but again they weren't talking about the same stuff I was, because they hadn't seen it. Some of them were all set to stamp out bathing suits and negligees, and, if possible, any depictions of the female body whatsoever. God, it was implied, did not approve of female bodies, and sex of any kind, including that practised by bumblebees, should be shoved back into the dark, where it belonged. I had more than a suspicion that *Lady Chatterley's Lover*, Margaret Laurence's *The Diviners*, and indeed most books by most serious modern authors would have ended up as confetti if left in the hands of these callers.

4   For me, these two experiences illustrate the two poles of the emotionally heated debate that is now thundering around this

issue. They also underline the desirability and even the necessity of defining the terms. "Pornography" is now one of those catchalls, like "Marxism" and "feminism," that have become so broad they can mean almost anything, ranging from certain verses in the Bible, ads for skin lotion and sex tests for children to the contents of *Penthouse*, Naughty '90s postcards and films with titles containing the word *Nazi* that show vicious scenes of torture and killing. It's easy to say that sensible people can tell the difference. Unfortunately, opinions on what constitutes a sensible person vary.

But even sensible people tend to lose their cool when they start 5
talking about this subject. They soon stop talking and start yelling, and the name calling begins. Those in favor of censorship (which may include groups not noticeably in agreement on other issues, such as some feminists and religious fundamentalists) accuse the others of exploiting women through the use of degrading images, contributing to the corruption of children, and adding to the general climate of violence and threat in which both women and children live in this society; or, though they may not give much of a hoot about actual women and children, they invoke moral standards and God's supposed aversion to "filth," "smut" and deviated *perversion*, which may mean ankles.

The camp in favor of total "freedom of expression" often comes 6
out howling as loud as the Romans would have if told they could no longer have innocent fun watching the lions eat up Christians. It too may include segments of the population who are not natural bedfellows: those who proclaim their God-given right to freedom, including the freedom to tote guns, drive when drunk, drool over chicken porn and get off on videotapes of women being raped and beaten, may be waving the same anticensorship banner as responsible liberals who fear the return of Mrs. Grundy, or gay groups for whom sexual emancipation involves the concept of "sexual theatre." *Whatever turns you on* is a handy motto, as is *A man's home is his castle* (and if it includes a dungeon with beautiful maidens strung up in chains and bleeding from every pore, that's his business).

Meanwhile, theoreticians theorize and speculators speculate. Is 7
today's pornography yet another indication of the hatred of the body, the deep mind–body split, which is supposed to pervade Western Christian society? Is it a backlash against the women's movement by men who are threatened by uppity female behavior in real life, so like to fantasize about women done up like outsize parcels, being turned into hamburger, kneeling at their feet in slavelike adoration or sucking off guns? Is it a sign of collective impotence, of a generation of men who can't relate to real women at all but have to make do with bits of celluloid and paper? Is the current

flood just a result of smart marketing and aggressive promotion by the money men in what has now become a multibillion-dollar industry? If they were selling movies about men getting their testicles stuck full of knitting needles by women with swastikas on their sleeves, would they do as well, or is this penchant somehow peculiarly male? If so, why? Is pornography a power trip rather than a sex one? Some say that those ropes, chains, muzzles and other restraining devices are an argument for the immense power female sexuality still wields in the male imagination: you don't put these things on dogs unless you're afraid of them. Others, more literary, wonder about the shift from the 19th-century Magic Woman or Femme Fatale image to the lollipop-licker, airhead or turkey-carcass treatment of women in porn today. The proporners don't care much about theory; they merely demand product. The antiporners don't care about it in the final analysis either; there's dirt on the street, and they want it cleaned up, now.

8   It seems to me that this conversation, with its *You're-a-prude/ You're-a-pervert* dialectic, will never get anywhere as long as we continue to think of this material as just "entertainment." Possibly we're deluded by the packaging, the format: magazine, book, movie, theatrical presentation. We're used to thinking of these things as part of the "entertainment industry," and we're used to thinking of ourselves as free adult people who ought to be able to see any kind of "entertainment" we want to. That was what the First Choice pay-TV debate was all about. After all, it's only entertainment, right? Entertainment means fun, and only a killjoy would be antifun. What's the harm?

9   This is obviously the central question: *What's the harm?* If there isn't any real harm to any real people, then the antiporners can tsk-tsk and/or throw up as much as they like, but they can't rightfully expect more legal controls or sanctions. However, the no harm position is far from being proven.

10   (For instance, there's a clear-cut case for banning—as the federal government has proposed—movies, photos and videos that depict children engaging in sex with adults: real children are used to make the movies, and hardly anybody thinks this is ethical. The possibilities for coercion are too great.)

11   To shift the viewpoint, I'd like to suggest three other models for looking at "pornography"—and here I mean the violent kind.

12   Those who find the idea of regulating pornographic materials repugnant because they think it's Fascist or Communist or otherwise not in accordance with the principles of an open democratic society should consider that Canada has made it illegal to disseminate material that may lead to hatred toward any group because of

race or religion. I suggest that if pornography of the violent kind depicted these acts being done predominantly to Chinese, to blacks, to Catholics, it would be off the market immediately, under the present laws. Why is hate literature illegal? Because whoever made the law thought that such material might incite real people to do real awful things to other real people. The human brain is to a certain extent a computer: garbage in, garbage out. We only hear about the extreme cases (like that of American multimurderer Ted Bundy) in which pornography has contributed to the death and/or mutilation of women and/or men. Although pornography is not the only factor involved in the creation of such deviance, it certainly has upped the ante by suggesting both a variety of techniques and the social acceptability of such actions. Nobody knows yet what effect this stuff is having on the less psychotic.

Studies have shown that a large part of the market for all kinds 13 of porn, soft and hard, is drawn from the 16-to-21-year-old population of young men. Boys used to learn about sex on the street, or (in Italy, according to Fellini movies) from friendly whores, or, in more genteel surroundings, from girls, their parents, or, once upon a time, in school, more or less. Now porn has been added, and sex education in the schools is rapidly being phased out. The buck has been passed, and boys are being taught that all women secretly like to be raped and that real men get high on scooping out women's digestive tracts.

Boys learn their concept of masculinity from other men: is this 14 what most men want them to be learning? If word gets around that rapists are "normal" and even admirable men, will boys feel that in order to be normal, admirable and masculine they will have to be rapists? Human beings are enormously flexible, and how they turn out depends a lot on how they're educated, by the society in which they're immersed as well as by their teachers. In a society that advertises and glorifies rape or even implicitly condones it, more women get raped. It becomes socially acceptable. And at a time when men and the traditional male role have taken a lot of flak and men are confused and casting around for an acceptable way of being male (and, in some cases, not getting much comfort from women on that score), this must be at times a pleasing thought.

It would be naïve to think of violent pornography as just harm- 15 less entertainment. It's also an educational tool and a powerful propaganda device. What happens when boy educated on porn meets girl brought up on Harlequin romances? The clash of expectations can be heard around the block. She wants him to get down on his knees with a ring, he wants her to get down on all fours with a ring in her nose. Can this marriage be saved?

16   Pornography has certain things in common with such addictive substances as alcohol and drugs; for some, though by no means for all, it induces chemical changes in the body, which the user finds exciting and pleasurable. It also appears to attract a "hard core" of habitual users and a penumbra of those who use it occasionally but aren't dependent on it in any way. There are also significant numbers of men who aren't much interested in it, not because they're undersexed but because real life is satisfying their needs, which may not require as many appliances as those of users.

17   For the "hard core," pornography may function as alcohol does for the alcoholic: tolerance develops, and a little is no longer enough. This may account for the short viewing time and fast turnover in porn theatres. Mary Brown, chairwoman of the Ontario Board of Film Censors, estimates that for every one mainstream movie requesting entrance to Ontario, there is one porno flick. Not only the quantity consumed but the quality of explicitness must escalate, which may account for the growing violence: once the big deal was breasts, then it was genitals, then copulation, then that was no longer enough and the hard users had to have more. The ultimate kick is death, and after that, as the Marquis de Sade so boringly demonstrated, multiple death.

18   The existence of alcoholism has not led us to ban social drinking. On the other hand, we do have laws about drinking and driving, excessive drunkenness and other abuses of alcohol that may result in injury or death to others.

19   This leads us back to the key question: what's the harm? Nobody knows, but this society should find out fast, before the saturation point is reached. The Scandinavian studies that showed a connection between depictions of sexual violence and increased impulse toward it on the part of male viewers would be a starting point, but many more questions remain to be raised as well as answered. What, for instance, is the crucial difference between men who are users and men who are not? Does using affect a man's relationship with actual women, and, if so, adversely? Is there a clear line between erotica and violent pornography, or are they on an escalating continuum? Is this a "men versus women" issue, with all men secretly siding with the proporners and all women secretly siding against? (I think not; there *are* lots of men who don't think that running their true love through the Cuisinart is the best way they can think of to spend a Saturday night, and they're just as nauseated by films of someone else doing it as women are.) Is pornography merely an expression of the sexual confusion of this age or an active contributor to it?

Nobody wants to go back to the age of official repression, when 20 even piano legs were referred to as "limbs" and had to wear pantaloons to be decent. Neither do we want to end up in George Orwell's 1984, in which pornography is turned out by the State to keep the proles in a state of torpor, sex itself is considered dirty and the approved practice is only for reproduction. But Rome under the emperors isn't such a good model either.

If all men and women respected each other, if sex were consid- 21 ered joyful and life-enhancing instead of a wallow in germ-filled glop, if everyone were in love all the time, if, in other words, many people's lives were more satisfactory for them than they appear to be now, pornography might just go away on its own. But since this is obviously not happening, we as a society are going to have to make some informed and responsible decisions.

Hunger

MAGGIE HELWIG

Maggie Helwig (b. 1961) is a Canadian writer living in Toronto. Her books include *Where She Was Standing* (2001), *Real Bodies* (2002), and *One Building in the Earth: New and Selected Poems* (2002).

Consider that it is now normal for North American women to 1 have eating disorders. Consider that anorexia—deliberate starvation—and bulimia—self-induced vomiting—and obsessive patterns for weight-controlling exercise are now the ordinary thing for young women, and are spreading at a frightening rate to older women, to men, to ethnic groups and social classes that were once "immune." Consider that some surveys suggest that 80 per cent of the women on an average university campus have borderline-to-severe eating disorders; that it is almost impossible to get treatment unless the problem is life-threatening; that, in fact, if it is not life-threatening it is not considered a problem at all. I once sat in a seminar on nutritional aspects of anorexia, and ended up listening to people tell me how to keep my weight down. All this is happening in one of the richest countries in the world, a society devoted to consumption. Amazing as it may seem, we have normalized anorexia and bulimia, even turned them into an industry.

2   We've also trivialized them: made them into nothing more than an exaggerated conformity with basically acceptable standards of behavior. Everyone wants to be thin and pretty, after all. Some people take it a little too far; you have to get them back on the right track, but it's all a question of knowing just how far is proper.

3   The consumer society has gone so far we can even buy into hunger.

4   But that is not what it's about. You do not stuff yourself with food and force yourself to vomit just because of fashion magazines. You do not reduce yourself to the condition of a skeleton in order to be attractive. This is not just a problem of proportion. This is the nightmare of consumerism acted out in women's bodies.

5   This is what we are saying as we starve: it is not all right. It is not all right. It is not all right.

6   There've always been strange or disordered patterns of eating, associated mainly with religious extremism or psychological problems (which some, not myself, would say were the same thing). But the complex of ideas, fears, angers and actions that make up contemporary anorexia and bulimia seems to be of fairly recent origin. Anorexia did not exist as a recognized pattern until the 1960s, and bulimia not until later than that—and at first they were deeply shocking. The idea that privileged young women (the first group to be affected) were voluntarily starving themselves, sometimes to death, or regularly sticking their fingers down their throats to make themselves throw up, shook the culture badly. It was a fad, in a sense, the illness of the month, but it was also a scandal, and a source of something like horror.

7   Before this, though, before anorexia had a widely recognized name, one of the first women to succumb to it had made her own scandalous stand, and left a body of writing that still has a lot to say about the real meaning of voluntary hunger.

8   Simone Weil was a brilliant, disturbed, wildly wrong-headed and astonishingly perceptive young French woman who died from the complications of self-starvation in America during World War II, at the age of 34. She never, of course, wrote directly about her refusal to eat—typically for any anorexic, she insisted she ate perfectly adequate amounts. But throughout her philosophical and theological writing (almost all of it fragments and essays collected after her death), she examines and uses the symbolism of hunger, eating and food.

9   Food occupied, in fact, a rather important and valued position in her philosophy—she once referred to food as "the irrefutable proof of the reality of the universe," and at another time said that the foods served at Easter and Christmas, the turkey and *marron*

glacés, were "the true meaning of the feast"; although she could also take the more conventional puritan position that desire for food is a "base motive." She spoke often of eating God (acceptable enough in a Christian context) and of being eaten by God (considerably less so). The great tragedy of our lives, she said, is that we cannot really eat God; and also "it may be that vice, depravity and crime are almost always . . . attempts to eat beauty."

But it is her use of the symbolism of hunger that explains her 10 death. "We have to go down into ourselves to the abode of the desire which is not imaginary. Hunger: we imagine kinds of food, but the hunger itself is real: we have to fasten onto the hunger."

Hunger, then, was a search for reality, for the irreducible need 11 that lies beyond all imaginary satisfactions. Weil was deeply perturbed by the "materialism" of her culture; though she probably could not have begun to imagine the number of imaginary and illusory "satisfactions" now available. Simply, she wanted truth. She wanted to reduce herself to the point where she would *know* what needs, and what foods, were real and true.

Similarly, though deeply drawn to the Catholic faith, she re- 12 fused to be baptized and to take Communion (to, in fact, eat God). "I cannot help wondering whether in these days when so large a proportion of humanity is sunk in materialism, God does not want there to be some men and women who have given themselves to him and to Christ and who yet remain outside the Church." For the sake of honesty, of truth, she maintained her hunger.

Weil, a mystic and a political activist simultaneously until the 13 end of her short life—she was one of the first French intellectuals to join the Communist party and one of the first to leave, fought in the Spanish Civil War and worked in auto factories—could not bear to have life be less than a total spiritual and political statement. And her statement of protest, of dissatisfaction, her statement of hunger, finally destroyed her.

The term anorexia nervosa was coined in the 19th century, but 14 it was not until sometime in the 1960s that significant—and constantly increasing—numbers of well-off young women began dying of starvation, and not until the early 1970s that it became public knowledge.

It is the nature of our times that the explanations proffered were 15 psychological and individualistic; yet, even so, it was understood as being, on some level, an act of protest. And of course symbolically, it could hardly be other—it was, simply, a hunger strike. The most common interpretation, at that point, was that it was a sort of adolescent rebellion against parental control, an attempt, particularly, to escape from an overcontrolling mother. It was a fairly acceptable paradigm for the period, although many mothers were justifiably disturbed; sometimes deeply and unnecessarily hurt. The theory still has some currency, and is not entirely devoid of truth.

16   But can it be an accident that this happened almost precisely to coincide with the growth of the consumer society, a world based on a level of material consumption that, by the end of the 1960s, had become very nearly uncontrollable? Or with the strange, underground guilt that has made "conspicuous consumption" a matter of consuming vast amounts and *hiding it*, of million-dollar minimalism? With the development of what is possibly the most emotionally depleted society in history, where the only "satisfactions" seem to be the imaginary ones, the material buy-offs?

17   To be skeletally, horribly thin makes one strong statement. It says, I am hungry. What I have been given is not sufficient, not real, not true, not acceptable. I am starving. To reject food, whether by refusing it or by vomiting it back, says simply, I will not consume. I will not participate. This is not real.

18   Hunger is the central nightmare image of our society. Of all the icons of horror the last few generations have offered us, we have chosen, above all, pictures of hunger—the emaciated prisoners of Auschwitz and Belsen, Ethiopian children with bloated bellies and stick-figure limbs. We carry in our heads these nightmares of the extreme edge of hunger.

19   And while we may not admit to guilt about our level of consumption in general, we admit freely to guilt about eating, easily equate food with "sin." We cannot accept hunger of our own, cannot afford to consider it.

20   It is, traditionally, women who carry our nightmares. It was women who became possessed by the Devil, women who suffered from "hysterical disorders," women who, in all popular culture, are the targets of the "monster." One of the roles women are cast in is that of those who act out the subconscious fears of their society. And it is women above all, in this time, who carry our hunger.

21   It is the starving women who embody the extremity of hunger that terrifies and fascinates us, and who insist that they are not hungry. It is the women sticking their fingers down their throats who act out the equation of food and sin, who deny hunger and yet embody endless, unfulfilled appetite. It is these women who live through every implication of our consumption and our hunger, our guilt and ambiguity and our awful need for something real to fill us.

22   We have too much; and it is poison.

23   It was first—in fact exclusively—feminist writers who began to explore the symbolic language of anorexia and bulimia: Sheila

MacLeod (*The Art of Starvation*), Susie Orbach (*Hunger Strike*), and others. However, as their work began to appear, a new presentation of eating disorders was entering the general consciousness, one that would no longer permit them to be understood as protest at *any* level.

For, as eating disorders became increasingly widespread, they also became increasingly trivialized, incorporated into a framework already "understood" all too well. Feminist writers had, early on, noted that anorexia had to be linked with the increasing thinness of models and other glamor icons, as part of a larger cultural trend. This is true enough as a starting point, for the symbolic struggle being waged in women's bodies happens on many levels, and is not limited to pathology cases. Unfortunately, this single starting point was seized by "women's magazines" and popularizing accounts in general. Anorexia was now understandable, almost safe really, it was just fashion gone out of control. Why, these women were *accepting* the culture, they just needed a sense of proportion. What a relief. 24

Now it could be condoned. Now it could, in fact, become the basis for an industry; could be incorporated neatly into consumer society. According to Jane Fonda the solution to bulimia is to remain equally unhealthily thin by buying the 20-minute workout and becoming an obsessive fitness follower (at least for those who can afford it). The diet clinic industry, the Nutrisystem package, the aerobics boom. An advertising industry, that plays equally off desire and guilt, for they now reinforce each other. Thousands upon thousands of starving, tormented women, not "sick" enough to be taken seriously, not really troubled at all. 25

One does not reduce oneself to the condition of a skeleton in order to be fashionable. One does not binge and vomit daily as an acceptable means of weight control. One does not even approach or imagine or dream of these things if one is not in some sort of trouble. If it were as simple as fashion, surely we would not be so ashamed to speak of these things, we would not feel that either way, whether we eat or do not eat, we are doing something wrong. 26

I was anorexic for eight years. I nearly died. It was certainly no help to me to be told I was taking fashion too far—I knew perfectly well that had nothing to do with it. It did not help much to be told I was trying to escape from my mother, since I lived away from home and was in only occasional contact with my family; it did not help much to be approached on an individualistic, psychological level. In fact, the first person I was able to go to for help was a charismatic Catholic, who at least understood that I was speaking in symbols of spiritual hunger. 27

28   I knew that I had something to say, that things were not all right, that I had to make that concretely, physically obvious. I did not hate or look down on my body—I spoke through it and with it.

29   Women are taught to take guilt, concern, problems, onto themselves personally; and especially onto their bodies. But we are trying to talk about something that is only partly personal. Until we find new ways of saying it and find the courage to talk to the world about the world, we will speak destruction to ourselves.

30   We must come to know what we are saying—and say it.

An Athlete's Lament

LAURA ROBINSON

Laura Robinson was a national-level cyclist, Nordic skier, and Canadian rowing champion. She is the author of *She Shoots, She Scores: Canadian Perspective on Women in Sports* (1997) and *Crossing the Line: Sexual Assault in Canada's National Sport* (1998). As a freelance journalist, she has contributed articles to *The Globe and Mail, The Toronto Star, Canadian Living, Saturday Night*, and *Ms. Magazine*. Robinson also writes and produces for CBC Radio and Television, the Women's Television Network, and the National Film Board.

PART ONE: FASTEST, HIGHEST, GROSSEST

1   When I was in grade eight and living in a Toronto suburb, some of the boys in my class rode their bicycles over to my house for a visit. It was an April evening in 1972, the air warm and calm, but alive with the promise of summer. I looked out the front door and saw a line of ten-speeds propped against our house. Glistening under the sun room lights, they seemed to be speed itself.

2   That was it. I was smitten. My body and mind were acting together. Probably my soul was involved too. I *had* to have a ten-speed. My coaster bike had never intimated anything about speed. I went to find the person who made all the big decisions in my life.

3   She wasn't buying me any new bike, my mother told me, when my sister's old one was perfectly capable of getting me to school. If I wanted a new one that bad, I'd have to start saving my baby-sitting money, and quit spending so much on clothes.

Fair enough. By the end of June, I had my ten-speed. I was   4
really lucky, too, because my brother, David, who was just eighteen
months younger than I, also yearned for a new bike. He'd been
saving his paper route money.

That summer, we passed from being kids to another magical   5
age—no longer children and not yet adults—and we took the first
real step away from home. Even my mother changed her tune.
Initially, she wanted to know why on earth we needed ten-speeds
when one speed had been just fine up to now. But once we had
them, she suggested we join the Mississauga Cycling Club. My
mother, the chain smoker, who would drive three blocks for
another carton of cigarettes. My mother, the queen of "do as I say,
not as I do," was recruiting us into a club where a cigarette would
never touch our teen-age lips. Though the irony was lost on us, we
signed up, and on a Tuesday evening in June, headed out to our
first cycling competition.

A couple of kilometres from our front door at the first stoplight,   6
two other cyclists, older guys, lined up with us while we waited for
the light to change. My brother sized the bikes up. They were way
better than ours, and one guy had an Italian accent, a sure give-
away that he was a real cyclist.

I learned quickly, after the first encounter, to look at the lines of   7
the bike frame and the way the derailleurs and brakes sit on it. The
angles, the wheel base, the gear ratios on the rear hub and, of
course, the name of the bike signaled in an instant that this was the
genuine article. But if the rider on it didn't have the legs—smooth,
tanned, ropey, layered muscles, twitching until the light changed, it
didn't matter how good the bike was: the person on it was not a
real cyclist.

My brother had bought his bike out of a Consumer's Distribut-   8
ing catalogue. Mine came from the hardware store. It cost me
eighty-eight dollars. For us, that was very expensive, but on the
grand scale of bicycles as finely crafted works of art, our bikes
didn't even register. They were anchors. Mine had a gear ratio on
the rear hub the size of a pie plate—unacceptable in this aerody-
namic world. My brother had toe clips, but I didn't. Just regular
pedals with reflectors on them. And, of course, my bicycle was
much too big for me; in 1972 you couldn't buy a ten-speed from a
hardware store, or anywhere else, that wasn't made for a man at
least six feet tall.

But all this was immaterial to us at the time. My brother and I   9
were riding to our first bike race with two grown-up cyclists. When
the light changed and we took off, I felt as if I had just opened a big
door to a new life.

10   On that summer evening I started to learn that sport wasn't what was on television or what I read about in newspapers. All that hype about yards gained and lost, all those guys screaming into microphones about great saves and incredible catches and phenomenal touchdowns—that wasn't sport. It was some sort of malignant male mutation. After all, men were virtually the only athletes who ever appeared on TV, and they didn't have any real connection to me—or to anyone else. They disappeared if you turned the TV off or threw out the paper. They didn't care about their fans; they cared about getting paid. How can you relate to nebulous images that don't know, or care, if you exist in the first place?

11   I was to learn that sport is about staying power. About a place where your body meets your soul and spirit. Sport is lonely and friendly all at once. Even when you're riding elbow to elbow in a pack, you can still feel alone. There are thousands of physical journeys to be made while cycling, but it's the human journey taking place in the subconscious that defines the experience.

12   Sport is about living from the inside out. It isn't about sitting in the seats of a stadium separated from the action—it *is* the action. So if you want to be a good athlete, you have to climb inside yourself and see what you're made of. Do you have what it takes? Are you going to find something very deep that will keep you going when your legs, your lungs, and your heart urge you to stop?

13   In the twenty-five years I've been riding, my bicycles have transported me to a world where anything seemed possible if I was willing to sweat enough. I'd find myself looking at a hill, thinking I can't possibly make it up, but I would, and I'd sail down the other side, leaning into corners and flying around curves. For a kid with endless energy, the first couple of years were magical. But the faster I got and the higher I rose in competitive sport, the more I realized the terrible price women had to pay to make it to the top level. For us, it was a hostile place where doing our best didn't necessarily count. Some days the pain and pressure of being female at a competition where only men mattered were overwhelming. Though I stuck it out for nearly twenty years, it wasn't until I quit that I regained the spiritual joys of those early years. But all of this—both lovely and terrible—stretched far ahead as I rode to my first time trial on that lovely summer evening.

14   A time trial is a race against the clock. Cyclists go off one at a time, usually a minute apart. The rider ahead of you is called your minuteman, and if you can see her, you can use her as a rabbit you try to catch. But really, you race against yourself, and once everyone's time has been tabulated, you find out who was the fastest.

This time trial was ten miles long. It was a perfect square, 15
ending where it began, on the farm roads west of Mississauga. At
the start line the riders were held up on their bikes by someone
who grasped the back of the saddle while they got comfortable in
their toe clips. Since I didn't have toe clips, I just waited, perched
on my bike, while a man straddled the back wheel, and held onto
my saddle. "Don't be nervous," he said in a tony British accent.
"Keep your head down, and go like stink."

The timer counted down from ten and I was off. I don't 16
remember much. I know I got chased by a dog and outsprinted him.
The course didn't feel like ten miles; before I knew it, the finish line
was coming up. I pedaled as hard as I could, and it was over.

There were a few boys from Scouts there[;] a father and son 17
who had French accents, real cycling shorts, and really good
bikes[;] the two men my brother and I rode over with, whose names
were Angelo and Duanne[;] and probably some other boys and
men I can't remember. Through all these years in sport, there were
always clusters of boys and men. They became generic guys to me.

When the timer had recorded our speeds, Angelo had the 18
fastest time for men, and much to the surprise of everyone, one of
the new boys had the fastest time for the teenagers. The timer
walked over to me and told me I had beaten all the other boys. Part
of me said, "Wow, I'm faster than those guys," but in my gut I felt
sick. Once again, I had been mistaken for a boy.

Today, I can hardly remember what the girly-girl culture I'd left 19
behind was like, except that girls weren't supposed to know much
or do much besides agree with the boys. I'm forever grateful that I
didn't have to grow up like most girls—on the sidelines.

At the time, I looked at the girls in my school who were in high 20
demand. They had beautiful clothes, wore make-up, and laughed
when boys said something that was supposed to be funny.

I wondered how a bike helmet or ski toque could fit over their 21
hairdos. In gym class they had to run around the track in baggy
blue one-piece rompers just like the rest of us. But their faces turned
into splotchy red and white maps before they'd even completed
one lap; mascara mixed with sweat, formed rivers and tributaries
that ran from their eyes. Nothing moved in their legs. It was as if
someone had stolen their strength and their muscles. They dropped
out of phys ed as soon as it was no longer compulsory, and
watched their boyfriends on the football team for the rest of their
high-school years. Looking back, I wonder if they were ever able to
make a friend of their own body.

If this was the alternative to feeling at home in your sweat, I 22
wanted no part of it. Yet I never once imagined myself anything but

female. How could riding a bike possibly change your sex? Nonetheless, if I was going to continue to ride, I'd have to join the world
of boys and men. . . .

23   Once I started racing for real—going beyond local time trials,
so I could see just how far and fast I could go—things changed.
Many of the men involved in cycling thought the presence of
women contaminated their sacred sport. . . .

24   The only way women seemed to be accepted was if we were
sleeping with the decision makers. I watched other young women
pair off with much older men—important men who chose the team
or coached it. I don't think they all did it to make the team. Some
were so good, they couldn't have helped but make it. No, it had
something to do with being a female without a man in a man's
world. Men could open a door for you or they could slam it in your
face. They knew I didn't like what they were doing to the other
girls. I didn't sit beside them on the long trips to the races or during
meals. I didn't want to get within an arm's length of those men.
They accused me of not being a team player.

25   Just as boys didn't need to be told that sport was for them, girls
weren't told specifically to have sex with older men, but we certainly got the message. We needed a man to help us onto the medal
podium. We weren't capable of doing it ourselves.

26   Questions were asked about the girls who didn't find a nice
older man to guide them. I was made to feel uncomfortable and
uneasy, but there was no language to explain why. Girls who went
out with boys our own age or girls our own age—there was no language for that either—started to look abnormal.

27   I feel so lucky to have escaped from sport without having been
broken by these men. The women they got to will bear the scars for
the rest of their lives. A trust was betrayed—the trust between
coach and athlete—at a time when girls were trying to become
women. Many survivors have eating disorders. Their coach-lover
wanted them to remain as girl-like as possible. As they matured
into women, their natural and beautiful shape was picked to pieces.
Their weight was announced at dinner to the whole team while
they tried vainly to eat. I know so many women athletes who did
everything from starving to changing into frilly clothes right after
the race, in an attempt to satisfy their coach-lovers. But their emaciated bodies were a metaphor for what was happening to their
minds and spirits. The damage was often permanent.

28   These predators, the ones who called themselves coaches, controlled their girls as surely as pimps control street walkers. They
had the power to stave off womanhood in maturing bodies and
control the desire for sex. Their girls would never desire another

man as long as they could be kept emotionally hungry for the coach-lover. When the coach-lover used one athlete up—when she either smartened up and left him or lost out to a new protégé—he soon had another human being to dominate.

But those private relationships were only one way men tried to break us. There was a public fight too. Sometimes race organizers refused to hold events for women at all. They'd tell us to leave the race site, that we were trespassing, even though the course was on city streets. When we fought for equal prize money, they mounted a smear campaign against us. In 1989, the women's Tour of Niagara was three stages long and offered $1,500 in prize money. When we arrived for the first eighty-kilometre race, there were no washrooms, and no water. We used the fields for washrooms and filled our water bottles from a farmer's hose. We paid for our food, travel and accommodation. Much as I like riding in the country, it's not conducive to crowds and fans. No one watched us race. The men's equivalent was the Tour du Canada—a week-long stage race that offered $50,000. The organizers paid for travel and meals; the races were held in both country and city. The last stage ended before the crowds at the Canadian National Exhibition in Toronto. 29

The men who ran the Ontario Cycling Association swore they wouldn't allow equal prize money. When I protested they told me I hadn't contributed anything to cycling. Why did I expect women to have equality? We hadn't earned it. In meetings, their faces turned red and the veins on their necks bulged. Once a man's wife had to restrain him from taking a swing at me. Even my own brother, the one I rode to my first bike race with, told me I was a step away from being burned at the stake as far as the other guys were concerned. The Toronto city councillor who supported us in our fight received two letters threatening rape and a death threat in the final days of the battle. I stopped riding home by myself after bike races. I stopped feeling safe. 30

Only lesbians would make such selfish demands, many male cyclists told me. And yet, if any men agreed with us, obviously we had slept with them. Whether our struggle was private or public, the physicality of women athletes was defined sexually. It was as if it didn't matter how fast we were—our speed didn't satisfy the men in charge. If anything, it frightened them. They wanted to capture our bodies. They wouldn't allow sport—the place we felt so much freedom—to free us. But what they didn't realize was how strong they made us. Each time they put up a barrier, we cleared it. With each delay in the equality they said we'd have to earn, we developed a patience as strong as steel. We should thank them for the inner resolve they inadvertently built in us during those horrible times. . . . 31

32   Ironically, I was also spending more time competing on the fierce circuit in the United States. Just as with everything else for Canadians, if you want to see if you've got what it takes, you have to go south. Once I passed that test, I realized just how far away I was from those quiet Mississauga roads I started out on. Once after a race in Nutley, New Jersey, I was trying to wash the dirt off my legs, but it wouldn't come off. The roads were layered with automobile emissions, so when we rode and whipped the grime up off the street, it caked on our sweaty legs. Later I stood on the sidewalk waiting for the men's race to start. All kinds of candy bar wrappers, popcorn bags and cigarette butts came floating down the gutter. What did all this crap have to do with the freedom I had originally found in cycling? When I started, I was gulping fresh air, pedaling under the shade of gracious old trees. I raced birds as they flew beside me. But all I could see around me now was a grimy American eastern seaboard town.

33   It took several more years, but I came to realize that competitive sport was not good for my health. After all the years, all the fights, the name calling and the tears, I decided I didn't have to race. It was probably on one of those lovely long rides that the thought hit me. Why not just ride? In the spring of 1991 I left bike racing behind. It would have been nice to race that season so I'd have a full twenty years behind me, but I had no interest in start lines any more. . . .

34   But when I quit, I started to feel again how exquisite riding a bike could be. I wasn't just free from the unhappy and unfriendly people in the sport; I was free from nervous sessions in the washroom before the race, free from weekends tied up with competition and travel, and finally free from the ride-till-you-die syndrome.

PART TWO: PATHFINDERS

35   Today, I have the best of all worlds. In the spring . . . I teach bike safety to kids. . . . Maybe some of them will have the kind of magical years I had when I was their age and started really cycling. In the winter, I teach kids how to cross-country ski. I like teaching in the far north—that way, I can ski early in the season and I get to meet kids I would never otherwise encounter. I work at a ski camp in LaRonge, Saskatchewan, with about fifteen other instructors. Once we're finished teaching for the day, we have our own little races that are by no means uncompetitive. They're just the right kind of challenge. . . .

36   In the north, time has a different rhythm from the time in the city. It takes longer. There are only a couple of generations between the people who lived with the land and the kids I'm teaching. The

Dene children come from a tradition of following the caribou that lasted until the fifties, when white people forced their great-grandparents to settle in hamlets. Many of the children—Cree and Dene—still have a strong connection to the way the earth lives and breathes. Everyone who knows anything about the north knows there are certain times of the year when everything closes and everyone goes hunting.

So for these kids, moving through the woods swiftly and grace-fully just might mean a little more than it would to, say, someone from Toronto who goes to a crowded ski trail that's impossible to get lost on. There's a journey through the woods for everyone, but people who live in urban areas may not be able to make it. They don't know how to listen to the trees, or the wind, or watch for changes in the snow. There is no heartbeat for them. They're lost. 37

Most white people don't think of themselves as part of nature—that the way their bodies run is like the pulse of each season. Nature is separate from their being. The ancestors of the Europeans who "settled" North America don't go to the woods. For most, the rhythm of nature is lost. They destroyed it. So great is their alienation, they don't even like living in their own bodies, let alone the wilderness. Yet there is a sense of identity in the woods, something that makes you feel in tune, especially if you come from a people whose existence, until quite recently, was intrinsically tied to the land. I think the kids in LaRonge can maintain that tie, so for me the sport of nordic skiing is not just a way of moving physically, but culturally and spiritually on a journey into the land and into your soul. 38

I once asked a school ski coach what he wanted the kids to take with them from being on his team. He replied, "I want them to feel what it's like to be larger than life. I want them to have worked all day long on the glide phase of the offset skate and then have some-thing magical happen as they start to glide." 39

That, too, is what I want for kids in sport. I want them to glide, and soar, and ski curves and corners they never imagined they could get around. I want them to test themselves—see how much faster, higher and farther they can go. 40

But do I want them to enter the winning-is-the-only-thing system I endured? These kids can't afford their own skis, let alone compete in a sport where a winter's worth of wax, traveling and racing equipment costs thousands. And that's only the beginning. Am I naive enough to believe lecherous coaches don't exist any-more? That native kids won't be discriminated against? That the white, competitive culture they'll have to perform in will do no harm to their spirit? 41

42   So do you give kids the opportunity to learn about what's in their hearts—whether it's skiing, dancing, music or painting—and not tell them about that other world where they can push their limits to the fullest? What if they have to trade their souls for that world? I still can't answer that question. It's a pity the traffic is going in the wrong direction. White people should be spending more time finding out how First Nations live a life in sport.

43   As a journalist, I have covered Aboriginal sport since 1990, and I've never been to an event that didn't include drumming, the recognition of elders, and a prayer for the athletes and their families. Willy Littlechild, who was the first Aboriginal person in Canada to obtain a physical education degree and for several years was the MP for Wetaskiwin, Alberta, says that for Cree people, dancing and running are very similar. "You celebrate thanksgiving to the Great Spirit, by dance or by running. They are a very spiritual part of our existence, and important in the development of our pride. The ceremonial run and the powwow dance are almost the same for us in giving thanks."

44   I got to experience that first-hand in the fall of 1992. I was covering a sacred run from Wasauksing to Neyaashiinigmiing—from the east side of Georgian Bay to "a place almost surrounded by water" on the west shore—for CBC Radio Sports. The organizers were short of runners, and invited me to join in. Seven runners— four adults and three kids—were to cover two hundred and sixty kilometres. Before we left, elders from Wasauksing folded up messages they wanted the runners to read when they reached Neyaashiinigmiing and placed them inside a staff. It wasn't much larger than a relay baton, but it contained a sacred bundle that we weren't to open and it was wrapped in the four colours of humanity: red, black, white and yellow. The elders did a sweetgrass smudging ceremony for the runners, and we were off.

45   The ceremonial or sacred run is a long distance event many people take part in. Much like a relay team, they pass the staff to one another, but instead of running a set distance, they go as far as they can, often surprising themselves with their endurance. Traditional runners spend years learning from elders and teachers about the responsibilities of being a First Nation person, of being an athlete and a carrier of culture and messages. Alcohol is forbidden, not just on the runs, but in life. So are drugs.

46   The roots of the run are buried so deeply in ritual and tradition that no amount of assimilation could destroy them. Spiritual runners would go from nation to nation, passing messages about powwows, councils and war, often covering hundreds of kilometres. Their footprints are in the earth forever and that's why they are still with us.

Meanwhile, I was running the best leg of the journey. I'd already 47 gone twelve kilometres before night settled in and my next turn rolled around at midnight. I received the staff and continued to run through the lakes district. The moon shone back from the water. At times I could see my shadow. It was like running through velvet.

A van and a small car followed the runners. About 1:00 a.m., I 48 handed the staff to another runner, folded myself up in the back of the car, and fell asleep. It was my turn again just before dawn, but when I tried to stretch out of the back seat, all I felt was pain. I should have known better. Twenty-two kilometres worth of lactic acid (the enemy of all athletes) had settled into my muscles. Every injury I had ever sustained came back for a visit.

Now the run wasn't so romantic. It was hard. We had a sunrise 49 sweetgrass ceremony at which we asked for help. Two runners from Christian Island joined us, only to misunderstand the rules and run eighteen kilometres without the staff. This distance couldn't be counted; we had to honour the runners of the past and that meant *with* the staff. Our youngest runner, Lester Taboboneung, was only eleven. It was his first run, and like the rest of the kids, he was worn out and limping.

"Who cares if they didn't carry the staff?" I told the chief runner. 50 "It's not as if they had cars and cellular telephones, but we're using them. Let's just get where we're supposed to go as fast as we can. I'm injured and the kids are injured; they just won't tell you."

"Our ancestors must have had injuries and they kept running. 51 We're supposed to understand what they felt like," he replied.

We retraced these eighteen kilometres, but our pace was decid- 52 edly slower. All I wanted was a shower and place big enough to stretch and sleep. I was hungry, sweaty, smelly, cramped, stiff and sore. We forced ourselves to keep going. Yet whenever we came to roadkill, everything stopped. An off-duty runner would get out of the car and gently pull the animal off the road. "Why do you do that?" I asked. "He is our brother," the chief runner replied, looking at me oddly as if I should have figured it out for myself. "We can't leave him there."

Eventually, I started to understand. Everything I'd done in 53 sport was about getting to the finish line the fastest way I could. Never mind roadkill, if I had heard a crash behind me in a bike race, I immediately turned on the speed to try to get a jump on those caught behind the crash. I wouldn't have stopped and helped anyone back up on her bike. It wasn't my fault she didn't know how to ride a straight line. If you don't finish first, I was taught, examine every detail of your preparation to figure out what you did wrong.

54   But this sacred run was about finishing as much as any race I'd ever been in. It was also as difficult as any race I'd ever been in. The difference—and, for me, much of the difficulty—was that time didn't matter. What we did between the start and the finish mattered.

55   With sixty kilometres to go, we were met by five runners with fresh legs. Someone had used that sacred cellular phone to call ahead for help. From this point, everything moved swiftly. With five kilometres to go, the kids, who could barely walk earlier in the day, piled out of the car and started running. Lester was handed the staff as we ran down a graceful hill that led into the park where the gathering at Neyaashiinigmiing waited. The drums were stronger and stronger as we neared the cedar encampment. One thousand people cheered. The runners read the elders' messages, which were about such contemporary concerns as land claims, staying clear of drugs and alcohol, and being proud to be First Nations.

56   Watching the kids made me feel as if I'd completed a circle. I'd started out like them—young and excited. Now I was feeling the way Duanne and Angelo must have felt when they took my brother and me cycling and skiing—really happy to see kids figure out they can go farther than they imagined.

57   You can have the World Series. I'll take the feeling you get when you watch an eleven-year-old run when he thinks he can't, then sprint into an encampment and deliver the staff he and many others have carried for the past twenty-seven hours. Then this shy little guy finds it in himself to speak to one thousand people, mainly adults, about land claims and other important matters. He speaks in Ojibway and English.

58   During our time together on the run, I wondered what might be going on in Lester's mind. At such a young age, he had been honoured by the elders and allowed to carry their messages. He ran through the day and night, as his people had millennia before, when it was so hard to keep pushing one foot ahead of the other and his body kept begging him to stop.

59   There is a very small fraction of time when a runner has neither foot on the ground. It's a time when he flies, when he runs free of gravity. And so, I wondered, did Lester hear the seemingly endless road that stretched ahead of him whisper as he ran? Did he hear it say there would be unbearable times when he would have to run on the painful and parched path that stretched into the future? But also that at other times it would whisper to him and say, Lester Taboboneung, you will have the strength and the spirit to become the wind.

The Way of All Flesh: The Worm Is at Work in Us All

JUDY STOFFMAN

Judy Stoffman is the literary reporter for *The Toronto Star*. Born in Hungary, she came to Vancouver as a child refugee in 1957. She has degrees in English from the University of British Columbia and Sussex University in England. She has worked for the CBC, *Canadian Living*, *The Globe and Mail*, and the now-defunct *Weekend* magazine, where "The Way of All Flesh" originally appeared.

When a man of 25 is told that aging is inexorable, inevitable, universal, he will nod somewhat impatiently at being told something so obvious. In fact, he has little idea of the meaning of the words. It has nothing to do with him. Why should it? He has had no tangible evidence yet that his body, as the poet Rilke said, enfolds old age and death as the fruit enfolds a stone. [1]

The earliest deposits of fat in the aorta, the trunk artery carrying blood away from the heart, occur in the eighth year of life, but who can peer into his own aorta at this first sign of approaching debility? The young man has seen old people but he secretly believes himself to be the exception on whom the curse will never fall. "Never will the skin of my neck hang loose. My grip will never weaken. I will stand tall and walk with long strides as long as I live." The young girl scarcely pays attention to her clothes; she scorns makeup. Her confidence in her body is boundless; smooth skin and a flat stomach will compensate, she knows, for any lapses in fashion or grooming. She stays up all night, as careless of her energy as of her looks, believing both will last forever. [2]

In our early 20s, the lung capacity, the rapidity of motor responses and physical endurance are at their peak. This is the athlete's finest hour. Cindy Nicholas of Toronto was 19 when she first swam the English Channel in both directions. The tennis star Bjorn Borg was 23 when he triumphed . . . at Wimbledon for the fourth time. [3]

It is not only *athletic* prowess that is at its height between 20 and 30. James Boswell, writing in his journal in 1763 after he had finally won the favors of the actress Louisa, has left us this happy description of the sexual prowess of a 23-year-old: "I was in full flow of health and my bounding blood beat quick in high alarms. Five times was I fairly lost in a supreme rapture. Louisa was madly fond of me; she declared I was a prodigy, and asked me if this was [4] extraordinary in human nature. I said twice as much might be, but this was not, although in my own mind I was somewhat proud of my performance."

5   In our early 30s we are dumbfounded to discover the first grey hair at the temples. We pull out the strange filament and look at it closely, trying to grasp its meaning. It means simply that the pigment has disappeared from the hair shaft, never to return. It means also—but this thought we push away—that in 20 years or so we'll relinquish our identity as a blonde or a redhead. By 57, one out of four people is completely grey. Of all the changes wrought by time this is the most harmless, except to our vanity.

6   In this decade one also begins to notice the loss of upper register hearing, that is, the responsiveness to high frequency tones, but not all the changes are for the worse, not yet. Women don't reach their sexual prime until about 38, because their sexual response is learned rather than innate. The hand grip of both sexes increases in strength until 35, and intellectual powers are never stronger than at that age. There is a sense in the 30s of hitting your stride, of coming into your own. When Sigmund Freud was 38 an older colleague, Josef Breuer, wrote: "Freud's intellect is soaring at its highest. I gaze after him as a hen at a hawk."

7   Gail Sheehy in her book *Passages* calls the interval between 35 and 45 the Deadline Decade. It is the time we begin to sense danger. The body continually flashes us signals that time is running out. We must perform our quaint deeds, keep our promises, get on with our allotted tasks.

8   Signal: The woman attempts to become pregnant at 40 and finds she cannot. Though she menstruates each month, menstruation being merely the shedding of the inner lining of the womb, she may not be ovulating regularly.

9   Signal: Both men and women discover that, although they have not changed their eating habits over the years, they are much heavier than formerly. The man is paunchy around the waist; the woman no longer has those slim thighs and slender arms. A 120-pound woman needs 2,000 calories daily to maintain her weight when she is 25, 1,700 to maintain the same weight at 45, and only 1,500 calories at 65. A 170-pound man needs 3,100 calories daily at 25, 300 fewer a day at 45 and 450 calories fewer still at 65. This decreasing calorie need signals that the body consumes its fuel ever more slowly; the cellular fires are damped and our sense of energy diminishes.

10   In his mid-40s the man notices he can no longer run up the stairs three at a time. He is more easily winded and his joints are

not as flexible as they once were. The strength of his hands has declined somewhat. The man feels humiliated: "I will not let this happen to me. I will turn back the tide and master my body." He starts going to the gym, playing squash, lifting weights. He takes up jogging. Though he may find it neither easy nor pleasant, terror drives him past pain. A regular exercise program can retard some of the symptoms of aging by improving the circulation and increasing the lung capacity, thereby raising our stamina and energy level, but no amount of exercise will make a 48-year-old 26 again. Take John Keeley of Mystic, Connecticut. In 1957, when he was 26, he won the Boston marathon with a time of 2:20. [In 1979,] fit and 48, [he was] as fiercely competitive as ever, yet it took him almost 30 minutes longer to run the same marathon.

In the middle of the fourth decade, the man whose eyesight has   11
always been good will pick up a book and notice that he is holding it farther from his face than usual. The condition is presbyopia, a loss of the flexibility of the lens which makes adjustment from distant to near vision increasingly difficult. It's harder now to zoom in for a closeup. It also takes longer for the eyes to recover from glare; between 16 and 90, recovery time from exposure to glare is doubled every 13 years.

In our 50s, we notice that food is less and less tasty; our taste   12
buds are starting to lose their acuity. The aged Queen Victoria was wont to complain that strawberries were not as sweet as when she was a girl.

Little is known about the causes of aging. We do not know if we are   13
born with a biochemical messenger programmed to keep the cells and tissues alive, a messenger that eventually gets lost, or if there is a "death hormone," absent from birth but later secreted by the thymus or by the mysterious pineal gland, or if, perhaps, aging results from a fatal flaw in the body's immunity system. The belief that the body is a machine whose parts wear out is erroneous, for the machine does not have the body's capacity for self-repair.

"A man is as old as his arteries," observed Sir William Osler.   14
From the 50s on, there's a progressive hardening and narrowing of the arteries due to the gradual lifelong accumulation of calcium and fats along the arterial walls. Arteriosclerosis eventually affects the majority of the population in the affluent countries of the West. Lucky the man or woman who, through a combination of good genes and good nutrition, can escape it, for it is the most evil change of all. As the flow of blood carrying oxygen and nutrients to the muscles, the brain, the kidneys and other organs diminishes,

these organs begin to starve. Although all aging organs lose weight, there is less shrinkage of organs such as the liver and kidneys, the cells of which regenerate, than there is shrinkage of the brain and the muscles, the cells of which, once lost, are lost forever.

15   For the woman it is now an ordeal to be asked her age. There is a fine tracery of lines around her eyes, a furrow in her brow even when she smiles. The bloom is off her cheeks. Around the age of 50 she will buy her last box of sanitary pads. The body's production of estrogen and progesterone which govern menstruation (and also help to protect her from heart attack and the effects of stress) will have ceased almost completely. She may suffer palpitations, suddenly break into a sweat; her moods may shift abruptly. She looks in the mirror and asks, "Am I still a woman?" Eventually she becomes reconciled to her new self and even acknowledges its advantages: no more fears about pregnancy. "In any case," she laughs, "I still have not bad legs."

16   The man, too, will undergo a change. One night in his early 50s he has some trouble achieving a complete erection, and his powers of recovery are not what they once were. Whereas at 20 he was ready to make love again less than half an hour after doing so, it may now take two hours or more; he was not previously aware that his level of testosterone, the male hormone, has been gradually declining since the age of 20. He may develop headaches, be unable to sleep, become anxious about his performance, anticipate failure and so bring on what is called secondary impotence—impotence of psychological rather than physical origin. According to Masters and Johnson, 25 percent of all men are impotent by 65 and 50 percent by 75, yet this cannot be called an inevitable feature of aging. A loving, undemanding partner and a sense of confidence can do wonders. "The susceptibility of the human male to the power of suggestion with regard to his sexual prowess," observe Masters and Johnson, "is almost unbelievable."

17   After the menopause, the woman ages more rapidly. Her bones start to lose calcium, becoming brittle and porous. The walls of the vagina become thinner and drier; sexual intercourse now may be painful unless her partner is slow and gentle. The sweat glands begin to atrophy and the sebaceous glands that lubricate the skin decline; the complexion becomes thinner and drier and wrinkles appear around the mouth. The skin, which in youth varies from about one-fiftieth of an inch on the eyelids to about a third of an inch on the palms and the soles of the feet, loses 50 percent of its thickness between the ages of 20 and 80. The woman no longer buys sleeveless dresses and avoids shorts. The girl who once dis-

dained cosmetics is now a woman whose dressing table is covered with lotions, night creams and makeup.

Perhaps no one has written about the sensation of nearing 60   18 with more brutal honesty than the French novelist Simone de Beauvoir: "While I was able to look at my face without displeasure, I gave it no thought. I loathe my appearance now: the eyebrows slipping down toward the eyes, the bags underneath, the excessive fullness of the cheeks and the air of sadness around the mouth that wrinkles always bring. . . . Death is no longer a brutal event in the far distance; it haunts my sleep."

In his early 60s the man's calves are shrunken, his muscles   19 stringy looking. The legs of the woman, too, are no longer shapely. Both start to lose their sense of smell and both lose most of the hair in the pubic area and the underarms. Hair, however, may make its appearance in new places, such as the woman's chin. Liver spots appear on the hands, the arms, the face; they are made of coagulated melanin, the coloring matter of the skin. The acid secretions of the stomach decrease, making digestion slow and more difficult.

Halfway through the 60s comes compulsory retirement for   20 most men and working women, forcing upon the superannuated worker the realization that society now views him as useless and unproductive. The man who formerly gave orders to a staff of 20 now finds himself underfoot as his wife attempts to clean the house or get the shopping done. The woman fares a little better since there is a continuity in her pattern of performing a myriad of essential household tasks. Now they must both set new goals or see themselves wither mentally. The unsinkable American journalist I. F. Stone, when he retired in 1971 from editing I. F. Stone's Weekly, began to teach himself Greek and is now reading Plato in the original. When Somerset Maugham read that the Roman senator Cato the Elder learned Greek when he was 80, he remarked: "Old age is ready to undertake tasks that youth shirked because they would take too long."

However active we are, the fact of old age can no longer be   21 evaded from about 65 onward. Not everyone is as strong minded about this as de Beauvoir. When she made public in her memoirs her horror at her own deterioration, her readers were scandalized. She received hundreds of letters telling her that there is no such thing as old age, that some are just younger than others. Repeatedly she heard the hollow reassurance, "You're as young as you feel." But she considers this a lie. Our subjective reality, our inner sense of self, is not the only reality. There is also an objective reality, how we are seen by society. We receive our revelation of old age from others.

The woman whose figure is still trim may sense that a man is following her in the street; drawing abreast, the man catches sight of her face—and hurries on. The man of 68 may be told by a younger woman to whom he is attracted: "You remind me of my father."

22   Madame de Sévigné, the 17th-century French writer, struggled to rid herself of the illusion of perpetual youth. At 63 she wrote: "I have been dragged to this inevitable point where old age must be undergone: I see it there before me; I have reached it; and I should at least like so to arrange matters that I do not move on, that I do not travel further along this path of the infirmities, pains, losses of memory and the disfigurement. But I hear a voice saying: 'You must go along, whatever you may say; or indeed if you will not then you must die, which is an extremity from which nature recoils.'"

23   Now the man and the woman have their 70th birthday party. It is a sad affair because so many of their friends are missing, felled by strokes, heart attacks or cancers. Now the hands of the clock begin to race. The skeleton continues to degenerate from loss of calcium. The spine becomes compressed and there is a slight stoop nothing can prevent. Inches are lost from one's height. The joints may become thickened and creaking; in the morning the woman can't seem to get moving until she's had a hot bath. She has osteoarthritis. This, like the other age-related diseases, arteriosclerosis and diabetes, can and should be treated, but it can never be cured. The nails, particularly the toenails, become thick and lifeless because the circulation in the lower limbs is now poor. The man has difficulty learning new things because of the progressive loss of neurons from the brain. The woman goes to the store and forgets what she has come to buy. The two old people are often constipated because the involuntary muscles are weaker now. To make it worse, their children are always saying, "Sit down, rest, take it easy." Their digestive tract would be toned up if they went for a long walk or even a swim, although they feel a little foolish in bathing suits.

24   In his late 70s, the man develops glaucoma, pressure in the eyeball caused by the failure of aqueous humour to drain away; this can now be treated with a steroid related to cortisone. The lenses in the eyes of the woman may thicken and become fibrous, blurring her vision. She has cataracts, but artificial lenses can now be implanted using cryosurgery. There is no reason to lose one's sight just as there's no reason to lose one's teeth; regular, lifelong dental care can prevent tooth loss. What can't be prevented is the yellowing of teeth, brought about by the shrinking of the living chamber within the tooth which supplies the outer enamel with moisture.

25   Between 75 and 85 the body loses most of its subcutaneous fat. On her 80th birthday the woman's granddaughter embraces her

and marvels: "How thin and frail and shrunken she is! Could this narrow, bony chest be the same warm, firm bosom to which she clasped me as a child?" Her children urge her to eat but she has no enjoyment of food now. Her mouth secretes little saliva, so she has difficulty tasting and swallowing. The loss of fat and shrinking muscles in the 80s diminish the body's capacity for homeostasis, that is, righting any physiological imbalance. The old man, if he is cold, can barely shiver (shivering serves to restore body heat). If he lives long enough, the man will have an enlarged prostate which causes the urinary stream to slow to a trickle. The man and the woman probably both wear hearing aids now; without a hearing aid, they hear vowels clearly but not consonants; if someone says "fat," they think they've heard the word "that."

At 80, the speed of nerve impulses is 10 percent less than it was   26
at 25, the kidney filtration rate is down by 30 percent, the pumping efficiency of the heart is only 60 percent of what it was, and the maximum breathing capacity, 40 percent.

The old couple is fortunate in still being able to express physi-   27
cally the love they've built up over a lifetime. The old man may be capable of an erection once or twice a week (Charlie Chaplin fathered the last of his children when he was 81), but he rarely has the urge to climax. When he does, he sometimes has the sensation of seepage rather than a triumphant explosion. Old people who say they are relieved that they are now free of the torments of sexual desire are usually the ones who found sex a troublesome function all their lives; those who found joy and renewal in the act will cling to their libido. Many older writers and artists have expressed the conviction that continued sexuality is linked to continued cre-ativity: "There was a time when I was cruelly tormented, indeed obsessed by desire," wrote the novelist André Gide at the age of 73, "and I prayed, 'Oh let the moment come when my subjugated flesh will allow me to give myself entirely to. . . .' But to what? To art? To pure thought? To God? How ignorant I was! How mad! It was the same as believing that the flame would burn brighter in a lamp with no oil left. Even today it is my carnal self that feeds the flame, and now I pray that I may retain carnal desire until I die."

Aging, says an American gerontologist, "is not a simple slope   28
which everyone slides down at the same speed; it is a flight of irregular stairs down which some journey more quickly than others." Now we arrive at the bottom of the stairs. The old man and the old woman whose progress we have been tracing will die either of a cancer (usually of the lungs, bowel or intestines) or of a stroke, a heart attack or in consequence of a fall. The man slips in the

bathroom and breaks his thigh bone. But worse than the fracture is the enforced bed rest in the hospital which will probably bring on bed sores, infections, further weakening of the muscles and finally, what Osler called "an old man's best friend": pneumonia. At 25 we have so much vitality that if a little is sapped by illness, there is still plenty left over. At 85 a little is all we have.

29   And then the light goes out.
        The sheet is pulled over the face.

30   In the last book of Marcel Proust's remarkable work *Remembrance of Things Past*, the narrator, returning after a long absence from Paris, attends a party of his friends throughout which he has the impression of being at a masked ball: "I did not understand why I could not immediately recognize the master of the house, and the guests, who seemed to have made themselves up, in a way that completely changed their appearance. The Prince had rigged himself up with a white beard and what looked like leaden soles which made his feet drag heavily. A name was mentioned to me and I was dumbfounded at the thought that it applied to the blonde waltzing girl I had once known and to the stout, white haired lady now walking just in front of me. We did not see our own appearance, but each like a facing mirror, saw the other's." The narrator is overcome by a simple but powerful truth: the old are not a different species. "It is out of young men who last long enough," wrote Proust, "that life makes its old men."

31   The wrinkled old man who lies with the sheet over his face was once the young man who vowed, "My grip will never weaken. I will walk with long strides and stand tall as long as I live." The young man who believed himself to be the exception.

The Case for Curling Up with a Book

CAROL SHIELDS

Novelist, poet, and playwright Carol Shields was born in Oak Park, Illinois, in 1935. She is the winner of a Pulitzer Prize, the Governor General's Award, the Orange Prize, the Charles Taylor Prize, and the National Book Critics Circle Award. Her most recent works include a biography of Jane Austen and the novel *Unless*. Shields lives in Victoria, British Columbia.

S ome years ago a Canadian politician, one of our more admirable   1
figures, announced that he was cutting back on his public life
because it interfered with his reading. *His reading*—notice the
possessive pronoun, like saying his arm or his leg—and notice too,
the assumption that human beings carry, like a kind of cerebral brief
case, this built-in commitment to time and energy[:] *their reading*.

I'm told that people no longer know how to curl up with a   2
book. The body has forgotten how to curl. Either we snack on
paperbacks while waiting for the bus or we hunch over our books
with a yellow underliner in hand. Or, more and more, we sit before
a screen and "interact."

Curling up with a book can be accomplished in a variety of   3
ways: in bed for instance, with a towel on a sunlit beach, or from an
armchair parked next to a good reading lamp. What it absolutely
requires is a block of uninterrupted time, solitary time and our
society sometimes looks with pity on the solitary, that woman alone
at the movies, that poor man sitting by himself at his restaurant
table. Our hearts go out to them, but reading, by definition, can
only be done alone. I would like to make the case today for solitary
time, for a life with space enough to curl up with a book.

Reading, at least since human beings learned to read silently   4
(and what a cognitive shift that was!) requires an extraordinary
effort at paying attention, at remaining alert. The object of our
attention matters less, in a sense, than the purity of our awareness.
As the American writer Sven Birkerts says, it is better, better in
terms of touching the self within us, that we move from a state of
half-distraction to one of full attention. When we read with attention, an inner circuit of the brain is satisfyingly completed. We feel
our perceptions sharpen and acquire edge. Reading, as many of
you have discovered, is one of the very few things you can do only
by shining your full awareness on the task. We can make love,
cook, listen to music, shop for groceries, add up columns of figures
all with our brain, our self that is, divided and distracted. But print
on the page demands all of us. It is so complex, its cognitive cir-
cuitry so demanding; the black strokes on the white page must be
apprehended and translated into ideas, and ideas fitted into patterns, the patterns then shifted and analyzed. The eye travels backward for a moment; this in itself is a technical marvel, rereading a
sentence or a paragraph, extracting the sense, the intention, the
essence of what is offered.

And ironically, this singleness of focus delivers a doubleness of   5
perception. You are invited into a moment sheathed in nothing but
itself. Reading a novel, *curled up* with a novel, you are simultaneously

in your arm chair and in, for instance, the garden of Virginia Woolf in the year 1927, or a shabby Manitoba farmhouse conjured by Margaret Laurence, . . . participating fully in another world while remaining conscious of the core of your self, that self that may be hardwired into our bodies or else developed slowly, created over the long distance of our lives.

6   We are connected through our work, through our familial chain and, by way of the Internet, to virtually everyone in the world. So what of the private self which comes tantalizingly alive under the circle of the reading lamp, that self that we only occasionally touch and then with trepidation. We use the expression "being lost in a book," but we are really closer to a state of being found. Curled up with a novel about an East Indian family for instance, we are not so much escaping our own splintered and decentred world as we are enlarging our sense of self, our multiplying possibilities and expanded experience. People are, after all, tragically limited: we can live in only so many places, work at a small number of jobs or professions; we can love only a finite number of people. Reading, and particularly the reading of fiction . . . lets us be other, to touch and taste the other, to sense the shock and satisfaction of otherness. A novel lets us be ourselves and yet enter another person's boundaried world, to share in a private gaze between reader and writer. *Your* reading, and here comes the possessive pronoun again, can be part of your life and there will be times when it may be the best part. . . .

7   [A] written text, as opposed to electronic information, has formal order, tone, voice, irony, persuasion. We can inhabit a book; we can possess it and be possessed by it. The critic and scholar Martha Nussbaum believes that attentive readers of serious fiction cannot help but be compassionate and ethical citizens. The rhythms of prose train the empathetic imagination and the rational emotions. . . .

8   Almost all of [us are] plugged into the electronic world in one way or another, reliant on it for its millions of bytes of information. But a factoid, a nugget of pure information, or even the ever-widening web of information, while enabling us to perform, does relatively little to nourish us. A computer connects facts but cannot reflect upon them. There is no depth, no embeddedness. It is, literally, software, plaintext, language prefabricated and sorted into byte sizes. It does not, in short, aspire; it rarely sings. Enemies of the book want to see information freed from the prison of the printed page, putting faith instead in free floating information and this would be fine if we weren't human beings, historical beings, thinking beings with a hunger for diversion, for narrative, for consolation, for exhortation.

We need literature on the page because it allows us to experi-   9
ence more fully, to imagine more deeply, enabling us to live more
freely. Reading, [we] are in touch with [our best selves], and I think,
too, that reading shortens the distance we must travel to discover
that our most private perceptions are, in fact, universally felt. *Your*
reading will intersect with the axis of *my* reading and of his reading
and of her reading. Reading, then, offers us the ultimate website,
where attention, awareness, reflection, understanding, clarity, and
civility come together in a transformative experience.

GLOSSARY

List of Useful Terms

ABSTRACT and **CONCRETE** are terms used to describe two kinds of nouns. *Abstract* nouns name ideas, terms, feelings, qualities, measurements—concepts we understand through our minds. For example, *idea, term, feeling, quality,* and *measurement* are all abstract words. *Concrete* nouns, on the other hand, name things we perceive through our senses: we can see, hear, touch, taste, or smell what they stand for. *Author, rhythm, penguin, apple,* and *smoke* are all concrete nouns.

An **ALLUSION** is a reference to something—a person, a concept, a quotation, or a character—from literature, history, mythology, politics, or any other field familiar to your readers. For instance, in an essay on different kinds of employees, we might call one individual "a Drew Carey type." Immediately, the reader can picture a big, gregarious, funny character.

The secret of the effective use of allusions is to allude to events, books, people, or quotations that are known to your readers. Suppose one of the references in an essay on kinds of employees is to "a Dunstan Ramsay type." Can you picture this type? Are you any better informed? If not, the allusion is a poor one.

Be sure your allusions are clear and unambiguous. A reference to "King" could mean Mackenzie King, B. B. King, or Martin Luther King, Jr. Who knows? Imagine the confusion if the reader has the wrong King in mind.

AMBIGUITY: An ambiguous statement is one that has at least two different and conflicting interpretations. Similarly, an ambiguous action is one that can be understood in various ways. When it's used deliberately and carefully, ambiguity can add richness of meaning to your writing; however, most of the time ambiguity is not planned. It is the result of imprecise use of language. For instance, the statement "He never has enough money" could mean that he is always broke, or that he is never satisfied no matter how much money he has. As a general rule, it is wise to avoid ambiguity in your writing.

An **ANALOGY** is a comparison. Writers explain complicated or unfamiliar concepts by comparing them to simple or familiar ones. For instance, one could draw an analogy between life's experience and a race: the stages of life—infancy, childhood, adolescence, maturity, old age—become the laps of the race, and the problems or crises of life become the hurdles of an obstacle course. If we "fall down," we have let a problem get the better of us; if we "get up again," we are refusing to let a problem beat us. See Jeffrey Moussaieff Masson's "Dear Dad" (page 83) for an extended analogy between penguins and humans. Analogies are often used for stylistic or dramatic effect, as well as to explain or illustrate a point.

ANALYSIS means looking at the parts of something individually and considering how they contribute to the whole. In essay writing, the common kinds of analysis are process analysis and causal analysis. See the introductions to Unit 2 and Unit 5 for more detailed explanations.

An **ANECDOTE** is a short account of an event or incident—often humorous—that is used to catch the reader's interest and illustrate a point. Writers frequently use this technique to introduce an essay. See the first paragraph of Brent Staples's "Just Walk On By" (page 169) for an example of the effective use of anecdote.

ARGUMENT: See RHETORICAL MODES.

The **AUDIENCE** is the writer's intended reader or readers. Knowledge of their level of understanding, interests, and expectations is critically important to the writer. TONE, level of vocabulary, the amount of detail included, even the organizational structure, will all be influenced by the needs of the audience.

You know instinctively that when you speak or write to children, you use simple, direct language and, usually, short sentences. You adapt your style to suit your listeners. Before you begin to write, think about your readers' knowledge of your topic, their educational background, and their probable age level. Never talk down to your readers, but don't talk over their heads, either, or they will stop reading in frustration.

For example, suppose you are preparing an article on the appeal of sports cars to the public. For a popular fashion magazine, you would probably stress reliability, style, and comfort, and you would support your thesis with examples of stylish women who love the sports cars they drive. You would not include much technical automotive jargon. If you are writing about the same topic for a general-audience magazine, however, you would include more specifics about price, ease and cost of maintenance, fuel consumption, and reliability under various weather and road conditions, with detailed figures comparing several popular makes. And if you are writing for a publication such as *Popular Mechanics* or *Road and Track,* you would stress performance, handling under high speed or unusual road conditions, and the ease or difficulty with which owners could maintain their cars themselves.

The **BODY** of any piece of writing is the part that comes between the INTRODUCTION and the CONCLUSION. In a PARAGRAPH, the body consists of sentences supporting and developing the TOPIC SENTENCE. In an essay, the body consists of paragraphs supporting and developing the thesis statement.

CHRONOLOGICAL ORDER means time order; items or ideas that are introduced chronologically are discussed in order of *time sequence*. Historical accounts are usually presented chronologically. In a chronological sequencing, connectives such as *first, second, third, next, then, after that,* and *finally* help to keep your reader on track. See the introduction to Unit 2 (page 65) for further details.

A **CLICHÉ** is a phrase or expression that has been used so often it has lost its impact. A phrase that you can fill in automatically after reading the first two or three words is a cliché. Consider, for example, the expressions *better late than* _____ , *easier said than* _____ , and *as stubborn as a* _____ . The endings are so predictable that readers can (and do) skip over them.

CLIMACTIC ORDER is an arrangement of key ideas in order of importance. In this ordering pattern, writers arrange their KEY IDEAS so that the most important or strongest idea comes last. Thus, the paper builds up to a climax.

COHERENCE is the clear connection established among the key ideas of a piece of writing. In a coherent paper, one paragraph leads logically to the next. Ideas are clearly sequenced within a paragraph and between paragraphs. The topic is consistent throughout; and the writer has supplied carefully chosen and logical TRANSITIONS such as *also, however, nevertheless, on the other hand, first, second,* and *thus.* If a paper is coherent, it is probably unified as well. (See UNITY.)

COLLOQUIALISM: Colloquial language is the language we speak. Expressions such as *guys, okay, a lot,* and *kids* are acceptable in informal speech but are usually not appropriate in essays, papers, or reports. Contractions (such as *they're, isn't, it's,* and *let's*) and abbreviations (such as *TV, ads,* and *photos*) that are often used in speech are appropriate in writing only if the writer is consciously trying to achieve a casual, informal effect.

CONCLUSION: The conclusion of any piece of writing determines what will stay with your reader; therefore, it should be both logical and memorable. A good conclusion contributes to the overall UNITY of the piece, so a conclusion is no place to throw in a new point you just thought of, or a few leftover details. Your conclusion should reinforce your THESIS, but it should not simply restate it or repeat it word for word, which is even more boring. Here are five effective strategies you can choose from when writing a conclusion:

1. *Refer back to your introduction.* This does not mean simply repeating the opening lines of your paper; instead, allude to its content and draw the connections for your reader. See the conclusion of "Metamorphosis" (page 68).

2. *Ask a rhetorical question*—one that is intended to emphasize a point, not to elicit an answer. See the concluding paragraph of "Listen Up" (page 110).

3. *Issue a challenge.* See the conclusion of "She Said, He Said" (page 137).

4. *Highlight the value or significance of your topic.* See the last paragraph of "Why Write?" (page 241).

5. *Conclude with a relevant, thought-provoking quotation.*

There are several other techniques you can use to conclude effectively: provide a suggestion for change, offer a solution, make a prediction, or end with an ANECDOTE that illustrates your thesis. Whatever strategy you choose, you should leave your reader with a sense that your paper is finished and complete, not that it has just "ended."

CONCRETE: See ABSTRACT/CONCRETE.

CONNOTATION and **DENOTATION:** The *denotation* of a word is its literal or dictionary meaning. *Connotation* refers to the emotional overtones the word has in the reader's mind. Some words have only a few connotations, while others have many. For instance, "house" is a word whose denotative meaning is familiar to all and that has few connotations. "Home," on the other hand, is also denotatively familiar, but has rich connotative meanings that differ from reader to reader.

To take another example, the word "prison" is denotatively a "place of confinement for lawbreakers convicted of serious crimes." But the connotations of the word are much deeper and broader: when we hear or read the word "prison," we think of colours like grey and black; we hear sounds of clanging doors or wailing sirens; and we associate with the word emotions like anger, fear, despair, or loneliness. A careful writer will not use this word lightly: to refer to your workplace as a "prison" is a strong statement. It would not be appropriate to use this phrase simply because you don't like the location or the lunch break.

CONTEXT is the verbal background of a word or phrase—the words that come before and after it and fix its meaning. For example, the word "period," which has many different meanings, means a particular kind of sentence in Eva Hoffman's "Lost in Translation" (Further Reading, page 309).

When a word or phrase is taken *out of context,* it is often difficult to determine what it originally meant. Therefore, when you are quoting from another writer, be sure to include enough of the context so that the meaning is clear to your reader.

DEDUCTION is the logical process of applying a general statement to a specific instance and reasoning through to a conclusion about that instance. See also INDUCTION.

DESCRIPTION: See RHETORICAL MODES.

DICTION refers to the writer's choice and arrangement of words in a piece of writing. Effective diction depends upon the writer's choosing a level of vocabulary suited to both the reader and the topic. Good writers do not carelessly mix formal with colloquial language, standard English with dialect or slang, or informal language with technical JARGON or archaisms (outmoded, antique phrases). Good diction is that which is appropriate to the topic, the reader, and the writer's purpose. Writing for a general audience about the closing of a local grocery store, a careful writer would not say, "The retail establishment for the purveyance of merchandise relative to the sustaining of life has cemented its portals," which is pretentious nonsense (see GOBBLEDYGOOK). "The corner store has been closed" conveys the same meaning concisely and appropriately.

EMPHASIS: A writer can emphasize or highlight important points in several ways: *repetition; placement* (the essay's first and last sections are the most prominent positions); or *phrasing.* Careful phrasing can call attention to a particular point. Parallel structure, a very short sentence or paragraph, even a deliberate sentence fragment are all emphatic devices. A writer can also add emphasis by developing an idea at greater length, or by calling attention to its significance directly, by inserting expressions such as "most important" or "significantly." TONE, particularly IRONY or even sarcasm, can be used to add emphasis. Finally, distinctive diction is an emphatic device. See Danny Irvine's "A Tree-Planting Primer" (page 89) and Mark Kingwell's "What Is the Good Life?" (page 280) for good examples of distinctive diction.

EVIDENCE in a piece of writing functions the same way it does in a court of law: it proves the point. Evidence can consist of statistical data, examples, references to authorities in the field, surveys, illustrations, quotations, or facts. Charts, graphs, and maps are also forms of evidence and are well suited to particular kinds of reports.

A point cannot be effectively explained, let alone proved, without evidence. For instance, it is not enough to say that computers are displacing many workers. You need to find specific examples of companies, jobs, and statistics to prove the connection. After all, the number of dogs in Canada has increased almost as much as the number of computers. Does that prove that dogs breed computers? What makes a paper credible and convincing is the evidence presented and the COHERENCE with which it is presented. See Wade Davis's "The End of the Wild" (page 44) for an example of the effective use of several kinds of evidence.

EXPOSITION: See RHETORICAL MODES.

FIGURES OF SPEECH are words or phrases that mean something more than the literal meanings of the individual words or phrases. Writers choose to use figurative language when they want the reader to associate one thing with another. Some of the more common figures of speech include SIMILES, METAPHORS, PERSONIFICATIONS, and PUNS.

GENERAL and **SPECIFIC:** *General* words refer to classes or groups of things. "Animal" is a general word; so is "fruit." *Specific* words refer to individual members of a class or group; e.g., "penguin" or "lemon." Good writing is a careful blend of general and specific language. (See also ABSTRACT/CONCRETE.)

GOBBLEDYGOOK is a type of JARGON characterized by wordy, pretentious language. Writing that has chains of vague, abstract words and long, complicated sentences—sound without meaning—is gobbledygook. See the example included under DICTION.

ILLUSTRATION: See the introduction to Unit 1.

INDUCTION is the logical process of looking at a number of specific instances and reasoning through to a general conclusion about them. See also DEDUCTION.

INTRODUCTION: The introduction to any piece of writing is crucial to its success. A good introduction identifies the THESIS of the piece, establishes the TONE, and secures the reader's attention. The introduction is the hook with which you catch your reader's interest and make the reader want to read what you have to say. Here are five different attention-getters you can use:

1. *Begin with a story related to your topic.* The story could be an anecdote (a factual, often humorous account of an incident) or a scenario (an account of an imagined situation). See the first paragraph of Antanas Sileika's "The View from Italy: Puritans 'R Us" (page 145) for an anecdotal introduction and the first two paragraphs of Thomas Hurka's "Should Morality Be a Struggle?" (page 155) for a scenario.

2. *Begin with a striking fact or startling statistic.* See the first paragraph of "Listen Up" in Unit 3.

3. *Set up a comparision or contrast to hook your reader.* See the introduction to Jeffrey Moussaieff Masson's "Dear Dad" (page 83) for a comparison and the introduction to R. G. Des Dixon's "Martha: One Pillowcase Short of a Pair" (page 73) for a contrast.

4. *Begin by stating a common opinion that you intend to challenge.* See "Why Write?" (page 240).

5. *Begin with a question or series of questions.* See the introduction to "The Trouble with Readers" (page 161).

Other strategies you might want to experiment with include beginning with a relevant quotation, offering a definition (make sure it's yours, not the dictionary's), or even telling a joke. You know how important first impressions are when you meet someone. Treat your introductory paragraph with the same care you would take when you want to make a good first impression on a person. If you bait the hook attractively, your reader will want to read on.

IRONY is a way of saying one thing while meaning something else, often the opposite of what the words themselves signify. To call a hopelessly ugly painting a masterpiece is an example of irony. For an extended example of verbal irony, see "A Tree-Planting Primer," page 89. Situations can also be ironic: in "Toothpaste" (page 117), we learn that a health and beauty product is made from disgusting materials; in "The Telephone" (page 174), the instrument that was supposed to enhance the life of a village in fact destroys it.

Irony is an effective technique because it forces readers to think about the relationship between seemingly incompatible things or ideas. Jessica Mitford's "Behind the Formaldehyde Curtain" (page 95) is a well-known piece of extended irony. Although she seems on the surface to be enthusiastic about the processes of embalming and restoration, Mitford forces her readers to consider the possibility that these practices are barbaric.

JARGON is the specialized language used within a particular trade, discipline, or profession. Among members of that trade or profession, jargon is appropriate; indeed, highly technical language is an efficient, time-saving means of communication. Outside the context of the trade or profession, however, jargon is inappropriate because it inhibits rather than promotes the listener's or reader's understanding. Another meaning of jargon, the meaning usually intended when the word is used in this text, is GOBBLEDYGOOK.

KEY IDEAS are the main points into which the development of a THESIS is divided. (See also PARAGRAPH.)

A **METAPHOR** is a figurative rather than a literal comparison. An effective metaphor is one that draws a fresh, imaginative connection between two dissimilar things. Dennis Dermody, for example, writes that a movie theatre is "a jungle . . . filled with a lot of really stupid animals" ("Sit Down and Shut Up or Don't Sit by Me," page 114). An apt, unusual metaphor makes the writer's idea memorable.

NARRATION: See RHETORICAL MODES.

ORDER refers to the arrangement of information or key ideas in a piece of prose. While you are still in the planning stages, choose the order most appropriate to your topic or THESIS. There are four arrangements to choose from:

1. *Chronological order* means in order of time, from first to last.
2. *Climactic order* means in order of importance, leading up to the climax. Usually you present your strongest or most important point last, your second-strongest point first, and the others in between, where they will attract less attention.
3. *Causal* or *logical order* means that the points are connected in such a way that one point must be explained before the next can be understood. Often used in causal analysis, this order is appropriate when there is a direct and logical connection between one point and the next.
4. *Random order* is a shopping-list kind of arrangement: the points can be presented in any order. Random order is appropriate only when the points are all equal in significance and not logically or causally linked.

A **PARAGRAPH** is a unit of composition, usually from five to twelve sentences long, all dealing with one point or KEY IDEA. In an essay, you present several KEY IDEAS, all related to your topic. Each key idea is developed in one or more paragraphs.

Most paragraphs have a *topic sentence*—a sentence that states clearly what point the paragraph is about. It is often the first or second sentence of the paragraph. The rest of the paragraph consists of sentences that develop the point, perhaps with examples, description, definition, quotation, comparison, or a combination of these strategies. There should be no sentence in the paragraph that is not clearly related to its key idea. Each paragraph should lead smoothly into the next (see TRANSITION), and it should also possess internal COHERENCE and UNITY. The essays of Bertrand Russell (page 124) and Wade Davis (page 44) deserve careful analysis: their paragraphs are models of form.

PARALLELISM means similarity of grammatical structure. In a sentence, for example, all items in a series would be written in the same grammatical form: single words, phrases, or clauses. Julius Caesar's famous pronouncement, "I came, I saw, I conquered," is a classic example of parallelism.

Parallelism creates symmetry that is pleasing to the reader. Lack of parallelism, on the other hand, can be jarring: "His favourite sports are skiing, skating, and he particularly loves to sail." Such potholes in your prose should be fixed up before you hand in a paper. For example, "What Carol says, she means; and she delivers what she promises, too" would be much more effective if rewritten in parallel form: "What Carol says, she means; what she promises, she delivers."

Because the human mind responds favourably to the repetition of rhythm, parallelism is an effective device for adding EMPHASIS. "Adam and Eve Redux" (page 142) contains numerous examples of parallelism in DICTION SYNTAX, and content.

TO **PARAPHRASE** is to put another writer's ideas into your own words. You must acknowledge the original writer as the source of the idea. If you don't, you are guilty of plagiarism.

Paraphrasing is essential when you are writing a research paper. Once you have gathered the information you need from various sources and organized your ideas into an appropriate order, you write the paper, drawing on your sources for supporting evidence but expressing the sources' ideas in your own words.

A paraphrase should reflect both the meaning and the general TONE of the original. It may be the same length or shorter than the original (but it is not a PRÉCIS).

PERSONIFICATION is a figure of speech in which the writer gives human qualities to an inanimate object or an abstract idea. For instance, if you write "The brakes screeched when I hit them," you are comparing the sound of the car's brakes to a human voice. Strive for original and insightful personifications; otherwise, you will be trapped by clichés such as "The solution to the problem was staring me in the face."

PERSUASION: See RHETORICAL MODES and the introduction to Unit 7.

POINT OF VIEW, in EXPOSITION, means the narrative angle of the essay: who's telling the story? (In PERSUASION and ARGUMENT, point of view can also mean the writer's opinion in the essay.)

If the writer identifies himself as "I," the essay is written from the first-person point of view. In this case, we expect to encounter the writer's own opinions and first-hand experiences. All the essays in Unit 1 are written in the first person.

If the writer is not grammatically "present," the essay is witten from the third-person point of view. Most of the essays in Units 2 to 8 are written primarily in the third person. The writer uses "one," "he/she," and "they," and the result is a more formal piece than one written in the first person.

A careful writer maintains point of view consistently throughout an essay; if a shift occurs, it should be for a good reason, with a particular effect in mind. Careless shifts in point of view confuse the reader. See paragraph 9 of Lewis Thomas's "Altruism" (page 220) for an example of a purposeful change in point of view.

A **PRÉCIS** is a condensed SUMMARY of an article or essay. It is one-quarter to one-third the length of the original. The examples and ILLUSTRATIONS are omitted, and the prose is tightened up as much as possible. All the KEY IDEAS are included; most of the development is not.

A **PUN** is a word or phrase that brings to the reader's mind two different meanings. Max Eastman, in *Enjoyment of Laughter*, classifies puns into three sorts: atrocious, witty, and poetic. The person who wrote "How does Dolly Parton stack up against Mae West?" was guilty of an atrocious pun. Lawrence Steinberg's title "Bound to Bicker" (page 162) contains a witty pun, as does Paul Quarrington's "Home Ice" (page 76). Poetic puns, such as those in Lorne Rubenstein's "Passion Play" (page 314), go beyond the merely humorous double meaning and offer the reader a concise, original comparison of two entities, qualities, or ideas.

PURPOSE means the writer's intent: to inform, to persuade, or to amuse, or a combination of these. See RHETORICAL MODES.

RHETORICAL MODES: The word "rhetoric" means the art of using language effectively. There are four classic modes, or kinds, of writing: exposition, narration, description, and argument. The writer's choice of mode is often dependent on his or her PURPOSE.

Exposition is writing intended to inform or explain. If the writer's purpose is to inform, this mode is a likely choice. Expository writing can be personal or impersonal, serious or light-hearted. The various methods of exposition (such as definition, comparison, process analysis, and the rest) are sometimes called rhetorical patterns.

Narration tells a story. It is the mode used for fiction. Examples of narrative writing are often found within expository prose: in ANECDOTES or ILLUSTRATIONS, for example. Michael Ignatieff's "Deficits" and Basil

Johnston's "Bush League Business" (pages 37 and 30, respectively) are good examples of the use of narration to help explain a THESIS.

Description is used to make a reader see, hear, taste, smell, or feel something. Good descriptive writing re-creates a sensory experience in the reader's imagination. Descriptive writing is often used to help develop points in a piece of EXPOSITION or ARGUMENT. In addition to the essays in Unit 1, see the essays by David Bodanis (page 117), Germaine Greer (page 137), and Anwar F. Accawi (page 174) for examples of effective description.

Argument, sometimes called *persuasion,* is writing that sets out not only to explain something but to convince the reader of the validity of the writer's opinion on an issue. Sometimes its purpose goes even further, and the writer attempts to motivate the reader to act in some way. Like exposition, argument conveys information to the reader, but not solely for the purpose of making a topic clear. Argument seeks to reinforce or to change a reader's opinion about an issue.

SATIRE is a form of humour, sometimes light-hearted, sometimes biting, in which the writer deliberately attacks and ridicules something: a person, a political decision, an event, an institution, a philosophy, or a system. The satirist uses exaggeration, ridicule, and IRONY to achieve his or her effect. There is often a social purpose in satire: the writer points to the difference between the ideal—a world based on common sense and moral standards—and the real, which may be silly, vicious, alienating, or immoral, depending on the object of the satirist's attack. The essays by Jessica Mitford (page 95) and Judy Brady (page 121) are examples of satire.

A **SIMILE** is a stated or explicit comparison between two things. Most similes are introduced by *like* or *as*. In the following sentence, Douglas Coupland uses two similes to describe the raw beauty of the Yukon landscape: "Glaciers drape like mink over feldspar ridges like broken backs" ("The Yukon," page 20).

SPECIFIC: See GENERAL/SPECIFIC.

A **STEREOTYPE** refers to a character, a situation, or an idea that is trite, unoriginal, and conventional. Stereotypes are based on automatic, widely known, and usually incorrect assumptions: women are poor drivers; truck drivers are illiterate; teenagers are boors. Stereotypical notions about races and nationalities are particularly dangerous: think of the well-known "Newfie" jokes, for example.

A careful writer avoids stereotypes, unless he or she is using them for satiric purposes. Unthinking acceptance of others' assumptions is a sure sign of a lazy mind. See Pat Capponi's "Dispatches from the Poverty Line" (page 23) and Neil Bissoondath's "I'm Not Racist But . . ." (page 211) for detailed explorations of various stereotypes.

STYLE is the distinctive way a person writes. When two writers approach the same topic, even if they share many of the same ideas, the resulting works will be different. That difference is the result of personal style. DIC-

TION, sentence structure, sentence length, TONE, and level of formality all contribute to an individual's style. Compare Mario Vargas Llosa's "With Pens Drawn" (page 276) and Carol Shields's "The Case for Curling Up with a Book" (Further Reading, page 346) as examples of different stylistic treatments of a similar topic.

Good writers adapt their style to their AUDIENCE; one doesn't write the same way in the business world as one does in the academic world, for example. In this sense, "good style" means one that suits the writer's PURPOSE, topic, and audience. An informal and humorous style full of slang expressions would be inappropriate in a paper on teenage suicide; similarly, a formal style would not be suitable for a promotional piece on new toys for the holiday season.

A **SUMMARY** is a brief statement, in sentence or paragraph form, of the KEY IDEAS of an article or essay. Compare PRÉCIS and PARAPHRASE.

SYNTAX means the arrangement of words in a sentence. Good syntax means not only grammatical correctness, but also effective word order and variety of sentence patterns. Good writers use short sentences and long ones, simple sentences and complex ones, and natural-order sentences and inverted-order ones. The choice depends on the meaning the writer wishes to convey.

A **THESIS** is the main idea or point about a topic that the writer wants to communicate to the reader in an essay. It is often expressed in a *thesis statement*. (See "How to Write to Be Understood," page xviii.) Professional writers sometimes do not directly state their thesis. Inexperienced writers would do well *not* to follow their example. A clearly stated thesis—one that expresses the central idea that everything in the essay is designed to support and explain—is the best guide you can provide for your reader. A good thesis statement also helps the writer stay focused.

TONE reflects the writer's attitude to the topic and to his or her intended audience. For instance, a writer who is looking back with longing to the past will use a nostalgic tone. An angry writer might use an indignant, outraged tone, or an understated, ironic tone—depending on the topic and purpose of the piece.

Through DICTION, POINT OF VIEW, sentence structure, PARAGRAPH development, and STYLE, a writer modulates his or her message to suit the knowledge, attitude, and taste of the target audience. Contrast the aggressive, even abrasive tone of Dennis Dermody's "Sit Down and Shut Up or Don't Sit by Me" (page 114) with the poignant yet positive tone of Brent Staples's "Just Walk On By" (page 169). Other examples of superb control of tone are Jessica Mitford's scathing "Behind the Formaldehyde Curtain" (page 95), Michael Ignatieff's sympathetic "Deficits" (page 37), and Judy Brady's ironic "Why I Want a Wife" (page 121).

A **TOPIC SENTENCE** is a sentence that identifies the point, or key idea, developed in a paragraph. The topic sentence is usually found at or near the beginning of the paragraph.

TRANSITIONS are linking words or phrases. They help connect a writer's sentences and paragraphs so that the whole piece flows smoothly and logically. Here are some of the most common transitions used to show relationships between ideas:

1. *to show a time relation:* first, second, third, next, before, during, after, now, then, finally, last

2. *to add an idea or example:* in addition, also, another, furthermore, similarly, for example, for instance

3. *to show contrast:* although, but, however, instead, nevertheless, on the other hand, in contrast, on the contrary

4. *to show a cause–effect relation:* as a result, consequently, because, since, therefore, thus

   See also COHERENCE.

UNITY: A piece of writing has unity if all its parts work together to contribute to the ultimate effect. A unified piece (paragraph, essay) has one topic and tone. Unity is an important quality of a good paragraph, essay, or article: each sentence must be related to and develop the key idea expressed in the TOPIC SENTENCE.

COPYRIGHT ACKNOWLEDGMENTS

Introduction, page xxxiii: "Cycling in the 1890s," by Katherine Murtha, in *Canadian Woman Studies*, vol. 21, no. 3 (Winter 2001/Spring 2002), pp. 119–121.

Unit 1, page 8: "A Cultural Exchange," by Brian Green; **10:** "Baba and Me," by Shandi Mitchell, 2001. Published originally in *Confluences*. Reprinted by permission of the author; **14:** "Edith," from *Drumblair: Memories of a Jamaican Childhood,* by Rachel Manley, published by Vintage Books, 1997. Reprinted by permission of the author; **20:** "The Yukon," from *Souvenir of Canada,* by Douglas Coupland. Copyright © 2002 by Douglas Coupland. Published by Douglas & McIntyre Ltd. Reprinted by permission of the publisher; **23:** Excerpt from *Dispatches from the Poverty Line,* by Pat Capponi. Copyright © 1997 by Pat Capponi. Reprinted with permission of Penguin Books Canada Limited; **30:** "Bush League Business," from *Indian School Days,* by Basil Johnston. Copyright © 1988. Reprinted with the permission of the author; **37:** "Deficits," from *Scar Tissue,* by Michael Ignatieff. Copyright © 1989 by Michael Ignatieff. Reprinted with permission; **44:** "The End of the Wild," by Wade Davis, from *The Clouded Leopard,* by Wade Davis. Copyright © 1998 by Wade Davis. Published by Douglas & McIntyre. Reprinted by permission of the publisher; **55:** "The Rake," by David Mamet. Copyright © 1993 by David Mamet, from *A Whore's Profession.* Reprinted with the permission of The Wylie Agency, Inc.

Unit 2, page 67: "Metamorphosis," by Sarah Norton; **69:** "The Magic of Moviegoing," by Rick Groen, *The Globe and Mail,* 4 January 2002. Reprinted with permission from The Globe and Mail; **73:** "Martha: One Pillowcase Short of a Pair," by R. G. Des Dixon, *The Globe and Mail,* 21 June 1998. Reprinted with permission; **76:** "Home Ice," by Paul Quarrington. Copyright © 1990 by Paul Quarrington. Reprinted with permission of Livingston Cooke, Inc; **83:** "Dear Dad," from *The Emperor's Embrace,* by Jeffrey Moussaieff Masson. Copyright 1999 by Jeffrey Masson; **89:** "A Tree-Planting Primer," by Danny Irvine. Reprinted with permission of the author; **95:** "Behind the Formaldehyde Curtain," by Jessica Mitford. Copyright © 1963, 1978 by Jessica Mitford. All rights reserved. Reprinted with permission of the Estate of Jessica Mitford.

AUTHOR INDEX